Arms Sales and Regional Stability

An Assessment

an IISS strategic dossier

published by

The International Institute for Strategic Studies

ARUNDEL HOUSE | 6 TEMPLE PLACE | LONDON | WC2R 2PG | UK

an IISS *strategic dossier*

Arms Sales and Regional Stability

An Assessment

The International Institute for Strategic Studies

ARUNDEL HOUSE | 6 TEMPLE PLACE | LONDON | WC2R 2PG | UK

EDITORS **Douglas Barrie, Dr Bastian Giegerich, Fenella McGerty**
ASSOCIATE EDITOR **Gregory Brooks, Jill Lally, Alasdair McKay, Jana Phillips, Adam Walters and Nicholas Woodroof**
CONTRIBUTORS **Douglas Barrie, Lucie Beraud-Sudreau, Charlotte Le Breton, Bastian Giegerich, Una Hakvag, Yuka Koshino, Fenella McGerty, William Natter III, Cecilie Sendstad, Simona Soare**
DESIGN, PRODUCTION, INFORMATION GRAPHICS **Alessandra Beluffi, Ravi Gopar, Jade Panganiban, James Parker, Kelly Verity**
RESEARCH SUPPORT **Charlotte Le Breton, Haena Jo, Tom Waldwyn**

This publication has been prepared by the Director-General and Chief Executive of the International Institute for Strategic Studies (IISS) and his staff. It incorporates commissioned contributions from recognised subject experts, which were reviewed by a range of experts in the field. The IISS would like to thank the various individuals who contributed their expertise to the compilation of this dossier. The responsibility for the contents is ours alone. The views expressed herein do not, and indeed cannot, represent a consensus of views among the worldwide membership of the Institute as a whole.

First published December 2022 by the International Institute for Strategic Studies.

Printed and bound in the UK by Hobbs the Printers Ltd.

British Library Cataloguing in Publication Data
A catalogue record for this book is available from the British Library

Library of Congress Cataloging in Publication Data
A catalogue record for this book has been requested

ISBN 978-1-032-52597-6

About The International Institute for Strategic Studies

The IISS is an independent centre for research, information and debate on the problems of conflict, however caused, that have, or potentially have, an important military content. The Council and Staff of the Institute are international and its membership is drawn from over 100 countries. The Institute is independent, and it alone decides what activities to conduct. It owes no allegiance to any government, any group of governments or any political or other organisation. The IISS stresses rigorous research with a forward-looking policy orientation that can improve wider public understanding of international security problems and influence the development of sounder public policy.

Contents

Common abbreviations

AAM	air-to-air missile
AECA	Arms Export Control Act
ATT	Arms Trade Treaty
AWACS	Airborne Warning and Control System
CAAT	Campaign Against the Arms Trade
CALCM	conventional air-launched cruise missile
CAT	Conventional Arms Transfer
CMC	Central Military Commission
COCOM	combatant commands
DESO	Defence Export Services Organisation
DIT	Department for International Trade
DSCA	Defense Security Cooperation Agency
DSE	Defence and Security Exports
DSIS	Defence and Security Industrial Strategy
DTIB	Defence Technological and Industrial Base
ECJU	Export Control Joint Unit
EDD	Equipment Development Department
FCAS	Future Combat Air System
FMS	Foreign Military Sales
GNA	Goldwater-Nichols Department of Defense Reorganization Act of 1986
ISR	intelligence, surveillance and reconnaissance
LAC	Line of Actual Control
LACMs	land-attack cruise missiles
MCMVs	mine countermeasures vessels
MGCS	Main Ground Combat System
MTCR	Missile Technology Control Regime
NDAA	National Defense Authorization Act
NDPG	National Defence Program Guidelines
NEC	National Economic Council
NSC	National Security Council
OEM	original equipment manufacturer
PMC	private military company
R&D	research and development
UAV	uninhabited aerial vehicle

INTRODUCTION – ARMS SALES AND REGIONAL STABILITY

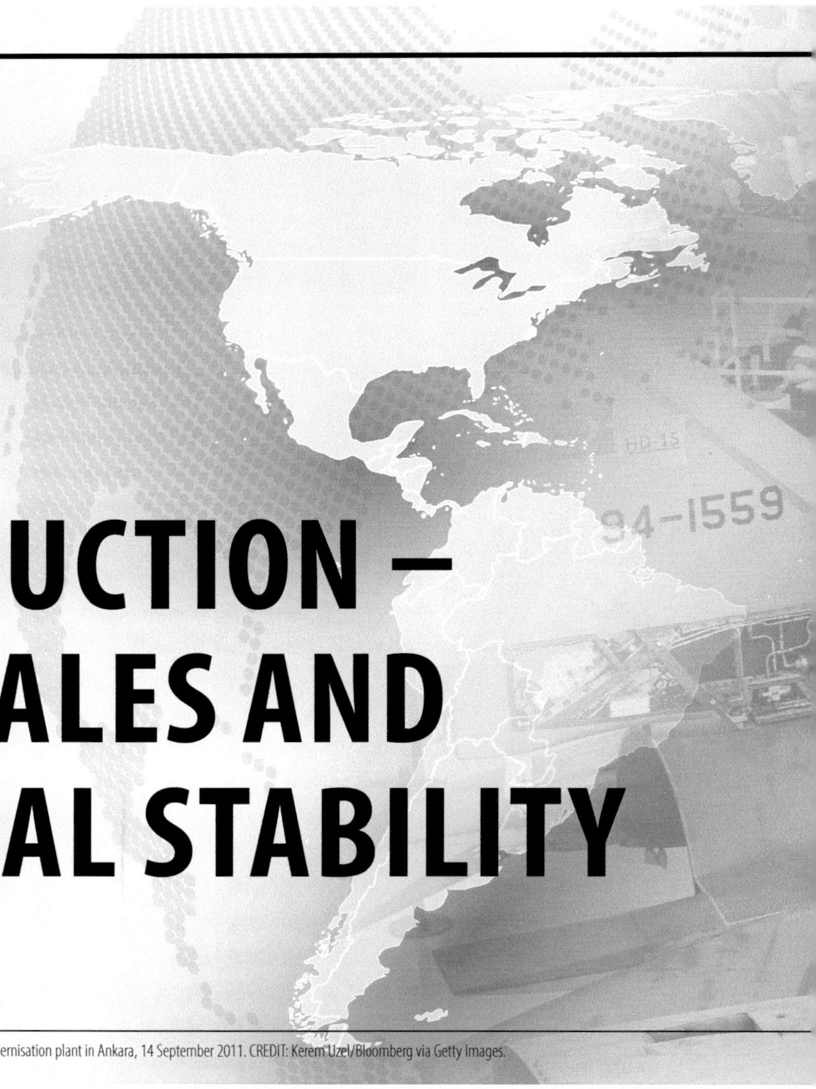

INSIDE TURKISH AEROSPACE INDUSTRIES PLANT

Technicians work on F-16s at the Turkish Aerospace Industries Inc. modernisation plant in Ankara, 14 September 2011. CREDIT: Kerem Uzel/Bloomberg via Getty Images.

CHAPTER 1

Influence and income are the two broad drivers behind countries selling advanced weapons to other countries. Influence is spread through defence and security relationships with allies or partner countries, cemented by arms sales, and it reverberates in the regions in which these relationships are situated, and domestically in both the seller and buyer nations. Direct and indirect economic and technological development benefits also underpin national policies regarding weapons sales to customer states.[1]

The debate over arms sales is polarised. At one end of the spectrum are advocacy groups who argue that the arms trade is morally reprehensible and without benefit,[2] a view often enmeshed with a tacit or explicit embrace of pacifism and leading to calls for the trade's abolition. At the other end is a purely transactional approach that views weapons as just another commodity to be sold. National arms-export policies, for the most part, attempt to navigate between these two poles with liberal and restrictive rules recognisable within national and transnational structures. The assessed effect of weapons sales on the stability of the client country's region contributes to, and sometimes determines, the outcome of policy deliberations. Such an evaluation is part of the boilerplate of US Defense Security Cooperation Agency (DSCA) notification of a possible arms export when it notes: 'the proposed sale of this equipment and support will not alter the basic military balance in the region'.[3]

This International Institute for Strategic Studies (IISS) dossier will consider the decision-making architecture of the key weapons-manufacturing nations, the multiple and sometimes contradictory building blocks of the processes, the government departments and

QATAR NATIONAL DAY
A Qatar Emiri Air Force F-15 *Eagle* performs in the sky above Qatar's capital Doha as the Gulf state marks its National Day, 18 December 2021. CREDIT: AFP via Getty Images.

bureaucracies involved, and how the impact of a potential sale is evaluated. It will explore the interplay between national defence industries and political elites and the extent to which this influences decision-making.

While few states would ever openly admit to supplying weaponry knowing it would be destabilising or indeed that less stability was an aim, there are recent instances where this can be argued to be the outcome. The far more common contention in the policy debate is that a weapons sale will not have a detrimental effect on stability, or indeed that it will contribute to enhancing regional stability. This dossier will examine the merits and demerits of such claims.

This volume's starting point is the end of the Cold War and of superpower confrontation. While the fall of the Berlin Wall may seem a convenient place to begin, this choice is not arbitrary: the approach to arms sales adopted by all the manufacturing nations considered by the study was influenced, moderated and shaped by the collapse of the Soviet Union and the shift this caused in the global security environment. The Cold War's immediate aftermath was marked by considerable industrial upheaval, especially but not exclusively in the United States.[4] Some companies exited the defence sector, while others merged or were acquired as industry responded to reductions in Washington's defence expenditure in the 1990s. During the confrontation between NATO and the Warsaw Pact countries, the sale of advanced US weaponry was arguably seen as improving alliance capabilities. But in the following years, the economic benefit of defence exports, substituting for reduced domestic demand, carried greater influence. In Russia in the 1990s defence exports were the only means of sustaining national production since the domestic orderbook had collapsed.[5] China emerged as a defence exporter and Russia re-emerged in due course. A number of European nations sharpened their defence export profiles, not always in alignment with the US.

The role of arms sales since the end of the Cold War will be reviewed in the remaining sections of this **Introduction**. National- and international-level developments over the past three decades will be explored to identify the continuing national imperatives in sustaining a domestic industrial base and how these relate to arms export ambitions and policy. It will consider the geopolitical and economic aims that are pursued within the ambit of the export of advanced weapons systems, and whether, and to what extent, such activity supports or detracts from foreign-policy and security goals.

Chapter Two will address the relationship between arms sales and regional security by examining what constitutes regional stability and whether it is the same as regional security, as well as how each concept relates to the notion of a regional balance of power. It will identify which factors contribute to, and even enhance, regional stability alongside those that may undermine or detract from the same and consider the concept of a 'regional security complex'. This chapter provides necessary context for the study's goal to help assess whether the broader implications of any proposed defence sale are adequately viewed in enhancing or undermining regional stability.

Chapters Three to **Five** are case studies of the US, China and Russia, the key suppliers with the capacity to develop and supply complex conventional weapons systems at the global level. The US is by value the largest arms-exporting nation by some considerable margin. **Chapter Three** will review the arms-sales policies of US administrations since the end of the Cold War, and how these have aligned, or otherwise, with foreign-policy goals. It will examine how the various relevant US government departments review potential export sales and the factors driving the decision-making process. Consideration will be given to the US approach to arms exports to the Middle East and the Indo-Pacific, and the implications for stability in these locales. Combat-aircraft sales and associated weapons packages, and the sale of uninhabited aerial vehicles (UAVs), will be the equipment focus. While the US chapter was concluded prior to the 23 February 2023 release of the latest Conventional Arms Transfer Policy, the underlying continuity, even given the increased emphasis on humanitarian concerns, will be readily apparent to readers.

China and Russia are the subjects of **Chapters Four and Five.** These chapters will examine their respective approaches to arms-export policy and the drivers behind decision-making. They will consider arms sales within the context of each nation's foreign policy and how this influences the decision-making process. The chapters will also discuss the relative differences in fortunes of the two nations' defence-aerospace industrial bases and how this may influence or shape aerospace arms exports in the future. How Russia's invasion of Ukraine may impact its future arms exports will also be given consideration.

Chapter Six will review the United Kingdom's approach to the sale of major weapons, predominantly in the defence-aerospace sector, and mainly to the Middle East. It will consider respective UK government arms-export policies from the 1990s onwards and the often vexed relationship with its key purchasing state in the Middle East, Saudi Arabia. It will also examine how the sale of major weapons systems sits within wider national defence-industrial political considerations.

The European Union's two largest arms exporters, France and Germany, are the focus of **Chapter Seven**. This chapter will discuss the differences and perhaps sometimes surprising similarities in policy outcomes between France and Germany. It will review the decision-making processes of the two states and how they assess whether a proposed sale of major weapons risks being destabilising.

Chapter Eight covers recent policy changes and political adjustments in Japan, a country that has recently begun to pursue weapons exports as a means to bolster its domestic industry as well as strengthen existing and develop new defence partnerships against a regional security context that is perceived to be increasingly challenging by leaders in Tokyo. The **Conclusion** draws together the main themes of the study and offers a number of comparative observations on the theme of arms exports and regional stability.

Scope of the dossier

This dossier aims to explore the relationship between major-weapons sales and regional stability or instability, whether there is a clear and direct causality, or whether the number of variables is such that any generalisation is unhelpfully reductive. It will also consider the shifting emphasis on some of the influencing factors on decision-making, such as an increased acknowledgement that human rights could be factored in to a greater extent, and how this may affect decision-making in the countries covered in this volume.

The ease of availability, the volume available of small and light arms combined with their illicit sale and acquisition along with the challenges of adequate control 'remain a defining factor in undermining peace and security'.[6] The capacity of such weapons to inflict human misery and economic hardship remains a vexing international issue and demands yet further attention. Small and light arms, however, are not the focus of this study. This dossier will instead consider what are sometimes described as 'major weapons' and their transfer between states. Major weapons cover air, land and sea platforms including combat aircraft and helicopters, and the associated missiles and munitions, main battle tanks, armoured vehicles, artillery, and guided weapons, ships, submarines and their related armaments.

Major weapons continue to be a particular feature of the international trade in armaments in part because, unlike small and light arms, only a comparatively limited number of countries can independently produce even some of the armaments previously mentioned. This group becomes even smaller when those states able to manufacture domestically all classes of conventional major weapons are considered. Alongside the primary producers, China, Russia and the United States, is a second tier that includes Europe's main weapons-manufacturing states – France, Germany, Italy, Spain, Sweden and the United Kingdom – along with South Korea and India in the Indo-Pacific. The last two states have only recently developed such capacities, and in the case of India the extent that it remains reliant on external support for some areas of defence technology is debatable. The emergence of new providers of some categories of major weapons has only complicated further the management and regulation of conventional-arms exports.

Within the major-weapons category, air systems are considered in more depth for this dossier than advanced armaments from the other domains. This is in part for brevity, and in part for significance, since in monetary and technological value the combat-air sector figures strongly in the export activities of many of the main suppliers of major weapons, most notably the US, France, the UK and Russia.

Given the scale and importance of the subject, a single publication will never be able to provide any definitive answers to what remains a challenging set of questions. The aim, however, is that this volume will contribute further to a better-informed debate. The IISS team conducted research interviews in 2021 and 2022 with government personnel, defence-industry representatives, experts in export law and other subject-matter experts in the private sector and the analytical community. These interviews were structured around a set of questions that examined the politics, mechanics and driving factors behind defence exports and what, if any, consideration was given to their impact on regional stability. Information gathered from these interviews informed the writing of this study and is referred to in anonymised form in chapter endnotes where appropriate.

68TH SESSION OF THE UNITED NATIONS GENERAL ASSEMBLY
US secretary of state John Kerry signs the UN Arms Trade Treaty, which seeks to regulate the international conventional-arms business, during the annual UN General Assembly in New York, 25 September 2013. CREDIT: Spencer Platt/Getty Images.

Why export major weapons?

Ideology, economic and industrial interests, shared security goals and geopolitical influence are interwoven, to varying degrees, in any political decision-making process on arms sales. The influence of each, however, is not fixed. This reflects in part national political priorities as well as the public perception regarding the legitimacy or otherwise of arms exports, in general or of a particular sale. In turn, all these factors are nested within a wider defence and security environment. The sale of the major-weapons category of armaments is overwhelmingly carried out between states, and involves the governments, the supplier nation's defence industry and the recipient armed service, its defence ministry and occasionally domestic industry. Such transactions are most often the subject of extensive national and international controls, which are, for the most part, legally binding at the national level and voluntary at the international level. As with nearly everything associated with arms exports, the effectiveness of the controls is disputed. At one extreme they are seen merely as a hindrance to business, and at the other they are seen as camouflage, serving only to legitimise the sale of advanced weapons for profit. But what is unarguable is the clear, continuing and, given Russia's February 2022 invasion of Ukraine, growing demand signals for major weapons systems among many states.

Legitimacy and the politics of arms sales

The United Nations Charter (Article 51)[7] asserts that UN member states have the right to individual and collective self-defence, and the notion of defence, at least narrowly, is predicated on holding a military capability and being willing to use armed force. In turn, such a force at the state level will include major weapons, and for most states this will mean purchasing to a lesser or greater extent such systems from a third-party provider. Very few countries have the defence-industrial capacity to domestically produce all classes of major weapons, whether armoured vehicles, combat aircraft, or surface or sub-surface combatants, or across all five domains: air, land, sea, cyber and space. Consequently, addressing such requirements entails acquiring the desired platform from one of a limited number of foreign producers. The choice of external supplier depends on multiple factors. But as previously suggested, political and security alignment, economic and industrial interests, and cost can all influence choices. While not mutually exclusive, not all these factors will always be considered, nor weighed equally, and weapons sales in some instances can help reconcile pragmatism with ideology.

This primes and sustains the global trade in major weapons, which in 2019 had an estimated value of USD118 billion.[8] The largest element of this figure was major weapons, with the United States dominating the export market.[9]

The UN has also attempted to reconcile the implications of a state's legitimate right to self-defence with the risks of an arms sales free-for-all. The 2013 Arms Trade Treaty[10] covered major, light and personal weapons categories and was intended to build on the UN Register of Conventional Arms. Arms control, however, and the broader goal of 'general and complete disarmament' [11] are not necessarily conterminous, and the idealism of the UN Office for Disarmament Affairs' aims is not necessarily embraced by those advocating arms control.

Arms-export policies are fundamentally political, and in liberal democracies they can and often do shift with changes in government, as the case-study chapters in this volume will show. Policy reviews are often, however, a matter of degree or nuance, rather than of basic principles. The level of oversight and the ability of the legislature to influence or question arms-export policy decisions also varies. In autocratic regimes the bureaucracy is even less transparent, even if there is a veneer of a legitimating process. Occasionally, however, there are genuine discontinuities, perhaps the most notable being US Democratic president Jimmy Carter's 1977 decision to pursue a policy of restraint over the export of conventional arms.[12] In 1997, two decades on from Carter's restraining order, Robin Cook, foreign secretary in the then newly elected UK Labour government, unveiled what was to become widely known, and sometimes derided, as its 'ethical foreign policy'. Cook said human rights would be at 'the heart of our foreign policy', and that the government would 'give a new momentum to arms control and disarmament'.[13] But realpolitik arguably thwarted Carter's goal and Cook's ambition. By 2000 Cook's ethical language had been dropped in favour of proposals for a 'more responsible arms trade'.[14]

Unless a maximalist position is assumed, either restraining or permissive, then decision-making depends on an assessment of multiple factors measured against national criteria and international norms. There is considerable criticism of the broad approach now taken to arms-export decision-making, including the contention that the process of the main arms exporters is weighted generally towards approval.[15] These arguments, however, can sometimes overlook, underplay or misrepresent the conventional deterrence value of the weapons system being supplied, and the value of considering the weapons or systems being supplied in a regional context.

Not all efforts to manage arms exports, however, are national, at least notionally. In 2008 the EU agreed what it described as the 'Common Position' on arms exports,[16] which covered the decision-making process and criteria concerning the export of weapons. Agreeing a collective position had echoes of the Carter administration's approach because it recognised the need for a multinational agreement to avoid one state simply undercutting another when securing weapons exports.

The Common Position can be viewed as an effort to establish a coherent approach to arms exports across all the EU's member states. Conversely, the lack of any capacity to enforce the criteria at the transnational level means it can also be read as a compromise because all decision-making and implementation rests at the member-state level.[17] This provides considerable latitude for states to interpret the criteria in such a way as to have the desired outcome, often in favour of a sale.

The economics of arms sales

At the risk of oversimplifying, there are arguably only two kinds of arms exporters: those that choose and those that must. The former have a large enough domestic market to make the foreign sale of export weapons an optional, but welcome, fillip to national acquisition numbers, whereas the latter require at least some promise of export sales to navigate national approval and funding processes in supporting the domestic development of major weapons. The economic case is intertwined with political decision-making, while the relative value and the return on investment in defence spending and associated exports remains polarising. In the air sector, only China, arguably Russia, and the US have air forces large enough, and therefore the resulting procurement-number needs, to support fully national defence-aerospace sectors at the original equipment manufacturer (OEM) level capable of meeting all domestic needs, even if this capacity is not always exercised.

Conversely, countries such as France and the UK, while still retaining the ability to design and produce major weapons – such as combat aircraft or main battle tanks – have greater incentives to amortise research and development expenses and reduce unit costs through exports. The allure of export sales has often been employed in lobbying for support of domestic development in preference to an off-the-shelf acquisition from overseas. This argument has and continues to be made regularly in the UK[18] and France by industry lobbyists and politicians, for example. The export market was also critical to Russia during the 1990s and early 2000s. Export sales provided sorely needed revenue at a time when domestic demand had collapsed because of wider economic problems. In the aerospace sector, China's repeat orders for the Sukhoi Su-27 *Flanker* combat aircraft provided badly needed work for industry, while the sale of the BMP-3 infantry fighting vehicle to the United Arab Emirates (UAE) has been described as saving Kurganmashzavod (Kurgan machine-building plant) from closure through a lack of orders.[19] Necessity, rather than ideological alignment, underpinned Moscow's conventional-arms export decisions in the 1990s.[20] A beneficiary of access to Russian aerospace technology in the 1990s and early 2000s, China is now emerging as a potential provider of major weapons in its own right.

Cost pressures, however, are also seeing some states try to sustain a national capacity through international cooperation. In Europe, the UK is a prime example of this. For instance, in the military-aircraft arena it has adopted multinational collaboration, in the land-vehicle domain it has purchased already existing armoured-vehicle designs, and the naval sector is in part again turning to international cooperation for primary surface-to-air missile systems for some classes of ship.

The economic value of weapons exports remains contested, with debate often polarised and analysis sometimes eliding into advocacy. Claims can appear inflated among those supporting exports and those opposed. The lack of transparency among many of the main weapons-exporting nations makes a clear-eyed assessment even more difficult.[21]

The Soviet Union's collapse and the dissolution of the Warsaw Pact greatly reduced the risk of peer or near-peer state-on-state conflict from the beginning of the 1990s. These developments had implications for US and European manufacturers of major weapons. Defence spending began to fall in the early 1990s in the US, while several allied nations also benefited from a 'peace dividend'. US defence spending as a percentage of gross domestic product (GDP) fell by nearly half during the period 1989–99, from 5.5% to 2.9% of GDP.[22] The challenge facing the sector was described by some as the most profound shift

PAKISTAN'S MILITARY VEHICLES
Pakistan's *Shaheen* long-range ballistic missiles during the Pakistan Day parade in Islamabad, 23 March 2022. CREDIT: GHULAM RASOOL/AFP via Getty Images.

it has seen since the end of the Second World War. In the US a wave of consolidation greatly reduced the number of companies involved in the defence sector – by the end of the 1990s there were only three military-aircraft manufacturers[23] – and greater emphasis was placed on defence exports to compensate for the domestic cuts.[24]

Consolidation also occurred among European defence manufacturers, but to a lesser extent, with national – rather than transnational – champions continuing to be prevalent. This was irrespective of political ambitions to foster consolidation at the European level. In 1998 the governments of France, Germany, Italy, Spain, Sweden and the United Kingdom signed a letter of intent on 'Measures to Facilitate the Restructuring of the European Defence Industry'.[25]

The absence of a consolidated European market, one that potentially has the volume demand to reduce the need for extra-European sales, underscores the continuing importance of defence exports for countries where domestic requirements alone are economically prohibitive. In the case of the UK, this has been compounded by the 2016 decision to leave the European Union and the wider economic impact of the withdrawal. Defence exports have, if anything, taken on even greater economic importance for the British government because of Brexit, and this prosperity logic is reflected in recent strategy documents examined in the UK chapter.

Arms exports are of a similar level of importance to France, described in 2018 by defence minister Florence Parly as 'the business model of our sovereignty'.[26] Like London, Paris uses defence exports to support a domestic industrial base that would otherwise be unaffordable to sustain. Parly's comment explicitly links arms sales with sovereignty, which in this case is the same as Paris's conception of strategic autonomy.[27] Without the continued export of major weapons, it would become increasingly difficult to sustain the levels of domestic research and development required to produce the next generation of weapons systems. In some cases, Paris is having to at least consider multinational development to spread investment costs, with the Future Combat Air System an example. France, Germany and Spain have partnered to work on a multi-role combat aircraft to enter service from 2040. The political impetus, however, is not fully mirrored in industry, where tensions over technology sharing and levels of participation have caused delay.[28]

Broad domestic conceptions of French and German strengths in part explain the differences in how arms exports are viewed politically. Germany is mostly perceived as an economic power rather than a military one. For Germany, the arms industry is arguably an economic, industrial issue, not a strategic or foreign-policy one, and defence companies themselves are considered economic rather than security actors. There is also less connectivity between the German defence industry and government in that a considerable element of the industry remains privately, rather than state, owned.

In 2020 US defence exports were valued at USD17.8bn[29] by the Aerospace Industries Association (AIA), with aerospace and defence representing 6.3% of all US export business that year.[30] In both the US and the UK, defence aerospace was the largest contributor by dollar value. The AIA figures for 2020 suggested defence aerospace represented 77% by value,[31] while in the UK the figure was 73.2%[32] for military aircraft. A notable difference, however, is the extent to which the Middle East is prevalent in sales figures. In the UK, the Middle East represented 60% of defence exports in the 2010–19 period;[33] based on AIA figures (US Defense Exports Stat Overview 2018) for the 2012–17 period, the Middle East only accounted for 27% of US defence exports. The Asia-Pacific market was the largest at 38%, with Europe third behind the Middle East at 22%.[34]

China and Russia are also in the top five arms-exporting states. In 2020 Moscow supplied military equipment it valued at USD15.6bn,[35] and in recent years India has been the country's largest customer.[36] Arms exports were a lifeline for much of Russia's defence industry in the 1990s and early 2000s as domestic acquisition collapsed. Recipients during this period included China, which benefitted from access to Russian defence-aerospace technology in helping to develop further its national military-aerospace sector. Beijing may well increasingly compete with Russia in markets that are either unwilling or unable to purchase US or European systems, and in some countries it may compete directly with the last two. Today, China counts Pakistan as its largest arms buyer.[37]

A question of stability

The cause-or-effect debate continues to roil around major-weapons sales. For anti-arms-trade campaigners, the sale of major weapons serves only to erode stability or contribute further to instability.[38] For others, the picture is more mixed depending on the recipient state. In considering the sale of a major weapons system, 'stability' is an oft-cited criterion, though the mechanisms and analysis to support a judgement are rarely fully available in the public domain.

Stability, in the defence and security context, explored in greater detail in the next chapter, is perhaps easiest to describe in negative terms. In a regional context it is the absence over time of state-on-state war, or any substantive risk of the outbreak of hostilities. Further positive stabilising factors could include the provision and use of political or diplomatic mechanisms to address any transnational concerns arising within the region. Established and publicly supported forms of government and an economy – post-industrial, industrial or agrarian – that provide for the broad needs of the populace are reinforcing factors. One of the many challenges in assessing the potential effect of a weapons sale on regional stability or instability is that it remains hostage to the vicissitudes of time. For example, a decade ago, who would have predicted a full-blown state-on-state war on Europe's immediate borders? A further historic example, the ramifications of which are still playing out, is this analysis from the US intelligence community in the early 1980s:

> Projected arms sales trends pose several potential problems for US interests. Military expansion in the region creates additional stresses within modernizing Gulf societies and may make military takeovers more likely ... Despite these dangers, the projected pattern of arms sales in the Persian Gulf has a number of positive implications for regional stability and US interests. Likely Western sales to North Yemen, Iran and Iraq will reduce their potential dependence on the USSR and will reduce the hostility of Baghdad and Tehran toward the West.[39]

Although coherent, the argument turned out to be wrong in many respects. Tehran would remain at least as hostile to the US, while a decade after the analysis the US led a coalition against Iraq in the Gulf War, and by the mid-1990s a reunified Yemen was embroiled in a short civil war. The last conflict was a harbinger of the decades of strife that followed.

Even the Trump administration, an outlier in much recent US domestic and foreign policy, cited 'interests in regional stability'[40] as a consideration in the export of major weapons. National Presidential Security Memorandum 10 identified the promotion of 'regional security' as an element of decision-making.[41] Despite the political distance between presidents Donald Trump and Barack Obama, the language around regional stability remained constant.[42] In considering arms-transfer decisions, both administrations used the same boilerplate language, reflecting 'the transfer's consistency with United States interests in regional stability'.[43] Stability as a stated key criterion is not restricted to US or European weapons-exporting nations. China identifies the requirement to 'not undermine peace, security and stability of the region concerned'[44] as one of its three criteria in assessing whether or not to approve an arms export. Russia, meanwhile, has over the past couple of decades been keen to be viewed as a responsible actor in its 'military technical cooperation' with export customers. The extent that this may change, as the ramifications of its invasion of Ukraine begin to materialise, has yet to become clear.

The lacklustre performance of Russian main battle tanks and other armoured vehicles in the Ukraine war may also influence the export market, as will the utility of portable anti-armour missiles in their defeat. Competition between the US and Russia over India's lucrative defence market could intensify further, for example, if Washington continues to try to build its share of New Delhi's procurements. The Indian Army's tank and armoured-vehicle inventory is almost all of Russian design.

The value of ground-based air defence has also again been underscored by the war, as has the ability to engage UAVs as well as crewed aircraft and helicopters. The value of UAVs in the intelligence, surveillance and reconnaissance (ISR) and armed roles, meanwhile, has only been reinforced further. The war has also been a reminder that a large inventory of major weapons systems is only one part of military capability, and that morale and fighting spirit are also important. Capability and intent are difficult to reconcile when considering the issue of stability in the context of weapons-sales policies and decision-making. As with much that is related to arms exports, it is often a matter of perspective. In reviewing a proposed sale, US policy guidance is to pay particular attention 'when considering transfers that involve power projection, anti-access or area denial capability, or the introduction of a capability that may increase regional tensions or contribute to an arms race'.[45]

One difficulty is that power-projection, anti-access and area-denial capabilities arguably are neither inherently offensive nor defensive, nor inherently stabilising or destabilising. All are context dependent. This view, however, is not universally shared. In, for example, *The Arms Production Dilemma*, the authors argue:

> Advanced combat aircraft are offense-capable systems whose deployment tends to erode confidence and increase fears of war ... their very power and versatility make them the most threatening and potentially destabilising form of weaponry after nuclear and chemical weapons and ballistic missiles.[46]

TURKISH AIRPOWER AT TEKNOFEST 2021
A Bayraktar *Akinci* UAV and an F-16 perform during the Aviation, Space and Technology Festival at Ataturk Airport in Istanbul, Turkey, 25 September 2021.
CREDIT: Coban/Anadolu Agency via Getty Images.

One could as easily suggest, given a multi-role combat aircraft's 'versatility', that its introduction into a region – in a particular set of circumstances – was instead stabilising. The underlying flaw in *The Arms Production Dilemma* is that it attempts to craft a universal argument that oversimplifies and misrepresents the nature of airpower. The argument put forward is not always wrong, but neither is it always right.

This, however, does not negate the potential significance of such weapons systems capable of being used for power projection. As a late 1980s US Directorate of Intelligence memo noted:

> dramatic increases in the long-range airstrike capabilities of several Middle Eastern countries are likely over the next few years and will – together with the acquisition of ballistic missiles by many of these same countries – contribute to the growing strategic vulnerability of states throughout the region.[47]

Vulnerability, if perceived to be mutual between competitor states, can be seen as stabilising. If the vulnerability is not viewed as mutual, but rather as a military advantage, then this is a risk to existing stability. Since the 1980s, the US has provided highly capable combat aircraft to the Gulf region, supplying at one point the most advanced variant of the Lockheed Martin F-16 *Fighting Falcon*, the Block 60, to the UAE, with a contract signature in 2000. More recently, in 2021, delivery of the Boeing F-15QA, an aircraft similar to the F-15EX *Eagle* II, began to Qatar. Capable conventional airpower among the Gulf Cooperation Council (GCC) states can be viewed as a deterrent to Iran's large holding of close-, short- and medium-range ballistic missiles, and as a preferable outcome to the GCC states pursuing a symmetric missile capability to that of Tehran. Had Washington decided against releasing either the F-16 Block 60 or the F-15QA, then the purchasing states in question would have been able to source broadly comparable combat aircraft from other providers. While the influence argument is often overstated, it does have value. In the case of the Block 60, for instance, the US was able to block the integration of the MBDA *Black Shaheen* air-launched land-attack cruise missile on the UAE's F-16,[48] restricting the missile to the less capable *Mirage* 2000, the other multi-role combat aircraft in the air force's inventory.[49]

From buyer to builder

While, as previously noted, very few states have the industrial capacity to address all their weapons-system needs, the international defence-industrial landscape is far from static. Seller–purchaser relationships can also be used by the latter over time as a mechanism through which to begin developing national areas of capability. Buyers requiring direct offsets on a weapons-system acquisition as part of the package can use this approach to begin nurturing domestic capacity in areas deemed to be of industrial and political value. Countries that now have a sovereign research, design and manufacturing capability in areas such as defence aerospace include Japan, South Korea and Turkey. All three began to build up national capacity through acquisition programmes with the US. In all three countries the F-16 has played a role, in the cases of South Korea and Turkey through direct acquisition and local final assembly, and in Japan as the basis for a 'domestic' design, the Mitsubishi F-2.[50] South Korea and Turkey are now weapons exporters, while Japan has begun tentatively to consider its role beyond national boundaries.

Japan, South Korea and, to a lesser extent, Turkey all shared the advantage of being industrialised, with a broad manufacturing sector and a workforce capable of supporting the requirements of weapons design, development and manufacture. None of the Gulf states yet has a comparable industrial base, though Saudi Arabia and the UAE have begun developing niche capabilities and have wider ambitions. One of the aims of Saudi Arabia's Vision 2030 is to greatly increase the amount of defence funding that is spent with domestic providers. The goal is to 'localise' 50% of the state's annual defence-equipment expenditure by the end of the decade.[51] How close to hitting, or by how far it misses, this target remains to be seen, although at the World Defense Show (WDS) in March 2022, Riyadh announced that localisation efforts reached 12% in 2021, up from 4% in 2016, further estimating that overall localisation will rise to 53% by 2030.[52]

Riyadh had ambitions to establish a final assembly line[53] as part of its 2007 purchase of 72 Eurofighter *Typhoon* multi-role fighter aircraft. Notionally, the first 24 aircraft would come off the line at BAE Systems' Warton site in northwest England, with the remainder to be put together from major sub-assemblies at a site in Saudi Arabia. Delays in selecting a site contributed to this overly ambitious target being dropped.[54] While any final assembly of a modern multi-role fighter has yet to be established in Saudi Arabia, there are multiple projects concerning the manufacture and assembly of Chinese-designed medium-altitude long-endurance UAVs.[55] The UAE has already established the capacity to design and build armed UAVs, with Algeria already an operator.[56]

Along with UAVs, the UAE has also established a tactical-missile manufacturing capacity as part of the EDGE Group. The initial building block of this capability was the purchase of the Denel Dynamics *Umbani* guided-bomb family.[57] Known in the UAE as *Al-Tariq*, it has already been sold to the Egyptian Air Force as well as being provided to the UAE Air Force.[58] Economic problems in South Africa and the resulting lack of defence funding provided a fertile recruitment environment, with numerous guided-weapons specialists joining EDGE from Denel Dynamics. EDGE's portfolio has expanded to include UAV-specific weapon designs, with powered stand-off missiles also in development as of 2022.[59] The UAE also aspires to a sovereign capability with regard to weapons systems,[60] although what this means in practical terms is still unclear. Given the comparatively small size of its domestic market, however, this would almost inevitably see the UAE become more active in the export arena to supplement domestic production numbers.[61]

Chinese, European, Russian and US defence companies are often no longer able to simply sell major weapons to key markets. Buyer states are moving increasingly beyond offset requirements to technology transfer or co-development as they look to build their domestic industry. The release or otherwise of sensitive technology and the capacity to independently modify software-dependent systems have sometimes been used as criteria for discrimination in acquisition decision-making. A proposed sale of the F-35A to the UAE was shelved in part because of the customer state's dislike of the technology restraints that Washington wished to impose as part of the deal.[62] In turn, the US was concerned about increasing ties between the UAE and China.[63] The upshot was that the UAE opted to purchase the *Rafale*, and also to begin to position on possibly accessing a French-led next-generation combat aircraft,[64] while putting the F-35 discussions on hold. The UAE also decided to buy a Chinese advanced jet trainer, the Hongdu L-15,[65] a move unlikely to have eased US concern.

From buyer to actor

US and European weapons sales into the Gulf region have traditionally been viewed as serving conventional deterrence purposes, and to build and help sustain security partnerships. The importance of access to Middle Eastern hydrocarbons to the US, until recently, was also a considerable factor in arms-sales policy, while the relationship between Israel and the US has underpinned Washington's regional decision-making. Sustaining Israel's qualitative military edge has been a long-standing criterion concerning US arms sales to the region.[66] Successive US administrations have seen a militarily strong Israel as supporting what stability there is in the area, notwithstanding the Israel Defense Forces' military incursions and the failure to resolve territorial disputes with the Palestinians.[67]

The Gulf states traditionally have not been extrovert in the use of military force beyond domestic boundaries; however, in recent years some have increasingly been willing to proactively exercise such a capacity.[68] This was perhaps first notable in the UAE's engagement in the war in Afghanistan in support of the US-led campaign. The air force deployed a small number of the F-16 Block 60 multi-role fighters,[69] along with regular Boeing C-17 *Globemaster* III heavy-transport-aircraft flights providing logistics back-up. The F-16s were used for close air support, with air crew gaining combat experience from the detachment.[70] The UAE[71] and Egypt[72] have been independent actors in supporting factions in Libya's civil war. The former was also a significant contributor to the Saudi-led 2015 intervention in Yemen's civil war, a conflict that has posed uncomfortable questions for some supplier nations to the UAE and Saudi Arabia.

The US Congress in 2018–19 attempted on several occasions to block weapons deliveries to Saudi Arabia, but Trump exercised his presidential veto.[73] The Biden administration subsequently put on hold Saudi orders for the Boeing GBU-39 Small Diameter Bomb, and likely also for the Raytheon *Paveway* IV precision-guided bomb.[74] The decision was described by the administration as part of an attempt to 'recalibrate our relationship' with Riyadh and to encourage a political resolution to the Yemen war.[75] The *Paveway* IV has previously been heralded as an export success by the UK: this variant was developed by US company Raytheon to meet a Royal Air Force requirement. The programme was highlighted in the 2018 report 'Growing the Contribution of Defence to UK Prosperity'.[76] While Saudi Arabia was not identified as a customer for the *Paveway* IV, it is assumed to have been the first export destination for the weapon.[77]

The war in Yemen, as well as human-rights abuses, also focused attention on French and German involvement in arms exports to the region. In 2018, the German government said it would halt export licences to countries taking part in the war.[78] Successive French governments, however, have continued to approve licences to Saudi Arabia and the UAE, with French President Emmanuel Macron criticising then German chancellor Angela Merkel's decision to suspend weapons sales to Saudi Arabia following the murder of Saudi journalist Jamal Khashoggi, in which the Saudi state was implicated.[79] In the case of Yemen, the French rationale for not halting sales to Saudi

BAE EUROFIGHTER *TYPHOON* ASSEMBLY PLANT
A BAE Eurofighter *Typhoon* jet in the final assembly hangar at the BAE Systems plant in Warton, UK, 27 February 2014. CREDIT: Chris Ratcliffe/Bloomberg via Getty Images.

Arabia and the UAE was that the weapons they exported were not meant to be used in the war.[80]

The UK's Defence and Security Industrial Strategy (DSIS) recognised what in narrow economic terms was an overdependence on one sector, the air sector, and even more so on one region.

> The UK is the second biggest exporter of defence products globally (after the US) ... However, the defence sector is extremely reliant on sales of air platforms to the Middle East and is all but unrepresented in exports to 17 of the 20 largest defence importers.[81]

Implicit within the DSIS was the potential difficulty of managing the supplier–purchaser relationship when the core customer base was too narrow. The sale of major weapons can provide an element of leverage or influence concerning the purchasing state's behaviour, but this can often be overstated. Any influence, however, will only be further diluted by overdependence on the part of the supplier state on a small number of key export partners, and the extent to which the relationship is considered 'strategic'. The latter factor, in particular, may have influenced French decision-making with regard to the UAE and Yemen.

Control limits

Efforts at international arms control stretch back to the beginning of the twentieth century, with a notable early achievement being the 1925 Geneva Protocol[82] that banned chemical and biological weapons. In the era of superpower confrontation between the US and the Soviet Union, bilateral nuclear-armed systems were the arms-control focus. In the conventional realm some categories of weapons were included as a result of being dual capable, for instance in the 1987 Missile Technology Control Regime (MTCR).[83] While the regime was aimed at constraining the proliferation of delivery systems capable of carrying a nuclear payload, ballistic and cruise missiles, some classes of UAVs, and their main subsystems were covered if they met range and payload thresholds specified by the regime. Launched by the G7, the MTCR now has 35 member states.[84] The regime, however, has sometimes been criticised as a form of cartel[85] attempting to limit non-signatory states' access to legitimate conventional defence technologies already in service with many of the signatories.

The first international treaty to encompass all the classes of major conventional weapons was the 2013 Arms Trade Treaty (ATT). The culmination of over a decade's lobbying, the treaty text was approved by the United Nations General Assembly on 2 April 2013 and was implemented as of 24 December 2014.[86] The ATT is arguably a success in simply coming into being, but like the EU's Common Position, the treaty remains dependent on national implementation mechanisms. There were also notable abstentions, including China and Russia. Beijing did accede to the treaty in 2020.[87] Conversely, while the US was a 2013 signatory, Trump viewed the ATT as 'badly misguided'[88] and said he would not pursue ratification.[89] The Biden administration has been reviewing the US Conventional Arms Transfer Policy, but as of autumn 2022 this had yet to be made public. Whether the work may revise the US position on the ATT is not yet known.

War over the air

The global air sector is estimated by the British government to have 'accounted for almost two-thirds of all defence exports' by value in the period 2010–19.[90] In 2020, US defence exports in the air sector were three times those of the other sectors combined according to figures from the AIA. The AIA attributed USD13.7bn in exports to the defence-aerospace sector in 2020, with a further USD4.1bn attributed to non-aerospace defence products.[91]

The dominance of the sector is still greater in the UK. In estimating defence exports for 2020, ADS, the defence and security industry's trade body, suggested the air sector would contribute 91% of the anticipated total, while land would contribute 6% and the maritime domain 3%.[92] Such a percentage spread is not an anomaly and reflects UK defence-industry performance over the previous decade, in which the aerospace sector represented 91% of orders and contracts from 2011–20, land business a further 5% and sea 4%.[93] During the same period, the Middle East was the UK's largest market: 58% of UK export orders and contracts were with this region.[94]

The market for combat aircraft is an oligopoly: a few large manufactures dominate the sector. France, Sweden, the UK, the US and Russia are the primary providers of combat aircraft. France in 2021–22 scored notable export sales success with the Dassault *Rafale* multi-role fighter.[95] Sweden is continuing to promote the Saab *Gripen* E, having secured Brazil as the export launch customer in 2014.[96] The UK and its three partners – Germany, Italy and Spain – continue to seek further export orders for the Eurofighter *Typhoon*. US export sales include the Lockheed Martin F-35 *Joint Strike Fighter*, the Boeing F-15 *Eagle*, F-16 *Fighting Falcon* and F/A-18E/F *Super Hornet*. Russia continues to seek exports for its Sukhoi Su-35 *Flanker* M and Su-30SM *Flanker* H along with the MiG MiG-29/35 *Fulcrum* family. Exports of combat aircraft also involve air-to-air and air-to-surface weapons packages as part of the initial deal, or as part of capability upgrades, that can at times be as controversial as the sale of a combat aircraft.

Russia's invasion of Ukraine will almost certainly have direct and indirect consequences for its weapons exports. Economic sanctions will at the very least make it more difficult for the Russian defence industry to access components and subsystems that it has previously used in export standard products. Another possibility is that the Russian government's behaviour will discourage some countries from buying from Moscow. It is also possible that Moscow, in an effort to bolster its export presence, will offer more capable systems than it previously would have been willing to release. A related issue is that Russia's focus will most likely shift to replenishing its own stocks and munitions to replace its losses and for use in the war against Ukraine. In turn, this might spur some target markets – for example India – further in their domestic-production ambitions.

The predominance in value of defence aerospace among those Western countries capable of manufacturing combat aircraft is in part a reflection simply of the high unit cost when compared to land systems, and the greater numbers procured when compared to naval platforms. Land-systems orders are often in triple figures, ships in single digits, and combat-aircraft exports can be in the tens but rarely exceed 100. In terms of unit cost, a modern main battle tank is in excess of USD10 million,[97] while a multi-role fighter aircraft is in the region of USD80m[98] and an advanced frigate can offer little change from USD1bn.[99] The largest combat-aircraft export sale in 2021, for example, was for the French *Rafale*, with the UAE order of 80[100] of the aircraft at an estimated cost of USD19bn.[101] An associated weapons package for an aircraft sale can comfortably also total hundreds of millions of dollars. A medium-range active-radar guided air-to-air missile (AAM) can cost around USD1m,[102] while a single loadout of AAMs for an aircraft could be near the unit cost of a main battle tank.

China has also previously sold combat aircraft, but these have tended to be of ageing designs that did not compare favourably with Western or Russian types. The Chengdu J-7, a derivative of the Soviet-era MiG-21 *Fishbed*, was by the mid-1980s the core of the People's Liberation Army Air Force's fighter capability. It supplied the J-7 to the Democratic People's Republic of Korea in 1982[103] and has exported the type since then in several guises to air forces unable either to afford or to access more capable US or European combat aircraft.

However, sustained investment by Beijing in its defence-aerospace sector since the mid-1990s means it is now able to offer more credible products for export. The delivery of the Chengdu J-10CE *Firebird* multi-role fighter to Pakistan,[104] a long-standing recipient of Chinese arms, marks a step change. The J-10C is a modern combat aircraft with advanced sensors and weapons. The Pakistan sale appears to include the PL-10 (CH-AA-9) imaging infrared guided AAM, and Islamabad has become the first export customer for the PL-15 (CH-AA-10), a medium- to long-range AAM. Both missiles are on a par with the most capable Western equivalents offered for export.[105] As with US and European equivalents, some of the performance characteristics of the export weapons will differ from the yet more capable domestic variants. China is almost certainly going to continue increasing its presence in the defence-exports arena, with the capacity to now offer considerably more capable systems than before.

Beijing has already enjoyed market success in adopting a permissive approach to the export of armed UAVs.[106] Washington had until 2019 maintained a far more restrictive approach to the release of such a capability to foreign customers, providing an opportunity that China was willing to exploit. Egypt, Saudi Arabia[107] and the UAE[108] had all expressed an interest in acquiring armed UAVs from the US; however, approval was not forthcoming. The US, and particularly the State Department, wanted to hold the line in adhering to the MTCR[109] and also did not want to be the first to provide such a capability in the region. The MTCR is a 35-nation accord intended to hamper the proliferation of delivery systems for weapons of mass destruction. Medium and large UAVs fell within Category I of the regime, which assumed a 'presumption of denial'. Decisions, however, are taken on a national basis, and exceptions are made. The UK, for instance, was the first export customer approved to receive a US armed UAV.[110] In July 2020 the US revised its position on UAV exports in its 'Updated UAS (Unmanned Aerial System) Policy'[111] which saw it shift to a moderately less restrictive approach.

The armed-UAV issue was representative of what might be termed an imitation dynamic. The United States' use of an armed version of the MQ-1 *Predator* at the start of its war in Afghanistan widened

***TOMAHAWK* MISSILE LAUNCH**
A RGM-109 *Tomahawk* cruise missile is launched from its Mark 41 vertical launch system aboard the destroyer USS *Fife* (DD-991) during Operation Desert Storm.
CREDIT: CORBIS/Corbis via Getty Images.

the utility of the UAV beyond the ISR realm and further piqued other nations' interest in exploring such a capability. As the utility of armed UAVs became increasingly apparent, acquisition ambitions only grew.

This, of course, is far from new. Following the outcome of the 1982 war between Argentina and the UK over the Falklands/Malvinas, and Israel's success against the Syrian Air Force and Syrian ground-based air defence, the US intelligence community suggested these events would have a clear effect on export-market weapons acquisitions.

> The dramatic effectiveness of high-technology weapons in the Falkland Islands conflict and in the recent Israeli experience in Lebanon will have a marked impact on global arsenals ... The control of arms transfers will be more difficult with increased demand and availability of advanced weapons.[112]

Another example of the US successfully utilising a military capability – thus pump-priming wider interest and helping to inadvertently drive export demand – is the use of conventionally armed land-attack cruise missiles in the 1991 war with Iraq. The use in 1991 of the AGM-86C Conventional Air-Launched Cruise Missile (CALCM) and the R/UGM-109 *Tomahawk* Land Attack Cruise Missiles (TLAM) in the opening attack on Iraq displayed the efficacy of cruise missiles, not least to multiple nations in the region. While, as of 2022, Washington has only sold the TLAM to the UK and has been comparatively restrictive in releasing air-launched cruise-missile types, other MTCR signatories have taken a more relaxed approach.

Having watched the US use of air-launched cruise missiles in the attacks on Iraq, the UAE was the first of several Gulf states to set about acquiring this capability, if at a shorter range. France and the UK agreed to sell a variant of the *SCALP* EG/*Storm Shadow* air-launched cruise missile to the UAE, despite US objections that even the variant being offered, the *Black Shaheen*, was a Category I MTCR weapon.[113] Subsequent to the UAE sale, Egypt, Kuwait, Qatar and Saudi Arabia have all purchased variants of the MBDA cruise missile.

Conclusion

That there is a relationship between the acquisition of major weapons and state-on-state war is self-evident: these are the primary arms with which forces will fight. But whether the relationship is causal remains contested. Is it inevitable that over time the purchase of modern weapons from a third party will always undermine regional stability, or further destabilise an area, and increase the risk of war? If this is true, then major arms-exporting states are simply enabling conflict. Measured against real-world experience, however, this does not appear to be the case. While the export of advanced arms can be fraught, the costs often very large, with the attendant risk of corruption, and the outcome of their sale over time contingent on an array of factors over which the supplier state has limited control, their provision is not de facto always destabilising or stabilising. Examples of both will be considered in later chapters of this volume.

NOTES

1 See, for example, Laurence Lustgarten, *Law and the Arms Trade: Weapons, Blood and Rules* (Oxford: Hart Publishing, 2020), p. 27.

2 See, for example, Campaign Against Arms Trade, 'About CAAT', https://caat.org.uk/about-caat/.

3 See, for example, Defense Security Cooperation Agency, 'Egypt TOW 2A Radio Frequency (RF) Missiles and Support', 19 May 2022, https://www.dsca.mil/press-media/major-arms-sales/egypt-tow-2a-radio-frequency-rf-missiles-and-support.

4 John Mintz, 'How a Dinner Led to a Feeding Frenzy', *Washington Post*, 4 July 1997, https://www.washingtonpost.com/archive/business/1997/07/04/how-a-dinner-led-to-a-feeding-frenzy/13961ba2-5908-4992-8335-c3c087cdebc6/.

5 Richard Connolly and Cecilie Sendstad, 'Russia's Role as an Arms Exporter: The Strategic and Economic Importance of Arms Exports for Russia', Chatham House, March 2017, p. 3, https://www.chathamhouse.org/sites/default/files/publications/research/2017-03-20-russia-arms-exporter-connolly-sendstad.pdf.

6 'Disarmament Chief Says Small Arms Remain Threat to Peace and Security', UN News, 6 October 2021, https://news.un.org/en/story/2021/10/1102372.

7 United Nations, 'Charter of the United Nations: Article 51', https://legal.un.org/repertory/art51.shtml.

8 Siemon T. Wezeman et al., 'International Arms Transfers and Developments in Arms Production', in SIPRI (ed.), *SIPRI Yearbook 2021: Armaments, Disarmament and International Security* (Oxford: Oxford University Press for SIPRI, 2021).

9 *Ibid.*

10 United Nations, 'The Arms Trade Treaty', https://thearmstradetreaty.org/hyper-images/file/ATT_English/ATT_English.pdf?templateId=137253.

11 United Nations Office for Disarmament Affairs, 'About Us', https://www.un.org/disarmament/about/.

12 Jimmy Carter, 'Conventional Arms Transfer Policy Statement by the President', The American Presidency Project, 19 May 1977, https://www.presidency.ucsb.edu/documents/conventional-arms-transfer-policy-statement-the-president.

13 'Robin Cook's speech on the government's ethical foreign policy', *Guardian*, 12 May 1997, https://www.theguardian.com/world/1997/may/12/indonesia.ethicalforeignpolicy.

14 Vikram Dodd and Ewen MacAskill, 'Labour drops "ethical" tag', *Guardian*, 4 September 2000, https://www.theguardian.com/politics/2000/sep/04/ethicalforeignpolicy.economy.

15 See, for example, Campaign Against Arms Trade, 'The Arms Trade', https://caat.org.uk/challenges/the-arms-trade/.

16 EUR-Lex, 'Council Common Position 2008/944/CFSP of 8 December 2008 Defining Common Rules Governing Control of Exports of Military Technology and Equipment', 8 December 2008, https://eur-lex.europa.eu/legal-content/EN/TXT/?uri=CELEX%3A32008E0944.

17 *Ibid.*

18 PWC, 'Assessment of the Expected Economic Impact of the Tempest Programme (2021–2050) Final Report', May 2021, p. 4.

19 Mikhail Barabanov, 'Russian Arms Deliveries to Arab Countries of the Persian Gulf Region', *Moscow Defence Brief*, vol. 4, 2008, p. 15.

20 Alexander A. Sergounin and Sergey V. Subbotin, 'Russia's Arms Transfers to East Asia in the 1990s (Oxford: Oxford University Press for SIPRI, 1999), p. 13, https://www.sipri.org/sites/default/files/files/RR/SIPRIRR15.pdf.

21 Lustgarten, *Law and the Arms Trade: Weapons, Blood and Rules*, p. 105.

22 SIPRI, 'Military Expenditure by Country as a Percentage of Gross Domestic Product, 1988–2002', 2018, https://www.sipri.org/sites/default/files/3_Data%20for%20all%20countries%20from%201988%E2%80%932017%20as%20a%20share%20of%20GDP.pdf.

23 Amy J. Boatner, 'Consolidation of the Aerospace and Defense Industries: The Effect of the Big Three Mergers in the United States Defense Industry', *Journal of Air Law and Commerce*, vol. 64, no. 3, 1999, p. 915, https://scholar.smu.edu/cgi/viewcontent.cgi?article=1521&context=jalc.

24 United States General Accounting Office, 'Military Exports: A Comparison of Government Support in the United States and Three Major Competitors', 18 May 1995, p. 1, https://www.gao.gov/assets/nsiad-95-86.pdf.

25 HM Government, 'Framework Agreement Concerning Measures to Facilitate the Restructuring and Operation of the European Defence Industry', 27 July 2000, p. 3, https://assets.publishing.service.gov.uk/government/uploads/system/uploads/attachment_data/file/518178/TS0033_2001.pdf.

26 Florence Parly, 'Présentation du plan transformation de la DGA' [Presentation of the DGA's Transformation Plan], DGA, 9 July 2018 (updated 14 September 2018), https://www.ixarm.com/fr/nouveautes/presentation-du-plan-de-transformation-de-la-dga.

27 See, for example, Lucie Béraud-Sudreau, *French Arms Exports: The Business of Sovereignty* (Abingdon: Routledge for the IISS, 2020).

28 Sylvia Pfeifer and Sarah White, 'Divisions risk undermining windfall for Europe's defence industry', *Financial Times*, 30 March 2022, https://www.ft.com/content/ac1a8318-9e3c-4ee9-9fce-c9a7d5cadda8.

29 Aerospace Industries Association, '2021 Facts & Figures: US Aerospace & Defense',

2021, p. 11, https://www.aia-aerospace.org/wp-content/uploads/2021-Facts-and-Figures-U.S.-Aerospace-and-Defense.pdf.

30 *Ibid.*, p. 10.

31 *Ibid.*, p. 11.

32 UK Defence Solutions Centre, 'Joint Economic Data Hub: Annual Economic Report', March 2022, p. 8, https://jedhub.org/report.

33 HM Government, 'Defence and Security Industrial Strategy: A Strategic Approach to the UK's Defence and Security Industrial Sectors', CP 410, March 2021, p. 75, https://assets.publishing.service.gov.uk/government/uploads/system/uploads/attachment_data/file/971983/Defence_and_Security_Industrial_Strategy_-_FINAL.pdf.

34 Aerospace Industries Association, 'US Defense Exports: Statistical Overview & Economic Impact Analysis 2018', p. 4.

35 BBC Monitoring, 'Russia signed arms contracts worth USD10 Billion in 2021', 14 November 2021, https://monitoring.bbc.co.uk/product/c203122c.

36 Peter D. Wezeman, Alexandra Kuimova and Siemon T. Wezeman, 'Trends in International Arms Transfers, 2020', SIPRI, March 2021, https://sipri.org/sites/default/files/2021-03/fs_2103_at_2020.pdf.

37 *Ibid.*

38 Campaign Against Arms Trade, 'The Arms Trade'.

39 Central Intelligence Agency, 'Arms Transfers to the Persian Gulf: Trends and Implications', August 1982, released by Directorate of Intelligence, pp. iii–iv, https://www.cia.gov/readingroom/docs/CIA-RDP83B00851R000100090003-4.pdf.

40 Presidential Memoranda, 'National Security Presidential Memorandum Concerning U.S. Conventional Arms Transfer Policy', 19 April 2018, https://irp.fas.org/offdocs/nspm/nspm-10.pdf.

41 *Ibid.*

42 White House, 'Presidential Policy Directive – United States Conventional Arms Transfer Policy', 15 January 2014, https://irp.fas.org/offdocs/ppd/ppd-27.html.

43 *Ibid.*

44 Ministry of Foreign Affairs of the People's Republic of China, 'Statement of the People's Republic of China to the Sixth Conference of State Parties to the Arms Trade Treaty', 20 August 2020, https://www.fmprc.gov.cn/mfa_eng/wjb_663304/zzjg_663340/jks_665232/kjfywj_665252/202008/t20200820_599769.html.

45 Presidential Memoranda, 'National Security Presidential Memorandum Concerning U.S. Conventional Arms Transfer Policy'.

46 Randall Forsberg (ed.), *The Arms Production Dilemma: Contraction and Restraint in the World Combat Aircraft Industry* (Cambridge, MA: MIT Press, 1994), p. 8.

47 Central Intelligence Agency, 'Middle East: Increasing Regional Strategic Airstrike Capabilities', 19 October 1988, released by Directorate of Intelligence, https://www.cia.gov/readingroom/docs/CIA-RDP05-00761R000101130001-8.pdf.

48 Douglas Barrie, 'Perseverance pays off for Paris in the UAE, Moscow's gambit falters', IISS Military Balance Blog, 26 November 2021, https://www.iiss.org/blogs/military-balance/2021/11/uae-combat-aircraft-25-years-in-the-making.

49 *Ibid.*

50 Lockheed Martin, 'F-2 Support Fighter', https://www.lockheedmartin.com/en-us/products/f-2.html.

51 Government of Saudi Arabia, 'Vision 2030', p. 48, https://www.vision2030.gov.sa/media/rc0b5oy1/saudi_vision203.pdf.

52 IISS, 'World Defence Show and Riyadh Defense Forum Report', March 2022.

53 'Saudi Arabia agrees major Typhoon deal with UK', Jane's, 17 September 2007, https://customer.janes.com/Janes/Display/jdin74319-jdin-2007.

54 Robert Wall, 'Saudi Arabia Agrees to Buy More Typhoon Combat Jets', *Wall Street Journal*, 9 March 2018, https://www.wsj.com/articles/saudi-arabia-agrees-to-buy-more-typhoon-combat-jets-1520617435.

55 Agnes Helou, 'Chinese and Saudi firms create joint venture to make military drones in the kingdom', *Defense News*, 9 March 2022, https://www.defensenews.com/unmanned/2022/03/09/chinese-and-saudi-firms-create-joint-venture-to-make-military-drones-in-the-kingdom/.

56 Jon Lake, 'Addcom Adds to Algerian Force', Times Aerospace, https://www.timesaerospace.aero/features/defence/adcom-adds-to-algerian-force.

57 Guy Martin, 'AL TARIQ Unveils New Warhead for Its Guided Bomb Range', defenceWeb, 30 November 2021, https://www.defenceweb.co.za/featured/al-tariq-unveils-new-warhead-for-its-guided-bomb-range/.

58 *Ibid.*

59 EDGE Group, 'Missiles & Weapons', https://edgegroup.ae/cluster/missiles-weapons.

60 Haena Jo, 'Can the UAE emerge as a leading global defense supplier?', *Defense News*, 15 February 2021, https://www.defensenews.com/digital-show-dailies/idex/2021/02/15/can-the-uae-emerge-as-a-leading-global-defense-supplier/.

61 *Ibid.*

62 'UAE told the U.S. it will suspend talks on F-35 jets – Emirati official', Reuters, 14 December 2021, https://www.reuters.com/business/aerospace-defense/uae-threatens-pull-out-23-bln-f-35-drone-deal-with-us-wsj-2021-12-14/.

63 David Schenker, 'Want to Sell F-35s to the UAE? Time to Address the China Factor', *National Interest*, 23 April 2021, https://nationalinterest.org/feature/want-sell-f-35s-uae-time-address-china-factor-183383.

64 Barrie, 'Perseverance pays off for Paris in the UAE, Moscow's gambit falters'.

65 'UAE Acquiring Chinese L-15 Jet Trainer', Aviation Week Network, 23 February 2022, https://aviationweek.com/defense-space/aircraft-propulsion/uae-acquiring-chinese-l-15-jet-trainer.

66 Jeremy M. Sharp et al., 'Israel's Qualitative Military Edge and Possible U.S. Arms Sales to the United Arab Emirates', R46580, Congressional Research Service, 26 October 2020, p. 1, https://crsreports.congress.gov/product/pdf/R/R46580.

67 Amos Yadlin and Assaf Orion, 'Israel's New Strategy: Why a Post-American Middle East Means a Greater Role in Regional Security', *Foreign Affairs*, 18 February 2022, https://www.foreignaffairs.com/articles/middle-east/2022-02-18/israels-new-strategy.

68 Karen E. Young, 'The Emerging Interventionists of the GCC', LSE Middle East

Centre Series Paper No. 02, LSE Middle East Centre, December 2013, http://eprints.lse.ac.uk/55079/.

69 Rajiv Chandrasekaran, 'In the UAE, the United States has a quiet, potent ally nicknamed "Little Sparta"', *Washington Post*, 9 November 2014, https://www.washingtonpost.com/world/national-security/in-the-uae-the-united-states-has-a-quiet-potent-ally-nicknamed-little-sparta/2014/11/08/3fc6a50c-643a-11e4-836c-83bc4f26eb67_story.html.

70 *Ibid.*

71 Emadeddin Badi, 'Russia Isn't the Only One Getting Its Hands Dirty in Libya', *Foreign Policy*, 21 April 2020, https://foreignpolicy.com/2020/04/21/libyan-civil-war-france-uae-khalifa-haftar/.

72 Alessia Melcangi, 'Egypt Recalibrated Its Strategy in Libya Because of Turkey', Atlantic Council, 1 June 2021, https://www.atlanticcouncil.org/blogs/menasource/egypt-recalibrated-its-strategy-in-libya-because-of-turkey/.

73 'Trump uses veto to unblock $8bn weapons sale to Saudi Arabia', BBC, 25 July 2019, https://www.bbc.co.uk/news/world-us-canada-49106989.

74 Joe Gould and Aaron Mehta, 'Boeing, Raytheon missile sales to Saudi Arabia paused by Biden administration', *Defense News*, 5 February 2021, https://www.defensenews.com/global/mideast-africa/2021/02/05/boeing-raytheon-missile-sales-to-saudi-arabia-canceled-by-biden-administration/.

75 Timothy Alan Betts, 'Remarks to the Defense Trade Advisory Group', US Department of State, 4 November 2021, https://www.state.gov/remarks-to-the-defense-trade-advisory-group/.

76 Phillip Dunne MP, 'Growing the Contribution of Defence to UK Prosperity', July 2018, p. 21, https://assets.publishing.service.gov.uk/government/uploads/system/uploads/attachment_data/file/723679/20180709_MOD_Philip_Dunne_Review_FOR_WEB_PUB.pdf.

77 Nicholas de Larrinaga, 'Saudi Arabia Becomes First Paveway IV Export Customer,' *Janes Defence Weekly*, 26 March 2014, https://customer.janes.com/Janes/Display/jdw54948-jdw-2014.

78 Koalitionsvertrag zwischen CDU, CSU und SPD, 'Ein neuer Aufbruch für Europa, Eine neue Dynamik für Deutschland, Ein neuer Zusammenhalt für unser Land' [A New Beginning for Europe, a New Dynamic for Germany, a New Cohesion for Our Country], 12 March 2018, p. 149, https://www.cdu.de/system/tdf/media/dokumente/koalitionsvertrag_2018.pdf?file=1.

79 'Macron accuse implicitement Merkel de "démagogie" sur les livraisons d'armes à Ryad' [Macron Implicitly Accuses Merkel of 'Demagogy' on Arms Deliveries to Riyadh], *Le Point*, 26 October 2018, https://www.lepoint.fr/politique/macron-accuse-implicitement-merkel-de-demagogie-sur-les-livraisons-d-armes-a-ryad-26-10-2018-2266348_20.php.

80 'Yémen: les armes françaises servent au Moyen-Orient' [Yemen: French Weapons Are Used in the Middle East], Franceinfo, 9 February 2018, https://www.francetvinfo.fr/monde/proche-orient/yemen/yemen-les-armes-francaises-servent-au-moyen-orient_2603056.html.

81 HM Government, 'Defence and Security Industrial Strategy: A Strategic Approach to the UK's Defence and Security Industrial Sectors', p.75, https://assets.publishing.service.gov.uk/government/uploads/system/uploads/attachment_data/file/971983/Defence_and_Security_Industrial_Strategy_-_FINAL.pdf.

82 United Nations Office for Disarmament Affairs, '1925 Geneva Protocol', https://www.un.org/disarmament/wmd/bio/1925-geneva-protocol/.

83 Missile Technology Control Regime, 'Frequently Asked Questions', https://mtcr.info/frequently-asked-questions-faqs/.

84 *Ibid.*

85 Andrew Feickert, 'Missile Technology Control Regime (MTCR) and the International Code of Conduct Against Ballistic Missile Proliferation (ICOC): Background and Issues for Congress', RL31848, Congressional Research Service, 8 April 2003, p.8, https://crsreports.congress.gov/product/pdf/RL/RL31848/3.

86 United Nations Office for Disarmament Affairs, 'Arms Trade Treaty', https://www.un.org/disarmament/convarms/arms-trade-treaty-2/.

87 Ministry of Foreign Affairs of the People's Republic of China, 'Statement of the People's Republic of China to the Sixth Conference of States Parties to the Arms Trade Treaty'.

88 'The Latest: Trump says "arms trade treaty" misguided', Associated Press, 27 April 2019, https://apnews.com/article/25e979767bef495c8e7395b3a9c2958e.

89 *Ibid.*

90 HM Government, 'UK Defence and Security Export Statistics: 2020', 26 October 2021, chart 9, https://www.gov.uk/government/statistics/uk-defence-and-security-exports-for-2020/uk-defence-and-security-export-statistics-for-2020.

91 Aerospace Industries Association, '2021 Facts & Figures: US Aerospace & Defense', p.11.

92 ADS, 'Industry Facts & Figures 2021', p. 11, https://www.adsgroup.org.uk/industry-issues/facts-figures-2021/.

93 HM Government, 'UK Defence and Security Export Statistics: 2020', chart 9.

94 *Ibid.*, chart 7.

95 Douglas Barrie et al., 'European Combat Air Power: A Snapshot', IISS, March 2022, p.18, https://www.iiss.org/blogs/research-paper/2022/03/european-combat-air-power-a-snapshot.

96 'The First Serial Production Gripen E Fighters are in Brazil', Saab, 6 April 2022, https://www.saab.com/newsroom/press-releases/2022/the-first-serial-production-gripen-e-fighters-are-in-brazil.

97 Ministry of National Defence, 'Abrams for Poland – We Reinforce the Potential of the Polish Armed Forces', 5 April 2022, https://www.gov.pl/web/national-defence/abrams-for-poland---we-reinforce-the-potential-of-the-polish-armed-forces.

98 US Department of Defense, 'F-35 Lightning II Joint Strike Fighter (JSF) Program (F-35)', December 2019, p.80, https://www.esd.whs.mil/Portals/54/Documents/FOID/Reading%20

Room/Selected_Acquisition_Reports/FY_2019_SARS/20-F-0568_DOC_32_F-35_SAR_Dec_2019_Full.pdf.

99 Pierre Tran, 'France takes delivery of its 5th FREMM', *Defense News*, 25 July 2018, https://www.defensenews.com/naval/2018/07/25/france-takes-delivery-of-its-5th-fremm/.

100 Barrie et al., 'European Combat Air Power: A Snapshot', p.18.

101 Samy Adghirni, 'UAE Buys 80 French Rafale Fighter Jets in $19 Billion Deal', Bloomberg, 3 December 2021, https://www.bloomberg.com/news/articles/2021-12-03/france-s-macron-signs-deal-to-sell-80-rafale-jets-to-the-uae.

102 US Department of Defense, 'Selected Acquisition Report: AIM-120 Advanced Medium Range Air-to-Air Missile (AMRAAM)', p.37, https://www.esd.whs.mil/Portals/54/Documents/FOID/Reading%20Room/Selected_Acquisition_Reports/FY_2018_SARS/19-F-1098_DOC_14_AMRAAM_SAR_Dec_2018.pdf.

103 Central Intelligence Agency, 'North Korea: Jet Fighter Production', April 1984, released by Directorate of Intelligence, https://www.cia.gov/readingroom/docs/CIA-RDP85T00310R000100060006-4.pdf.

104 Gareth Jennings, 'Pakistan Receives First J-10 Fighters From China', *Jane's Defence Weekly*, 11 March 2022, https://customer.janes.com/Janes/Display/BSP_14812-JDW.

105 'Chinese and Russian Air-Launched Weapons: A Test for Western Air Dominance', in IISS (ed.), *The Military Balance 2018* (Abingdon: Routledge for the IISS, 2018), https://www.iiss.org/publications/the-military-balance/the-military-balance-2018/mb2018-01-essays-1.

106 John Chipman, 'John Chipman's Military Balance launch event remarks', IISS, 15 February 2022, https://www.iiss.org/blogs/analysis/2022/02/john-chipmans-military-balance-launch-event-remarks.

107 'Saudi Intelligence Chief Talks Security with Brennan Delegation', 22 March 2009, released by WikiLeaks as Cable 09RIYADH445_a, https://wikileaks.org/plusd/cables09RIYADH445_a.html.

108 'Shaykh Mohamed bin Zayed Rejects Unarmed Predator Proposal', 27 June 2004, released by WikiLeaks as Cable 04ABUDHABI2113_a.

109 US Department of State, 'U.S. Export Policy for Military Unmanned Aerial Systems', 17 February 2015, https://2009-2017.state.gov/r/pa/prs/ps/2015/02/237541.htm.

110 Craig Hoyle, 'UK cheers the Reaper UAV', Flight Global, 16 June 2008, https://www.flightglobal.com/uk-cheers-the-reaper-uav/80945.article.

111 US Department of State, 'U.S. Policy on the Export of Unmanned Aerial Systems', https://2017-2021.state.gov/u-s-policy-on-the-export-of-unmanned-aerial-systems-2/index.html.

112 Central Intelligence Agency, 'The Falklands Islands and Lebanon Crises: Impact on Global High-technology Arms Transfers', August 1982, released by Directorate of Intelligence, p.iii, https://www.cia.gov/readingroom/docs/CIA-RDP83B00851R000100080002-6.pdf.

113 Jeffrey Lewis, 'Storm Shadow, Saudi & the MTCR', Arms Control Wonk, 31 May 2011, https://www.armscontrolwonk.com/archive/204051/saudi-arabia-storm-shadow-the-mtcr/.

REGIONAL STABILITY

LITHUANIA TO DELIVER THE TURKISH-MADE *BAYRAKTAR* TB2 UAV TO UKRAINE

The Turkish *Bayraktar* TB2 named '*Vanagas*' (*Hawk*) is presented in Siauliai Air Base in Lithuania, 6 July 2022. CREDIT: Paulius Peleckis/Getty Images.

CHAPTER 2

'Turkish drone power is heating up frozen conflicts', an explanatory video promoted by Turkey's national broadcaster, TRT World, rather breathlessly declared in October 2020.[1] The background was the deployment by Azerbaijan of Turkish armed uninhabited aerial vehicles (UAVs) in the war with Armenia, which, while sometimes overinterpreted in its importance for the campaign, did give Azerbaijan's forces an asymmetric advantage. A year later, in October 2021, Ukraine's armed forces struck for the first time a separatist artillery position with weapons from a *Bayraktar* TB2 UAV supplied by Turkey. The following day Dmitry Peskov, spokesperson for the Kremlin, declared with reference to Turkey's armed UAV export 'that deliveries of these types of weapons to the Ukrainian military can potentially destabilize the situation'.[2]

It was of course Russia's direct and indirect support for separatists in Ukraine's east since 2014 that was the initial destabilising force, and the situation was only worsened by Russia's full-scale war of aggression against Ukraine that began in February 2022. Russia's own sluggish progress regarding armed UAVs has been a feature of both episodes.[3] In their different ways, what Peskov and the TRT World moderator alluded to was that arms exports can change a local or regional balance of military power and can thus have implications for the onset or continuation of armed conflict.

2022 CHANGCHUN AIR SHOW
A Chengdu J-20 combat aircraft at Changchun Air Show in Changchun, Jilin Province of China, 23 August 2022. CREDIT: Zhang Hui/VCG via Getty Images.

Stabilising or destabilising?

This issue is well understood by arms-exporting nations, and regional stability often sits at the intersection of risk assessments, conducted before an export licence is granted or denied, that consider the strategic interests of the exporting nation. In principle, arms exports can both strengthen regional stability and undermine it. Arms exports are often undertaken with the explicit goal of strengthening the capabilities and the deterrence posture of the exporting state's allies, and thus influencing the existing regional balance of power in a way that is favourable to the exporter's interests. However, if perceived as escalatory or overtly offensive in nature by other powers in the recipient's region or by the exporting nation's strategic adversaries, arms sales can contribute to arms racing and increase the risks of armed conflict. Furthermore, there is the risk that weapons, once exported, might fall into the wrong hands, or could be used to commit human-rights violations.

Given that it might be in the interest of the exporting country to strengthen its allies' capabilities, deter adversaries or more generally influence regional security in a way that is favourable to that state's interests, it is a given that regional stability cannot be simply a status quo concept when it comes to arms-export control. For instance, it is very likely that some arms-exports decisions are explicitly made with the motivation to shift an existing regional balance of power – thus, not all change is bad. But even in situations where countries are in active armed conflict, the specifics of the case in question need to be carefully considered so that a judgement can be formed on what impact an arms-export decision might have, for instance, whether those exports might lead to an end of hostilities (usually through the victory of one side) or to their continuation (by levelling the capability playing field).

Another important determining factor is whether a rapid conclusion or extended conflict is in the interest of the sending and the receiving nation, with the latter being a legitimate and legal aim in cases of self-defence under UN Charter Article 51. Nevertheless, it is concerning that little insight exists 'into how much impact the risk assessment process has on decisions to approve arms sales'.[4] The point of risk assessments conducted by governments is to determine whether the benefits of an arms-export decision are likely to outweigh the risks – it is not to establish a benchmark where an export decision can only go ahead when there is no associated risk at all.

While the debate about arms sales and regional stability is often influenced by normative or even ideological undercurrents on the side of both supporters and opponents, there is usually little detail on what is meant by the term regional stability. There is even less granularity on the assumed cause and effect relationship that might inform risk assessments and thus arms-export decision-making and policy. On balance, regional-stability concerns will always be highly context specific as a factor influencing export decisions, given that arms exports generate both potential benefits and potential risks. In that sense, regional stability is akin to human-rights concerns or issues regarding technology diffusion.

This chapter will provide an outline of the structure of the global arms trade in order to establish reference points relating to regional stability in the export policies of several countries and discuss what constitutes regional security and the factors that can contribute to, or undermine, stability. To conclude, it will examine the difficulty of translating theoretical concerns for regional stability into practical guidance with reference to existing literature in the field.

Tiers of arms suppliers and regional stability

Arms exporters are often grouped broadly into three tiers. Each is banded by various policy, defence-industrial, defence-technological and economic criteria. Within each tier, the main motivating factors arguably differ,[5] which translates into distinct approaches to arms-export restrictions.[6]

China, Russia and the United States are first-tier suppliers because they are global actors that can sustain the technological, industrial and organisational infrastructure as well as the knowledge and skills development of complex conventional weapons systems. In these countries, there is considerable domestic demand for such capabilities as well as significant investment in defence. As such, political, geopolitical and economic motivations all underpin first-tier suppliers' arms-export strategies.

Unsurprisingly, the three first-tier suppliers are also among the world's top five arms-exporting nations, supplying the largest volumes of major conventional weapons.[7] They differ to an extent in willingness to release their most advanced major weapons. For instance, in the aerospace realm Beijing and Washington both operate combat-aircraft types that are not available for export, respectively the Chengdu J-20 and the Lockheed Martin F-22 *Raptor*, while Moscow has sought, so far unsuccessfully, to export its Sukhoi Su-57 *Felon* to India. The first-tier countries also differ in their willingness to release certain types of weaponry. As previously indicated, China and the US have taken divergent approaches to armed UAV exports.[8]

A broader group of second-tier suppliers – which includes France, Germany and the United Kingdom – retain the industrial, organisational and technological skills to indigenously develop major weapons systems. But these states increasingly lack the domestic volumes to sustain such programmes. The prevalent motivation for arms-export strategies in second-tier suppliers is industrial and economic – notably, the need to generate sufficient revenues to maintain and invest in their research and development base to stay competitive.

There are significantly more second-tier suppliers than first-tier ones, which can make arms-export contracts more competitive. For instance, second-tier and first-tier providers may compete to secure export orders, which can, at least in principle, incentivise a more liberal approach to arms-export controls.

Third-tier suppliers have limited industrial and organisational capacity as well as skills to sustain cutting-edge innovation over the long term and are generally reliant on capacity transfers and localised production licences. These suppliers are not globally competitive and their arms-export policies are determined by pressing needs to ensure the economic resources to maintain their sovereign military-industrial bases. Their defence-industrial bases remain highly dependent on external revenues. Examples of third-tier suppliers include Belarus, the Czech Republic and Serbia.[9]

Advanced military technology and regional stability

Other approaches focus on the types of national arms exports (i.e., offensive versus defensive weapons) and the impact on regional stability. This debate has featured prominently in media and academic analysis regarding US and allied support for Ukraine since the limited Russian invasion of the country and the annexation of Crimea in 2014 and more broadly since Russia invaded Ukraine a second time on 24 February 2022.[10]

Beyond the offensive versus defensive weapons debate, arms exports can also be structured into three categories based on the type and scope of military technology that is transferred and which may then have a different potential impact on regional stability.

- The first category is represented by materiel transfers, such as the export of major conventional weapons systems in all domains of warfare, along with ammunition and training (to use the equipment) and maintenance.
- The second category refers to design transfers, notably those of the major conventional weapons systems, or at least elements of their design and production plans.
- The third category of transfers refers to the export of technology, designs, skills and manufacturing capacity.

As a purchasing state increasingly looks to build or develop further a national defence-industrial base, it may attempt to leverage its buying power with supplier states. It may initially attempt to move from a category-one acquisition to one that includes final assembly, and eventually seek the transfer of design capacity.[11] India and South Korea are examples here, as they prefer associations with prominent first- and second-tier arms suppliers for technological, geopolitical and international-status reasons.[12]

Much arms-trade literature does not consider fully the link between different types of arms exports (beyond offensive versus defensive) on regional stability and conflict patterns. Nevertheless, capacity transfers – although far rarer – are potentially permanent and can have a long-term impact on the regional balance of power. Such transfers also give more agency to regional actors than arms suppliers in settling regional disputes and consequently have a longer-term impact on regional stability or instability.

By contrast, material transfers are cyclical, temporary (even if lasting decades) and depend more on the interests of the arms supplier, thus sustaining any agency the supplier nation has in influencing regional stability through arms exports.

Assessing arms exports' impact on regional stability

Adherence to national rules can sometimes appear notional, with arms-export decision-making slanted towards positive outcomes. This is often discussed in arms-export literature through reference to 'restraint' in relation to specific arms exports on a case-by-case basis. As such, this approach is only able to establish a weak link between different arms-export policies and their impact on regional stability by emphasising that regional stability does not carry the same weight in the arms-export criteria for international actors. Studies often highlight restraint in exporting arms to volatile regions as the variable most conducive to greater regional stability. This is typically thought to apply to all types of state arms-export regimes, various arms suppliers and different interests that motivate the export operations

SAUDI NATIONAL DAY
The Royal Saudi Air Force performs fly-past during celebrations ahead of Saudi Arabia's 92nd National Day in Riyadh, 22 September 2022.
CREDIT: FAYEZ NURELDINE/AFP via Getty Images.

of significant conventional-weapons suppliers. Restraint, however, across all categories of relevant stakeholders is unlikely to be possible, nor does it guarantee a positive outcome in terms of regional stability.

When examining the possible impact – negative or positive – of a major-weapons sale on regional stability, it is useful to acknowledge the co-dependency between the supply and demand sides, covering their respective agency and interests in any weapons acquisition. This may include relations between the supplier and the recipient of arms exports. Such relations could take the form of formal and informal military alliances, collective-defence arrangements, common interoperability requirements, standardisation of military equipment initiatives, common or joint operations, common threat responses, basing rights/strategic location and logistical support. Other factors in supplier–recipient relations can include the alignment of geopolitical interests, for example territorial revisionism or ideological convergence. A further category of factors regarding the notion of co-dependency and the impact that arms exports have on regional stability includes supportability and cost-management measures. These could cover participation in multinational co-design, co-development and/or co-production; a bilateral or multinational supply chain; development- and production-cost offsetting by economies of scale; and cost-sharing of upgrades. The multinational elements of the US Lockheed Martin F-35 *Lightning* II programme is an example of this co-dependency.

The gap between the ideals of national arms-export policies and the practice of arms exports has been a constant, as this chapter and others in this dossier have noted. In this context, what could be termed the 'elasticity' of the implementation of national arms-export regulations has as much of an effect on regional stability as the type of said national regulations, their respective strength or otherwise, and indeed with regard to whether the supplier sits in the first, second or third tier.

This elasticity should entail the exercise of flexibility and proportionality in arms-export decisions, depending on structural balance-of-power conditions and recipients' legitimate defence needs. But such decisions must comply with national arms-export regulations and international law at the time the export is granted and delivered, as well as post-delivery. The lack of national arms-export regulations, as well as violations and corrupt practices surrounding their implementation, should not be confused with 'elasticity'.

The notion of elasticity can be used to explain variations in the practice of national arms-export regulations by accommodating flexibility and proportionality in arms-exports decision-making. At the same time, it can also be used to explore how individual arms-exports decisions have, in context, facilitated regional stability or contributed to regional instability. The more elastic national arms-export controls are, the more they positively contribute to regional stability by enabling flexible and proportional supplies based on the recipient's need and the structural conditions of the regional balance of power.

This chapter does not consider stability to derive solely from the absence of inter-state conflict or crises, but rather from ensuring a balance of power between actors – during times of peace, crisis and war – which ensures the respect of the international and regional rule of law. This means that if national export controls are not sufficiently elastic to accommodate structural and strategic needs, exports of arms may have a negative impact on regional stability.

Rather than scrutinising uniquely the strength of national arms-export regulations or the level of compliance with regulations, the impact of arms exports on regional stability can be considered as a function of co-dependency. This sits between the interests and agencies of supplier and recipient, which in turn are shaped by the structure of the arms market in specific regions.

For example, in regions where there is a diversity of arms suppliers (first, second and third tier), with dispersed patterns of exports, unilateral restraint from exporting weapons does not always lead to enhanced regional stability. Moreover, considerations around whether arms exports enable human-rights violations, bolster repressive authoritarian regimes[13] or cause regional instability are often framed in terms of reputational rather than security costs.[14]

Take the Middle East, for example. Exercising restraint when supplying Middle Eastern countries with weapons systems could prove ineffective because these states already have several available suppliers of major conventional weapons systems to choose from, including all but one of the countries considered in this volume: China, France, Russia, the UK and the US. It could also be counterproductive if suppliers like Russia and China favour actors that harbour revisionist goals that could further disrupt regional stability, such as Iran.

In regions where there is a limited number of arms suppliers (particularly first-tier ones) which have overlapping or concentrated patterns of arms exports (i.e., two or more first- and second-tier suppliers sell weaponry to one of two or more countries involved in regional competition), restraint also may not support greater regional stability unless it is exercised collectively by all first-tier suppliers.

The 2020 war between Armenia and Azerbaijan: imported instability?

Between 27 September and 10 November 2020, Armenia and Azerbaijan fought a state-on-state war in and around the disputed Nagorno-Karabakh region, resulting in the deaths of some 6,000 soldiers. Following Azerbaijan's clear success on the battlefield, the war ended with a ceasefire agreement brokered by Russia. The countries had previously fought a war from 1988 to 1994 and tensions had been simmering since, with, for example, notable clashes between the conflict parties in April 2016.

International attempts to negotiate a peaceful settlement of the Nagorno-Karabakh issue continued under the so-called OSCE Minsk Group – established in 1994 and chaired by France, Russia and the United States – but were unsuccessful. In light of the stalled international conflict-management efforts and against the background of unresolved territorial issues, both Armenia and Azerbaijan began to make significant investments in their armed forces. According to the IISS Military Balance+ database, Armenia's defence budget grew in constant USD terms from 348 million in 2010 to 593m in 2020. Azerbaijan increased its spending on the same metric from USD1.38 billion in 2010 to USD2.61bn in 2020. In 2020, Armenia spent 4.97% of its GDP on defence, whereas Azerbaijan spent 5.31% in the same year.[15] Given the limited defence-industrial bases of both countries, Yerevan and Baku are dependent on international arms deliveries to modernise and improve their military capabilities in terms of equipment and technology.

Russia has been Armenia's key supplier, providing in the decade from 2010 to 2020 armoured vehicles, short-range and point-defence surface-to-air missile systems, anti-tank weapons, short-range ballistic-missile launchers, multiple-rocket launchers and a small number of ground-attack aircraft. Azerbaijan has been able to access a wider supplier base, most notably Israel and Turkey, while also purchasing equipment from Russia, including main battle tanks and other armoured vehicles, multiple-rocket launchers, artillery, anti-tank weaponry and attack helicopters. Israel supplied Azerbaijan with a range of UAVs and loitering munitions as well as short-range ballistic-missile launchers. Turkey sold multiple-rocket launchers and transferred a small number of *Bayraktar* TB2 armed UAVs.[16] Turkey likely provided support through the use of the TB2. A small number only of TB2s were employed during the war, likely in air-to-surface attack roles. The Azerbaijani Armed Forces had other non-armed UAVs for intelligence, surveillance and reconnaissance (ISR) roles. The primary munition likely used with the TB2 was the Roketsan MAM-L, a 22-kilogram semi-active laser-guided unpowered weapon.

Media commentary on the 2020 conflict attributed Azerbaijan's eventual success on the battlefield largely to UAVs and loitering munitions. In reality, well-planned and executed tactics paired with external support and use of ISR assets in combination with armed UAVs and loitering munitions were key to Azerbaijan's victory.[17] Azerbaijan was also willing to suffer considerable casualties among its ground forces in pursuit of its goals. Nevertheless, the asymmetry created by Azerbaijan's sourcing of ISR and armed UAVs and loitering munitions through international suppliers is regularly cited among the factors contributing to the outbreak of hostilities in 2020.[18] These imports, so the argument goes, altered the military balance between the two countries, which had in any case already been characterised by accelerating spending patterns on both sides (if slanted in favour of Azerbaijan), and created a window for offensive action on the part of the latter. It remains an open question whether Armenia acquiring more weapons would have acted as a deterrent towards Azerbaijan. Arms racing, however, is not a recipe for long-term regional stability.

Part of the picture is also a protracted and ultimately unsuccessful negotiation process, with the lack of progress fuelling resentment and a pattern of increasingly fervent rhetoric from senior politicians. The emergence of Turkey as a declared and powerful partner for Azerbaijan altered the geopolitical constellation which had previously been dominated by Russia's alignment with Armenia.[19]

Table 2.1: **Selected defence procurement since 2010**

Contract date	Equipment	Type	Quantity	Prime contractor	Deliveries
Armenia					
c. 2012	T-72B1	Main battle tank (MBT)	35	Russian government surplus	2013
	n.k.	Armoured vehicle	110		
2015	9K720 *Iskander*-E (RS-SS-26 *Stone*)	Short-range ballistic missile	≥2	KB Mashinostroyenia	2016
2015	9A52 *Smerch*	300mm multiple rocket launcher (MRL)	6	Splav	2016
2015	9K135 *Kornet*-E (RS-AT-14 *Spriggan*)	Man-portable anti-tank missiles	n.k.	KBP Instrument Design Bureau	2017
c 2018	9K33 *Osa*-AK (RS-SA-8 *Gecko*)	Point-defence surface-to-air missile (SAM) system	≥4	Russian government surplus	2019
c 2018	9K331MKM *Tor*-M2KM (RS-SA-15 *Gauntlet*)	Short-range SAM system	≥2	Almaz-Antey	2019
2019	Su-30SM *Flanker* H	Fighter/ground-attack aircraft	4	Irkut Corporation	2019
Azerbaijan					
c. 2010	T-72	MBT	93	Belarusian government surplus	2011–12
2010	Mi-35M *Hind*	Attack helicopter	24	Rostvertol	2011–13
2010	Mi-17-1V *Hip*	Multi-role helicopter	≥40	Kazan Helicopter Plant	2011–13
2011	T-90S	MBT	≥100	UralVagonZavod	2012–15
	BMP-3	Infantry fighting vehicle (IFV)	≥88	Kurganmashzavod	
	TOS-1A	220mm MRL	≥18	UralVagonZavod	
	9A52 *Smerch*	300mm MRL	≥18	Splav	
	2S19 *Msta*-S	152mm self-propelled howitzer	≥18	UralVagonZavod	
	2S31 *Vena*	120mm self-propelled gun/mortar	≥18	Kurganmashzavod	
2011	*Tufan* (*Sa'ar* 62)	Guided-missile patrol craft	6	Israel Shipyards	2015–19
	Shaldag V	Fast guided-missile patrol boat	6		
2012	*Abisr* (*Barak*-MRAD)	SAM system	n.k.	Israel Aerospace Industries (IAI)	2016
2013	T-300 *Kasirga*	302mm MRL	21	Roketsan	2015–16
2013	BTR-82A	IFV	230	Arzamas Machine-Building Plant	2012–16
2014	9P157-2 *Khrizantema*-S (RS-AT-15 *Springer*)	Self-propelled anti-tank missile system	n.k.	KB Mashinostroyenia	2017
2016	DANA M1M	152mm self-propelled howitzer	≥9	Excalibur Army	2017
	RM-70 *Vampir*	122mm MRL	≥8		
c. 2017	*Spear*	120mm self-propelled mortar	≥3	Elbit Systems	2018
c. 2017	*Hermes* 900	Medium intelligence, surveillance and reconnaissance (ISR) uninhabited air vehicle (UAV)	≥1	Elbit Systems	2018
c. 2017	*Barak*-LRAD	Self-propelled medium-range SAM system	n.k.	IAI	2018
c. 2017	*Polonez*	300mm MRL	≥6	Precise Electromechanics Factory	2018
c. 2017	LORA	Short-range ballistic missile	≥2	IAI	2018
c. 2020	*Bayraktar* TB2	Medium combat ISR UAV	n.k.	Baykar	2020

Source: IISS, *Military Balance 2023*

GERMANY'S DEFENCE WHITE PAPER
Ursula von der Leyen presents the new White Paper at *Bundespressekonferenz* in Berlin, Germany, 13 July 2016. CREDIT: Cuneyt Karadag/Anadolu Agency/Getty Images.

Regional stability as a reference point for policy

While arms-exporting nations commonly mention regional stability in their strategy documents – such as in defence White Papers or defence strategies, or specific arms-export policy materials – they usually do not include a definition of what it is. Occasionally, the wider discussion in those documents suggests some causes of regional instability (such as poverty, environmental degradation, organised crime, terrorism and armed conflict), and sometimes governments identify those partners they intend to work with to strengthen regional security. More specific reference points for strategy and policy are the effects of arms build-ups or the introduction of game-changing military capabilities by various regional actors. Within national strategy documents, arms build-ups, arms transfers and arms exports are identified as sometimes being linked to international and regional (in) stability, usually in the context of sections that underline the need for effective arms control and restrictive arms-export policies. What is a universal feature, though, is the absence of detail.

The US Conventional Arms Transfer Policy, for example, makes only one reference to regional stability, stating that any transfer must be consistent 'with United States interests in regional stability especially when considering transfers that involve power projection, anti-access or area denial capability, or the introduction of a capability that may increase regional tensions or contribute to an arms race'.[20] It furthermore clarifies that another criterion to be assessed is the effect of any transfer 'on the technological advantage of the United States, including the recipient's ability to protect sensitive technology'.[21]

The UK's 2021 Integrated Review of Security, Defence, Development and Foreign Policy, entitled 'Global Britain in a Competitive Age', makes several references to efforts to strengthen regional stability and to working more closely with partners to achieve this end. But only once, in a footnote on counter-proliferation, does the document elaborate that regional stability could be undermined by the spread of advanced military technology. The accompanying defence command paper, 'Defence in a Competitive Age', does not add further detail.[22] However, the assessment of the effect of arms exports on regional stability has been a long-established practice for the UK. For example, an explanation of the process provided by the government to Parliament in 2000 clarified that assessments of the adverse effects on regional stability would take into account

> the balance of forces between the states of the region concerned, their relative expenditure on defence, the potential for the equipment significantly to enhance the effectiveness of existing capabilities or to improve force projection, and the need not to introduce into the region new capabilities which would be likely to lead to increased tension.[23]

This wording was repeated in 2014 as still being adequate after an EU Common Position was adopted in 2008 (and of relevance to the UK until it formally left the European Union) and after the UK signed the Arms Trade Treaty in 2013.[24] However, the Strategic Export Licensing Criteria announced by the UK at the end of 2021 removes references to the EU Common Position and also downgrades concerns for regional stability among the criteria for UK decision-makers (see Chapter 6).

The EU adopted a Common Position on arms exports in December 2008, outlining criteria which would obstruct the granting of an export licence. For instance, the fourth criterion covers the preservation of regional peace, security and stability. It then specifies that any export should not adversely affect regional stability in any significant way.[25] The User Guide for the Common Position, published by the EU, provides some useful guidance on what to look for when forming a judgement on this criterion, suggesting the key point was

> whether supplying the recipient country with the equipment will significantly improve its military capability, and if it does, would a neighbouring country as a result be put under threat of conflict. Where there are existing tensions in the region, would supplying this equipment enhance the recipient country's capability by introducing a new piece of equipment into the region which could threaten a neighbouring country.[26]

The User Guide, furthermore, indicates that any judgement needs to take into consideration the motivation for the purchase (whether it will replace an existing capability or introduce a new capability) as well as the nature of the equipment to be exported (if it would upset an existing balance of power and be perceived as threatening by neighbours). It also considers the intentions of the end user (whether it could be used in the spirit of the regional-stability criterion).

The Common Position presents an important reference point for EU member states. The German defence White Paper published in 2016 declared that

> arms build-up can undermine the stability of the international system and, indirectly, also the security of Europe and Germany. Build-ups of conventional armaments can change the military balance at the regional and global levels and increase the risk of violent interstate conflicts. This can be considerably exacerbated by the development of new technologies that are not yet part of current arms control regimes.

Germany considers a restrictive arms-export policy as being 'the precondition, the means and the basis for peaceful conflict resolution and disarmament'.[27] Before also listing the criteria of the EU Common Position, Dutch arms-export policy states that

> an advance assessment will always be made for every transaction requiring a licence, to determine whether there is a risk that a potential trading partner will use equipment or knowledge in an undesirable way, for example to violate human rights or heighten domestic or regional instability.[28]

Of course, the fact that the EU Common Position exists and is referenced does not imply that member-state governments will actually reach the same judgement when it comes to practical decisions. In fact, the German White Paper calls for a further harmonisation of member-state arms-export guidelines.[29]

Germany has been an attractive case study for policy analysts because it is generally perceived to pursue a restrictive security and defence policy, while nevertheless managing to reliably rank among the leading arms exporters globally in terms of value. In analysing German arms trade from 1992 to 2013, Hendrik Platte and Dirk Leuffen find that normative issues seem to have played only a minor role in German arms-export decision-making. In contrast, security-political considerations seem to hold greater importance, while commercial considerations have the strongest impact on arms-trade policy.[30] Writing in the late 1980s, peace researchers like Michael Brzoska suggested German arms-export policy has gradually become more permissive as a result of a 'dynamic interactive process', which includes politicians, the foreign-policy elite, Germany's arms-export bureaucracy and the country's arms industry.[31] Germany established the so-called 'Political Principles' in 1971 to guide the decision-making process regarding arms exports. These were revised in 1982, 2000 and 2019 and are due to be revised again before the end of 2022. While the 1971 Principles excluded the delivery of weapons of war to non-NATO states,[32] the 1982 version introduced the caveat that these exports might be permissible if, for example, Germany's vital interests as well as NATO's interests warranted it.[33] Since then, the Political Principles have introduced a range of norms and regulations, allowing exports to non-NATO/EU states under certain conditions.

The German 2019 Political Principles explicitly acknowledge the EU criteria as an integral constituent but nevertheless introduce additional constraints compared to the EU position. For example, on human rights, the EU Common Position provides for a refusal to export if there is a 'clear risk' that the goods in question could be used for internal repression (Art. 2 (2)a).[34] The German Political Principles only demand 'reasonable cause' to suspect the weapons or equipment in question will be used for internal repression or for other persistent and systematic violations of human rights.[35]

With regard to involvement in external conflicts, the Common Position calls on governments to deny arms exports to states if there is a 'clear risk' that the weapons or military equipment will be used 'aggressively against another country or to assert by force a territorial claim'.[36] To assess this risk, the Common Position provides a list of criteria to consider (Art. 2, 4. a–d). The German Political Principles take a more restrictive stance and exclude the possibility of exports to countries that are already engaged in armed conflicts. This restriction also applies if there is a risk of an armed conflict breaking out or if the export would cause, sustain or exacerbate existing tensions or conflicts.

Whereas the German Principles exclude economic interests as a decisive factor for any export-licensing decision, the Common Position explicitly refers to the consideration of economic, social, commercial and industry interests in the decision-making process (although not in a dominant way, overriding the criteria established to constrain exports). As mandated by the Political Principles, the German government publishes an annual report on Military

CHINA'S DEFENCE WHITE PAPER
An official distributes copies of China's latest defence White Paper to journalists in Beijing, 24 July 2019. CREDIT: Kyodo News Stills via Getty Images.

Equipment Exports (*Rüstungsexportbericht*). However, this official report only provides approved values and does not outline the reasons and justifications for export decisions.[37] The German Political Principles have 'earned Germany the reputation of a high-regulation country'.[38]

But in practice this high-regulation environment has been less of a constraint on arms exports from Germany than might be expected. For example, across different German governments, the authorisation of arms exports to Saudi Arabia has been justified by highlighting Saudi Arabia's role as an anchor of stability in the region and the necessity of ensuring a strategic balance vis-à-vis Iran in order to maintain regional stability and security.[39] Saudi Arabia's involvement in the Yemen conflict did not initially lead to German arms exports ceasing, as a strict reading of the German guidelines would suggest. Rather, it was the political fallout from the 2018 murder of Jamal Khashoggi that led to a halt in exports. Prior to the incident, Saudi Arabia continued to receive arms exports, such as eight German patrol vessels.[40] German arms exports to Saudi Arabia fell from a volume of EUR415m in 2018 to EUR830,000 in 2019 as a result.[41] Egypt presents a similar pattern: EU foreign ministers issued an export ban in 2013 when the internal situation in the country deteriorated.[42] Nonetheless, German arms exports picked up again in 2014 and in 2020. Egypt, despite its involvement in the conflict in Libya, received the already completed patrol boats, which had been destined for Saudi Arabia.[43] These instances suggest that 'even temporary halts on arms exports have been justified not due to concerns about regional instability, but due to poor human rights records in importing countries'.[44]

Nevertheless, there is evidence that Germany does indeed make use of the provisions of the Political Guidelines and the EU Common Position. For example, German arms exports to Turkey have usually been justified using an alliance-political rationale, referring to Turkey's NATO membership and candidacy for EU membership. Yet, in light of internal developments in Turkey and increasing tensions with Greece in the Aegean between November 2016 and March 2017, the German government denied export licences for 11 different projects, compared to only eight rejections in the period between 2010 and 2015.[45] Exports were denied on the grounds of inadequate 'respect for human rights and international humanitarian law', and the criterion relating to the 'internal situation in the country of final destination, as a function of the existence of tensions and armed conflict'.[46] Moreover, after the Turkish intervention in Syria in 2018, arms exports were temporarily suspended, and in 2019 the German government denied applications for arms-export licences.[47]

However, regional security concerns in the context of arms exports are not limited to NATO or EU member states. For example, the 2018 defence White Paper of the Republic of Korea stated that Seoul would 'actively participate in the international community's non-proliferation efforts to contribute to regional stability and global peace while bolstering the foundation for international cooperation for the security of the Korean Peninsula'.[48]

But even countries not among the global partners of leading Western arms-exporting nations pay tribute to the idea. China's 2019 defence White Paper indicated Beijing would seek to contribute to the global strategic balance and stability, and China's export-control law specifies three criteria for arms-export policy, one being that exports would not 'undermine peace, security and stability of the region concerned and the world as a whole'.[49] Overall, regional stability as a policy reference point remains vague. Policy documents suggest that when it comes to regional stability, states appear to be primarily concerned with the effects of equipment or technology that would introduce a new capability into a regional military balance or generate greater force-projection capability in support of offensive military operations.

The meaning of regional security

There is a school of thought in security studies proposing that regional subsystems might exist around the globe where the security of one country within this subsystem is so closely tied to the security of the other states there that it is no longer accurate to focus on individual states as the referent objects of security. Instead, it would be more appropriate to think of regional security complexes, defined as a group of states so interdependent 'that their major security problems cannot reasonably be analyzed or resolved apart from one another'.[50] Another idea, originating in the 1950s and associated with the writings of political scientist Karl W. Deutsch, is that through processes of cooperation and even integration states may develop into security communities where armed force is no longer an acceptable means of resolving conflicts and instead disputes are settled in other ways.[51]

While these concepts have been prominent in academic discourse, the notion of regional stability in the context of arms-export policy has a lot less to do with interdependence and political community and much more to do with geographically bounded balances of military power. It is more appropriate, therefore, to think of a region simply as 'a territorial subsystem of the global system'.[52] As the review of policy documents above suggests, regional stability does not have a settled definition. But the governments concerned seem to focus on general notions such as the absence of war and the avoidance of significant capability asymmetries that might trigger conflict in a geographically defined area.[53] Regional stability is therefore not merely a shorthand for maintaining the status quo when it comes to arms exports.

Arms exports can serve to avoid the disturbance of regional stability as much as they can serve to create that stability in the first place. Thus, the effects of arms exports on regional stability are highly context specific as it is just as plausible that the diffusion of capability will remove incentives to engage in armed conflict as it is that it will create them. It should be noted, however, that the local or regional balance of power is a very crude guide to evaluate the likelihood of armed conflict, especially if it is disconnected from an in-depth assessment of the historical and current political and economic relations of the region in question. Exploring such relations might unearth any number of factors that could drive decision-makers towards conflict, just as a simple misinterpretation of the existing military balance might do.[54]

It is notable that analysts, who have tried to devise metrics to measure how risky a certain arms sale was and to provide frameworks to assess the risks of exports that might be discussed, do not attempt to measure regional stability directly in any way. To capture the risks associated with arms sales, A. Trevor Thrall, Jordan Cohen and Caroline Dorminey focus on corruption, the political stability of the recipient state, the behaviour of a government towards its own citizens and associated human-rights issues, as well as whether the state in question is engaged in inter-state conflict or facing significant terrorist or insurgent risks.[55] Seeking to understand how conflict-prone specific arms exports are – defined as the effect of an export on either prolonging existing conflict or increasing the likelihood of armed conflict – Beata Cichocka and Ian Mitchell measure risk in recipient states using a number of proxy variables focused on income levels, democracy and militarisation. The assumption is that exports to low-income, militarised autocracies would be conflict prone whereas exports to high-income democracies with a lower proportion spent on defence would be less so. These studies generate some very interesting and sometimes counter-intuitive empirical results when the methodologies are applied to recent datasets of arms sales from a number of exporting states. Cichocka and Mitchell's data, for example, suggests the UK has been a more responsible exporter than Sweden and Germany, who in turn appear more responsible (i.e., engaged in less conflict-prone exports) than Canada, China, France, Russia and the US.[56] The underlying methodologies are certainly contentious and the data is a snapshot in time. Furthermore, these risk-assessment frameworks do not factor in regional stability and in general focus more on the absence of war or conflict and governance questions and less on the balance of power and capabilities, issues that have been prominent in policy documents.

Observations on the empirical relationship between arms exports and regional stability

While existing work considers regional stability to be both a potential benefit and a potential risk of arms exports, there is very little evidence to suggest the risk assessment element is driving decisions. Thrall, Cohen and Dorminey, for example, find in relation to US arms sales 'evidence that strategic interests and economic considerations significantly impact arms sales but no evidence that risk assessment does so'. They continue to argue that

> the most powerful explanatory factors for the pattern and volume of sales are whether a country is an ally of the United States, the level of trade conducted between a country and the United States, and how much a country spends on its military each year ... we found no signs that the risk of negative downstream consequences impacts weapons sales even in cases where the strategic benefits appear to be marginal.[57]

Gregory S. Sanjian's work using data on US and Soviet exports to India and Pakistan, Iran and Iraq, and Ethiopia and Somalia between 1950 and 1991 found that 'weapons shipments of the US and the USSR were profoundly destabilising, while those of third parties had generally little impact'. The conclusion the author draws is that

NORTH KOREA MILITARY AVIATION FESTIVAL
A MiG-21 aircraft taxiing during the first Wonsan Friendship Air Festival in Kangwŏn Province, North Korea. CREDIT: ED JONES/AFP via Getty Images.

> even if the Superpowers had wanted to reduce conflict and imbalance among their clients, the policy of dispensing arms was not likely to achieve those objectives ... [their] weapons did not just fail to lesson conflict and imbalance between the dyad rivals; they actually intensified those problems.[58]

There is a lot to unpack from these findings. Firstly, the bipolar structure of the Cold War created several regional rivalries and a number of client-state relationships between some of the actors involved and the dominant powers, and arms suppliers, of the day. The data for that period seems to suggest that in this bipolar context, the arms-exporting powers behaved in a way that proved destabilising for several regional security contexts and undermined regional stability. The main reason advanced by scholars is that some of the exports created military imbalances among the importing countries that intensified rivalries which on occasion led to conflict and war. It should be noted, however, that some of the work focused directly on existing regional rivalries and thus a regional security context where tensions were already notable and, in some cases, high. In addition, decision-makers at the time will have also had to consider the risks of not taking action (in the sense of preventing exports) and the possible effects of that course. Therefore, it is difficult to judge whether the effects observed by scholars were intentional – attempts to shift the regional balance of power in the context of the wider bloc confrontation – or failures of risk assessment.

At a minimum, a conclusion to be drawn from previous studies is that a bipolar international system might encourage export behaviour that tolerates a significant amount of regional instability underneath a stable bipolar global balance of power. Of course, it will be hard for any bureaucratic arms-export decision-making process to clearly define exactly how much risk would be acceptable in specific regional contexts and at specific points in time. The IISS Military Balance+ dataset, covering the equipment holdings of 171 countries around the world, contains plenty of examples of weapons systems and platforms that have been in active service for 50 years or more. Many of these systems will be obsolete and would represent little value in terms of capability if used today, but their existence illustrates the fact that the in-service life of equipment can span several decades, during which the relationships and political and security contexts can change completely and in ways that might be unforeseen.

The difficulties of modelling – or even imagining – those potential future realities make it likely that long-term risks will struggle to receive the same attention as short-term benefits during the arms-export decision-making process.[59] A recent example of these changes over time are the security and defence policies of several states in the Middle East and North Africa. Countries like Qatar, Saudi Arabia and the United Arab Emirates (UAE) have a long-standing track record of investing in high-end military capabilities from a number of international suppliers. But until a few years ago, their foreign policies were comparatively introvert, and their militaries did not engage in much independent operational activity outside of established multilateral frameworks.

While there were human-rights concerns, there was also the argument to support ruling regimes in their attempt to balance Iran and in general provide stability in their own countries. During the latter half of the previous decade (the 2010s), however, these countries developed increasingly extrovert foreign policies and began to use their armed forces for forms of power projection and military crisis management. Qatar, Saudi Arabia and the UAE have become involved both in Libya's conflict and in the Yemeni civil war. On occasion, they have supported different sides, which has caused a number of arms-exporting governments – including France, Germany, the UK and the US – to either temporarily halt or restrict arms-export activity. This is because arms exports were seen as contributing to the further escalation of conflicts in the region and to a number of civilian casualties. Some analysts interpret the changes in the security-policy behaviour of some Arab nations as a 'militarization of [their] foreign policies' which should lead to a permanent stop to arms exports.[60] This view is not universal, however, and exporting governments, at least judged based on their decisions, seem to assess risks and rewards differently and might have different underlying perceptions of the threats posed by regional instability.[61]

The United States has often been treated in the literature as a prime example of a 'hegemonic exporter' which puts strategic considerations first, followed by commercial factors, with normative drivers lagging some distance behind.[62] While research suggests this logic held during the Cold War, since its conclusion the data implies a greater consideration of human rights in US decision-making.[63] France, on the other hand, has often been treated and presented as a trading state that puts commercial and business interests first, prioritising the survival and growth of its advanced domestic arms industry.[64] In contrast to some of the findings referenced above, recent empirical work suggests that this trading-state motivation does not necessarily lead to destabilising export behaviour. Cécile Fauconnet and her co-authors suggest France is less likely to export arms to recipient countries that do not respect human rights. In addition, France exports less often weapons systems which the authors categorise as 'destabilizing' (including aircraft and armoured vehicles).[65]

In general, some effort has been put into understanding the effects of arms exports on democratic development, human rights and inter-state conflict, all of which, as mentioned above, have an assumed link to regional stability. Scholarly work does suggest, for example, that there is a point where, statistically, the volume of imported arms has a negative effect on democratic development in recipient nations, but if imports stay below that level there is no effect either way.[66] The need for a more nuanced analysis of arms imports is also supported by Richard Johnson, whose work shows that the impact of arms transfers on human rights depends on the types of weapons that are imported. According to Johnson, the import of transport aircraft, transport helicopters and combat helicopters is positively related to human-rights developments, whereas the import of offensive armoured vehicles is negatively related.[67]

Looking at inter-state conflict, David Kinsella's analysis suggests that major-power arms transfers during the Cold War could encourage both assertive and more restrained behaviour. In particular, Soviet arms transfers to revisionist client states tended to exacerbate rivalries in the Middle East and the Persian Gulf, whereas American transfer programmes with status quo-oriented states served to deter escalatory behaviour by regional rivals.[68] In a later study, Kinsella reconfirms the de-escalatory effect great-power arms transfers can have, and attributes this to the arms-transfer dependence between those powers and client states. Due to the prospect of arms shipments being curtailed by disapproving suppliers when they are needed the most, namely during regional crises, dependent client states have tended to self-restrain their foreign-policy behaviour.[69]

With regard to intra-state conflict, the literature suggests that arms imports are unlikely to be the root cause of an outbreak of hostilities, but they can contribute to or reinforce a dynamic towards conflict that is already established and under way in a country.[70] While not suggesting there is a causal link between arms exports and political violence, work spanning war and other forms of armed conflict (under the heading political violence) nevertheless posits that restraint on the side of suppliers would help reduce the likelihood of an outbreak of conflict.[71]

Conclusion

Regional stability is a factor, and sometimes an important one, in national arms-export-policy decision-making. Assessing its value in this process, however, is often made difficult by the lack of transparency both in the weighting it is given within bureaucratic decision-making and indeed in how stability or instability is defined by each state. Furthermore, the extent that any process attempts to project forward the implication of a major-weapons sale over time remains uncertain. A state in a region deemed stable in the 2020s could look very different in the 2030s. Conversely, the judicious provision of major weapons into a region at risk of becoming destabilised could redress a potential imbalance.

NOTES

1 TRT World, 'Decoded: Turkey's Drone Power', https://www.trtworld.com/video/news-videos/decoded-turkeys-drone-power/5f90120e46e7130017c16ccf.

2 'Kremlin says Turkish drones risk destabilising situation in east Ukraine', Reuters, 27 October 2021, www.reuters.com/world/middle-east/kremlin-says-turkish-drones-risk-destabilising-situation-east-ukraine-2021-10-27/.

3 For an assessment of Russia's UAV efforts, see Julian Cooper, 'The Nagorno-Karabakh War: a spur to moscow's UAV efforts?', IISS, 31 March 2021, https://www.iiss.org/blogs/research-paper/2021/03/nagorno-karabakh-war-moscow-uav-efforts.

4 A. Trevor Thrall, Jordan Cohen and Caroline Dorminey, 'Power, Profit, or Prudence? US Arms Sales since 9/11', *Strategic Studies Quarterly*, vol. 535, no. 1, September 1994, p. 102.

5 Michael Brzoska and Frederic S. Pearson, 'Developments in the Global Supply of Arms: Opportunity and Motivation', *The Annals of the American Academy of Political and Social Science*, September 1994, 58–72, https://doi.org/10.1177/0002716294535001005; Stephanie Neuman, 'International Stratification and Third World Military Industries', *International Organization*, vol. 38, no. 1, Winter 1984, pp. 167–97, https://doi.org/10.1017/S0020818300004306; Kieth Krause, 'The Political Economy of the International Arms Transfer System: The Diffusion of Military Technique via Arms Transfers', *International Journal*, vol. 45, no. 3, Summer 1990, pp. 687–722, https://doi.org/10.2307/40202695; and Barry Buzan and Eric Herring, *The Arms Dynamic in World Politics* (Boulder, CO: Lynne Reinner, 1998).

6 Lucie Béraud-Sudreau and Hugo Meijer, 'Enjeux stratégiques et économiques des politiques d'exportation d'armement: Une comparaison franco-américaine [Strategic and Economic Issues of Arms Export Policies: A Franco-American Comparison], *Révue Internationale de Politique Comparée*, vol. 23, no. 1, 2016, pp. 57–84, https://doi.org/10.3917/ripc.231.0057.

7 Pieter D. Wezeman, Alexandra Kuimova and Siemon T. Wezeman, 'Trends in International Arms Transfers, 2021', SIPRI, March 2022, https://www.sipri.org/sites/default/files/2022-03/fs_2203_at_2021.pdf.

8 Kelvin Wong, 'Winning streak: China hits stride in armed MALE UAV Exports', *Jane's International Defence Review*, 23 April 2022, https://customer.janes.com/Janes/Display/FG_2741436-IDR; and David Hambling, 'Russia Enters Military Drone Export Market With Sale to Myanmar', *Forbes*, 25 January 2021, https://www.forbes.com/sites/davidhambling/2021/01/25/russia-enters-military-drone-export-market-with-sale-to-burma/?sh=6ddc6e35208d.

9 SIPRI Arms Transfers Database, https://www.sipri.org/databases/armstransfers.

10 Stephen Biddle, 'Is there a difference between "defensive" and "offensive" weapons?', *Washington Post*, 28 April 2022, https://www.washingtonpost.com/politics/2022/04/28/ukraine-russia-military-warfare-offensive-defensive-weaponry/; Eric Schmitt and Julian E. Barnes, 'Ukraine's Demands for More Weapons Clash With U.S. Concerns', *New York Times*, 12 July 2022, https://www.nytimes.com/2022/07/12/us/politics/ukraine-us-weapons.html; Barbara Starr, 'Pentagon Reviewing Industry Proposals for Innovative Weapons Ideas to Send to Ukraine', CNN, 30 June 2022, https://edition.cnn.com/2022/06/30/politics/pentagon-technology-ukraine-usa/index.html; and David M. Herszenhorn, Lily Bayer and Hans Von Der Burchard, 'Germany to send Ukraine weapons in historic shift on military aid', Politico, 26 February 2022, https://www.politico.eu/article/ukraine-war-russia-germany-still-blocking-arms-supplies/.

11 Buzan and Herring, *The Arms Dynamic in World Politics*, pp. 40–1.

12 See, for example, Dana P. Eyre and Mark C. Suchman, 'Status, Norms, and the Proliferation of Conventional Weapons: An Institutional Theory Approach', in Peter Katzenstein (ed.), *The Culture of National Security: Norms and Identity in World Politics* (New York: Columbia University Press, 1996), pp. 79–113.

13 Shannon Lindsey Blanton, 'Foreign Policy in Transition? Human Rights, Democracy, and U.S. Arms Exports', *International Studies Quarterly*, vol. 49, no. 4, December 2005, pp. 647–67.

14 See, for example, Gregory Sanders, 'Arms Trade Reform Options for the New Administration,' *CSIS*, February 2021, p. 2, https://csis-website-prod.s3.amazonaws.com/s3fs-public/publication/210205_Sanders_T46_Formatted.pdf; Jennifer Erickson, *Dangerous Trade: Arms Exports, Human Rights, and International Reputation* (New York: Columbia University Press, 2015), pp. 1–3; and Jennifer Erickson, 'Market Imperative Meets Normative Power: Human Rights and European Arms Transfer Policy', *European Journal of International Relations*, vol. 19, no. 2, 2011, pp. 209–34.

15 All figures from IISS Military Balance+, accessed 28 June 2022, https://milbalplus.iiss.org/.

16 Procurement data drawn from IISS Military Balance+, accessed 28 June 2022.

17 Douglas Barrie and Niklas Ebert, 'Armed UAVs: an asset, but not alone all-conquering', IISS Military Balance Blog, 5 July 2021, https://www.iiss.org/blogs/military-balance/2021/07/nagorno-karabakh-armed-uavs.

18 Jordan Smith, Pieter D. Wezeman and Alexandra Kuimova, 'Arms Transfers to Conflict Zones: The Case of Nagorno-Karabakh', SIPRI, 30 April

2021, https://sipri.org/commentary/topical-backgrounder/2021/arms-transfers-conflict-zones-case-nagorno-karabakh.

19 Azer Babayev, 'Nagorno-Karabakh: Why Did the Second Armenia-Azerbaijan War Start?', PRIF Blog, 5 November 2020, https://blog.prif.org/2020/11/05/nagorno-karabakh-why-the-second-armenia-azerbaijan-war-started/.

20 US Department of State, 'Conventional Arms Transfer Policy', 17 December 2018, https://www.state.gov/conventional-arms-transfer-cat-policy/.

21 *Ibid.*

22 HM Government, 'Global Britain in a Competitive Age: The Integrated Review of Security, Defence, Development and Foreign Policy', CP 403, March 2021, p. 84, https://assets.publishing.service.gov.uk/government/uploads/system/uploads/attachment_data/file/975077/Global_Britain_in_a_Competitive_Age-_the_Integrated_Review_of_Security__Defence__Development_and_Foreign_Policy.pdf; and UK Ministry of Defence, 'Defence in a Competitive Age', CP 411, March 2021, https://assets.publishing.service.gov.uk/government/uploads/system/uploads/attachment_data/file/974661/CP411_-Defence_Command_Plan.pdf.

23 Hansard, 'Consolidated EU and National Arms Export Licensing Criteria', 26 October 2000, column 200W, https://assets.publishing.service.gov.uk/government/uploads/system/uploads/attachment_data/file/432246/consolidated-eu-and-national-arms-export-licensing-criteria.doc.

24 Hansard, 'Consolidated EU and National Arms Export Licensing Criteria', 25 March 2014, https://publications.parliament.uk/pa/cm201314/cmhansrd/cm140325/wmstext/140325m0001.htm.

25 The Council of the European Union, 'Council Common Position 2008/944/CFSP of 8 December 2008 Defining Common Rules Governing Control of Exports of Military Technology and Equipment', *Official Journal of the European Union*, 13 December 2012, https://eur-lex.europa.eu/LexUriServ/LexUriServ.do?uri=OJ:L:2008:335:0099:0103:EN:PDF.

26 European Union, 'User's Guide to Common Position 2008/944/CFSP Defining Common Rules Governing the Control of Exports of Military Technology and Equipment', 16 September 2019, p. 87, https://www.consilium.europa.eu/media/40659/st12189-en19.pdf.

27 Both quotes are from Federal Government of Germany, 'White Paper on German Security Policy and the Future of the Bundeswehr', July 2016, pp. 40–1, https://issat.dcaf.ch/download/111704/2027268/2016%20White%20Paper.pdf.

28 Government of the Netherlands, 'Dutch Export Policy on Strategic Goods in 2020', September 2021, p. 6, https://www.government.nl/documents/reports/2021/09/09/dutch-export-control-policy-in-2020.

29 Federal Government of Germany, 'White Paper on German Security Policy and the Future of the Bundeswehr', p. 74.

30 Hendrik Platte and Dirk Leuffen, 'German Arms Exports: Between Normative Aspirations and Political Reality', *German Politics*, vol. 25, no. 4, 2016, pp. 561–80.

31 Michael Brzoska, 'The Erosion of Restraint in West German Arms Transfer Policy', *Journal of Peace Research*, vol. 26, no. 2, 1989, pp. 165–77.

32 Bundesministerium für Wirtschaft und Energie, 'Politische Grundsätze der Bundesregierung für den Export von Kriegswaffen und sonstige Rüstungsgüter' [Political principles of the federal government for the export of war weapons and other armaments], 16 June 1971, http://ruestungsexport-info.de/fileadmin/media/Dokumente/R%C3%BCstungsexporte___Recht/Politische_Grunds%C3%A4tze/Politische-Grundsaetze-1971.pdf

33 Bundesministerium für Wirtschaft und Energie, 'Politische Grundsätze der Bundesregierung für den Export von Kriegswaffen und sonstige Rüstungsgüter vom 28.4.1982' [Political principles of the Federal Government for the export of war weapons and other armaments of April 28, 1982], 28 April 1982, http://ruestungsexport-info.de/fileadmin/media/Dokumente/R%C3%BCstungsexporte___Recht/Politische_Grunds%C3%A4tze/Politische-Grundsaetze-1982.pdf

34 European Union, 'Council Common Position 2008/944/CFSP of 8 December 2008 Defining Common Rules Governing Control of Exports of Military Technology and Equipment', 17 September 2019, https://eur-lex.europa.eu/legal-content/EN/TXT/PDF/?uri=CELEX:02008E0944-20190917&from=EN.

35 Bundesministerium für Wirtschaft und Klimaschutz, 'Politische Grundsätze der Bundesregierung für den Export von Kriegswaffen und sonstigen Rüstungsgütern' [Political principles of the federal government for the export of war weapons and other armaments], https://www.bmwi.de/Redaktion/DE/Downloads/P-R/politische-grundsaetze-fuer-den-export-von-kriegswaffen-und-sonstigen-ruestungsguetern.pdf?__blob=publicationFile.

36 The Council of the European Union, 'Council Common Position 2008/944/CFSP of 8 December 2008 Defining Common Rules Governing Control of Exports of Military Technology and Equipment', article 2, paragraph 4.

37 Bernhard Moltmann 'Im Dunkeln ist gut munkeln: Oder: Die Not mit der Transparenz in der deutschen Rüstungsexportpolitik' [Rumor is good in the dark: Or: The need for transparency in German arms export policy], *HSFK Standpunkte,* no. 1, 2011, pp. 1–12; and Christian Mölling, 'Für eine sicherheitspolitische Begründung deutscher Rüstungsexporte' [Für eine sicherheitspolitische Begründung deutscher Rüstungsexporte'], *SWP-Aktuell,* no. 66, November 2013, p. 2.

38 Hendrik Platte and Dirk Leuffen, 'German Arms Exports: Between Normative Aspirations and Political Reality', *German Politics*, vol. 25, no. 4, 2016, p. 563.

39 Simone Wisotzki, 'Deutsche Rüstungsexporte in alle Welt? Eine Bilanz der vergangenen 30 Jahre' [German Arms Exports to the World? Taking Stock of the Past 30 Years], Leibniz-Institut Hessische Stiftung Friedens- und Konfliktforschung

im Auftrag von Greenpeace e.V., March 2020, p. 13, https://www.greenpeace.de/publikationen/2020-07-19_studie_deutsche_ruestungsexporte.pdf; 'Saudi-Arabien – "Ein Stabilitätsanker in der Region"' [Saudi Arabia – 'An Anchor of Stability in the Region'], Welt, 9 July 2011, https://www.welt.de/politik/deutschland/article13476959/Saudi-Arabien-Ein-Stabilitaetsanker-in-der-Region.html; and 'Bundesregierung verteidigt Rüstungsexporte nach Saudi-Arabien' [Federal government defends arms exports to Saudi Arabia], Der Spiegel, 20 November 2013, https://www.spiegel.de/politik/deutschland/bundesregierung-verteidigt-ruestungsexporte-nach-saudi-arabien-a-934734.html.

40 'Acht deutsche Patrouillenboote für Saudi-Arabien' [Eight German patrol boats for Saudi Arabia], DW, 23 March 2018, https://www.dw.com/de/acht-deutsche-patrouillenboote-f%C3%BCr-saudi-arabien/a-43095872.

41 'Stopp für Rüstungsexporte nach Saudi-Arabien verlängert' [Suspension of arms exports to Saudi Arabia extended], DW, 10 December 2020, https://www.dw.com/de/stopp-f%C3%BCr-r%C3%BCstungsexporte-nach-saudi-arabien-verl%C3%A4ngert/a-55893545.

42 'Merkel plädiert für Stopp von Waffenexporten' [Merkel calls for arms exports to be stopped], Der Spiegel, 18 August 2013, https://www.spiegel.de/politik/ausland/aegypten-merkel-will-mit-waffenexport-stopp-druck-machen-a-917234.html.

43 'Regierung genehmigt Export von Patrouillenbooten nach Ägypten' [Government approves export of patrol boats to Egypt], *ZEIT Online*, 2 November 2020, https://www.zeit.de/wirtschaft/2020-11/ruestungsexporte-patroullienboote-luerssen-werft-aegypten-exportstopp-saudi-arabien-bundesregierung; and Hans Uwe Mergner, 'Ägypten übernimmt für Saudi-Arabien bestimmte Patrouillenboote' [Egypt takes over patrol boats destined for Saudi Arabia], Europäische Sicherheit & Technik, 6 November 2020, https://esut.de/2020/11/meldungen/23959/aegypten-uebernimmt-fuer-saudi-arabien-bestimmte-patrouillenboote/.

44 Yannik Hüllinghorst and Stephan Roll, 'German Arms Exports and the Militarisation of Arab States' Foreign Policies, *SWP Comment*, no. 6, January 2021, 2021, p.4, https://www.swp-berlin.org/publications/products/comments/2021C06_GermanArmsExports.pdf; and Wisotzki, 'Deutsche Rüstungsexporte in alle Welt? Eine Bilanz der vergangenen 30 Jahre', p.14.

45 Markus Bayer et al., 'Türkei', BICC, 25 July 2022, p.10, https://www.ruestungsexport.info/user/pages/04.laenderberichte/tuerkei/2022_Tuerkei.pdf.

46 Simone Wisotzki, *German Arms Exports to the World? Taking Stock of the Past 30 Years* (Frankfurt am Main: Peace Research Institute Frankfurt, 2020), pp. 6, 11–12, https://www.hsfk.de/fileadmin/HSFK/hsfk_downloads/PRIF_Report_07_20.pdf; and Markus Bayer et al., 'Türkei', pp. 10–11.

47 Wisotzki, *German Arms Exports to the World? Taking Stock of the Past 30 Years*, pp. 11–13; and Bundesministerium für Wirtschaft und Energie, 'Bericht der Bundesregierung über ihre Exportpolitik für konventionelle Rüstungsgüter im Jahre 2019' [Report of the Federal Government on Its Export Policy for Conventional Armaments in 2019], June 2020, p.24, https://www.bmwk.de/Redaktion/DE/Publikationen/Aussenwirtschaft/ruestungsexportbericht-2019.pdf?__blob=publicationFile&v=12.

48 Ministry of National Defense Republic of Korea, 'Defense White Paper', 2018, p. 209, https://www.mnd.go.kr/user/mndEN/upload/pblictn/PBLICTNEBOOK_201908070153390840.pdf.

49 State China Aerospace Studies Institute, *In Their Own Words: China's National Defense in the New Era* (Beijing: Foreign Languages Press, 2019), https://www.airuniversity.af.edu/CASI/Display/Article/2538677/in-their-own-words-2019-chinas-national-defense-in-the-new-era/; and Ministry of Foreign Affairs of the People's Republic of China, 'General Statement by H.E. Ambassador Li Song at the Fifth Conference of State Parties to the Arms Trade Treaty', 26 August 2019, https://www.fmprc.gov.cn/mfa_eng/wjdt_665385/zyjh_665391/201908/t20190828_678766.html.

50 Barry Buzan, Ole Wæver and Jaap de Wilde, *Security: A New Framework for Analysis* (Boulder, CO: Lynne Rienner, 1998), p. 11–2; and, see also, Barry Buzan, *People, States, and Fear: An Agenda for International Security Studies in the Post-Cold War Era* (Boulder, CO: Lynne Rienner, 1991).

51 Karl W. Deutsch et al., *Political Community and the North Atlantic Area: International Organization in the Light of Historical Experience* (Princeton, NJ: Princeton University Press, 1957).

52 Fungisai Nota, 'Theory of Regional Stability as a Public Good: Examples from Southern Africa', *The Economics of Peace and Security Journal*, vol. 4, no. 2, 2009, p. 6.

53 See also Jonathan D. Pollack, 'Changes and Prospects for the Structure of Regional Stability in East Asia: A U.S. Perspective', Brookings, 25 January 2016, https://www.brookings.edu/on-the-record/changes-and-prospects-for-the-structure-of-regional-stability-in-east-asia-a-u-s-perspective/.

54 Louis J. Cantori and Steven L. Spiegel, 'The Analysis of Regional International Politics: The Integration Versus the Empirical Systems Approach', *International Organization*, vol. 24, no. 4, Autumn 1973, pp. 465–94; and Austin Long, 'Proliferation and Strategic Stability in the Middle East', in Elbridge A. Colby and Michael S. Gerson (eds), *Strategic Stability: Contending Interpretations* (Carlisle, PA: Strategic Studies Institute and U.S. Army War College Press, 2013), pp. 383–432, https://www.jstor.org/stable/resrep12086.13#metadata_info_tab_contents.

55 A. Trevor Thrall, Jordan Cohen and Caroline Dorminey, 'Power, Profit, or Prudence? US Arms Sales since 9/11', *Strategic Studies Quarterly*, Summer 2020, pp. 100–26.

56 Beata Cichocka and Ian Mitchell, 'Undermining Global Security: Measuring

the Risk of Arms Exports and Commitment to Development', 24 February 2021, Center for Global Development, https://www.cgdev.org/blog/undermining-global-security-measuring-risk-arms-exports-and-commitment-development.

57 Thrall, Cohen and Dorminey, 'Power, Profit, or Prudence? US Arms Sales since 9/11', pp. 100, 114.

58 Gregory S. Sanjian, 'Promoting Stability or Instability? Arms Transfers and Regional Rivalries, 1950–1991', *International Studies Quarterly*, vol. 43, no. 4, December 1999, pp. 641, 668; and, see also, Anna Stavrianakis, 'Licensed to Kill: The United Kingdom's Arms Export Licensing Process, *The Economics of Peace and Security Journal*, vol. 3, no. 1, 2008, p. 33.

59 Thrall, Cohen and Dorminey acknowledge this factor in their analysis. They propose a 'red flag' system in which arms exports are blocked if the importing nations fall into one of several high-risk categories relating to governance, state fragility or conflict risk. See Thrall, Cohen and Dorminey, 'Power, Profit, or Prudence? US Arms Sales since 9/11', p. 119.

60 Hüllinghorst and Roll, 'German Arms Exports and the Militarisation of Arab States' Foreign Policies'.

61 Beth Oppenheim, 'Europe Is at War Over Arms Exports', *Foreign Policy*, 18 September 2019, https://foreignpolicy.com/2019/09/18/europe-is-at-war-over-arms-exports/.

62 See, for example, Béraud-Sudreau and Meijer, 'Enjeux stratégiques et économiques des politiques d'exportation d'armement: Une comparaison franco-américaine' [Strategic and economic issues of arms export policies A Franco-American comparison], p. 72.

63 Blanton, 'Foreign Policy in Transition? Human Rights, Democracy, and U.S. Arms Exports'.

64 See, for example, Béraud-Sudreau, *French Arms Exports: The Business of Sovereignty*.

65 Cécile Fauconnet, Julien Malizard and Antoine Pietri, 'French Arms Exports and Intrastate Conflicts: An Empirical', *Defence and Peace Economics*, vol. 30, no. 2, pp. 176–96.

66 Shannon L. Blanton, 'The Transfer of Arms and the Diffusion of Democracy: Do Arms Promote or Undermine the "Third Wave"?', *The Social Science Journal*, vol. 36, no. 3, 1999, pp. 413–29.

67 Richard Johnson, 'The Role and Capabilities of Major Weapon Systems Transferred Between 1950 and 2010: Empirical Examinations of an Arms Transfer Data', *Defence and Peace Economics*, vol. 28, no. 3, 2017, pp. 272–97.

68 David Kinsella, 'Nested Rivalries: Superpower Competition, Arms Transfers, and Regional Conflict, 1950–1990', *International Interactions*, vol. 21, no. 2, 1995, pp. 109–25.

69 David Kinsella, 'Arms Transfer Dependence and Foreign Policy Conflict', *Journal of Peace Research*, vol. 35, no. 1, 1998, pp. 7–23.

70 Oliver Pamp et al., 'The Build-Up of Coercive Capacities: Arms Imports and the Outbreak of Violent Intrastate Conflicts', *Journal of Peace Research*, vol. 55, no. 4, 2018, pp. 430–44.

71 Cassady Craft and Joseph P. Smaldone, 'The Arms Trade and the Incidence of Political Violence in Sub-Saharan Africa, 1967–97', *Journal of Peace Research*, vol. 39, no. 6, 2002, pp. 692–710.

AN IISS STRATEGIC DOSSIER

THE UNITED STATES

Source: IISS

CHAPTER 3

Map 3.1: **Selected* combat-aircraft sales to the Middle East, North Africa and Asia from the US**

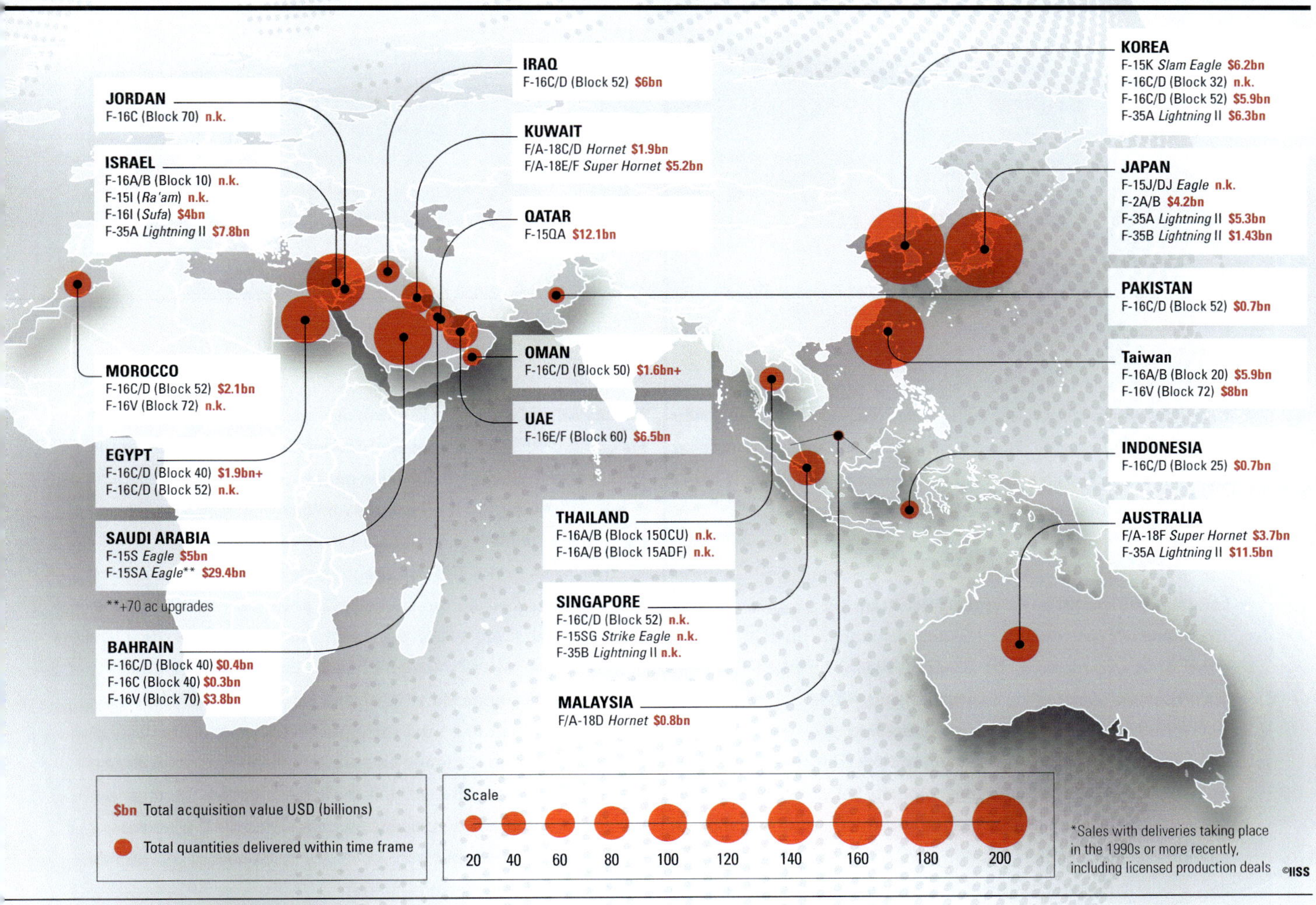

Since the end of the Soviet Union over 30 years ago, the United States has occupied an unparalleled position as the world's largest exporter of advanced weaponry, with arms transfers worth more than USD34 billion in 2021 alone.[1] Such exports have been driven by multiple political decision-making considerations, including promoting and leveraging the military strength of US allies; assuming or aligning with region-specific security concerns; responding militarily to threats as warranted (or inferred); encouraging pro-democracy interests and initiatives; and supporting domestic industry.

Regional stability has been a constant fixture among these considerations – though not always with the same precedence, nor necessarily the same levels of interpretation – for successive US administrations. This consideration has sometimes been accompanied by vigorous public debate and disagreement. Washington's Foreign Military Sales (FMS) Program has generated transfers – or transfer approvals – that have been, and continue to be, subject to considerable public scrutiny. This is a product of a values-based exercise, one tempered and ever-governed by rules, regulations and procedures established (directly or indirectly) by the US Congress.

Arms sales to the Middle East and the Indo-Pacific region have a history of on occasion being contentious in Congress. In 1981 congressional opponents raised concerns about president Ronald Reagan's proposed sale of the Boeing E-3 Airborne Warning and Control System,[2] and the same can be said about president George H.W. Bush's proposed transfer of F-16s to Taiwan amid the 1992 election cycle.[3] More recently, in 2019, president Donald Trump vetoed

PRESIDENT JIMMY CARTER
US president Jimmy Carter in his private study, 21 November 1978. Carter wanted to shift to a more restrictive arms export policy and looked to craft a multinational approach.
CREDIT: Hum Images/Universal Images Group via Getty Images.

three congressional resolutions blocking weapons sales to Saudi Arabia.[4] In January 2021, President Joe Biden announced a pause on weapons sales to Saudi Arabia and the United Arab Emirates (UAE) in part due to congressional concerns.[5]

Congressional power and the executive branch

The prominent position of the US Congress in the transfer of conventional arms derives from the US Constitution, America's founding document and supreme social contract. Article I asserts that 'Congress shall have Power … to regulate commerce with foreign nations', and Article IV states that Congress shall 'make all needful rules and regulations respecting the territory or other property belonging to the United States'.[6] As a result of original decree and through the evolution of modern practice, Congress has emerged as the world's most influential national legislative body for considering the sale of major weapons.

Congress has, over time, established an oversight regime regarding the transfer of US-origin defence articles and services. At the height of the Cold War, for instance, it authored the Foreign Assistance Act of 1961, and later approved the Arms Export Control Act of 1976 (AECA).[7] AECA, as amended, has endured the test of time and currently provides not only the authoritative bedrock but also the critical context for US FMS and all arms-related legislative and administrative activities.

Despite such a prominent role, Congress is not omnipotent with respect to all arms-trade activity – at least not in a practical sense. In practice, the initiation and delivery of security assistance abroad is a task and burden placed on the executive branch – that is, the bureaucracy and structures of the state tasked with implementing policy, requiring the involvement of personnel from both the Department of State (DoS) and the Department of Defense (DoD).

The ultimate responsibility for management of US FMS rests with the secretary of state, while the department's Bureau of Political and Military Affairs (S/PM) is tasked with overseeing the administration of FMS through the Defense Security Cooperation Agency (DSCA) at the DoD. This arrangement in turn relies on the respective military departments – the Army, the Navy and the Air Force – to staff, resource and execute sales within the programme.

The White House also has a central role in major-weapons sales. Five modern American presidents have issued formal Conventional Arms Transfer (CAT) Policy documents to set goals, guide planning and drive greater interdepartmental coordination in a manner consistent with congressional ideals and fiat (and President Biden has signalled his intent to be the sixth). Yet on-site arms-related assessments, recommendations and end-use compliance measures remain reliant on mid-level staff execution and DSCA direction. This organisational design and process places considerable trust in the judgement and ability of rank-and-file personnel to understand and consistently promote US national-security interests.

US foreign arms-related transfer activities are therefore initiated, assessed, approved and executed by a vast number of security-assistance and security-cooperation specialists across a broad array of offices. All this occurs in a manner consistent with – and ultimately accountable to – a set of statutes, public laws and policy declarations established and profoundly influenced by Congress. Still, the extent to which the totality of the effort correctly accounts for and promotes US national-security interests, alliances and regional security concerns remains worthy of further examination.

Arms-export process, organisation and authority

With a declaration of conventional-arms transfers as 'an exceptional foreign policy implement' and a specific appeal for restraint in their use, president Jimmy Carter released the first national-level policy on conventional-arms transfers in May 1977.[8] A reflection of the relatively new 1976 AECA, PD/NSC-13 feted and advanced congressional

THE PENTAGON
The US Department of Defense is one of the main, but far from the only, government offices that has an important input into decisions regarding the sale of major weapons.
CREDIT: Bill Clark/CQ-Roll Call, Inc via Getty Images.

priorities, especially with respect to the promotion of multilateralism and human rights, the fostering of regional stability and the protection of sophisticated weaponry. Despite its forward-looking nature, however, neither the 1970s-era Congress nor the Carter administration could envision the geopolitical shifts on the horizon, nor could either anticipate the full nature of the professional changes relevant to US foreign policy and FMS about to transpire within the greater US national-security community.

Against the backdrop of the 1980s Cold War and as part and parcel of the new federal process soon to evolve, Congress approved and sent to president Reagan for signature the Goldwater–Nichols Defense Reorganization Act of 1986 (GNA).[9] The Act was designed to strengthen the US military joint staff and elevate and empower both the role and authority of each regionally focused geographical combatant command (COCOM). It set in motion a shift in the ways and means of DoD and DoS overseas engagement – perhaps more than originally imagined.[10] After its enactment, the resident military staffs at each geographical COCOM grew ever-more influential relative to their respective counterparts in the Pentagon, especially with respect to theatre campaign planning, the development of war-fighting requirements and direct engagement with foreign nations.[11] With respect to FMS recommendations, the empowered and reformed COCOM staffs subsequently aligned with the transnational and regionally based approach (and Bureau structure) at State Department headquarters, thus facilitating a greater focus on regional stability concerns overseas.[12]

To support and staff this empowered and expanded role of the COCOMs, Congress also created and enforced a professional-development pipeline more attuned to broader 'joint' training, experience and assignments. Senior-level promotions were linked to a new joint military professional-education requirement (with the curriculum extended to include DoS and other federal employees).[13] Additional refinement of the military profession occurred with the creation of the joint specialist officer designation and the wider use of 'jointness' as a term within policy directives and federal statutes.[14] By design, therefore, COCOM staff positions eventually grew to be more attractive assignments for aspiring generals and admirals.

The Defense Security Cooperation Agency

With change being a watchword during the immediate post-Cold War era, the Clinton administration unveiled the Defense Reform Initiative (DRI) in early 1997, an effort that further professionalised the FMS system and produced both the DSCA and the term 'security cooperation'.[15] Formed by, with and through an expansion of the Defense Security Assistance Agency, and placed as a direct report to the under secretary of defense for policy, the DSCA became the lead Pentagon office for guiding FMS policy compliance, implementation and liaison with the DoS and each implementing agency within the DoD (the Army, the Navy, etc.). Pursuant to the DRI, the DSCA also became responsible for administering Foreign Military Financing (FMF) and international military education and training.

To execute and meet both FMS-related and security-cooperation objectives, the DSCA:

- initiated a regular (i.e., near-daily) distribution process for sending policy memoranda to relevant stakeholder offices;
- refined a security-cooperation training and education curriculum for what became the Defense Security Cooperation University;[16]
- created and maintained an online archive of official (and pertinent) information;
- sponsored ad hoc travelling survey teams; and
- established security-cooperation offices overseas to engage potential recipient nations about potential sales and other related activities.[17]

Figure 3.1: **Annual values of Direct Commercial Sales (authorisations) to Asia, the Middle East and North Africa (MENA) and the rest of the world, 1999–2020**

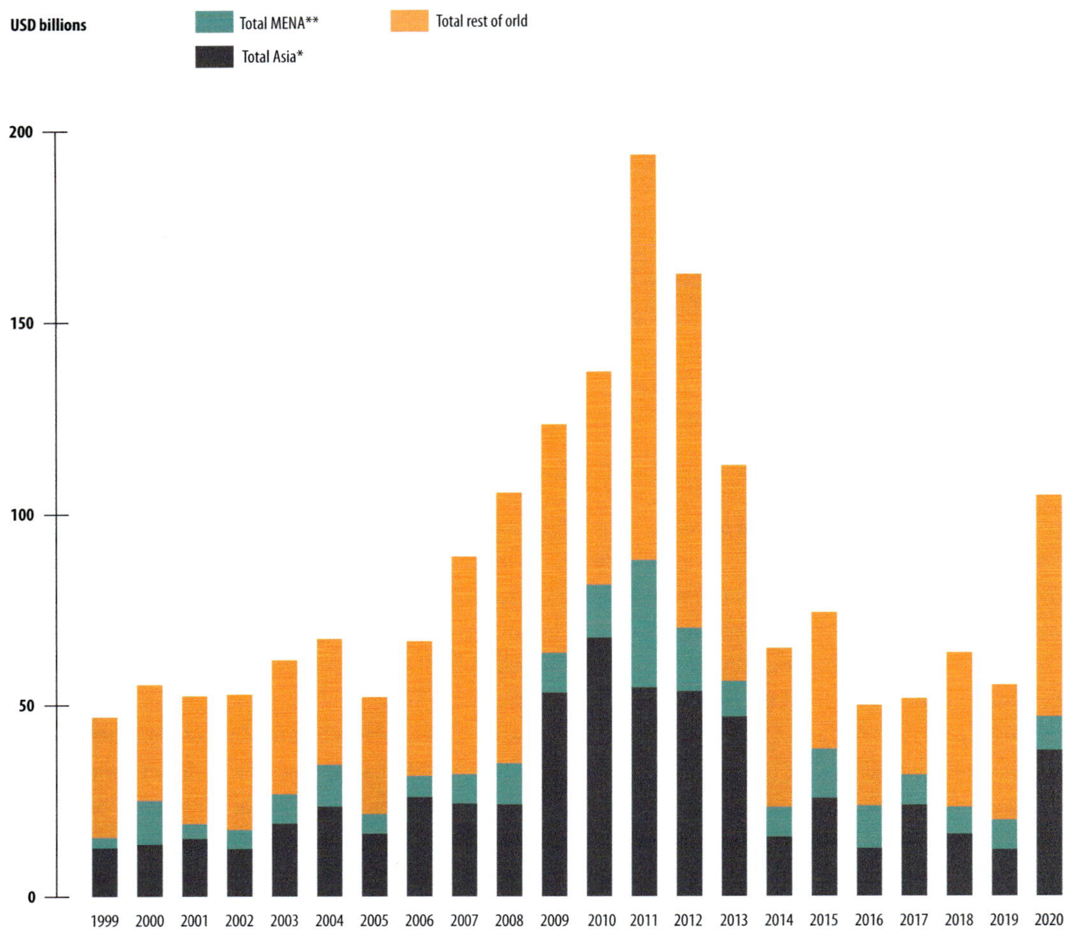

*Afghanistan, Australia, Bangladesh, Brunei, Cambodia, China, Fiji, India, Indonesia, Japan, South Korea , Laos, Malaysia, Mongolia, Nepal, New Zealand, Pakistan, Philippines, Singapore, Sri Lanka, Taiwan, Thailand, Timor Leste, Vietnam. **Algeria, Bahrain, Egypt, Iran, Iraq, Israel, Jordan, Kuwait, Lebanon, Libya, Morocco, Oman, Qatar, Saudi Arabia, Syria, Tunisia, UAE, Yemen.

Source: IISS

This approach and construct remain in place today. Since 2011, moreover (and only in response to specific combatant-command requests), DSCA resources and deploys Expeditionary Requirements Generation Teams (consisting of seasoned personnel) to help COCOM staffs clarify, propose and tailor security-related approaches to both country-specific and regionally based FMS-related issues.[18]

The Bureau of Political and Military Affairs

By delegation of the statutory authority conferred specifically on the secretary of state, the Bureau of Political and Military Affairs is the primary State Department office responsible for oversight and execution of security assistance and security cooperation, with the DSCA providing administrative support. To execute these duties, S/PM relies on its subordinate Office of Regional Security and Arms Transfers. These bodies ensure proper collaboration and coordination between the State Department and the Department of Defense, and throughout and across all other relevant bureaus and offices within State headquarters (e.g., the Bureau of East Asian and Pacific Affairs).

In practice, each FMS proposal (or 'Case') forwarded by the DSCA to the Regional Security and Arms Transfers Office is reviewed with US foreign-policy and national-security objectives in mind. At times, this review has proven to be lengthy and complex, requiring extensive discussions between bureau and COCOM staffs, security-cooperation personnel, as well as with representatives from foreign governments, congressional offices and private defence firms. On occasion, this review has also involved more extensive collaboration with senior staff at a designated implementation agency (within the Office of the Secretary of the Navy, for example), to explore in greater detail concerns about partnership capacity, military inter-operability, nation-to-nation relationship building, and US industrial-base considerations.[19] All the while, the secretary of state retains primacy of position within the inter-agency community regarding any proposed FMS sale in an effort to ensure a greater emphasis on US foreign-policy objectives.

The importance of FMS and its management

An important foreign-policy tool of the federal government, the US FMS Program has been developed and executed as a form of security assistance since the 1970s in accordance with guidelines established by law. First authorised and defined by Congress as part of the 1976 Arms Export Control Act, security assistance involves the provision of

> defense articles, military training, and other defense-related services by grant, loan, credit, or cash sales in furtherance of national policies and objectives ... funded and authorized by Department of State [and] administered by Department of Defense/Defense Security Cooperation Agency.[20]

The term security cooperation would follow two decades later, within amendments to Title 10 of the US Statutory Code, the intention being to support Building Partnership Capacity (BPC) initiatives within allied militaries.[21] The primary 'train and equip' or BPC security-cooperation effort authorised under Title 10 authority is currently known as the '333 Program' (previously '1206'). Its execution has required cooperation with, and the ultimate deferral to, the State Department in an effort to maintain consistency with US foreign-policy objectives.

Congress

With the Foreign Assistance Act and the Arms Export Control Act acknowledged and accepted as established law, the practice of congressional FMS oversight has materialised mostly in one of two ways: when FMS cases have been presented to Capitol Hill for review (formally and informally), and during annual deliberations of authorisation and appropriations measures governing the departments of State and Defense.

With respect to case-by-case oversight, the speaker of the House and both the Senate Foreign Relations (SFRC) and House Foreign Affairs (HFAC) committees have occupied central roles, with all three engaging in constant monitoring of potential arms-sales cases. However, once a formal notice of a potential sale is delivered, there is only a limited amount of time for review and action – no more than 15 or 30 days (depending on the identity and status of the proposed recipient state). Immediate cross-bicameral collaboration between the leadership of the Senate and the House of Representatives is thus required.[22] To be sure, the narrowness of this window places a premium on pre-notice monitoring by the respective offices.[23]

Over the past 30 years, the appropriations panels and Armed Services committees in each legislative body have played a clear role in the longer deliberation process that involves the review of annual departmental funding (at the DoD and DoS). The increased involvement of the Armed Services committees is understandable as it coincides with the DoD's increasingly important role in executing FMS during the post-GNA era; the expansion of security-cooperation efforts since the late 1980s; and the consistent prominence of the National Defense Authorization Act (NDAA) – an act that has been approved and enacted each and every year since 1961.[24] Given such dependable regularity, the NDAA has been, and continues to be, the primary legislative vehicle for advancing not only regular programmatic management tweaks but also new initiatives in the field of security assistance and security cooperation. It served, for example, as the legislative vessel in 2016 for the creation of the '333 Program'.[25]

In practice, the SFRC and HFAC leadership and other interested congressional parties are afforded the opportunity to introduce and amend provisions during the NDAA deliberation process. This allows them to bring their respective perspectives and areas of expertise to bear on various arms-related matters.[26] Furthermore, FMS-related provisions can be included within the appropriations measures each year.[27]

Brave new world

The Soviet Union's collapse at the end of 1991 precipitated far-reaching geopolitical changes, including a reshaping of the major-weapons export market. Previously well-known arms-export leaders fell off the pace or disappeared altogether. The United States' relative share of sales rose rapidly, while the market shrank from a Cold War annual high in 1987 of USD40.6bn to a low of USD20.2bn in 1994 (in constant 1990 USD).[28] Moscow-directed exports also dropped precipitously and by 1994 represented only 6% of the total market. That same year Washington's share of exports soared above 50%.[29]

This period also saw a shift in the make-up of the leading global importers. While Saudi Arabia remained at or near the top of arms recipients in both the 1980s and 1990s, several other countries emerged as significant recipient states. In the early 1990s, Kuwait, Malaysia, South Korea, Taiwan and Thailand all rose through the ranks, with much of the procurement originating from the US. Former Soviet client states, including Afghanistan, Angola, Iraq and Syria, trended downward, while Libya, Cuba and Vietnam vanished altogether from the list of recipients.[30]

Alongside the end of the Soviet Union, two further events would influence Washington's international-engagement strategy, and thus FMS policy, throughout the 1990s. China's brutal suppression of Tiananmen Square pro-democracy protesters in 1989 hardened US-Sino relations and affected FMS-related decisions. Only 14 months later, Iraq invaded Kuwait.

The impact of and fallout from these three events – which were the consequences of decisions made in Moscow, Beijing and Baghdad – would influence and tax the political bandwidth of the Bush administration for years.

Timeline 3.1: **Selected* combat-aircraft sales to the Middle East and North Africa from the US**

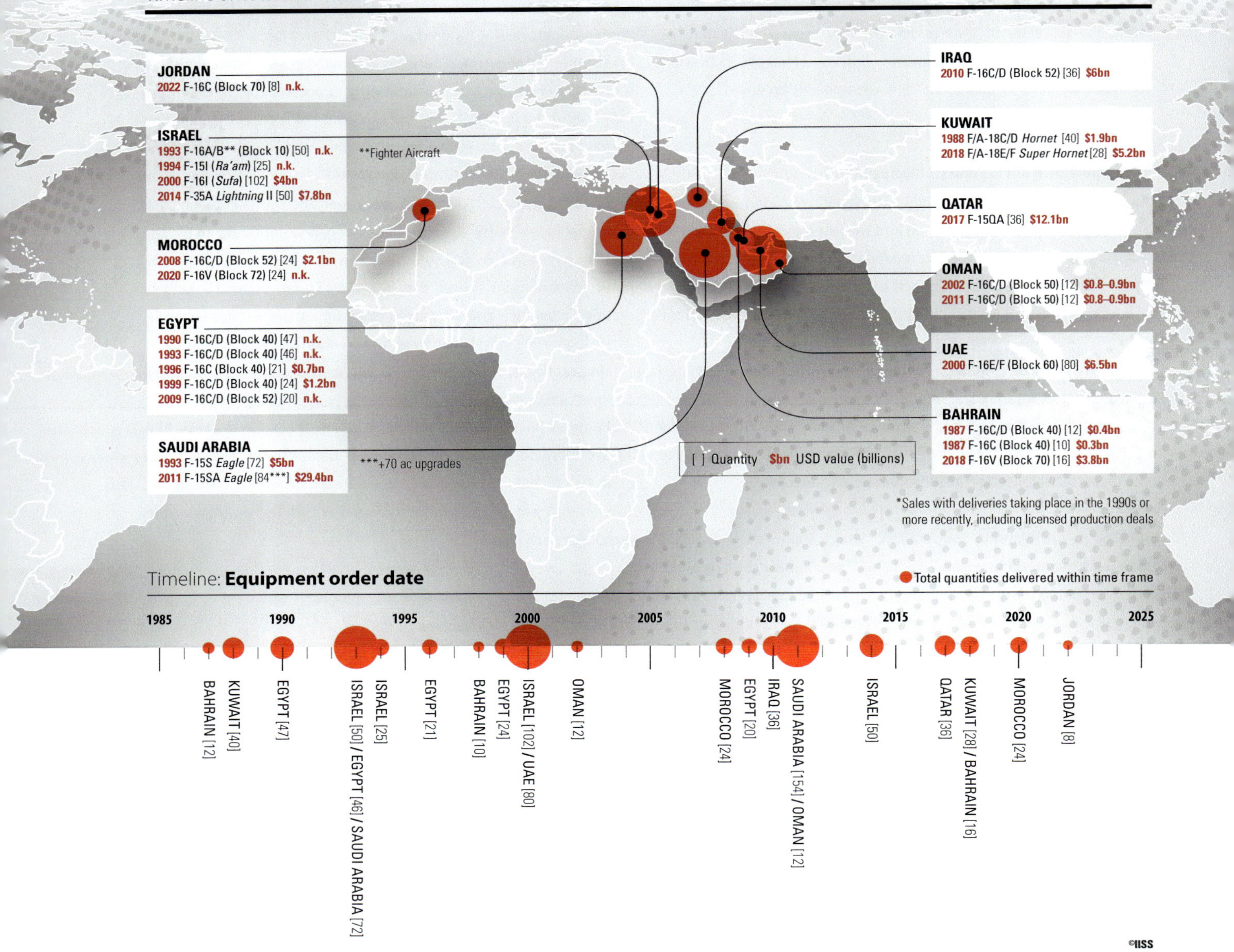

Source: IISS

The early 1990s and the Bush administration

George H.W. Bush entered office at the beginning of 1989 with the goal of strengthening democratic ideals all across the world.[31] Improved cross-Atlantic relations with an ailing Soviet Union had begun to give the Reagan administration greater flexibility to address issues beyond those of traditional super-power military confrontation, a legacy that Bush aimed to pursue in his advocacy of pro-trade and pro-democracy policies abroad.[32] But the decisions and developments in Moscow, Baghdad and Beijing soon limited such ambitions and focused and intensified the demands on senior-level attention.[33] The president and his team consequently prioritised efforts to craft an enduring post-Cold War architecture for Europe. With respect to the Tiananmen protests and wider unrest in China, the administration opted to prioritise the perseverance of the larger US-Sino diplomatic relationship. Baghdad's seizure of Kuwait in 1990 soon led to *Operation Desert Shield* and *Operation Desert Storm*.[34]

Nevertheless, all three regional challenges served as reminders of the importance of security matters within the conduct of international affairs. They brought forth for debate not only the foundational concepts of state sovereignty and ideals of political association but also the need to respect and grasp anew the potencies and limitations of military force abroad – especially those of the US military.[35]

In Europe, Bush administration officials were challenged with the possibilities of German unification (and the benefits and limitations of expanding NATO membership); the nuances of ongoing Moscow–Washington–NATO posturing; deliberations at the United Nations; and the promises and consequences of disarmament pacts, nuclear and otherwise (such as Open Skies, START I and II, and the nearly completed CFE Treaty).[36] Saddam Hussein's invasion of Kuwait threatened 40% of the world's potential oil supply, compelling administration officials to plan for and rally an international coalition in opposition.[37] In time, and under the auspices of UN Security Council authorisation,[38] as many as 38 foreign nations would pledge military and financial commitments to the US-led effort – the largest political–military alliance constituted since the end of the Second World War.[39]

Security matters, especially debates about the use of military force abroad, would continue to receive the lion's share of senior-level attention as the Bush administration approached the mid-point of its term.[40] Even though the Gulf War would conclude by March 1991 and the Soviet Union would cease to officially exist by the end of that same year, the challenges associated with ensuring an effective security presence in these regions would persist. The evolving post-Cold War geopolitical climate, such as it was, would greatly impact Washington's future security-assistance and security-cooperation decisions.

Box 3.1: **NSDD-5**

NSDD-5 called for the use of such transfers to:

- strengthen and revitalise mutual security relationships;
- demonstrate an enduring interest in the security of US friends and partners around the world; and
- foster regional stability, as (and where) appropriate.

To bring forth these principles in a practical way, NSDD-5 also urged due consideration of:

- the nature of military threats facing a prospective arms recipient;
- the potential improvement a specific arms transfer might provide to a recipient's capacity for participating in US-sponsored collective-security efforts (known today as building partnership capacity);
- a recipient's existing and potential capacity for countering external aggression;
- the ability of a proposed transfer to promote and maintain regional stability; and
- the extent to which a proposed transfer might align with and positively contribute to US interests and objectives.

Bush and arms exports

Bush did not initially follow Reagan in promulgating a revised conventional-arms transfer policy when he took office, and instead relied on the former's 1981 National Security Decision Directive – NSDD-5 – and remained true to its stated goals.[41]

However, a recalibration of NSDD-5 occurred on 2 October 1989, when president Bush signed and issued National Security Directive 26 (NSD-26), a memorandum establishing US foreign-policy objectives for Iran and Iraq. The memorandum, 'U.S. Policy Toward the Persian Gulf', expressly encouraged US military exports to Gulf Cooperation Council (GCC) members. The document directed the secretaries of state and defense to jointly 'develop a strategy for a long-term program of arms sales to Saudi Arabia and the other GCC states'.[42] The new directive essentially redefined US national security to be dependent on both access to Gulf-produced oil *and* the inherent capacity of GCC allies to defend themselves against external aggression. To support this two-pronged goal, NSD-26 also called on the National Security Council (NSC) to further discourage Soviet arms sales to the region and, perhaps most importantly, recalled the need to respect Israeli military strength (relative to neighbouring Arab countries).[43]

The administration prioritised the underlying thrust of NSD-26 even more after Iraq's invasion of Kuwait in late 1990, even if some aspects of the document appeared immaterial or outdated. Unfettered Western access to oil and the sustainment of military support to allies in the Gulf region would remain important goals to guide US foreign policy for years to come.

But as a list of principles or as a road map to guide future weapons transfers, Bush's NSD-26 fell short. In contrast, the Reagan-era NSDD-5 provided a more relevant and actionable post-Gulf War guide and instruction set. Indeed, Reagan's NSDD-5 CAT Policy characterised conventional-arms transfers as 'an essential element of [the United States'] global defense posture and an indispensable component of its foreign policy'.[44]

Post-Gulf War arms sales

Iraq's invasion of Kuwait represented a threat to nearby Arab regimes, especially Saudi Arabia, and led to a shift in how many Middle Eastern states viewed security issues. More generally, the successful US intervention in Iraq and pledge to remain more militarily engaged in the region made Arab states reconsider their long-standing alignment against Israel. After the war, Arab regimes grew more interested in the defence of their own respective borders.

Secretary of state James Baker looked to build on the outcome of the war to 'show what American diplomacy could accomplish in the wake of sweeping military successes' and to 'win the peace', and began a vigorous pursuit of negotiations in an attempt to ease Arab–Israeli tensions.[45] In parallel, the administration negotiated and announced several FMS initiatives to improve the capacity of US allies in the Middle East to defend themselves. Two separate but related FMS packages of advanced fighter aircraft were announced by Washington in 1991, with F-16C Block 40 aircraft approved for Egypt, and ex-US Air Force (USAF) McDonnell Douglas F-15A and B aircraft approved for Israel.[46]

PRESIDENT BILL CLINTON
US president Bill Clinton signing the Comprehensive Test Ban Treaty, 24 September 1996. Clinton continued to pursue a relatively liberal approach to conventional arms sales.
CREDIT: Timothy A. Clary/AFP via Getty Images.

An effort to improve the Saudis' military capability was also under way with further sales of the General Dynamics M1 *Abrams* alongside upgrades to the Kingdom's E-3 airborne warning and control system (AWACS) fleet. The administration would subsequently announce another large FMS package the following year, with Riyadh agreeing to buy 72 F-15 combat aircraft, spares and related support for more than USD9bn. The Washington–Riyadh FMS deals amounted to more than USD13bn and would represent the majority of all US FMS for 1992.[47] Iraq, however, was not the only threat to regional stability as far as Washington or its regional partners were concerned. Iran's antagonistic relations with its neighbours remained a problem, and Tehran also seemed interested in bolstering its armed forces in the wake of US success in Iraq.[48] Given Tehran's then-unacknowledged (but strongly suspected and later confirmed) support for Hizbullah militants in Lebanon, Shia-led Iran quickly supplanted Iraq as the primary security concern for Tel Aviv and the region's Sunni-led Arab capitals. The military-modernisation effort in the Gulf region had entered a new phase.

In the Indo-Pacific, the nature of the challenge posed by China was also changing. The 1992 delivery of the Sukhoi Su-27SK *Flanker* B from Russia to the People's Liberation Army Air Force (PLAAF) marked the start of a broader modernisation programme that continues to this day. In November of that year the US and Taiwan signed an agreement covering the acquisition of 120 F-16A and 30 F-16B aircraft as a significant part of a wholesale air-force upgrade.[49]

The Clinton years

President Bill Clinton assumed office hot on the heels of a campaign that was critical of his predecessor's approach to economic and foreign affairs. Clinton argued that Bush's mismanagement of the economy had disenfranchised too many Americans and that his international engagements – especially those concerning Moscow and Beijing – had failed to promote pro-democracy initiatives and concerns. In essence, his campaign platform had been a strong endorsement of the classic liberal internationalist agenda.[50]

Once inaugurated, president Clinton turned most of his attention to domestic concerns and adopted many of his predecessor's security-related initiatives only when and where necessary.[51] Clinton viewed the realm of foreign policy as primarily a means for promoting American trade and in 1993 established the National Economic Council (NEC). A forum for senior advisers, the NEC became equal in stature to and modelled on the NSC.[52] The new president subsequently prioritised a balanced federal budget and the completion of trade accords and sought new trade-related deals (through the Asia-Pacific Economic Cooperation forum, for instance). Clinton also set a course for China's eventual inclusion in the World Trade Organization and for continuing most-favoured-nation trade status to Beijing – thereby further prioritising economic interests and muting both the pro-democracy and security-related initiatives he had touted earlier during the election campaign.[53]

For the Clinton administration, ensuring greater market access around the world would be the means for improving America's security, as asserted in the 1995 National Security Strategy, entitled 'Engagement and Enlargement'.[54] The combination of greater economic integration and interdependence was viewed as a disincentive for armed conflict.[55]

Nevertheless, Clinton's preference for diplomatic cooperation on a grand scale, prioritising arms-control and trade agreements, and for the pursuit of peace agreements would eventually lead to the US exhibiting a greater level of confidence and boldness on the world stage. Before the end of Clinton's terms in office, his administration would expand NATO membership, sign the Comprehensive Test-Ban Treaty (1996), and negotiate and sign more than 300 trade pacts. Clinton would attribute America's robust and successful economic expansion during his presidency to these acts. Only weeks before yielding the baton to his successor, for instance, Clinton claimed that international trade had bolstered nearly 25% of the domestic American economy. He further implied that trade sparked, sustained and would be required to maintain future US global leadership.[56]

Clinton's CAT Policy

Clinton's 1995 Presidential Decision Directive (PDD)/NSC-34 on conventional-arms export policy attempted to align national economic interests more closely with security concerns. It was the broadest and lengthiest of all the CAT documents to date – extending in length to ten pages, more than four times that of the inaugural document authored by president Carter.[57] While being lengthier than the Carter document, PDD/NSC-34 incorporated many of the same themes, particularly in terms of 'restraint'[58] and in the emphasis on striking a multilateral[59] approach, with the notion of establishing an 'Inner Circle'[60] of like-minded nations to better coordinate policies on major-weapons exports. In the then-confidential memorandum introducing the CAT Policy, Clinton wrote:

> the U.S. should pursue, on a case-by-case informal basis within an inner circle of close allies, a strategy of linking increased arms and technology cooperation, and market access, to greater cooperation in restraining conventional arms transfers to countries outside the circle. This strategy will be implemented on an informal, case-by-case basis with our closest allies (e.g., France, the UK and Germany).[61]

PDD/NSC-34 also echoed an earlier (and still classified) PDD/NSC memo related to non-proliferation and export-control policy (PDD/NSC-13) by calling for restraint in the treatment of sensitive technologies and geographical regions as well as encouraging greater transparency and multilateralism when securing US foreign-policy objectives.

The Clinton administration regarded arms sales as a 'legitimate instrument'[62] of foreign policy and couched them as 'inevitable'. Clinton's tone was some distance from the 'essential element' and 'indispensable component' language used in Reagan's NSDD-5 (and later adopted by George H.W. Bush).[63] It also proved more ambitious than Bush's Middle Eastern arms-control proposal in that it looked to broaden the regional approach and asserted an 'expectation' that any possible negative economic effect of arms sales in the recipient country should play a larger role in future CAT decisions.[64]

PDD/NSC-34 described the world's post-Gulf War arms market as one dominated by Washington and presented this characterisation as both a justification and an opportunity for securing greater public transparency in the trade of all weapons. It further emphasised greater employment of cooperative multilateral approaches as a way to simultaneously promote confidence between recipient states and reduce fears that might result from perceived security imbalances among them. The document appealed to the US inter-agency community for greater support of democratic initiatives and market reforms wherever possible and to better mitigate risks when dealing with potential 'rogue' and 'pariah' nations.[65]

Box 3.2: **NSC-34**

NSC-34 specifically identified five goals in finalising CAT decisions:

- ensuring US technological advantage over adversaries;
- assisting allies to deter and defend themselves against aggression, while promoting inter-operability with US forces;
- preserving regional balances of military forces in areas critical to US interests, especially in Central Europe, the Persian Gulf and Northeast Asia, while also preventing the proliferation of weapons of mass destruction (WMD);
- promoting peaceful conflict resolution, arms control, human rights and regional stability, and promoting the totality of US foreign-policy objectives, such as the expansion of democracy; and
- facilitating the ability of the US defence-industrial base to meet US defence requirements and maintain long-term military-technological superiority at lower costs.

In a salute to the ideas of greater openness and internationalism, the Clinton CAT directive incorporated much of the founding language of the UN, of the Helsinki Final Act, from the Paris Charter, from the Organization for Security and Co-operation in Europe (OSCE), as well as from the 1991 Madrid Middle East Peace Conference. Greater transparency in the sale of arms had been established as a goal by the UN in 1991, for example, with an endorsement by unanimous vote and the creation of the (still-active) Register of Conventional Arms.[66] Greater openness had already been demonstrated by the OSCE as well. Greater deference to human rights had already been promoted, too, within the Helsinki 'Decalogue'.[67] The 1990 Paris Charter – an echo of Helsinki and a harbinger of the 1995 OSCE – also contained language urging the world community to embrace a greater degree of multilateralism in all international engagements.[68]

As for allusions to the future, PDD/NSC-34 declared 'the U.S. will use the negotiation of the COCOM successor regime as a way to advance transparency in transfers' and to promote restraint, with 'COCOM' in this case a reference to the Cold War-era Coordinating Committee on export controls established by the US and the United Kingdom in the late 1940s.[69] Clinton had therefore anticipated the establishment of the Wassenaar Arrangement on Export Controls for Conventional Arms and Dual-Use Goods and Technologies as the successor of COCOM. Still in force, Wassenaar currently consists of 42 active members.[70]

Figure 3.2: **Annual values of Foreign Military Sales (FMS) to the Middle East, North Africa, Asia and the rest of the world, 2016–2021**

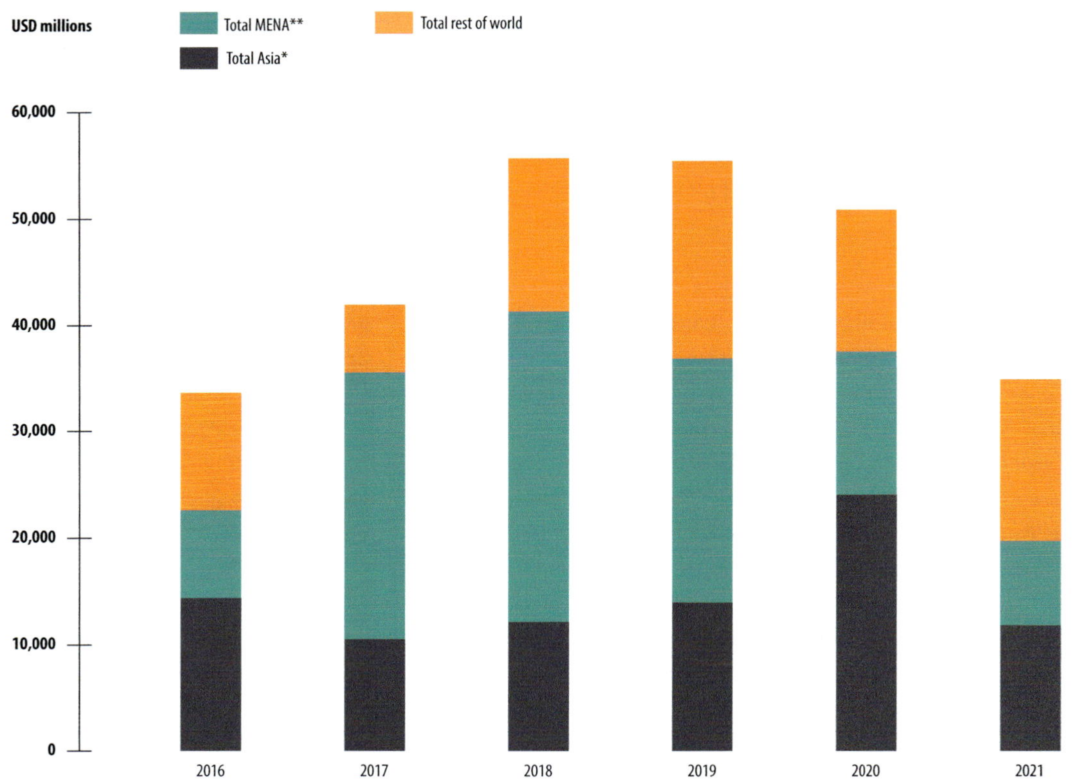

*Afghanistan, Australia, Bangladesh, Brunei, Cambodia, China, Fiji, India, Indonesia, Japan, South Korea, Laos, Malaysia, Mongolia, Nepal, New Zealand, Pakistan, Philippines, Singapore, Sri Lanka, Taiwan, Thailand, Timor Leste, Vietnam. **Algeria, Bahrain, Egypt, Iran, Iraq, Israel, Jordan, Kuwait, Lebanon, Libya, Morocco, Oman, Qatar, Saudi Arabia, Syria, Tunisia, UAE, Yemen.

Source: IISS

Along with the measured language and the goal of restraint, however, PDD/NSC-34 advocated greater support of US industry in pursuing overseas sales opportunities, laying bare an inherent tension within the policy. It authorised the tasking of US government personnel at home and abroad to support American industry marketing efforts abroad, listing 12 specific criteria for making export decisions on a case-by-case basis. These included promoting US strategic and foreign-policy objectives around the world; improving military-to-military inter-operability between the US and recipient nations; increasing US geopolitical access (and leverage); improving allied confidence-building measures; and exploring greater allied burden-sharing opportunities to deal with evolving security concerns.[71]

Clinton and arms sales

Reflecting US dominance in the post-Cold War era, the Clinton administration would announce new aircraft deals with more than ten nations, including Malaysia, one of Moscow's traditional trading partners. The deals covered the sale and transfer of F-16s to Australia, Bahrain, Egypt, Israel, Jordan, Singapore, South Korea, Thailand and the UAE.[72] Clinton would also strike a new transfer package with Tel Aviv to provide an additional two dozen F-15Is to the Israeli Air Force. As domestic acquisition rates of the F-16 continued to decline during the mid-1990s, additional export sales gained greater relative importance for sustaining production and related services, even though the USAF didn't take delivery of its final F-16 until March 2005.[73] Meanwhile, several regionally based scares related to nuclear-arms development occurred in the Indo-Pacific, prompting leaders in Washington to reconsider all existing defence-posture and alliance-building schemes.

Firstly, North Korea suddenly withdrew from the 1994 six-party disarmament talks amid Western suspicion that Pyongyang had already acquired a nuclear weapon. Secondly, Pyongyang conducted a test in 1998 of a delivery system potentially capable of carrying a nuclear warhead, firing a long-range missile over Japan (and prompting objections from Tokyo).[74] Finally, India and Pakistan each conducted successful nuclear-weapons tests of their own.[75] The developments involving these three nations – North Korea, India and Pakistan – increased strategic uncertainty on the Asian continent. Clinton strategists thus began pursuing parallel (if not directly linked) tracks of strategic planning and engagement on nuclear and conventional matters, pursuing reassurance and disarmament talks

BUSH AND KARZAI
US president George W. Bush meeting with Afghanistan's leader Hamid Karzai on 15 December 2008. US Involvement in fighting in Afghanistan was to last two decades, becoming a US policy preoccupation. CREDIT: Musadeq Sadeq/AFP via Getty Images.

to address the former concern and initiating greater alliance-building outreach efforts and FMS-oriented transfers for the latter.

Meanwhile, the Indo-Pacific region became the largest market in the world for defence imports over the course of the Clinton administration. From 1994 to 1998, the region evolved to represent more than 40% of global arms sales by value, with Japan, South Korea and Taiwan (all US allies) collectively accounting for nearly three-quarters of the total.

The George W. Bush years

The Republican Party returned to government in 2001 with George W. Bush, the son of George H.W. Bush, as president. George W. Bush brought with him an experienced foreign-policy team, one far more comfortable with the use of military force as a vehicle for change in the international arena than that of his predecessor. With the abundance of conservative and neo-conservative talent and significant prior senior-level governing experience (much of it within the administration of the elder president Bush), George W. Bush's team was well poised to artfully redirect and reapply the ends and means of American national-security policy.

While the campaign had often mentioned a desire to effect regime change in Iraq, the true nature and full extent of Bush's national-security agenda remained unclear during much of the first year.[76] Would the president opt to follow his father's example in promoting stability and guarding the sanctity of nation-state sovereignty, or prove to be more idealistic in vision and conservative in action – indeed, 'Reaganesque' – in the framing and wielding of American power at home and abroad?

These questions were answered with the terrorist attack on the World Trade Center and the Pentagon on 11 September 2001. The administration immediately sought and received UN endorsement and congressional authorisation for military action against the culprits: Osama bin Laden and the al-Qaeda network. With the necessary endorsement measures secured within a week and after pleas for cooperation (and an ultimatum) were ignored by the Taliban, the president authorised armed strikes against targets in Afghanistan on 7 October 2001, initiated in concert with British forces.[77] Dubbed *Operation Enduring Freedom*, the effort began a 'global war on terrorism' and would become a cause célèbre for US counter-terrorism efforts elsewhere around the globe (i.e., in Asia, the Pacific, Central America and across Africa).

After describing an 'axis of evil' in the world consisting of Iran, Iraq and North Korea in 2002, Bush began moving beyond calls for regional stability and placed greater emphasis on the promotion of democracy in foreign lands. *Operation Enduring Freedom* would continue for the duration of his presidency, grow to involve several international organisations – including NATO and the European Union – and include 58 coalition partners. Surprisingly, and at odds with traditional neo-conservative thought, the administration had put itself at the forefront of a large multilateralist effort after 9/11 – albeit one based on a US interventionist agenda.[78] The interventionist spirit would again be evident nearly a year and a half later as Washington led a ten-nation military assault into Iraq. Not unlike the initial phases of *Operation Enduring Freedom* in Afghanistan, the opening phase of *Operation Iraqi Freedom* proved successful as coalition forces secured their immediate objectives and overthrew the host nation's government in relatively quick fashion. The success of the initial military operation was not extended, however, with Iraq increasingly torn apart by insurrection and civil conflict.

In both Afghanistan and Iraq, misalignments with, and disagreements about, strategic objectives and operational conduct gnawed away at coalition performance and camaraderie, undermined progress and stability, fuelled corruption, and allowed (and arguably caused) dissent and insurgencies to grow. By the end of Bush's first term, non-US coalition members had grown weary of both missions, a fatigue exacerbated by the apparent lack of progress, rising costs and casualty rates, and the US president's blunt, independent personal style. But both conflicts would dominate and tax the US national-security agenda for the remainder of the Bush presidency.[79]

The 9/11 attacks shook the Bush team and yet instilled in it a faith and confidence, if not arrogance, in using American stimulus to spearhead 'the spread of democracy and economic openness' throughout the greater Middle East.[80] This became a hallmark of the White House agenda; as Bush portentously stated in his second inauguration speech, 'the survival of liberty in our land depends on the success of liberty in other lands'.[81] This lofty approach had been evident many years earlier when the president had introduced the so-called Bush Doctrine of pre-emptive strike in anticipation of gathering threats, and also when he had proposed increases in foreign aid, presented a national strategy to combat the proliferation of WMD, developed the Pan-Sahel Initiative (a precursor to the Trans-Saharan Counterterrorism Partnership programme), and aggressively and successfully pursued numerous trade negotiations.

President Bush would continue to pursue a consistently broad internationalist approach throughout his tenure and finalise more than 15 bilateral free-trade agreements with the likes of Australia, Bahrain, Jordan, Morocco, Oman, Singapore and others by 2009.[82] He would also grant Kuwait and Bahrain exclusive 'major non-NATO ally' status, as well as improve relations with India, Japan, Pakistan, Qatar, South Korea and the UAE (and specifically waive nuclear-related sanctions imposed on both Islamabad and New Delhi).[83] The level of US bilateral collaboration with allies had thus grown in many ways over his eight years in office, even as the pro-democracy vision of liberal-democratic internationalism grew ever more remote within the major combat zones.

George W. Bush and arms exports

Despite his worldview differing sharply from Clinton's, Bush declined to promulgate a new CAT Policy. Instead, his administration relied on existing statutory authorities and simply aligned itself with some of the goals set out in the CAT directive issued by his predecessor.[84]

Perhaps this was due to the pressing nature and chaotic circumstances of the post-9/11 environment, which necessitated ad hoc and hurried security-related decisions, many of which could not be fully vetted or coordinated (irrespective of any overarching policy directive, Clinton's PDD/NSC-34 or otherwise). In November 2002, president Bush did call for a comprehensive, six-month review of defence-trade export policy in NSPD-19. As of 2022, however, no evidence exists that this review was completed.

The realities and pressing needs of the wars in Afghanistan and Iraq and the broader counter-terrorism operations around the globe dominated US national-security decision-making over the course of the Bush administration. From such a circumstantial backdrop the administration forged a new type of FMS philosophy based on greater allied collaboration in support of a specific set of goals in each respective campaign theatre. Some transfer deals would be approved as a token of gratitude in return for mission support (as in the case of a 2003 agreement with Jordan).[85] Others would be approved to help facilitate potential support of future missions or to undergird and preserve the larger coalition.[86]

While the US and its allies were embroiled for the most part in counter-insurgency wars against technologically unsophisticated – if nonetheless lethal – threats, the international appetite for major modern weaponry did not abate. Both Israel and Japan would commit to deals with the US in 2001 that had been initiated during the Clinton administration, with Tel Aviv announcing 52 new (and US-financed) F-16Is. Then, in 2002, both Oman and South Korea would secure deals with Washington valued at USD1.1bn and USD4.4bn, respectively. The Omani Air Force would receive 12 F-16Cs, and related spare engines, parts, radars, sensors, assorted weaponry and other support. In turn, Seoul would receive as many as 40 F-15Ks and a similar support package.[87]

With an alliance-expansion goal in mind, Washington agreed to the sale of 17 F-16 air-defence fighters to Jordan in 2003, partly in recognition of Amman's support of the US during *Operation Iraqi Freedom*.[88] The US also agreed to support the transfer of seven F-16As from Singapore to Thailand in 2004, with the transfer serving as a token of thanks for Singapore's earlier use of Thai training space. In 2005, both the administration and Congress also agreed to release 14 F-16As originally purchased by Pakistan in 1988, and later added another 18, with the subsequent lot consisting of the more modern 'C' variant. Singapore would again receive favourable treatment from Washington in 2007, this time in the form of a US commitment for 12 new F-15Es – redesignated 'F-15SGs'. Key allies Morocco, Turkey and Australia would also secure deals in 2007, with 24 and 30 Block 50/52 versions of F-16Cs approved for Rabat and Ankara, respectively, and 24 F/A-18Es earmarked for Canberra.[89]

By the end of his eight years in office, Bush would approve FMS packages valued at a remarkable amount of more than USD128.6bn. This era would prove notable in yet another respect, as international interest grew in uninhabited aerial vehicles (UAVs). This was likely a consequence of the US military's successful employment around the world of such capabilities, especially the medium-altitude/long-endurance (MALE) *Predators* and *Reapers*. Indonesia would purchase an unknown quantity of the Israeli-made MALE *Heron*-2 drones, for example, a model within the same family and mission niche as the *Predator*. Lebanon would procure at least eight of the short-range (yet performance-limited) *Mohajer* UAV systems from Iran. In 2007, Australia would request (and receive approval to buy) four US-produced long-endurance/low-altitude (yet relatively light and small) *Scan Eagle* UAV systems (also known as *Blackjack*).[90]

Cruise control and unavailable aerial vehicles

Land-attack cruise missiles (LACMs) and uninhabited aerial vehicles (UAVs) are two technology areas where the United States has historically followed a more limited release strategy than other providers, which has occasionally generated friction with allies and partners. In both cases, Washington's unilateral approach has failed to halt the acquisition of such capabilities around the world. From a US perspective, this has arguably had unintended and unwelcome consequences in both instances.

Washington, London and Paris have at various times disagreed over the provision of air-launched cruise missiles to the Gulf states,[91] while relations between Washington and Saudi Arabia and the United Arab Emirates (UAE) have been strained by US unwillingness to provide certain classes of UAVs.[92] US export policy regarding these technologies has also resulted in intra-governmental department tensions, primarily between the departments of Defense and State.

Regime regimen

Much of the United States' decision-making over the past few decades has been based on its approach to the 1987 Missile Technology Control Regime (MTCR),[93] a non-binding international accord intended to slow the acquisition of vehicles capable of delivering weapons of mass destruction. Established by the G7, the regime aims to restrict the export of delivery systems capable of a range of 300 kilometres with a 500-kilogram payload, parameters effectively drawn from the Soviet R-17 *Elbrus* (RS-SS-1c *Scud*) short-range ballistic missile. The MTCR is divided into two categories of governance: the first covers complete systems above the 300km/500kg criteria and the second covers systems falling below one of the two criteria, along with related subsystems. The former is predicated on an assumption of denial, while the latter allows for far greater national discretion. The sustainment of Israel's qualitative military edge also shapes the United States' export policy in the Middle East.

The MTCR is predominantly concerned with ballistic-missile proliferation, with cruise missiles and UAVs being lesser worries.[94] Technology developments in the latter two, however, have made them areas of greater strain, while the regime has at times struggled to accommodate the pace of demand-driven change.[95] In both cases, technological developments in the US helped prime broader international interest.

In the past 25 years, cruise missiles and UAVs have gone from being niche capabilities to becoming more commonplace in the inventories of many of the world's more capable militaries. The debut of US conventionally armed cruise missiles in the Gulf War only served to spur greater regional and global interest in the capability. Excepting Israel, no other Middle Eastern state at the time had the indigenous technology base to even consider developing a land-attack cruise-missile capability, even in the medium term. Consequently, by the mid-1990s, the UAE sought to acquire an air-launched land-attack cruise missile from abroad, with the country selecting the then Matra BAe Dynamics *Black Shaheen* variant of the *SCALP* EG/*Storm Shadow*.[96] In turn, the US adopted a more restrictive approach and raised concerns about the European missile's performance with regard to MTCR thresholds.[97]

This pattern was repeated with the provision of the *Storm Shadow* to the Royal Saudi Air Force and also with a subsequent sale proposed to Egypt. In the case of the sale to Riyadh, approval reportedly had to be given by then British prime minister Tony Blair.[98]

Publicly available material describes the *Storm Shadow* as having a range 'in excess of 250 kilometers'.[99] Though correct, the actual range figure is more than double this. In contrast, and in a manner more consistent with traditional interpretation of the MTCR, Washington has limited its LACM offerings to Riyadh and Abu Dhabi to the Boeing AGM-84H SLAM-ER, a shorter-range LACM than the *Storm Shadow* and one less than half the weight.

Not for sale

In the first decade of this century, the UAE and Saudi Arabia discussed with the US the possibility of acquiring armed UAVs. Neither country's attempts succeeded. In the case of the UAE, it rejected a counter-proposal for the transfer of the unarmed variant of the General Atomics RQ-1 *Predator* A,[100] amidst Abu Dhabi's warnings it would shop elsewhere for an armed model. Both Saudi Arabia and the UAE have since acquired armed UAVs from China. The UAE finally completed a deal in 2013 for the RQ-1E *Predator* XP, an unarmed version of the *Predator*.

The MTCR again played a part in US reticence to export MALE UAVs given their Category I designation. Furthermore, the US State Department was keen to avoid setting a precedent that would only encourage the widespread adoption of such a capability. While US policy limited the spread of US armed UAVs considerably, such restraint has also created a gap in the market for an unmet demand signal. This has been met in the Gulf region by China, which, in addition to sourcing Saudi Arabia and the UAE, has provided armed UAVs to Egypt, Iraq and Jordan. More recently, Turkey has also provided exports to the region. As of mid-2022, Iraq and Qatar are among the 22 countries that have either signed for or taken delivery of the Turkish *Bayraktar* TB2, a weapons-capable MALE UAV produced by Istanbul-based Baykar. Although China has never been an MTCR signatory, Turkey joined the regime in 1997, revealing a desire among some of its members to push the interpretations of the pact.

Attempts to update the MTCR to better accommodate UAV development have so far been unsuccessful.[101] Meanwhile, the US issued revised MTCR-related export guidance in 2018, easing the approval process for the sale of MALE and long-range UAVs.[102] This was followed in 2020 by Washington revising how it would consider UAVs with a maximum air speed of less than 800km/hour that previously would have fallen within MTCR Category I.[103] These would now be viewed as Category II items, allowing for greater discretion in export decision-making.

Timeline 3.2: **Selected* combat-aircraft sales to Asia from the US**

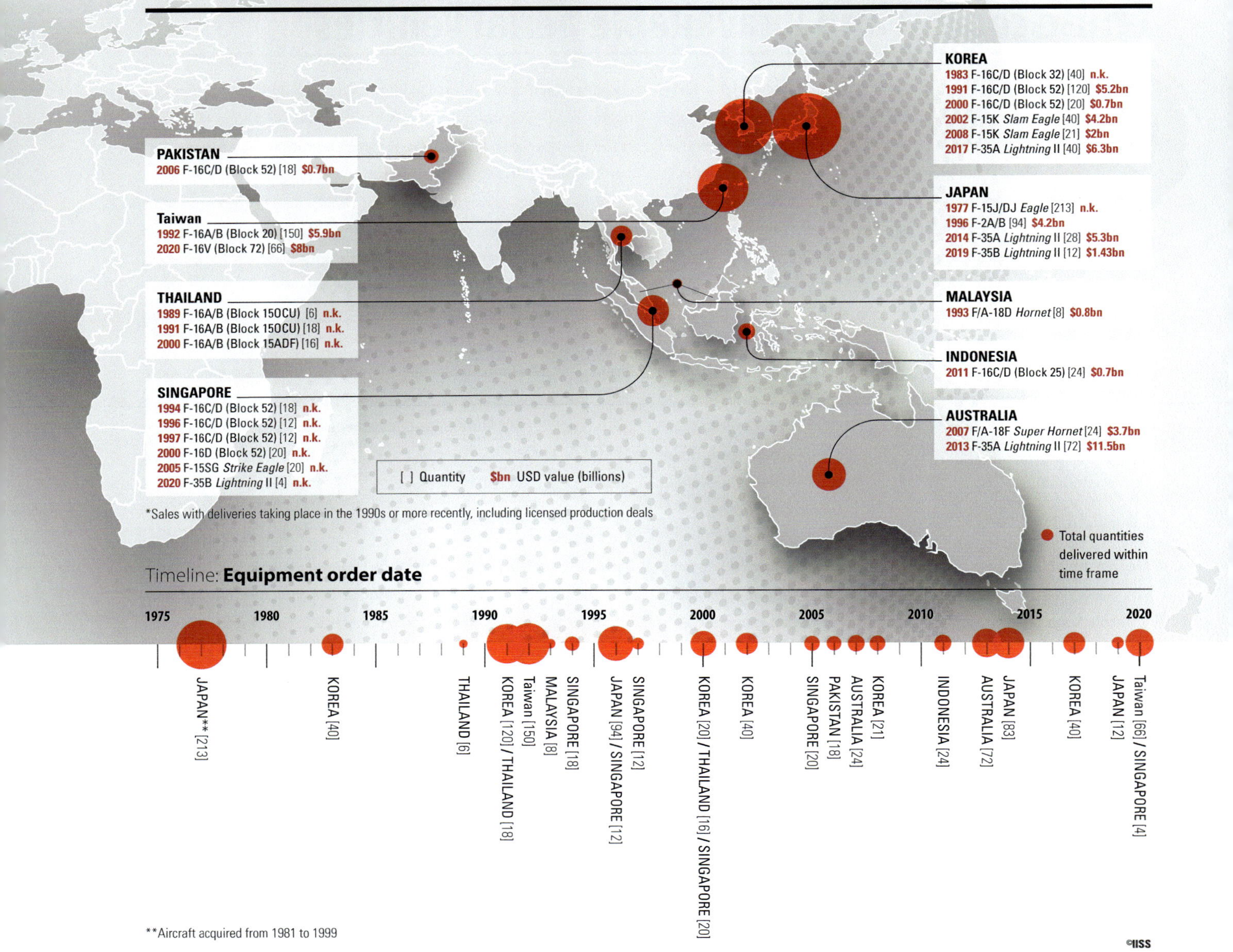

Source: IISS

The Obama years

In his inaugural speech, president Barack Obama described the 'sturdy alliances and enduring convictions' of America's triumph during the Cold War, which echoed a liberal-democratic internationalist theme from the Clinton era.[104] This was tempered, however, by his wish to avoid appearing overly partisan or parochial,[105] especially as he appealed to the global Muslim community during the first summer of his administration. In a June 2009 speech in Cairo, Obama stepped back from the unilateralist democracy-promotion crusade of his predecessor, and instead asserted America's respect for sovereignty, the rule of law, and a recognition of local culture, human dignity and individual agency around the world. He also called for a greater diplomatic consensus in a more interdependent world – indeed, more multilateralism – and made it clear he favoured negotiation and collaboration over confrontation. His vision was thus both internationalist and liberal, and one invested in the justness of international partnerships. This led Matthew N. Gobush to describe the Obama Doctrine as one of 'moral multilateralism', in that the president had assigned moral value to the concept of collective security.[106]

A moral multilateralist or not, Obama set out to reorient American priorities to address the circumstances of the wars abroad and a fiscal crisis at home. With change in mind, he quickly announced a US troop-reduction plan for Iraq to be completed by the end of August 2010. When that date arrived, he declared an end to the combat mission and pledged, and would subsequently achieve, a full withdrawal of all American troops by the end of 2011. Much to his chagrin, however, a US force would need to return in 2014 to help combat the resurgent Islamic State (ISIL/ISIS) terrorist group, one evidently enabled by the Syrian civil war. That September Obama announced the formation of ten-member international coalition and a comprehensive strategy to combat ISIS. Still in existence, this alliance has grown to include more than 60 countries and has involved extensive deployments of naval and air assets to the region, as well as the insertion of several thousand ground troops not only in Syria but also in neighbouring Iraq.[107]

While the efforts in Iraq and Afghanistan and in support of the wider counter-terrorism efforts represented a nearly full plate for the Obama team, other security matters around the world also required attention.

- North Korea appeared to have resumed a nuclear-enrichment programme, prompting the White House to publicly trumpet the importance of the US–South Korea alliance.
- In Iran, authorities cracked down on the Iranian Green Movement during protests against hardliner Mahmoud Ahmadinejad's presidential-election victory.
- In East Africa, internal conflict in Somalia continued to fuel upticks in piracy activities within the maritime environs.
- Across the Middle East and North Africa (MENA) region in the spring of 2011, several major social-media-fuelled uprisings occurred. In what would be called the 'Arab Spring', public protests first occurred in Tunisia before spreading to 17 other MENA nations (including Bahrain, Egypt, Libya, Syria, the UAE and Yemen). This series of uprisings would eventually spark regime change in four separate countries.
- In a harbinger of events to come, Russia annexed Crimea in 2014 and seized partial control of two Ukrainian administrative enclaves adjacent to the Russian border. Yet this development did not stop the Obama team and its allies from involving Moscow in a July 2015 nuclear-disarmament deal between Iran and China, France, Germany, Russia, the UK and the US (the so-called P5+1 Group).[108]

Box 3.3: **PPD-27**

As for national-security and foreign-policy goals, PPD-27 avowed that CAT decisions should:

- ensure that US military forces (and those of allies and partners) continue to enjoy technological superiority over adversaries;
- promote the acquisition of US systems to increase inter-operability with allies and partners, and lower the unit costs for all, thereby strengthening the US industrial base;
- enhance the ability of allies and partners to deter or defend themselves against aggression;
- encourage the maintenance and expansion of US security partnerships with those who share American interests, and encourage regional access in areas critical to US interests;
- promote regional stability, peaceful conflict resolution and arms control;
- prevent the proliferation of conventional weapons that could be used as delivery systems for WMD;
- promote cooperative counter-terrorism (CT), critical-infrastructure protection (CIP) and other homeland-security priorities;
- combat transnational crime and related threats to national security;
- support democratic governance and related US foreign-policy objectives; and
- ensure that arms transfers do not contribute to human-rights violations and violations of international humanitarian law.

Obama and arms sales

On 15 January 2014 Obama released Presidential Policy Directive-27 (PPD-27), nearly a year into his second term. Incorporating many of the same themes and objectives as Clinton's PDD/NSC-34, PPD-27 affirmed ten national-security and foreign-policy goals as well as 13 criteria for guiding future CAT decisions. The promotion of 'regional stability' was again a stated American goal, while 'arms control and transfer restraint' was identified as a 'critical element of U.S. conventional arms transfer policy'.[109]

Three national-security and foreign-policy goals asserted by the Obama administration in the 2014 memorandum were distinct. Firstly, PPD-27 specifically characterised cooperative (not just consonant) CT, CIP and other homeland-security initiatives as national-security priorities. Secondly, PPD-27 prioritised efforts to combat transnational crime as a unique foreign-policy and national-security objective. Thirdly, PPD-27 encouraged the maintenance and expansion of security partnerships with those nations sharing mutual interests and enjoying (or potentially enjoying) regional access in parts of the world viewed as critical to US national security.[110] Somewhat surprisingly, Clinton's policy had not specifically emphasised an expansion of partnerships in key regional areas of strategic importance.

As for the specific criteria in PPD-27 cited as the basis for making CAT decisions, they included:

- the appropriateness of such a transfer and the consistency with which it aligned with US regional stability interests;
- the impact such a transfer might have on US capabilities and in protecting its technological advantage;
- the economic, political or social impact a transfer might have on a recipient, and on the political or security environment of the greater region;
- the ability of a recipient nation to field the transferred deliverable;
- the risk of vulnerability involved and the degree of protection afforded by a recipient country in handling sensitive technology;

RSAF F-15SG
A Republic of Singapore Air Force Boeing F-15SG, 5 February 2018. The small island state has long been a customer of modern US weaponry. Credit: Seong Joon Cho/Bloomberg via Getty Images.

- a proposed recipient's past record relative to human rights (HR), democratisation, CT, counter-proliferation (CP), non-proliferation and the potential misuse of the arms to be transferred;
- the likelihood of HR abuses or serious violations of international humanitarian law;
- the availability of comparable systems from foreign suppliers; and
- the degree to which the potential transfer would support US strategic, foreign-policy and defence interests through access and influence, allied burden-sharing and inter-operability.

More broadly, PPD-27 unequivocally declared respect for the requirements, regulations and protocols contained in the Arms Export Control Act, the Foreign Assistance Act, the International Emergency Economic Powers Act, each annual iteration of the annual National Defense Authorization Act, all applicable export-control regimes and other relevant international commitments. The CAT Policy restated Washington's commitment to participate in both the UN Registry of Conventional Arms (UNROCA) and the Wassenaar Arrangement for maintaining transparency and promoting confidence and proliferation restraint. It also renewed Washington's pledge to work bilaterally and multilaterally to aid other potential suppliers in the establishment of similar export mechanisms of their own.

PPD-27 further declared that no conventional-weapons transfer would be approved if the US government had knowledge that a potential recipient had

- engaged in war crimes, genocide or crimes against humanity;
- directed attacks against legally protected civilians;
- displayed grave breaches of the Geneva Conventions of 1949; or
- engaged in serious violations of Common Article 3 of the Geneva Conventions of 1949.[111]

PPD-27 also stated that the US would exercise restraint in potential transfers if potential recipients had previously displayed questionable behaviour in any other areas related to human rights and dignity.[112] The Obama CAT Policy complemented, and included, many of the themes promoted and released only nine months earlier in PPD-23, the presidential directive entitled 'U.S. Security Sector Assistance Policy'.[113] PPD-27 in fact amplified the aspirational goals contained within PPD-23 in calling for greater cooperation with multilateral organisations and US allies; the promotion of collective security; more initiatives to build partner capacity; and for achieving greater respect of universal values, good governance and the rule of law. In the aggregate, the combination of these two directives – PPD-23 and PPD-27 – strongly emphasised and prioritised regionally based goals and solutions.

President Obama would negotiate a total of USD278bn-worth of foreign arms sales over the course of his eight years in office, more than twice that of his immediate predecessor and a higher amount than any other American administration since the end of the Second World War.[114] At first glance, this would appear to run wholly counter to the advocacy of a policy based on restraint. In terms of combat aircraft, however, several importing nations were coincidentally in the process of recapitalising their respective fleets, either through the purchase of additional numbers of types already held in inventory or through shifting to more advanced and more expensive designs. Export orders for the more costly Lockheed Martin F-35 were beginning to rise, for example, pushing up aggregate export values. In short, much of the spike in FMS value was a result of timing and coincidence.

The list of recipient countries receiving advanced US combat aircraft during Obama's presidency would increase to ten and include the additions of Iraq and Indonesia. Approvals of F-35A *Lightning* II transfers during this time included Australia, Israel, Japan, Singapore and South Korea. Additional F-16 orders were also booked for Egypt, Indonesia, Iraq and Oman. Israel, Saudi Arabia and Singapore would also request and receive approval for additional F-15C *Eagle*s during this period. In 2013, Australia would receive approval for 12 of the Boeing EA-18G *Growler*.[115]

Alongside crewed combat aircraft, uninhabited aerial systems (UASs) were an increasing focus of export interest. More than 11 countries sought and secured approval for the transfer of such capabilities during the tenure of the Obama administration. All these inquiries were for unarmed platforms to serve in intelligence, surveillance and reconnaissance (ISR) roles. But the sale of armed UASs (except to the UK) remained a line the US administration was unwilling to cross, despite several requests (particularly from Middle Eastern states).

Less problematic was the provision and sale of small, unarmed UAVs. The Philippines received approval in 2009 for such a deal, securing a pledge for two RQ-5 *Hunter* UAS out of existing US Army stocks. Australia would receive approval a year later for the transfer of ten RQ-7 *Shadow* 200s, another in-stock system from the US Army inventory.

Over the course of the next five years, seven countries would receive approval to acquire multiple systems of the Boeing-made RQ-21 *Scan Eagle*, a small and more modern unarmed UAV. These states were Cameroon, Iraq, Japan, Kenya, Malaysia, Pakistan and Singapore. Approval for larger ISR UAVs was also given, as the UAE requested an unarmed variant of the MQ-1 *Predator*, and South Korea received clearance for the RQ-4A *Global Hawk*.

The Trump years

Donald Trump was anything but a liberal-democratic internationalist. Both before and after his election he repudiated nearly all things associated with not only his predecessor, Barack Obama, but also his predecessor's predecessor, George W. Bush. He positioned himself as anti-establishment, campaigned on a platform entitled 'America First' and maintained this vision throughout his White House tenure.

Trump governed as a populist, a nationalist, a unilateralist, a non-interventionist, a protectionist and an isolationist. To the alarm of US allies, he threatened to cancel or withdraw from several multilateral pacts, including NATO, and carried through with such threats on several occasions, as with the Trans-Pacific Partnership, the Paris Climate Accords, the Intermediate-Range Nuclear Forces Treaty, the Iran nuclear agreement, and the North American Free Trade Agreement, or NAFTA (replacing it with a new deal). He also embraced grandiose brinkmanship, engaging in a tariff-based trade war with Beijing and increasing the number of naval deployments to the western Pacific to gain geopolitical advantage.[116] Such unpredictability and brash treatment of norms became a hallmark of his presidency, and labels he appeared to relish. In the main, his approach repudiated the post-Second World War international legacy of both major political parties in the US.

President Trump did facilitate three rounds of what became known as the 'Abraham Accords', establishing ties between Bahrain, Israel and the UAE, and between Bahrain, Morocco and Sudan. Counter to US diplomatic tradition, he recognised Jerusalem as the capital of Israel and directed the relocation of the American Embassy from Tel Aviv.[117] He also signed a peace agreement with the Taliban pledging to end US involvement in Afghanistan and to remove all American troops from that country by 1 May 2021.[118]

On the counter-terrorism front, Trump increased drone strikes in Africa, and both continued and intensified the 'global war on terror' and attacks against ISIS (leading to the killing of ISIS leader Abu Bakr al-Baghdadi).[119] In yet another remarkable and unprecedented move, Trump designated the *entire* Islamic Revolutionary Guard Corps (IRGC) a terrorist organisation (a force of more than 200,000 personnel).[120] After restoring (and increasing the scope and acuteness of) economic sanctions against Iran, he ever-so-boldly authorised the use of an attack drone over Baghdad to kill visiting Major General Qasem Soleimani, the long-time commander of Iran's Quds Force (the most elite and clandestine IRGC unit).[121]

Not all his moves proved successful, however, such as his attempts at rapprochement with North Korea (2018–19) and his removal of US troops from the Kurdish-controlled areas of northern Syria in late 2019, against the advice of senior defence advisers.[122] The former effort produced no agreement on nuclear disarmament, and the latter left the Kurds vulnerable to an attack from Turkish forces, a traditional adversary. The attack prompted president Trump to subsequently announce unilateral sanctions against Ankara, an awkward act given Turkey's status as a NATO ally.[123]

Trump and arms sales

There was no discernible strategy, doctrine, principle, identity or political philosophy driving the Trump administration's international engagement. The populist president appeared to be neither a US liberal nor a conservative in any consistent sense, nor internationally collaborative or multilateral. Against this background, a CAT Policy

PRESIDENT DONALD TRUMP
US president Donald Trump leaving *Marine One*, the presidential helicopter at the White House, 12 December 2020. Several major arms-sale successes were claimed by Trump, even if already in the pipeline. CREDIT: Al Drago/Getty Images.

update surprisingly emerged during the administration's second year incorporating and promoting collaboration, multilateralism and what appeared to be many traditional liberal internationalist principles.

On 19 April 2018, president Trump released National Security Presidential Memorandum-10 (NSPM-10) on United States Conventional Arms Transfer Policy, referring to such transfers as critical to maintaining a strong military, for advancing both US national and economic security postures, and for enabling American foreign-policy objectives.[124] By decree, NSPM-10 superseded PPD-27, the CAT Policy issued in 2014 by president Obama, and respectfully referenced the AECA of 1976, as amended (22 U.S.C. 2751 *et seq.*), for guidance.

For a president apparently keen on repudiating as many of his predecessor's policy initiatives as possible, NSPM-10 proved to be remarkably consistent with many elements of Obama's PPD-27. Many of the same goals, considerations, priorities and criteria promulgated in PPD-27 were replicated in NSPM-10. Indeed, the Trump policy contained large excerpts from the prior document, especially those referencing the promotion of allies, regional stability and the protection of human rights (as well as women's and gender-related rights). As for the contrast between the two, the most obvious manifested in the form of an omission, as the Trump document skipped mention of (and thus seemed unconcerned about) the status of 'democratization' efforts in foreign lands or even the practice of democracy itself. The Trump document, unsurprisingly, stressed the importance of the business element of weapons exports and the administration's role in supporting domestic industry in such deals.

NSPM-10 emphasised US industry concerns and notably departed from its predecessor in several additional ways. The new document pledged future support for increasing US competitiveness in key markets, for instance, although the identity or nature of what constituted such a distinction was not defined. The policy further asserted that 'the executive branch will advocate strongly on behalf of U.S. companies' when (or if) a proposed transfer is determined to be in the national interest, and promised to:

- 'maximize the ability of U.S. industry to grow and support [the capacity] of allies and partners';
- clarify and streamline industry-related regulatory procedures;
- increase federal contracting predictability and flexibility; and
- provide 'appropriate advocacy and trade promotion activities' for overseas initiatives.[125]

The Trump document introduced a standard for CAT decisions aimed at reducing the 'risk of national or coalition operations causing civilian harm' and stipulated that future transfer decisions should facilitate the capabilities and capacity of partner nations 'through sales and security cooperation efforts'.[126] Remarkably, NSPM-10 also declared that consideration would be given to the 'likelihood' a potential transfer decision might reduce a recipient's dependence on US adversaries – a further novel standard in the history of US CAT Policy evolution.

NSPM-10 required an action plan from the secretary of state within 60 days, one including recommendations on how to implement the goals and criteria outlined therein, and one drafted in a manner sensitive to the market challenges afflicting the US defence-industrial base. Completing the plan also required coordination with the secretaries of defense, commerce and energy, as well as the inclusion of an estimate and identification of financial and personnel resources. Concerning UAVs and UASs, NSPM-10 directed a review of export-policy rules and anticipated an adjustment to the approval process for such systems.

On 24 July 2020, the Trump administration concurrently (and surprisingly) announced a revised approach to reviewing UAS export applications and for meeting its responsibilities under the MTCR. The announcement immediately created a specific and novel sub-category for UASs flying at speeds below 800km/hour (for context, see earlier UAV text box). This effectively removed slower-moving UASs from the 'strong presumption of denial' category within the MTCR as far as Washington was concerned. Such exports still required federal review and approval but within a more favourable context. The policy revision essentially lowered the bar of approval for meeting US foreign-policy interests and objectives.

Industry welcomed the change in keeping with a general desire to improve a burdensome process.[127] However, the implementation and practical effect of the change is still unclear. Despite the policy shift on UASs/UAVs, the FMS pattern established during the Obama administration continued among the rank and file of the establishment. With few exceptions, transfers continued to favour the short-range, low-altitude *Scan Eagle* UAV system. For all intents and purposes, the Trump CAT Policy document appeared to produce little impact.

Meanwhile, the transfer of combat aircraft during the Trump administration continued and included approvals to seven foreign recipients: Bahrain, Israel, Japan, Kuwait, Qatar, Taiwan and Singapore. Moreover, specific aircraft models transferred included variants of the F-16, F-15, F/A-18 and F-35.[128]

The Biden years

As a disciple of the liberal-democratic internationalist tradition, President Biden has called for greater international cooperation to address multiple challenges in many realms, including energy, trade, the cyber domain, the environment, public health, diplomacy and defence.[129] For instance, he pointedly called for an energetic and concerted effort to repair the US alliance network during a 2019 campaign stop in New York, voicing special concern about and support for NATO and the idea of collective security.[130] As president, he has extended the New START Treaty with Russia, rejoined both the Paris Climate Accords and the World Health Organization, ordered a global posture review for the US military and announced a course correction in US foreign policy to 'better unite our democratic values with our diplomatic leadership'.[131]

Biden has also renewed the traditional US commitment to promote democracy and human rights. He immediately ordered a freeze on American support to offensive military operations in Yemen, amid considerable evidence of famine and widespread suffering among the non-combatant community. He also scheduled a 'Summit for Democracy' to discuss challenges around the world related to privacy, free speech, corruption, persecution, good governance and the rule of law.[132]

Yet in remarks consonant with (if less grave and softer in tone than) those of one of his predecessors, President Biden linked America's 'success' with the greater global community's success in a speech before the UN General Assembly. Here, he decided against promoting and using the more pointed and ambitious 'survival of liberty' theme voiced by George W. Bush during his second inauguration.[133]

Biden's words and deeds nevertheless remain consistent with the teachings of liberal-democratic internationalism. They suggest a preference for expanding trade, commerce and democracy throughout the family of nations by peaceful means. To date, the US president appears bent on positioning America mostly as a facilitator and as an exemplar for democracy-seeking aspirants around the world – à la Reagan's 'Shining City on a Hill' – rather than as a provocateur (or agent) of change at the forefront of military interventions overseas.[134] Indeed, less than six weeks into the job, Biden implored America to consider that 'our strength abroad requires us to build back better at home'.[135]

Biden's first major decision related to US overseas military commitments reflected these sentiments. He over-ruled the consensus of his national-security team and opted to honour Trump's pledge to withdraw from Afghanistan without any conditions – veering only from its proposed schedule and announcing an exit by the symbolic date of 11 September.[136]

But the sudden decision and poor execution caught many by surprise, raising questions not only about Biden's commitment to the notion of allied consultation but also about his judgement. For at least one prominent observer, 'multilateralism and alliance-first foreign policy in principle gave way to America-first unilateralism in practice'.[137] For another, President Biden's unwise acceptance of the Trump withdrawal plan and rejection of a more moderate option undermined the will and capacity of the Afghan government, hastened a Taliban victory and cast doubt on American credibility abroad.[138] Such concerns continued to dominate the public narrative until the president announced a successful anti-terrorist strike in Kabul against Ayman al-Zawahiri, a senior al-Qaeda leader and former associate of Osama bin Laden.[139]

In the greater Middle East, Biden's campaign rhetoric has awkwardly collided with new emergent realities resulting from broad economic and security-related trends or from the decisions of

PRESIDENT JOE BIDEN
US President Joe Biden attending the Jeddah Security and Development Summit, 16 July 2022. The Biden administration has suggested it will pursue an arms-export policy predicated more on the human-rights behaviour of recipient countries. CREDIT: Royal Hashemite Court/Anadolu Agency via Getty Images.

his predecessor and other world leaders.[140] Indeed, the spike in oil prices induced by the February 2022 Russian invasion of Ukraine has forced a reassessment of US–Saudi relations, and decades of military modernisation by regional powers in the Middle East have given rise to talk about UAE and Saudi independence and a divergence from US security policies.[141]

In the Indo-Pacific region and specifically with respect to China, Biden has mostly adopted the approach set out by his predecessor. For instance, Trump's anti-Beijing tariff regime designed to protect US intellectual property and trade advantage remains in place, and the effort led by the US Commerce Department to guard against the importation of compromised software continues. Moreover, the frequency of US naval deployments to the western Pacific has not receded and the strength of the US-led alliance system in the Eastern Hemisphere has not waned.[142] Indeed, the ties between the nations of the Quad – Australia, India, Japan and the US – have only deepened, and for good reason, as unsettling acts authorised by Beijing around the region appear to be on the rise.[143] Furthermore, the announcement of the AUKUS pact, a pledge between Australia, the UK and the US to jointly collaborate on mutual security matters and help produce a fleet of nuclear-powered submarines for Canberra, marks a new chapter in collective security for the Indo-Pacific theatre (although allied relationships elsewhere, such as with Paris, may have suffered).[144]

Meanwhile, the Russian invasion of Ukraine has sparked a period of considerable angst throughout the Atlantic Alliance, and the Biden White House spent much of early 2022 looking for an effective response to the crisis. In the end, solidarity within NATO has grown and prevailed in support of a neighbour suffering from an unprovoked attack.[145]

Biden and arms exports

During his 'America's Place in the World' speech at the State Department on 4 February 2021, President Biden announced a freeze on any and all US assistance to offensive military operations in Yemen.[146] As a consequence, agreements secured during the last few months of the Trump administration with Saudi Arabia and the UAE were halted pursuant to further review, delaying arms transfers valued in billions of US dollars.[147] The halt also precipitated a review and expected revision of the Trump CAT Policy. This process extended throughout summer, autumn and early winter of 2021 and continues as this chapter is finalised and goes to print. There are expectations it will lead to a greater emphasis being placed on human rights and at least one parallel call for comprehensive reform in all US security-assistance initiatives.

Despite a preference for greater emphasis on human rights, the Biden team announced a USD500 million maintenance contract to support Riyadh's helicopter fleet in October 2021, followed by a USD650m deal to transfer air-to-air missiles in November – both submitted to Congress for approval without any word about a forthcoming CAT Policy update.[148] Despite considerable concern and resistance, Congress approved the sales in December, enabled by several appeals to view them as a signal of America's resolve and commitment to allies in the region.[149] Only a few weeks prior, senior administration officials also announced plans to proceed with the multibillion-dollar F-35 sale to the UAE.[150]

At the time of writing, Washington continues to await a White House revision and release of an updated US policy on CAT. Meanwhile, the Biden team has proceeded to engage allies in all corners of the globe, in turn approving arms transfers to Ukraine (to a value of more than USD25.6bn),[151] Saudi Arabia (USD1.1bn) and Taiwan (USD1.2bn) as real-world conditions and perceived commitments to allies appear

F-35A
Fighter jet the F-35A *Lightning* flies above Avalon Airport in Melbourne, Australia, 1 March 2019. CREDIT: Michael Dodge/Getty Images.

to require a continuation of arms transfers.[152] As Beijing and Tehran continue to proceed with their respective military-modernisation efforts and related export programmes, the Biden administration will almost certainly find itself torn between the high-minded ideals of humanitarian concerns and the demands and requirements it faces in the security realm.[153]

Conclusion

As stated at the start of this chapter, the US remains the largest exporter of major weapons, and it is likely to remain so for the foreseeable future. It also has in place greater legislative oversight of and influence on the administration's arms-export decision-making than any of the other countries considered in this dossier. Overall, however, the existent scrutiny and oversight regime has not overly hampered the profits and success of the US defence industry in the global market.

The sale of major weapons remains an effective support tool of foreign and security policy, and at times represents a source of domestic friction and tension between many of the interested parties. This is not always publicly evident since a country's interest in a specific weapon or capability may be privately discouraged by US officials due to underlying security concerns. The practice of restraint on the part of Washington has not always been reciprocated by allies and regional partners. In the case of land-attack missiles in the Middle East, for instance, the US has adopted a more restrictive approach than its European counterparts, with the latter enjoying greater export success in the air-launched cruise-missile market. A similar market opportunity has developed in response to Washington's restrictive approach to the export of weaponised UAVs. In this case, however, Europe has been in no position to take advantage, even if a more liberal and trade-friendly approach were pursued. European manufacturers simply have not had a suitable product to offer. Instead, and more damagingly for US interests, China has provided armed UAVs to interested parties (including a number of states in the Middle East). NATO member Turkey has also emerged more recently as an exporter of armed UAVs.

NOTES

1 Defense Security Cooperation Agency, 'Historical Sales Book: Fiscal Years 1950–2021', US Department of Defense, pp. 1–5, https://www.dsca.mil/sites/default/files/dsca_historical_sales_book_FY21.pdf.

2 See US Secretary of State, 'Saudi AWACs and F-15 Enhancement Package', 16 April 1981, released by Directorate of Intelligence, https://www.cia.gov/readingroom/docs/CIA-RDP84B00049R000601540017-3.pdf.

3 *Ibid.*

4 US Secretary of State, 'Saudi AWACs and F-15 Enhancement Package'; and 'Trump uses veto to unblock $8bn weapons sale to Saudi Arabia', BBC News, 25 July 2019, https://www.bbc.co.uk/news/world-us-canada-49106989

5 Katrina Manson and Andrew England, 'Biden suspends arms sales to Saudi Arabia and UAE', *Financial Times*, 27 January 2021, https://www.ft.com/content/356df221-251f-4eba-a307-88e485ef1d45.

6 US Library of Congress, 'The US Constitution', https://constitution.congress.gov/constitution/.

7 See Govtrack, 'House Vote #87 in 1961 (87th Congress)', 31 August 1961, https://www.govtrack.us/congress/votes/87-1961/h87; and Govtrack, 'H.R. 13680 (94th)', https://www.govtrack.us/congress/bills/94/hr13680. US Congress approved and established AECA as a free-standing act within a provision of the International Security Assistance and Arms Export Control Act of 1976, as part of a complete revision and rewrite of the Foreign Military Sales Act of 1968. Congress also incorporated within AECA licensing authority for direct commercial sales in Section 38, 'Control of Arms Exports and Imports'.

8 White House, 'Presidential Directive/NSC-13', Jimmy Carter Presidential Library and Museum, 13 May 1997, https://www.jimmycarterlibrary.gov/assets/documents/directives/pd13.pdf.

9 See 99th Congress, 'Goldwater–Nichols Department of Defense Reorganization Act of October 4, 1986', 1 October 1986, https://history.defense.gov/Portals/70/Documents/dod_reforms/Goldwater-NicholsDoDReordAct1986.pdf.

10 See James R. Locher III, 'Taking Stock of Goldwater-Nichols', *Joint Forces Quarterly*, No. 13, Autumn 1996, pp. 10–17, https://ndupress.ndu.edu/portals/68/Documents/jfq/jfq-13.pdf; John P. White, 'Defense Organization Today', *Joint Forces Quarterly*, No. 13, Autumn 1996, pp. 18–22, https://ndupress.ndu.edu/portals/68/Documents/jfq/jfq-13.pdf; and David C. Jones, 'Past Organisational Problems', *Joint Forces Quarterly*, No. 13, Autumn 1996, pp. 23–28, https://ndupress.ndu.edu/portals/68/Documents/jfq/jfq-13.pdf.

11 See Archie D. Barrett, 'Empowering Eisenhower's Concept', *Joint Forces Quarterly*, Autumn 1996, No. 13, p. 13, https://ndupress.ndu.edu/portals/68/Documents/jfq/jfq-13.pdf; and Christopher D. Holmes and Francis J. Park, 'History of Joint Staff Strategic Planning, 1949–2020', Joint History and Research Office, pp. 9–10, https://www.jcs.mil/Portals/36/Documents/History/Dec21/SHS_14_History%20of%20Joint%20Staff%20Strategic%20Planning.pdf.

12 For the Department of State organisational chart, see US Department of State, 'Department of State Organisational Chart', February 2020, https://www.state.gov/wp-content/uploads/2020/02/Dept-Org-Chart-Feb-2020-508.pdf; and for further discussion on the rise of the regional perspective, see Holmes and Park, 'History of Joint Staff Strategic Planning, 1949–2020,' pp. 9–11.

13 See John J. Hamre, 'Reflections: Looking Back at the Need for Goldwater-Nichols', Center for Strategic and International Studies, 27 January 2016, https://www.csis.org/analysis/reflections-looking-back-need-goldwater-nichols; Kristy N. Kamarck, 'Goldwater-Nichols and the Evolution of Officer Joint Professional Military Development', R44340, Congressional Research Service, 13 January 2016, https://sgp.fas.org/crs/natsec/R44340.pdf; and US Code, Office of the Law Revision Counsel, '10 USC 668: Definitions', https://uscode.house.gov/view.xhtml?req=granuleid:USC-prelim-title10-section668&num=0&edition=prelim.

14 See Kristy N. Kamarack, 'Goldwater-Nichols and the Evolution of Officer Joint Professional Military Education', p. 10; and US Code, '10 USC 668: Definitions'.

15 See Defense Security Cooperation University, *Security Cooperation Management* (Arlington, VA: Defense Security Cooperation Agency, Department of Defense, 2022), especially chapter 1, https://www.dscu.edu/documents/publications/greenbook/01-Chapter.pdf?id=1.

16 For an overview of the Defense Security Cooperation University (DSCU), see Defense Security Cooperation University, 'About DSCU', https://www.dscu.edu/about.

17 Consisting of one or more individuals, SCOs are also referred to as Security Cooperation Offices and can take many forms. They can consist of all or part of the DoD contingent within an overseas US embassy and include certain liaison offices, military advisory groups and/or the defence attaché office. The important point is that once formed, the SCO represents and is empowered by the DSCA on SC-related matters. See the following DoD Directives (DoDD) and DoD Instructions (DoDI): US Department of Defense, 'Instruction 5132.13: Staffing of Security Cooperation Organizations (SCOs) and the Selection and Training of Security Cooperation Personnel', 9 January 2009 (updated 9 January 2009), https://www.esd.whs.mil/Portals/54/

Documents/DD/issuances/dodi/513213p.pdf; US Department of Defense, 'Instruction 5132.14: Assesment, Monitoring, and Evaluation Policy for the Security Cooperation Enterprise', 13 January 2017, https://open.defense.gov/portals/23/documents/foreignasst/dodi_513214_on_am&e.pdf; US Department of Defense, 'Directive 5205.75: DoD Operations at U.S. Embassies', 4 December 2013, https://www.esd.whs.mil/Portals/54/Documents/DD/issuances/dodd/520575p.pdf; and US Department of Defense, 'Directive 5132.03 DoD Policy and Responsibilities Relating to Security Cooperation', 29 December 2016, https://www.esd.whs.mil/Portals/54/Documents/DD/issuances/dodd/513203_dodd_2016.pdf.

18 Defense Security Cooperation University, *Security Cooperation Management*, especially chapter 5, https://www.dscu.edu/documents/publications/greenbook/05-Chapter.pdf?id=1.

19 As many as 11 DoD implementing agencies are listed in the DSCU textbook. The list includes the three Military Departments (MILDEPs) – the army, the navy and the air force – and many DoD agencies, such as the Missile Defense Agency, National Security Agency and DSCA. See Defense Security Cooperation University, *Security Cooperation Management*, especially chapter 5, p. 21, https://www.dscu.edu/documents/publications/greenbook/05-Chapter.pdf?id=1.

20 See US Department of Defense, 'Department of Defense Dictionary of Military and Associated Terms', JP 1-02, 8 November 2010 (updated 15 November 2014), p. 222, http://edocs.nps.edu/2014/December/jp1_02.pdf.

21 *Ibid.*, p. 223. BPC-like activities began in the 1980s (and arguably earlier) with DoD counter-narcotics and counter-terrorist assistance to foreign militaries, but 'security cooperation' as a term did not officially come into being until after 1997.

22 See Paul K. Kerr, 'Arms Sales: Congressional Review Process', RL31675, Congressional Research Service, 10 June 2022, https://crsreports.congress.gov/product/pdf/RL/RL31675.

23 The informal (and yet significant) influence of the other congressional leadership offices should also be noted: Senate majority leader, Senate minority leader and House of Representatives minority leader (and their respective and subordinate 'whip' offices), as each senator and representative feels compelled to represent their respective constituencies on all matters foreign and domestic.

24 Nese F. DeBruyne and Barbara Salazar Torreon, 'Defense Authorization and Appropriations Bills: FY1961–FY2018', Congressional Research Service, 19 April 2018, https://crsreports.congress.gov/product/pdf/RL/98-756/48.

25 Included in the NDAA for Fiscal Year 2017, see Legal Information Institute, '10 U.S. Code § 333 – Foreign Security Forces: Authority to Build Capacity', https://www.law.cornell.edu/uscode/text/10/333.

26 In the House of Representatives, the HFAC is officially granted sequential referral status during NDAA consideration by the speaker and the Rules Committee. In the Senate, the SFRC chair can bring any issue to the floor for a vote or debate unless cloture is invoked. See Mark J. Oleszek, 'Committee Jurisdiction and Referral in the House', R46251, 4 March 2020, Congressional Research Service, https://crsreports.congress.gov/product/pdf/R/R46251; and Mark J. Oleszek, 'Committee Jurisdiction and Referral in the Senate', R46815, 10 June 2021, https://crsreports.congress.gov/product/pdf/R/R46815.

27 For current security cooperation-related congressional reporting and notification requirements, see sections 8133–8139 of the Department of Defense Appropriations Act, 2022: House Committee on Rules, 'Rules Committee Print 117–35 Text of the House Amendment to the Senate Amendment to H.R. 2471', 8 March 2022, pp. 391–7, https://rules.house.gov/sites/democrats.rules.house.gov/files/BILLS-117HR2471SA-RCP-117-35.pdf.

28 Siemon T. Wezeman and Pieter D. Wezeman, 'Transfers of Major Conventional Weapons', in SIPIRI (ed.), *SIPRI Yearbook 1998: Armaments, Disarmament and International Security* (Oxford: Oxford University Press for SIPRI, 1998), p. 292, figure 8.1, https://www.sipri.org/sites/default/files/SIPRI%20Yearbook%201998.pdf.

29 The US share of world military exports peaked at above 60% in 1993. See US Department of State, 'World Military Expenditures and Arms Transfers 1998', US Government Printing Office, April 2000, p. 11, https://2009-2017.state.gov/documents/organization/110701.pdf.

30 See Richard F. Grimmett, 'Conventional Arms Transfers to the Third World, 1986–1993', Congressional Research Service, 29 July 1994, p. 58, https://digital.library.unt.edu/ark:/67531/metadc816823/m2/1/high_res_d/94-612_1994Jul29.pdf; and Ian Anthony, Pieter D. Wezeman and Siemon T. Wezeman, 'The Trade in Major Conventional Weapons', in SIPIRI (ed.), *SIPRI Yearbook 1995: Armaments, Disarmament and International Security* (Oxford: Oxford University Press for SIPRI, 1995), pp. 493–4, https://www.sipri.org/sites/default/files/SIPRI%20Yearbook%201995.pdf.

31 For his views on democratic ideals, containment and the nature of the times, see Bush's remarks in his Texas A&M Commencement address: George H.W. Bush, 'Remarks at the Texas A M University Commencement Ceremony in College Station', George H.W.

Bush Presidential Library and Museum, 12 May 1989, https://bush41library.tamu.edu/archives/public-papers/413.

32 The historical events leading up to the collapse of the Warsaw Pact provided more than ample justification for such a view. By 1990, for example, USD2.45trn of the USD3.34trn of all annual global commerce – or 73.0% – consisted of imports and exports between (and among) the US and the 21 other free-trading members of the industrialised world. For the original argument, see Tony Smith, *America's Mission: The United States and the Worldwide Struggle for Democracy in the Twentieth Century* (Princeton, NJ: Princeton University Press, 1994), pp. 327–8; and see also John B. McLenaghan and Chandrakant A. Patel (eds), *Direction of Trade Statistics: Yearbook 1991* (Washington DC: International Monetary Fund, 1991), p. 2, https://www.elibrary.imf.org/view/book/9781451981339/9781451981339.xml.

33 US Department of State, Office of the Historian, 'A Short History of the Department of State: Bush's Foreign Policy', https://history.state.gov/departmenthistory/short-history/bushi; and see also William J. Burns, *The Back Channel: A Memoir of American Diplomacy and the Case for Its Renewal* (New York: Random House, 2019), pp. 56–7, 75–6.

34 David Rothkopf, *Running the World: The Inside Story of the National Security Council and the Architects of American Power* (New York: Public Affairs, 2005), pp. 288–91; see also Michael Mandelbaum, *Mission Failure: America and the World in the Post-Cold War Era* (New York: Oxford University Press, 2016), pp. 20–4; and Zbigniew Brzezinski and Brent Scowcroft, America and the World: Conversations on the Future of American Foreign Policy (New York: Basic Books, 2008), p. 141.

35 For an excellent discussion on the senior-level diplomatic and administrative challenges and demands during this time, see Dennis Ross, *Statecraft: And How to Restore America's Standing in the World* (New York: Farrar, Straus and Giroux, 2007), pp. 3–99; and see also Burns, *The Back Channel: A Memoir of American Diplomacy and the Case for Its Renewal*, pp. 76–8.

36 The treaty on Conventional Armed Forces in Europe (CFE) negotiations culminated with a signing in November 1990. For an excellent discussion on the nature and pace of events unfolding during this period, see Rothkopf, *Running the World: The Inside Story of The National Security Council and The Architects of American Power*, pp. 260–301; and for an excellent discussion about the complex discussions between US, Soviet and German leaders regarding the unification of East and West Germany, see Ross, Statecraft: And How to Restore America's Standing in The World, pp. 29–47.

37 See Rothkopf, *Running the World: The Inside Story of The National Security Council and The Architects of American Power*, p. 295.

38 The UN Security Council would approve 12 resolutions related to the Iraqi invasion and occupation of Kuwait. UN Security Council Resolution (UNSCR) 678 proved to be the key decree. See United Nations Security Council Resolutions, 'Resolution 678', 29 November 1990, http://unscr.com/en/resolutions/678.

39 According to Michael Watkins and Susan Rosegrant, allied contributions amounted to USD53.7bn out of USD61.1bn total war costs, with Germany, Japan, Saudi Arabia and Kuwait providing the largest contributions. See World Atlas, 'Which Countries Were Involved In The Gulf War?', https://www.worldatlas.com/articles/which-countries-were-involved-in-the-gulf-war.html; Ross, *Statecraft: And How to Restore America's Standing in The World*, p. 89; and Burns, *The Back Channel: A Memoir of American Diplomacy and the Case for Its Renewal*, p. 60.

40 See Smith, *America's Mission: The United States and the Worldwide Struggle for Democracy in the Twentieth Century*, pp. 311–45; and Rothkopf, *Running the World: The Inside Story of the National Security Council and the Architects of American Power*, p. 290, specifically his reference to the 'collective desire of America's senior leadership not to add another crisis to their already too-full agenda'.

41 For Reagan's National Security Decision Directive (NSDD-5), see White House, 'National Security Decision Directive Number 5: Conventional Arms Transfer Policy', Ronald Reagan Presidential Library and Museum, 8 July 1981, https://www.reaganlibrary.gov/public/archives/reference/scanned-nsdds/nsdd5.pdf.

42 White House, 'National Security Directive 26: US Policy Toward the Persian Gulf', Federation of American Scientists, Intelligence Research Program, 2 October 1989, p. 3, https://irp.fas.org/offdocs/nsd/nsd26.pdf.

43 *Ibid.*

44 See White House, 'National Security Decision Directive Number 5: Conventional Arms Transfer Policy'.

45 See Burns, *The Back Channel: A Memoir of American Diplomacy and the Case for Its Renewal*, p. 68.

46 These deals would eventually lead to the delivery of 46 aircraft to Egypt, 80 to Turkey (in two separate instalments) and ten to Israel. See Ian Anthony, Pieter D Weseman and Siemon T Wezeman, 'The Trade in Major Conventional Weapons', in SIPRI (ed.), *SIPRI Yearbook 1996: Armaments, Disarmament and International Security* (Oxford: Oxford University Pres for SIPRI, 1996), pp. 487–530, appendix 11B, https://www.sipri.org/sites/default/files/SIPRI%20Yearbook%201996.pdf.

47 See US Arms Control and Disarmament Agency, *World Military Exports and Arms Transfers, 1993–1994*, February 1995, p. 151, table IV, https://2009-2017.state.gov/documents/organization/185647.pdf.

48 Anoushiravan Ehteshami, 'Iranian Rearmament Strategy Under President Rafsanjani', *Jane's Intelligence Review*, July 1992, p. 312.

49 See, for example, F-16.net, 'Republic of China/Taiwan', https://www.f-16.net/f-16_users_article19.html.

50 Woodrow Wilson is credited with originating the modern American version of the liberal internationalist agenda. For an extensive discussion on this, see Smith, *America's Mission: The United States and the Worldwide Struggle for Democracy in the Twentieth Century*, pp. 84–109, 327, 346–68.

51 Smith, *America's Mission: The United States and the Worldwide Struggle for Democracy in the Twentieth Century*, p. 324. For a discussion about Clinton's antipathy towards and reluctance to engage in traditional national-

security engagements see also Rothkopf, *Running the World: The Inside Story of the National Security Council and the Architects of American Power*, pp. 318–32.

52 Mandelbaum, *Mission Failure: America and the World in the Post-Cold War Era*, pp. 35–51; and Rothkopf, *Running the World: The Inside Story of the National Security Council and the Architects of American Power*, p. 306.

53 Rothkopf, *Running the World: The Inside Story of the National Security Council and the Architects of American Power*, pp. 355–62.

54 See White House, 'A National Security Strategy of Engagement and Enlargement', National Security Strategy Archive, February 1995, https://nssarchive.us/wp-content/uploads/2020/04/1995.pdf.

55 For a good discussion on the foundation of liberal internationalist theory, see Smith, *America's Mission: The United States and the Worldwide Struggle for Democracy in the Twentieth Century* (1994 edition), pp. 346–68; see also Mandelbaum, *Mission Failure: America and The World in The Post-Cold War Era*, pp. 316–19; and Jeffrey Sachs, 'International Economics: Unlocking the Mysteries of Globalization', *Foreign Policy*, Spring 1998, pp. 97–111.

56 See the White House, 'Clinton on Foreign Policy at University of Nebraska', Federation of American Scientists, 8 December 2000, https://web.archive.org/web/20150428115430/http://fas.org/news/usa/2000/usa-001208zws.htm.

57 See White House, 'Presidential Directive/NSC-13'.

58 See White House, 'Presidential Review Directive/NSC-34', Clinton Presidential Library and Museum, 21 May 1993, p. 2, https://clinton.presidentiallibraries.us/items/show/101150.

59 *Ibid.*, p. 4.

60 *Ibid.*, p. 5.

61 *Ibid.*

62 *Ibid.*

63 White House, 'National Security Decision Directive Number 5: Conventional Arms Transfer Policy'.

64 White House, 'Presidential Review Directive/NSC-34'.

65 *Ibid.*

66 See United Nations, 'United Nations Register of Conventional Arms', https://www.unroca.org; and SIPRI, *SIPRI Yearbook 1992: World Armaments and Disarmament* (Oxford: Oxford University Press, 1992), p. 299, https://www.sipri.org/sites/default/files/SIPRI%20Yearbook%201992.pdf.

67 For OSCE and Helsinki Principles Governing Conventional Arms Transfers, see OSCE, 'Principles Governing Conventional Arms Transfers', 25 November 1993, https://www.osce.org/files/f/documents/3/6/42313.pdf.

68 For an excellent discussion on the history of the Charter of Paris and the OSCE, see Christian Nünlist, Juhana Aunesluoma and Benno Zogg, 'The Road to the Charter of Paris: Historical Narratives and Lessons for the OSCE Today', OSCE Network, 2017, https://osce- network.net/fileadmin/user_upload/publications/RoadtoParisCharterFINALREPORT.pdf.

69 For more on COCOM, see Yoko Yasuhara, 'The Myth of Free Trade: The Origins of COCOM 1945–1950', *The Japanese Journal of American Studies*, vol. 4, 1991, p. 132, https://web.archive.org/web/20040730220532/http://wwwsoc.nii.ac.jp/jaas/periodicals/JJAS/PDF/1991/No.04-127.pdf.

70 For an overview of the Wassenaar Arrangement, see US Department of State, 'Wassenaar Arrangement on Export Controls for Conventional Arms and Dual-Use Goods and Technologies', 22 March 2004, https://2001-2009.state.gov/t/isn/rls/fs/30957.htm.

71 White House, 'Presidential Review Directive/NSC-34'.

72 SIPRI, *SIPRI Yearbook 1999: Armaments, Disarmament and International Security* (Oxford: Oxford University Press, 1999), https://www.sipri.org/sites/default/files/SIPRI%20Yearbook%201999.pdf; and SIPRI, SIPRI Yearbook 2001: Armaments, Disarmament and International Security (Oxford: Oxford University Press, 2001) https://www.sipri.org/yearbook/2001.

73 Susan Ferns, 'Air Force receives last F-16', Aeronautical Systems Center Public Affairs, 24 March 2005, https://www.af.mil/News/Article-Display/Article/134773/air-force-receives-last-f-16/.

74 See Global Security, 'Six-Party Talks', https://www.globalsecurity.org/wmd/world/dprk/6-party.htm; and Utpal Vyas, Ching-Chang Chen and Denny Roy (eds), *The North Korea Crisis and Regional Responses* (Honolulu, HI: East-West Center, 2015), pp. 3–33, https://www.eastwestcenter.org/system/tdf/private/northkoreacrisis.pdf?file=1.

75 See the Carey Sublette, 'Pakistan's Nuclear Weapons Program', Nuclear Weapons Archive, 10 September 2001, https://nuclear-weaponarchive.org/Pakistan/PakTests.html.

76 Michael R. Gordon and Bernard E. Trainor, *Cobra II: The Inside Story of the Invasion and Occupation of Iraq* (New York: Pantheon, 2006), pp. 13–14; see also Bob Woodward, *Plan of Attack* (New York: Simon and Schuster, 2004), p. 2; and Ross, *Statecraft: And How to Restore America's Standing in the World*, pp. 103–4.

77 UNSCR 1368 was approved on 12 September 2001, expressing the UN Security Council's 'readiness to take all necessary steps to respond', and US Congress approved the 'Authorization for Use of Military Force' (AUMF) two days later. To review UNSCR 1368, see United Nations Security Council, 'Resolution 1368 (2001)', 12 September 2001, http://unscr.com/en/resolutions/doc/1368. Enacted with president Bush's signature on 18 September 2001, the AUMF authorised 'all necessary and appropriate force against those nations, organizations, or persons [the president] determines planned, authorized, committed, or aided the terrorist attacks that occurred on September 11, 2001, or harbored such organizations of persons'. See 107th Congress, 'Joint Resolution', Government Printing Office, 18 September 2001, https://www.govinfo.gov/content/pkg/PLAW-107publ40/html/PLAW-107publ40.htm.

78 Daniel Deudney and G. John Ikenberry, 'Misplaced Restraint: The Quincy Coalition Versus Liberal Internationalism', *Survival: Global Politics and Strategy*, vol.63, no. 4, August–September 2021, pp. 18–21, https://www.iiss.org/blogs/

survival-blog/2021/08/quincy-coalition-liberal-internationalism.

79 Ross, *Statecraft: And How to Restore America's Standing in the World*, pp. 5–11.

80 Smith, *America's Mission: The United States and the Worldwide Struggle for Democracy* (2012 edition), p. 363.

81 Melvyn P. Leffler, 'September 11 in Retrospect: George W. Bush's Grand Strategy Reconsidered', *Foreign Affairs*, September/October 2011, https://www.foreignaffairs.com/articles/2011-08-19/september-11-retrospect.

82 White House Office of Communications, 'Policies of the Bush Administration 2001–2009', https://georgewbush-whitehouse.archives.gov/infocus/bushrecord/documents/Policies_of_the_Bush_Administration.pdf.

83 Alex Wagner, 'Bush Waives Nuclear-Related Sanctions on India, Pakistan', *Arms Control Today*, https://www.armscontrol.org/act/2001-10/press-releases/bush-waives-nuclear-related-sanctions-india-pakistan.

84 Partly out of organisational and bureaucratic inertia independent of electorally-inspired 'regime change', presidential directives are typically honoured throughout the executive branch from one US presidential administration to the next unless (or until) superseded or rescinded. Once drafted, reviewed, coordinated, approved, signed and distributed, such memoranda establish and promote within the interagency community a set of vocabulary, goals and overt criteria for careerists to leverage while considering and justifying transfer-related proposals.

85 See SIPRI, *SIPRI Yearbook 2021: Armaments, Disarmament and International Security* (Oxford: Oxford University Press for SIPRI, 2021), https://www.sipri.org/yearbook/2021.

86 *Ibid.*

87 See SIPRI, *SIPRI Yearbook 2005: Armaments, Disarmament and International Security* (Oxford: Oxford University Press for SIPRI, 2005), https://www.sipri.org/yearbook/2005.

88 SIPRI, *SIPRI Yearbook 2021: Armaments, Disarmament and International Security*.

89 *Ibid.*

90 *Ibid.*

91 Jeffrey Lewis, 'Storm Shadow, Saudi & the MTCR', Arms Control Wonk, 31 May 2011, https://www.armscontrolwonk.com/archive/204051/saudi-arabia-storm-shadow-the-mtcr/.

92 'Saudi Intelligence Chief Talks Security with Brennan Delegation', 22 March 2009, released by WikiLeaks as Cable 09RIYADH445_a, https://wikileaks.org/plusd/cables/09RIYADH445_a.html.

93 See, for example, US Senate, International Security, Proliferation and Federal Services Subcommittee, of the Committee Governmental Affairs, 'Cruise Missile and UAV Threats to the United States', US Government Printing Office, 11 June 2002, https://www.govinfo.gov/content/pkg/CHRG-107shrg80605/html/CHRG-107shrg80605.htm.

94 Dennis M Gormley and Richard Speier, 'Controlling Unmanned Air Vehicles: New Challenges', *Nonproliferation Review*, vol. 10, no. 2, 2003, pp. 66–79, https://www.tandfonline.com/doi/abs/10.1080/10736700308436931.

95 *Ibid.*

96 Jeffrey Lewis, 'Storm Shadow, Saudi & The MTCR'.

97 *Ibid.*

98 *Ibid.*

99 MBDA Missile Systems, 'Storm Shadow/SCALP', https://www.mbda-systems.com/product/storm-shadow-scalp/.

100 'Shaykh Mohammed bin Zayed Rejects Unarmed Predator Proposal', 27 June 2004, released by WikiLeaks as Cable 04ABUDHABI2113, https://wikileaks.org/plusd/cables/04ABUDHABI2113_a.html.

101 Paul K. Kerr, 'US-Proposed Missile Technology Regime Changes', IF11069, Congressional Research Service, 10 May 2022, https://sgp.fas.org/crs/nuke/IF11069.pdf.

102 *Ibid.*

103 *Ibid.*

104 White House, 'President Barack Obama's Inaugural Address', 21 January 2009, https://obamawhitehouse.archives.gov/blog/2009/01/21/president-barack-obamas-inaugural-address.

105 John P. Avlon, 'Obama Writes the Post-Partisan Playbook', Politico, 20 January 2009, https://www.politico.com/story/2009/01/obama-writes-the-post-partisan-play-book-017634.

106 Matthew N. Gobush, 'Moral Multilateralism: The Obama Doctrine's Christian Realism', *Providence*, 25 July 2016, https://providencemag.com/wp-content/uploads/Moral-Multilateralism-The-Obama-Doctrine's-Christian-Realism-Matthew-N-Gobush.pdf.

107 See US State Department, 'U.S. Relations with Syria', https://www.state.gov/u-s-relations-with-syria/; Associated Press, 'A Timeline of the US Involvement in Syria's Conflict', ABC News, https://abcnews.go.com/International/wireStory/timeline-us-involvement-syrias-conflict-60314701; and Denver Nicks, 'U.S. Forms Anti-ISIS Coalition at NATO Summit', *Time*, 5 September 2014.

108 US Department of State, 'Joint Comprehensive Plan of Action', https://2009-2017.state.gov/e/eb/tfs/spi/iran/jcpoa/index.htm.

109 White House, 'Presidential Policy Directive – United States Conventional Arms Transfer Policy', 15 January 2014, https://obamawhitehouse.archives.gov/the-press-office/2014/01/15/presidential-policy-directive-united-states-conventional-arms-transfer-p.

110 *Ibid.*

111 *Ibid.*

112 *Ibid.*

113 To review PPD-23, see White House, 'Fact Sheet: U.S. Security Sector Assistance Policy', 5 April 2013, https://obamawhitehouse.archives.gov/the-press-office/2013/04/05/fact-sheet-us-security-sector-assistance-policy.

114 Marcus Weisgerber and Caroline Houck, 'Obama's Final Arms-Export Tally More than Doubles Bush's', 8 November 2016, Defense One, https://www.defenseone.com/business/2016/11/obamas-final-arms-export-tally-more-doubles-bushs/133014/.

115 See SIPRI Trade Registers database, https://armstrade.sipri.org/armstrade/page/trade_register.php.

116 Associated Press Television News, 'US Navy deploys three aircraft carriers to Pacific

against China', Republic World, 14 June 2020, https://www.republicworld.com/world-news/us-news/us-navy-deploys-three-aircraft-carriers-to-pacific-against-china.html.

117 John Raine, 'Washington Returns to a Reordered Middle East', IISS, 31 March 2021, https://www.iiss.org/blogs/analysis/2021/03/washington-middle-east-geopolitics.

118 Eugene Kiely and Robert Farley, 'Timeline of U.S. Withdrawal from Afghanistan', FactCheck.org, 17 August 2021, https://www.factcheck.org/2021/08/timeline-of-u-s-withdrawal-from-afghanistan/.

119 'President Trump: "Abu Bakr al-Baghdadi is dead"', BBC News, 27 October 2019, https://www.bbc.com/news/av/world-50200383.

120 'Revolutionary Guard Corps: US labels Iran force as terrorists', BBC News, 8 April 2019, https://www.bbc.com/news/world-us-canada-47857140.

121 'Qasem Soleimani: US kills top Iranian general in Baghdad air strike', BBC News, 3 January 2020, https://www.bbc.com/news/world-middle-east-50979463.

122 Paul Sonne, Josh Dawsey and Missy Ryan, 'Mattis Resigns After Clash with Trump over Troop Withdrawal from Syria and Afghanistan', *Washington Post*, 20 December 2018, https://www.washingtonpost.com/world/national-security/trump-announces-mattis-will-leave-as-defense-secretary-at-the-end-of-february/2018/12/20/e1a846ee-e147-11e8-ab2c-b31dcd53ca6b_story.html.

123 'Turkey-Syria offensive: US sanctions Turkish ministries', BBC News, 15 October 2019, https://www.bbc.com/news/world-middle-east-50050264.

124 See Donald J. Trump, 'National Security Presidential Memorandum Regarding U.S. Conventional Arms Transfer Policy', Federation of American Scientists, 19 April 2018, https://irp.fas.org/offdocs/nspm/nspm-10.pdf.

125 *Ibid.*

126 *Ibid.*

127 Rachel Stohl, 'Defense Industry Cheers as the Trump Administration is Poised to Loosen Restrictions on Drone Exports', *Responsible Statecraft*, 25 June 2020, https://responsiblestatecraft.org/2020/06/25/defense-industry-cheers-trump-loosen-restrictions-drone-exports/.

128 See SIPRI, *SIPRI Yearbook 2021: Armaments, Disarmament and International Security.*

129 See Council on Foreign Relations, 'President-Elect Biden on Foreign Policy', 7 November 2020, https://www.cfr.org/election2020/candidate-tracker.

130 Joe Biden, 'Biden Harris Democrats', https://joebiden.com/AmericanLeadership/.

131 White House, 'Remarks by President Biden on America's Place in the World', 4 February 2021, https://www.whitehouse.gov/briefing-room/speeches-remarks/2021/02/04/remarks-by-president-biden-on-americas-place-in-the-world/.

132 *Ibid.*

133 White House, 'Remarks by President Biden Before the 76th Session of the United Nations General Assembly', 21 September 2021, https://www.whitehouse.gov/briefing-room/speeches-remarks/2021/09/21/remarks-by-president-biden-before-the-76th-session-of-the-united-nations-general-assembly/.

134 Speech by Ronald Regan, 'Shining City on a Hill' – Ronald Reagan, 1988 State of the Union Address, Washington DC, 25 January 1988, in C-SPAN, 30 August 2018, https://www.c-span.org/video/?c4746361/shining-city-hill-ronald-reagan-1988-state-union-address; and see also John Winthrop, 'City Upon a Hill', Digital History, 1630, http://www.digitalhistory.uh.edu/disp_textbook.cfm?smtID=3&psid=3918.

135 White House, 'Interim National Security Strategy', March 2021, p. 16, https://www.whitehouse.gov/wp-content/uploads/2021/03/NSC-1v2.pdf.

136 Terri Moon Cronk, 'Biden Announces Full U.S. Troop Withdrawl from Afghanistan by Sept. 11', US Department of Defense, 14 April 2021, https://www.defense.gov/News/News-Stories/Article/Article/2573268/biden-announces-full-us-troop-withdrawal-from-afghanistan-by-sept-11/.

137 Richard Haass, 'The Age of America First: Washington's Flawed New Foreign Policy Consensus', *Foreign Affairs*, November/December 2021, p. 93, https://www.foreignaffairs.com/articles/united-states/2021-09-29/biden-trump-age-america-first.

138 Rory Stewart, 'The Last Days of Intervention: Afghanistan and the Delusions of Maximalism', *Foreign Affairs*, November/December 2021, pp. 60–73, https://www.foreignaffairs.com/articles/afghanistan/2021-10-08/last-days-intervention.

139 'Biden announces U.S. operation killed al-Qaida leader who helped plan 9/11', Yahoo! News, 2 August 2022, https://news.yahoo.com/biden-announces-u-operation-killed-121430790.html; Judith Miller, 'Biden's Afghanistan Challenges Ahead After Zawahiri's Death', Fox News, 2 August 2022, https://www.foxnews.com/opinion/biden-afghanistan-challenges-ahead-after-zawahiris-death; and Brian Freeman, 'Zawahiri Killing reignites Afghanistan withdrawal debate before anniversary', Newsmax, 3 August 2022, https://www.newsmax.com/newsfront/zawahri-afghanistan-biden/2022/08/03/id/1081568/.

140 John Raine, 'Washington Returns to a Reordered Middle East', IISS, 31 March 2021, https://www.iiss.org/blogs/analysis/2021/03/washington-middle-east-geopolitics.

141 David B. Roberts, 'Lifting the Protection Curse: The Rise of the New Military Powers in the Middle East', *Survival: Global Politics and Strategy*, vol. 63, no. 2., April–May 2021, pp. 139–153; see also Judith Miller, 'Biden Confronts Saudi Prince on Khashoggi's Murder', Pundicity, 16 July 2022, https://judithmiller.com/26320/biden-saudi-khashoggi-murder.

142 Matt Pottinger, 'Beijing's American Hustle: How Chinese Grand Strategy Exploits US Power', *Foreign Affairs*, September–October 2021, pp. 102–14, https://www.foreignaffairs.com/articles/asia/2021-08-23/beijings-american-hustle; see also Tulip Naksompop Blauw, 'A Free and Open Indo-Pacific a Common Vision – US Secretary of Defence', Thai PBS World, 13 June 2022, https://www.thaipbsworld.

com/a-free-and-open-indo-pacific-a-common-vision-us-secretary-of-defence/; and Dzirhan Mahadzir, 'Japanese PM Kishida Lays out Indo-Pacific Strategy in Shangri-La Speech', USNI News, 13 June 2022, https://news.usni.org/2022/06/10/japanese-pm-kishida-lays-out-indo-pacific-strategy-in-shangri-la-speech.

143 See Justin Ong, 'Global Order in Potentially Most Dangerous Period Since WWII: Top US Commander', *Straits Times Singapore*, 11 June 2022, https://www.straitstimes.com/singapore/global-order-in-potentially-most-dangerous-period-since-wwii-top-us-commander; see also Oriana Skylar Mastro, 'The Taiwan Temptation: Why Beijing Might Resort to Force', *Foreign Affairs*, July–August 2021, pp. 58–67, https://www.foreignaffairs.com/articles/china/2021-06-03/china-taiwan-war-temptation; Tim Huxley and Lynn Kuok (eds.), *Asia-Pacific Regional Security Assessment 2022* (London: IISS, 2022), https://www.iiss.org/publications/strategic-dossiers/asia-pacific-regional-security-assessment-2022; and Simon McCarthy, 'China and Cambodia Break Ground at Naval Base in Show of "Iron-Clad" Relations', CNN, 9 June 2022, https://www.cnn.com/2022/06/09/asia/china-cambodia-naval-base-military-intl-hnk/index.html.

144 François Heisbourg, 'Euro-Atlantic Security and the China Nexus', *Survival: Global Politics and Strategy*, vol. 63, no. 6, December 2021–January 2022, pp. 45–62; and Haas, 'The Age of America First: Washington's Flawed New Foreign Policy Consensus', p. 93.

145 Nigel Gould-Davies, 'Putin's Strategic Failure', *Survival: Global Politics and Strategy*, vol. 64, no. 2, April–May 2022, pp. 7–16, https://www.iiss.org/blogs/survival-blog/2022/04/putins-strategic-failure.

146 White House, 'Remarks by President Biden on America's Place in the World'.

147 See 'Biden Administration Halts Arms Sales to UAE and Saudi Arabia', DW, 28 January 2021, https://www.dw.com/en/biden-administration-halts-arms-sales-to-uae-and-saudi-arabia/a-56365478; and Theresa Hitchens, 'UAE Arms Sales Deal Remains in Limbo Pending Biden Review', *Breaking Defense*, 5 August 2021, https://breakingdefense.com/2021/08/uae-arms-sale-remains-in-limbo-pending-biden-review/amp/.

148 See Stephanie Kirchgaessner and Bethan McKernan, 'Biden's $500 million Saudi deal contradicts policy on "offensive" weapons, critics say', *Guardian*, 27 October 2021, https://www.theguardian.com/us-news/2021/oct/27/joe-biden-saudi-arabia-arms-weapons-deal; and Kylie Atwood, 'Biden administration notifies Congress of $650 million arms sale to Saudi Arabia', CNN, 4 November 2021, https://www.cnn.com/2021/11/04/politics/us-saudi-arabia-arms-sale/index.html.

149 See Caroline Vakil, 'Senators Make Bipartisan Push to Block $650M Sale to Saudis', *Hill*, 18 November 2021, https://thehill.com/homenews/senate/582288-senators-make-bipartisan-push-to-block-650m-weapons-sale-to-saudis/; and Brian Slodysko, 'Senate rejects bipartisanship bid to stop $650M Saudi Arms sale', ABC News, 7 December 2021, https://abcnews.go.com/Politics/wireStory/senate-rejects-bipartisan-bid-stop-650m-saudi-arms-81611929.

150 See MEE staff, 'Biden administration "fully committed" to sale of F-35 warplanes to UAE, says official', Middle East Eye, 16 November 2021, https://www.middleeasteye.net/news/uae-arms-sale-biden-administration-fully-committed-official-says.

151 Lolita C. Baldor and Matthew Lee, 'US to send $3 billion in aid to Ukraine as war hits 6 months', Associated Press, 23 August 2022, https://apnews.com/article/us-ukraine-3-billion-dollar-aid-package-363cdbeb670626eb410d72e81bd8068c. https://www.msn.com/en-us/news/politics/house-approves-stopgap-funding-bill-with-ukraine-aid/ar-AA12rTzA

152 Ellen Knickmeyer and Lolita C. Baldor, 'US to send Ukraine another $1 billion in military aid', *Military Times*, 8 August 2022, https://www.militarytimes.com/news/pentagon-congress/2022/08/08/us-to-send-ukraine-another-1-billion-in-military-aid/.

153 See Francois Murphy, 'Exclusive: Iran expands advanced centrifuge work underground, IAEA report shows', Reuters, 8 June 2022, https://www.reuters.com/world/middle-east/iran-expands-advanced-centrifuge-work-underground-plant-iaea-says-2022-06-08/.

CHINA

Source: IISS

CHAPTER 4

Map 4.1: **Selected* combat-aircraft sales to the Middle East, North Africa and Asia from China**

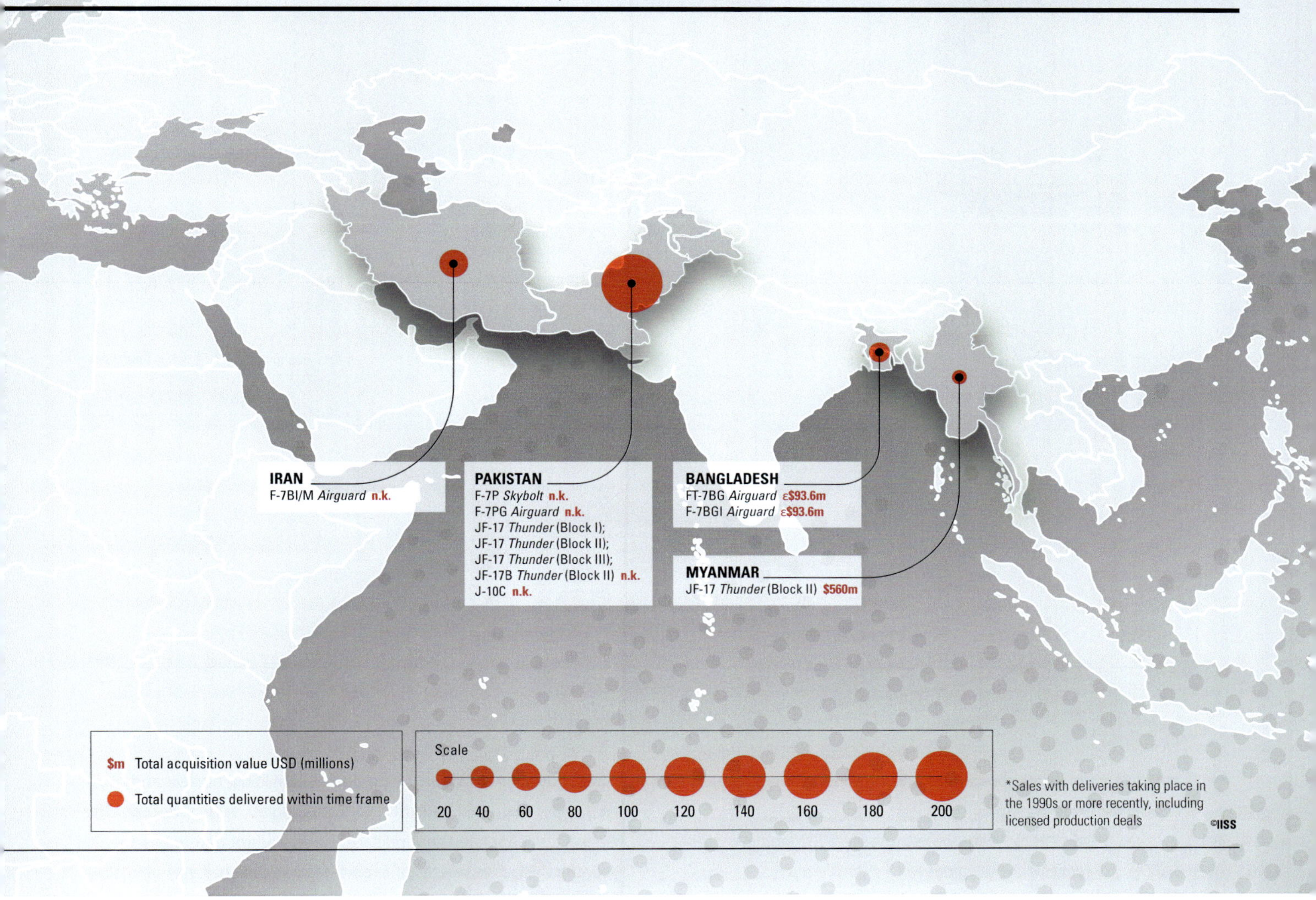

Between 2017 and 2021, China was the world's fourth-largest arms exporter. China's history in arms exports began in the 1950s, when it provided second-hand Soviet equipment to ideologically aligned partners. By 2022, China's arms exports had become more advanced technologically, were domestically produced and were exported widely. China's arms sales have historically been driven by ideological, strategic and economic motives. Over time, the ideological component of China's arms-exporting rationale has decreased in importance, while China's rise as a political and economic power has made geopolitical and economic considerations increasingly important in Beijing's calculations. As a result, China has sought to professionalise the institutional bureaucracy behind its arms-export system. Not only has China centralised the decision-making process that controls arms exports, but it has also passed an updated export-control law.[1] Moving forward, though, China's ability to balance its desire to export arms for geopolitical reasons will need to be measured against its ability to uphold its self-declared principles of non-interference, respect for sovereignty and territorial integrity.[2]

China's arms-export dynamics

Chinese arms exports can be understood by identifying factors determining their demand from external markets as well as domestic drivers. Chinese weapons are primarily exported according to domestic laws and play an important role in Beijing's foreign policy. However, the drivers behind arms exports have changed over time in accordance with shifts in domestic politics.

Timeline 4.1: **Selected* combat-aircraft sales to the Middle East, North Africa and Asia from China**

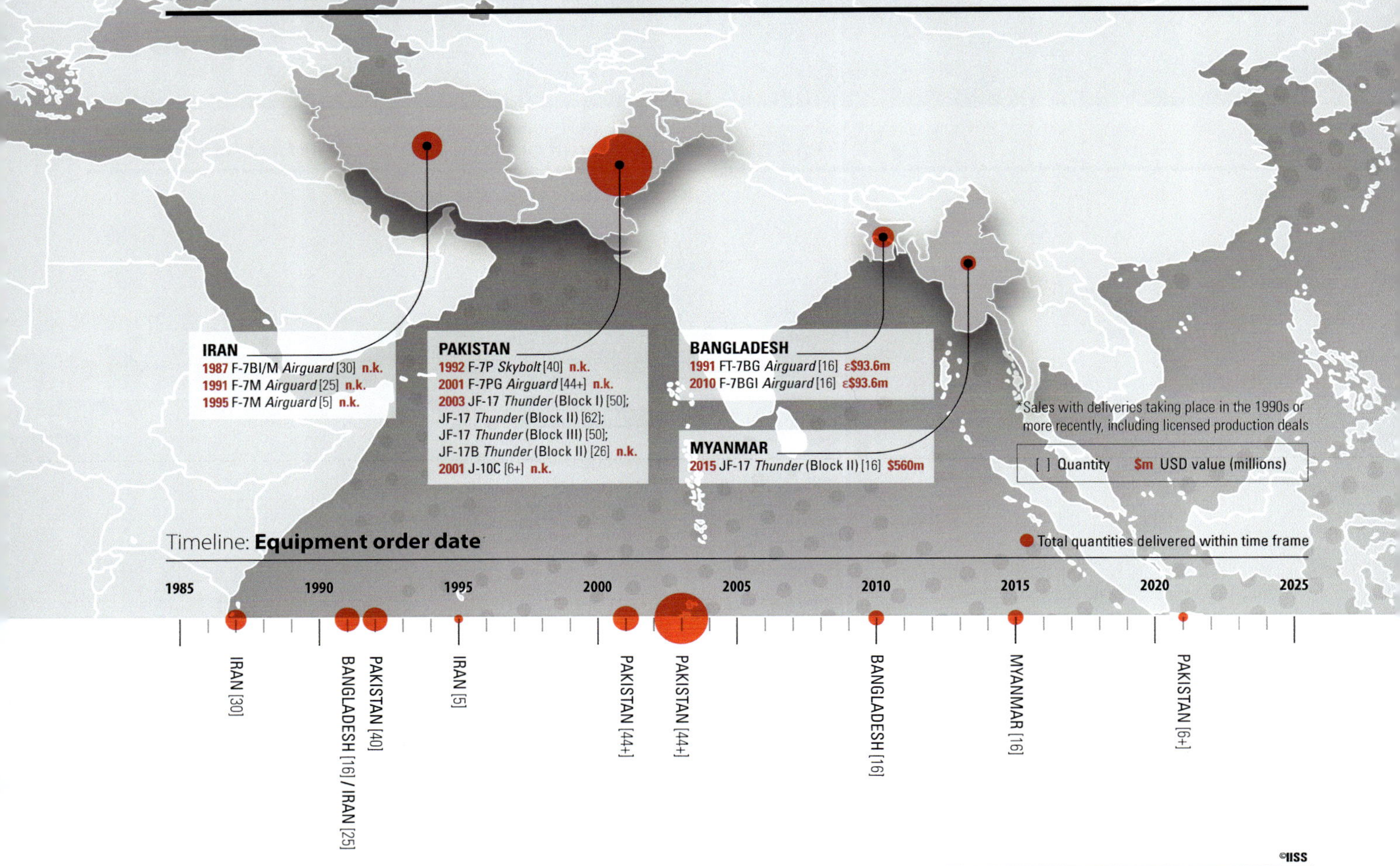

Source: IISS

In all of its weapons sales and transfers, China contends that it upholds three principles.[3]

- Firstly, exported weapons must serve the legitimate self-defence of the recipient.
- Secondly, the weapons exported must contribute to regional and global peace, security and stability.
- Thirdly, and finally, the weapons China exports must not be intended for interference in another country's internal affairs.

It is still unclear how these principles are applied and whether one takes priority over the others during decision-making.

China uses these principles as well as national regulations and limited participation in the UN Register on Conventional Arms and is reluctant to join the Wassenaar Arrangement to export weapons because of its own national interests. China's national regulation on arms exports is set out in the Regulation on Export Control of Military Items, which was passed in 1997 and revised in 2002.[4] However, in 2020, China passed a new Export Control Law at the Standing Committee of the 13th National People's Congress. This law replaced a number of previous export-control regulations and sought to regulate 'controlled items', including dual-use, military, nuclear and other national-security-related items, technologies and services.[5] The legislation stipulated that military export-control authorities should conduct risk assessments of export destinations that may ultimately 'endanger national security' or present non-proliferation risks. It also stipulated that exporting companies are inherently responsible for internal review and compliance mechanisms. This is reflected, for example, on Norinco's website, which currently hosts a section under 'sustainable development' titled 'non-proliferation exports and self-discipline'. This section was likely added to the website following the new export-control regulations as it was signed by Norinco Chairman Zheng Guanjie, who took up his position in 2020.

China's participation in international export-control regimes has been mixed. China has been a member of the UN Register of Conventional Arms since its creation and has contributed annual submissions semi-regularly, and at times has provided only basic information or incomplete records. In place of Wassenaar Arrangement membership, China has attempted to integrate international standards into its national laws and regulations on export controls. By doing so, China claims it upholds the 'spirit' of the Arrangement and abides by it

DENG XIAOPING
Deng Xiaoping at a rally celebrating the 50th anniversary of the founding of the People's Liberation Army, 1977. CREDIT: Sovfoto/Universal Images Group via Getty Images.

in principle without having signed it. This situation, of course, allows China to avoid participation in any multilateral review mechanism.

China is also not a signatory to the Missile Technology Control Regime (MTCR).[6] It has agreed in writing to adhere to its original guidelines and parameters but makes no mention of the agreement's annex on specific technologies and information on how to interpret the guidelines and parameters.[7] Moreover, China has not agreed to adhere to any revisions of the original document,[8] such as the 1993 expansion to cover all systems intended to deliver weapons of mass destruction (WMD).[9]

Ideological factors

Ideological factors played a dominant role in China's arms exports during the Cultural Revolution and the Mao era in general. From 1966 to 1978, Chinese arms exports were directed not only to countries within the Asia-Pacific but also more widely to those who China viewed as supporting a vision of 'world revolution'.[10] Arms exports were mostly directed to Cambodia, North Korea, Pakistan, Tanzania and Vietnam. In contrast to China's arms-export principles of today, these weapons were exported to both revolutionary governments and national-liberation fronts such as the Khmer Rouge in Cambodia and North Vietnam.[11] These exports were also an attempt to put China at the forefront of the Non-Aligned Movement and to compete with the Soviet Union following the deterioration of Sino-Russian relations. Concerning the former, Tanzania declared independence in 1962 and began receiving Chinese civilian aid in the form of infrastructure development in 1965. In 1970, China also transferred second-hand MiG-17 *Fresco* fighter aircraft, Type-59 tanks and Type-062 patrol craft to Tanzania's armed forces.[12] Chinese arms exports to Albania, North Korea and Pakistan also served the purpose of assisting countries which had similarly complicated or even adversarial relationships with Russia.[13] Arms transfers during the early 1970s were not driven by strong economic considerations and were instead given as gifts or through military aid. As noted by Lee, 'on certain occasions China even refused to accept payment for its arms and publicized military aid agreements between the PRC [People's Republic of China] and North Vietnam or Cambodia as friendly military aid with no profit gained'.[14]

However, this policy slowly weakened in the late 1970s when Deng Xiaoping gained power. Following the Cultural Revolution and investment in intensive Four Modernisations policies, China required foreign exchange to bolster its failing economy.[15] China's 'opening up reforms' (改革开放), which were led by Deng, resulted in a demilitarisation of Chinese foreign policy and a greater focus on economic development at home.[16]

During the Deng era, China's defence economy also shifted from being heavily dependent on Soviet-era weapons to increasing national production. Developing strategic technologies through programmes such as the 863 Program (also known as the State High-tech Development Plan) meant that China's peacetime defence production increased rapidly. As such, the drivers behind Chinese arms exports began to move beyond ideological considerations.

Strategic factors

According to Zhu, Chinese arms have traditionally also served a 'strategic' goal of supporting regional countries to reduce the threat of US hegemonism to China's periphery or to help China project influence globally through political and diplomatic means.[17]

Arms exports to regional countries helped China counter what it viewed as the threat of US hegemony in the Asia-Pacific, particularly during the Cold War. While ideological factors played a role in some of these cases, such as China's exports to North Vietnam and North Korea during the Vietnamese and Korean wars, they equally also helped prevent American and Soviet hegemony in China's neighbouring countries. Chinese exports to Iran in the 1980s of Type-59 towed guns, Type-63 towed multiple-rocket launchers (MRLs), Type-59 tanks and *Red Arrow*-73 anti-tank missiles could also be seen through the lens of anti-hegemonism. This is because by 'strengthening Iran, a threatening neighbour to the Soviets, China [added] to the difficulties facing Moscow'.[18]

Economic factors

In the 1980s, arms sales increasingly became a means to help fund China's military modernisation and military technological innovation. During the decade, China became the fifth-largest supplier of arms to the developing world. According to Bitzinger, 'deliveries of Chinese weapons systems grew 37 percent between 1982–1985 and 1986–1989, while arms transfer agreements from China to the Third World increased by more than 137 percent between these same two periods'.[19] Chinese weapons exports in the 1980s also diversified in type, to include surface-to-air missiles, anti-ship missiles, radar systems, submarines and tactical-bomber aircraft.[20] In 1988, China sold medium-range ballistic missiles to Saudi Arabia, and it transferred short-range ballistic missiles to Pakistan in 1992.[21]

It was during the 1980s that China also began to extend its arms exports further throughout the Asia-Pacific and Middle East. Algeria, Bangladesh, Iraq, Myanmar, Sri Lanka and Thailand became Chinese export markets. While some of these markets were geopolitically valuable to China because they allowed it to project political power and occupy regional political dynamics that may have otherwise been taken up by the Soviet Union (such as in Thailand), most of these cases reflected what was a growing and lucrative business for Beijing. According to Bitzinger, during the 1980s over 80% of Chinese arms sales were to the Middle East and South Asia.[22] Moreover, between 1982 and 1989 China became a weapons supplier to both Iran and Iraq, and during the Iran–Iraq War, the two countries accounted for 57% of China's arms exports. [23]

However, during this time, Chinese defence exports reflected what has been described as both 'historical glory and embarrassment in reality'.[24] Following the Soviet Union's dissolution, China's arms exports dwindled. China's weapons and platforms were based on Soviet weapons but were far behind the technological curve. China's defence industry, which had focussed on reverse-engineering Soviet weapons designs and exporting them at affordable prices to developing countries, was unable to develop a more modern weapons system domestically. Furthermore, the Western arms embargoes imposed on China following the 1989 Tiananmen Square protests and massacre worsened China's situation. Consequently, in the 1990s, China once again became a net arms importer – this time from Russia – and instigated wide-scale defence-industrial reforms to increase domestic innovative capability. This strategy worked. Through previous foreign-technology transfer practices from the West and reverse-engineering more advanced Russian weapons, Chinese arms exports picked up again in the 2000s, and China's defence industry has continued to produce increasingly advanced indigenous systems ever since.[25]

Since 2005, China's arms exports have diversified through North and sub-Saharan Africa, to Angola, Benin, Burundi, Cameroon, Central African Republic, Chad, Côte D'Ivoire, Democratic Republic of the Congo, Djibouti, Egypt, Ethiopia, Gabon, Ghana, Guinea, Kenya, Libya, Mali, Mauritania, Morocco, Mozambique, Namibia, Niger, Nigeria, Republic of Congo, Rwanda, Senegal, Seychelles, Sierra Leone, Somalia, Uganda, Zambia and Zimbabwe. In Latin America, Chinese arms have been exported to the Bahamas, Bolivia, Ecuador, Mexico, Peru, Trinidad and Tobago and Venezuela. China's regional exports also went beyond the traditional defence relationship with Iran and Iraq, and China has since 2005 exported to Egypt, Jordan, Kuwait, Qatar, Saudi Arabia, Syria, the United Arab Emirates (UAE) and even NATO-allied Turkey. In the Asia-Pacific, Bangladesh, Cambodia, Indonesia, Laos, Malaysia, Myanmar, Nepal, Pakistan, Papua New Guinea, Sri Lanka, Thailand and Timor-Leste have received Chinese weapons since 2005 in addition to the earlier presence of Chinese arms in Thailand, Cambodia and North Korea. Chinese weapons have also been exported to Afghanistan, Kazakhstan, Kyrgyzstan, Tajikistan and Turkmenistan, reportedly causing tension within the Sino-Russian relationship.

Unsurprisingly, China has failed to export weapon systems to the US or allied states, with very few exceptions. However, Chinese weapons have, in rare instances, been exported to Europe. In 2019, Serbia ordered nine CH-92 armed uninhabited aerial vehicles (UAVs). This was followed in 2022 by the delivery of the HQ-22 surface-to-air missile system to the same country.[26] Between 2016 and 2018, China also delivered six A-200 301mm towed MRLs and ten VN-3 armoured personnel vehicles to Belarus.[27]

A return to strategic drivers?

Since the 1990s and early 2000s, Chinese arms exports have benefited from a second wave of reverse-engineered Russian advanced equipment, which allowed China to simultaneously improve its domestic defence-industrial base and continue exporting a wide array of advanced weapons to a growing list of markets.

China's economic growth, along with its ability to build advanced major weapons, has given it a wider range of countries to export to, as well as more flexibility in its approach. As such, decisions regarding

CHINA'S J-10C MULTIPURPOSE AIR FIGHTER
A Chengdu J-10C combat aircraft on display during the 13th China International Aviation and Aerospace Exhibition, or Airshow China 2021, in Zhuhai in south China's Guangdong province.
CREDIT: Feature China/Future Publishing via Getty Images.

China's arms exports are based primarily on political and economic considerations and only rarely on ideological affinity.

In 2015 at the All-Military Diplomatic Work Conference, Chinese President Xi Jinping ordered that military diplomacy should play a more prominent role in China's foreign policy. Military diplomacy should also align with China's domestic- and foreign-policy priorities.[28] This directive was a step change for the People's Liberation Army (PLA) and Ministry of Defense (MOD), who had historically played only a minor role in foreign policy, which was traditionally directed predominantly by the Chinese Ministry of Foreign Affairs.

According to a statistical analysis of Chinese arms exports from 2013 to 2022, there has been an increasing correlation between countries receiving Chinese major weapons systems and membership of the Belt and Road Initiative (BRI). A 2018 IISS study found that only 31% of BRI member countries have received Chinese arms sales since 2013 (23 countries out of 74 that were linked to the BRI at that time).[29] However, an update to this data shows a stronger correlation. In 2022, of the 147 countries and territories that officially signed onto the BRI, 68 had received Chinese weapons since 2013 (roughly 46%).

This correlation alone, though, does not prove that Chinese arms exports are becoming more strategic in nature and serving greater geopolitical goals. For example, despite concerns over China's ability to leverage diplomatic defence relationships, United Nations voting in 2022 on motions in support of Ukraine and that condemn Russia shows that BRI member countries have largely chosen solidarity with China and its 'partner with no limits'. Indeed, on 7 April 2022, of the 147 countries and territories officially in the BRI, China and 18 others voted against suspending Russia from the UN Human Rights Council.[30] Only 57 BRI member countries (roughly 39%) voted in favour of Russia's suspension from the UN Human Rights Council. Notwithstanding these two examples, there are several different motivations behind voting patterns at the UN, as well as arms-import decisions in countries that have received Chinese weapons since 2013. Despite its defence-industrial and political strengths, Beijing must still contend with the domestic political factors in recipient countries, decisions about the requirements for weapons and other geopolitical considerations. As such, Chinese arms exports are unlikely to be decisive foreign-policy tools in and of themselves.

Arms exports have, however, played an important role in Chinese economic policy by facilitating access to natural resources in foreign markets. Rather than leveraging economic relationships through the BRI to expand its arms-exports reach, China has in some cases taken the opposite policy approach. For example, while Chinese arms deals are often heavily discounted or sold on credit, in some cases arms have been traded for access to oil or minerals. According to Chinese reporting, Venezuela received arms from China in return for partial payment in oil, while Uzbekistan and Turkmenistan have received Chinese long-range air-defence missile systems in exchange for natural gas.[31]

Chinese defence exports continue to serve an economic purpose by funding China's defence-industrial complex. As part of Xi's reforms of China's defence-industrial state-owned enterprises, companies have been instructed to rely more on their own sources of income to increase their competitiveness and invest in innovation and research and development.[32]

Xi rings the changes

As the types of weapons available and the geographical dispersion of arms sales have diversified, the processes and bureaucracy controlling exports have also shifted to become more centralised in order to address organisational and legal clarity.

China's defence-industrial complex was restructured in 1998 in an attempt to improve the sector's competitiveness and efficiency,

Figure 4.1: **Export decision-making tree**

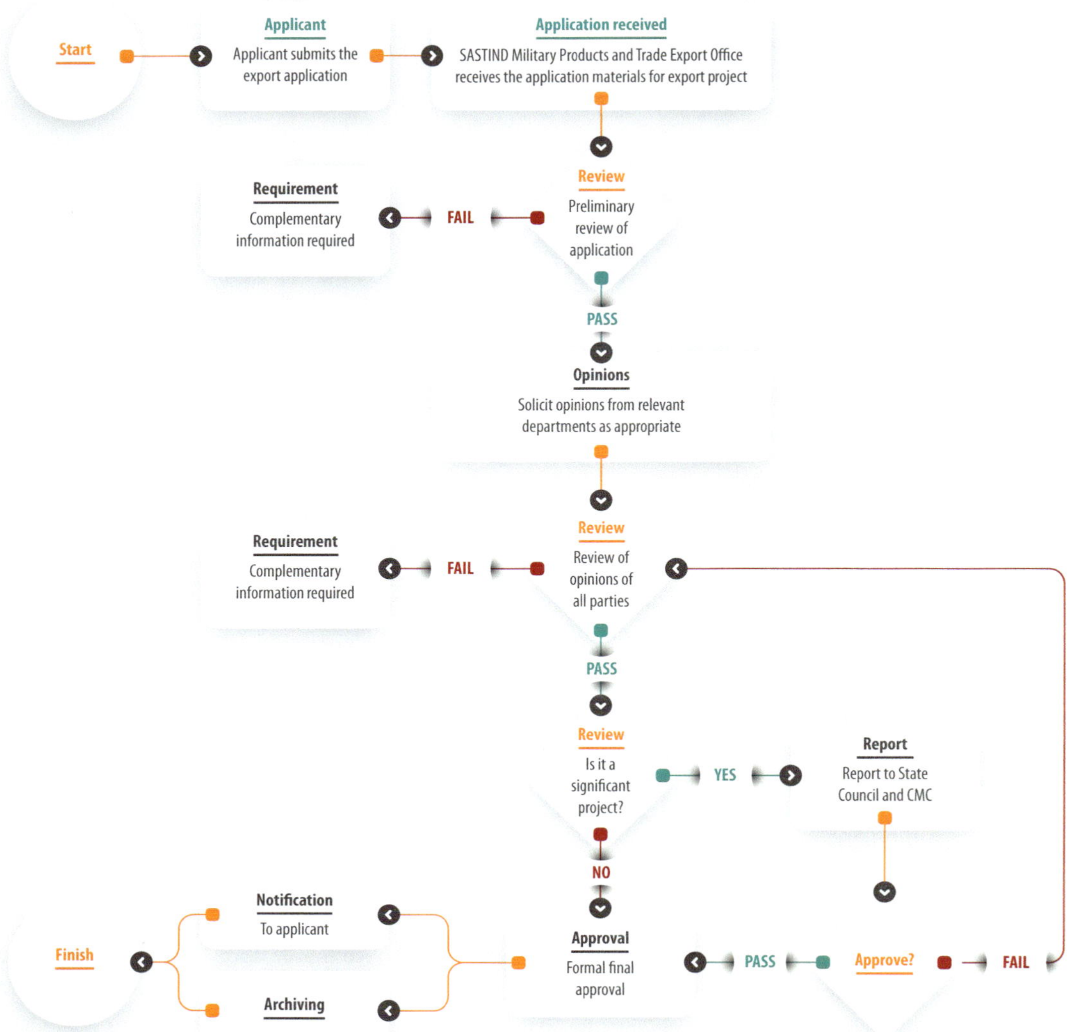

Source: IISS

de-commercialise the PLA and further distance the army from its previously close relationship with the complex. This reform also dissolved the influential State Administrative Committee on Military Products and Trade (SACMPT), and since the late 1990s a new structure has directed China's arms exports. The former arrangement saw the various agencies in place engage in arms exports at different and often competing levels, which illustrates the sometimes diverging interests and lack of clear central decision-making.

Until the late 1990s, Chinese arms exports were overseen by numerous government agencies, the PLA and China's defence-industrial complex. Each institution played a role in either the export-review process or the export of military products themselves. The process was driven by the State Council and its relevant organisations, on the one hand, and the Central Military Commission (CMC) and its subordinate departments, on the other.[33] At the top, the State Council, Central Military Commission and Military Products Export Leading Group provided oversight of leadership. Sitting in between the State Council and CMC, the SACMPT served as an inter-agency bureau and drafted the laws that governed arms exports. The SACMPT reported to the State Council and the CMC. The bureau was staffed by the Ministry of Foreign Affairs (MFA), State Commission on Science, Technology and Industry for National Defense (COSTIND), General Staff, Ministry of Foreign Trade and Economic Coordination (MOFTEC) and other departments.

The State Council reviewed exports that were considered of significant importance together with the CMC before approval. The Leading Group's role and make-up were unclear. Some analysts suggested this

CHINA HOLDS MILITARY PARADE TO COMMEMORATE THE END OF THE SECOND WORLD WAR IN ASIA
A GJ-1 UAV shown as part of the military parade to mark the 70th anniversary of the end of the Second World War in Beijing, China, 3 September 2015. CREDIT: Andy Wong - Pool /Getty Images.

group comprised elite decision-makers of the state and party organs who met to discuss controversial and sensitive exports, while others argued this group was ostensibly the SACMPT under a different name.

Six state and party agencies played a decision-making and procedural role in China's arms-export practice. COSTIND (which was replaced by the State Administration for Science, Technology and Industry for National Defense in 2008) oversaw the planning and regulation of the defence-industrial complex.[34] The General Armaments Department (GAD) under the CMC informed the PLA of arms-control issues, vetted the export of military products in conjunction with the MFA and played a policy role by deciding China's position in arms-control discussions.

The Ministry of National Defense's Foreign Affairs office was likely also charged with vetting arms-control decisions and policies, and probably competed for influence with the GAD. The MFA's Arms Control and Disarmament Department also played a leading role in formulating export policies and decisions on specific exports. However, the MFA was 'reportedly not well informed about China's sensitive exports and often found out about them after the fact' and 'traditionally … has taken a more conservative approach to China's conventional arms exports'.[35] While MOFTEC officials formed part of the SACMPT, MOFTEC was largely responsible for issuing broad-based trade laws that governed export control, but it played no role in licensing military-product exports. The General Administration of Customs (GAC) enforced export controls and ensured appropriate licences were in place before goods could be exported.

Within China's defence sector, military and defence-industrial enterprises both played a role in arms exports. Of the former, Poly Technologies Ltd had a civilian wing, but its military branch was an extension of the Equipment Division of the General Staff Department of the CMC and exported PLA surpluses. Other companies also existed but played a minor role. Chinese defence conglomerates conducted arms trade through subsidiary trading companies to access the international market. As China's defence conglomerates were subdivided (in recent years some have merged again), each conglomerate maintained its own corresponding export subsidiary.

Central control

Following the restructuring of China's defence-industrial complex in the late 1990s, and particularly since President Xi took office in 2013, the Chinese leadership has placed a renewed emphasis on the importance of centralisation of authority and the political power of the party over the state. This has impacted both the actors involved in the decision-making and regulatory processes of arms exports as well as the process itself.

Under the new system, the State Council, CMC and Leading Group have maintained their positions and responsibilities from the previous system. Operationally, the State Administration for Science, Technology and Industry for National Defence (SASTIND), the Ministry of Commerce (MOFCOM), the Ministry of Industry and Information Technology (MIIT), the GAC, the State Atomic Energy Agency, the Central Military Commission Equipment Development Department (CMC EDD) and other government agencies all play a role in reviewing and approving export-licence applications.

According to the SASTIND website, arms exports are currently decided by its Military Products Trade and Export Office. Following a successful preliminary review by SASTIND, applications for export licences are then sent to 'relevant departments as appropriate', which involves an opaque review process by various ministries. Though the departments included in this stage of the process are not directly identified by SASTIND on its website, the Export Control White Paper

Figure 4.2: **China: armed UAV exports**

Recipient	CH-3	CH-4	*Wing Loong* I	*Wing Loong* II	CH-92A	WJ-600
Algeria	YES	YES				
Egypt			YES			
Indonesia		YES				
Iraq		YES				
Jordan		YES				
Kazakhstan			YES			
Myanmar	YES					
Nigeria	YES			YES		
Pakistan	YES	YES				
Saudi Arabia		YES	YES			
Serbia					YES	
Sudan	YES	YES				
Turkmenistan	YES					YES
UAE			YES	YES		

Source: IISS

published by the State Council in 2021 outlines the relevant ministries involved depending on the nature of the export item.[36]

According to the White Paper, MOFCOM and the GAC are involved in all export-licence procedures, whether these are military, dual-use or civilian in nature. With regard to military exports and the export of dual-use missiles, SASTIND and the CMC EDD are responsible for formulating regulations regarding export controls of military and dual-use missiles and carrying out assessments of applications for the export of such items. For example, in 2020 SASTIND and the CMC EDD published a notice for commercial launch-vehicle producers with regard to the standardisation of development of such systems for the purpose of national innovation but also for quality control of exports.[37]

Following the input of the relevant agencies and departments, SASTIND and the CMC EDD undertake a 'comprehensive review' of the opinions of all parties involved. As in the previous export-licensing system, projects that are of a particularly sensitive political or strategic nature must receive both State Council and CMC approval. Considering SASTIND and the CMC EDD are already involved in the previous stages of the licensing process, this step could indicate higher political approval within the state and party system. However, it is unclear exactly how high this approval may go. If the application is approved, it goes through final administrative and archival steps before the process is completed.

A few issues remain with this process. Firstly, it would appear that within the previous system, various ministries vied for influential positions as part of the approval process. It seems that under the current process other ministries besides SASTIND and the CMC EDD provide secondary 'opinions'. However, as in the previous system, it is unclear which ministry's opinion is the most influential.

Secondly, the role of the MFA and the MOD is not mentioned in SASTIND's document or in the Export Control White Paper. It is likely that the MFA's Arms Control Department or the civilian and PLA sections of China's embassies abroad are involved in certain steps in the process.

Lastly, while the new documents describe the final approval required from the State Council and CMC for particularly sensitive exports, recent documents do not mention the Military Products Export Leading Group at all. Analysts have questioned whether this leading group actually existed in the first place, and it is unclear whether this group survived the reforms and Xi's leadership. However, a 2014 article on the Symposium on Military Trade in Defense Science and Technology Industry mentions that the symposium was attended by 'the main persons in charge of each military industry group, members of the leading group for the trade of military products, the International Cooperation Sub-Committee of SASTIND, the military trade department of the military industry group and the principles of military trade companies'.[38] This suggests that as early as 2014 the Leading Group still played an important, if ambiguous, role in China's arms exports.

China's UAV exports: policy and practice

Despite its ranking in terms of defence exports, there are very few areas where Chinese major weapons dominate. This is not the case, however, when it comes to the export of armed UAVs, including sales of such systems to the Middle East. The United States' unwillingness to approve armed UAV sales to the region, and more generally, provided China with an opportunity that it quickly capitalised on. Washington, as one of the founder signatories of the MTCR in 1987, was unwilling to release a weapons system it viewed as contrary to its commitments under the regime.

As with many of its military capabilities, China's UAV history began with a Soviet system, the Lavochkin La-17 (DR-1) target drone, which was acquired in the 1950s. It was not, however, until the 1990s and early 2000s that Beijing's UAV efforts really gathered momentum. As of 2022, China has developed a range of UAVs for surveillance and combat roles for its own military use, as well as a range of variants thereof. Of the latter, the *Caihong* (or *Rainbow*) series is manufactured by the China Aerospace Science and Technology Corporation (CASC), while the *Wing Loong* series is manufactured by Chengdu Aircraft Industry Group (CAIG). As well as benefiting from US reticence to release armed UAVs for export, China also had the advantage of being able to offer considerably lower-priced systems, albeit at lower levels of performance and capability. Chinese CH-3, CH-4A, CH-4B, *Wing Loong*-1 and *Wing Loong*-2 UAVs have been sold to Algeria, Egypt, Indonesia, Iraq, Jordan, Kazakhstan, Laos, Myanmar, Nigeria, Pakistan, Saudi Arabia, Serbia, Sudan, Turkmenistan, the UAE and Uzbekistan.[39] China has signed agreements to export UAVs on almost an annual basis between 2011 and 2020.

While the Chinese military has not participated in a conflict since a border skirmish with the Vietnamese military in 1979, Chinese UAVs have been used in combat by recipient militaries. This has provided Chinese producers and the military with insights into their combat effectiveness. Overall, anecdotal evidence suggests that the different UAVs have performed inconsistently. In 2015, the Iraqi military used a CH-4 UAV to strike an Islamic State (ISIS/ISIL) position in Ramadi. This was the first use of the CH-4 in combat.[40] Nigeria began using the CH-3 in its fight against Boko Haram militants as early as 2015.[41] During the course of its operations, it has lost a number of the CH-3s. Meanwhile, the Royal Jordanian Army and Air Force (RJAF) reportedly intended to sell their aircraft in 2019, despite having only received them two years prior. The RJAF reported in November 2018 that it was unhappy with the UAVs' performance.[42]

Some Chinese armed UAVs have, however, impacted local conflicts and regional power dynamics.[43] The UAE, for example, has deployed *Wing Loong*-2 UAVs to Al Khadim air base in eastern Libya in an effort to bolster the Libyan National Army. By not subscribing to international export-control regimes, Chinese arms suppliers have been able to take advantage of market opportunities in countries which Western competitors in UAV production would not export to, due to ethical or legal restrictions, or to countries that cannot afford Western alternatives. Ultimately, China's UAV exports have highlighted the loose application of the country's stated guiding principles on exports.

Conclusion

The drivers behind China's arms exports over the years have shifted from being ideological in nature to serving strategic and economic policy goals. As China's defence industry has modernised, in part through the help of a foreign-exchange influx due to its arms exports, the country has changed from being a net arms importer to an arms exporter. Despite the slight dip in China's arms export volume between 2011-2015 and 2016-2020, by 2020 China was the world's fifth largest defence exporter. As China's arms industry has modernised, Beijing has become willing and able to offer advanced military technology to recipients who would otherwise be unable to afford or qualify for similar types of technology from Western counterparts.

The Chinese government maintains that its arms exports are only approved based on principles of self-defence of the recipient, non-interference in another country's security and the maintenance of regional balances of power. In practice, however, Chinese arms exports have on occasion arguably had destabilising effects. While data from four years ago did not show a growing correlation between arms exports and Chinese foreign-policy initiatives, such as the BRI, more recent data has shown that the correlation had indeed become stronger by 2022. This may be due to President Xi's 2015 directive that the military and defence will play a larger and more prominent role in China's foreign-policy activities and help achieve China's goals. However, more research is required to qualify this correlation further and rule out other explanations.

Nevertheless, Chinese weapons may be influencing the balance of power between regional actors, particularly through exports of armed UAVs to the Middle East and Africa. Chinese weapons have already been used, both successfully and unsuccessfully, in combat scenarios in regional conflicts in the Middle East as well as West, North and the Horn of Africa. However, Western countries have criticised the spread of Chinese advanced military technology due to the lack of conditionality. It is unlikely that China will change its foreign-policy practices if they are contrary to its national interests. Nevertheless, China has taken steps in recent years to centralise and streamline its arms-export regulations and procedures. Such steps include stricter due-diligence and risk-assessment procedures for all parties involved.

But these new laws and regulations have only just come into force, so assessing their effectiveness and understanding their impact on Chinese arms-export behaviour will require further observation. For now, China's expanding bilateral defence relationships remain an evolving foreign-policy effort. These relations potentially offer further opportunities for China to fill capability gaps, including strengthened ties with Iran, an isolated Russia and even a new agreement with the Solomon Islands in the Pacific.

NOTES

1 The National People's Congress of the People's Republic of China, 'Export Control Law of the People's Republic of China', 17 October 2020, http://www.npc.gov.cn/npc/c30834/202010/cf4e0455f6424a38b5aecf8001712c43.shtml.

2 Permanent Mission of the People's Republic of China to the United Nations Office at Geneva and other international organizations in Switzerland, 'Statement of the People's Republic of China to the Sixth Conference of States Parties to the Arms Trade Treaty', 17 August 2020, https://www.mfa.gov.cn/ce/cegv/eng/dbtxwx/t1807021.htm.

3 State Administration for Science, Technology and Industry for National Defense, 'Military Export License - Project Approval', 18 July 2022, http://gfplatform.cnsa.gov.cn/n6195634/n6195706/n6195716/n6427863/n6428043/c6429055/content.html.

4 China Export Control Information, 'Regulations of the People's Republic of China on the Administration of the Export of Military Products', http://exportcontrol.mofcom.gov.cn/article/zcfg/gnzcfg/gzjgfxwj/202111/441.html.

5 National People's Congress of the People's Republic of China, 'Export Control Law of the People's Republic of China', 17 October 2020, http://www.npc.gov.cn/npc/c30834/202010/cf4e0455f6424a38b5aecf8001712c43.shtml.

6 Permanent Mission of the People's Republic of China to the United Nations Office at Geneva and Other International Organizations in Switzerland, 'Missile Technology Control Regime (MTCR)', https://www.mfa.gov.cn/ce/cegv//eng/cj/cjjblc/cjlc/t85378.htm.

7 GovInfo, 'Export Controls: Some Controls Over Missile-Related Technology Exports To China Are Weak (Letter Report, 04/17/95, GAO/NSIAD-95-82)', 17 April 1995, https://www.govinfo.gov/content/pkg/GAOREPORTS-NSIAD-95-82/html/GAOREPORTS-NSIAD-95-82.htm.

8 *Ibid.*

9 Permanent Mission of the People's Republic of China to the United Nations Office at Geneva and other international organizations in Switzerland, 'Missile Technology Control Regime (MTCR)', https://www.mfa.gov.cn/ce/cegv//eng/cj/cjjblc/cjlc/t85378.htm.

10 Zhu Qichao, 'The Evolution of International Arms Trade Motivation and the Game of National Strategy', AiSiXiang, 2006, https://m.aisixiang.com/data/11973.html.

11 Richard Bitzinger, 'Arms to Go', *International Security*, Vol. 17 No.2, 1992, pp. 84–111.

12 SIPRI Arms Transfer Database, 'Trade Register', 14 March 2022, https://armstrade.sipri.org/armstrade/page/trade_register.php.

13 Bitzinger, 'Arms to Go'.

14 Wei-china Lee, 'The Birth of a Salesman: China as an Arms Supplier', *Journal of Northeast Asian Studies,* vol. 5, no.4, Winter 1987.

15 Dennis J. Blasko, 'Always Faithful: The PLA reform from 1949 to 1989' in David Graff and Robin Higham (eds.), *A Military History of China,* (Lexington: University Press of Kentucky, 2012) p. 258.

16 Michael Raska and Richard Bitzinger, 'Strategic Contours of China's Arms Transfers', *Strategic Studies Quarterly*, Spring 2020.

17 Zhu Qichao, 'The Evolution of International Arms Trade Motivation and the Game of National Strategy', AiSiXiang, 2006, https://m.aisixiang.com/data/11973.html.

18 Lee, 'The Birth of a Salesman'.

19 Bitzinger, 'Arms to Go'.

20 SIPRI Arms Transfer Database, 'Trade Register', 14 March 2022, https://armstrade.sipri.org/armstrade/page/trade_register.php.

21 The US-China Economic and Security Review Commission, 'China's Reported Ballistic Missile Sale to Saudi Arabia: Background and Potential Implications', 16 June 2014, https://www.uscc.gov/sites/default/files/Research/Staff%20Report_China%27s%20Reported%20Ballistic%20Missile%20Sale%20to%20Saudi%20Arabia_0.pdf; and Congressional Record Online through the Government Printing Office, Pakistan Continues Missile Purchases From China and Escalates Tensions in South Asia', https://www.govinfo.gov/content/pkg/CREC-1994-09-29/html/CREC-1994-09-29-pt1-PgE20.htm.

22 Bitzinger, 'Arms to Go'.

23 SIPRI Arms Transfer Database, 'Trade Register', 14 March 2022, https://armstrade.sipri.org/armstrade/page/trade_register.php.

24 Zhu, 'The Evolution of International Arms Trade Motivation and the Game of National Strategy'.

25 Raska and Bitzinger, 'Strategic Contours of China's Arms Transfers'; Lucie Béraud-Sudreau and Meia Nouwens, 'China-Europe military Cooperation in the Twenty-First Century: From Friends to Frenemies?' in Roger Cliff and Roy D. Kamphausen (eds). *Enabling a More Externally Focussed and Operational PLA - 2020 PLA Conference Papers* (Carlisle Barracks, PA: USAWC Press, 2022).

26 Dusan Stujanovich, 'China makes semi-secret delivery of missiles to Sebia', AP News, 10 April 2022, https://apnews.com/article/russia-ukraine-europe-china-serbia-nato-682ab79c4239f14ecc1133ff5c7addc9; and SIPRI Arms Transfer Database, 'Trade Register', 14 March 2022, https://armstrade.sipri.org/armstrade/page/trade_register.php.

27 SIPRI Arms Transfer Database, 'Trade Register', 14 March 2022.

28 Cao Zhi, 'Xi Jinping: jin yi bu kai guang xin jun wai jiao xin ju mian' 习近平：进一步开创军外交新局面 [Xi Jinping: further create a new situation in military diplomacy], Xinhua, 29 January 2015,

http://www.xinhuanet.com/politics/2015-01/29/c_1114183775.htm.

29 Lucie Béraud-Sudreau and Meia Nouwens, 'Are arms exports a tool of Chinese Foreign Policy?', East Asia Forum, 7 July 2018, https://www.eastasiaforum.org/2018/07/07/are-arms-exports-a-tool-of-chinese-foreign-policy/.

30 UN News, 'UN General Assembly votes to suspend Russia from the Human Rights Council', 7 April 2022, https://news.un.org/en/story/2022/04/1115782; and IISS, 'IISS China Connects', https://chinaconnects.iiss.org/.

31 Ma Yao, 'How China becomes third-largest supplier of weapons worldwide?', China Military Online, 27 February 2018, http://english.chinamil.com.cn/ as cited in Raska and Bitzinger, 2020; Sina Military Online, 中国的武器还不被认可？有些国家已经被列入黑名单 ['Chinese weapons are not recognised yet? Some countries have been blacklisted'], 21 January 2019, https://mil.sina.cn/sd/2019-01-21/detail-ihqfskcn9151073.d.html?cre=tianyi&mod=wpage&loc=15&r=32&rfunc=59&tj=none&tr=32.

32 Lucie Beraud-Sudreau and Meia Nouwens, 'Weighing Giants: Taking stock of the expansion of China's defence industry', *Defence and Peace Economics*, vol. 31, no.2, 2021, https://www.tandfonline.com/doi/abs/10.1080/10242694.2019.1632536.

33 Bates Gill and Evan Medeiros, 'Chinese Arms Exports: Policy, Players and Process', US Army War College Monographs, 2000, 132. https://press.armywarcollege.edu/monographs/132.

34 James Mulvenon and Rebecca Samm Tyroler-Cooper, 'China's Defense Industry on the Path to Reform', The US-China Economic and Security Review Commission, October 2009, https://www.uscc.gov/sites/default/files/Research/Chinas_Defense_Industry_on_the_Path_of_Reform.pdf.

35 Gill and Madeiros, 'Chinese Arms Exports'.

36 The State Council Information Office of China, 'White Paper on Export Control in China', 21 December 2021, http://www.scio.gov.cn/m/zfbps/32832/Document/1718300/1718300.htm.

37 National Defense Science and Industry, 'Notice by the Equipment Development Department of the Central Military Commission of the State Administration of Science, Technology and Industry for National Defense on Promoting the Standardized and Orderly Development of Commercial Launch', 30 May 2019, http://www.gov.cn/zhengce/zhengceku/2020-03/24/content_5494956.htm.

38 news.enorth.com.cn, 'National Defense Technology Industry Military Products Trade Work Conference Held in Beijing', 18 February 2014, http://news.enorth.com.cn/system/2014/02/18/011683380.shtml.

39 SIPRI Arms Transfer Database, 'Trade Register', 14 March 2022, https://armstrade.sipri.org/armstrade/page/trade_register.php.

40 Partick Boehler and Gerry Doyle, 'Use by Iraqi Military May be a Boon for China-made Drones', *New York Times*, 17 December 2015, https://www.nytimes.com/2015/12/18/business/international/china-drone-export-iraq.html.

41 PopSci, 'Did An Armed Chinese-Made Drone Just Crash in Nigeria?', 28 January 2015, https://www.popsci.com/did-armed-chinese-made-drone-just-crash-nigeria/.

42 Garrett Reim, 'Jordan military tries to sell off 'knock-off' Chinese drones', FlightGlobal, 4 June 2019, https://www.flightglobal.com/helicopters/jordan-military-tries-to-sell-off-knock-off-chinese-drones/132985.article.

43 Sebastien Roblin, 'Chinese Drones Are Going to War All Over the Middle East and Africa', *National Interest*, 29 September 2019, https://nationalinterest.org/blog/buzz/chinese-drones-are-going-war-all-over-middle-east-and-africa-74246.

RUSSIA

Source: IISS

CHAPTER 5

Map 5.1: **Selected* combat-aircraft sales to the Middle East, North Africa and Asia from Russia**

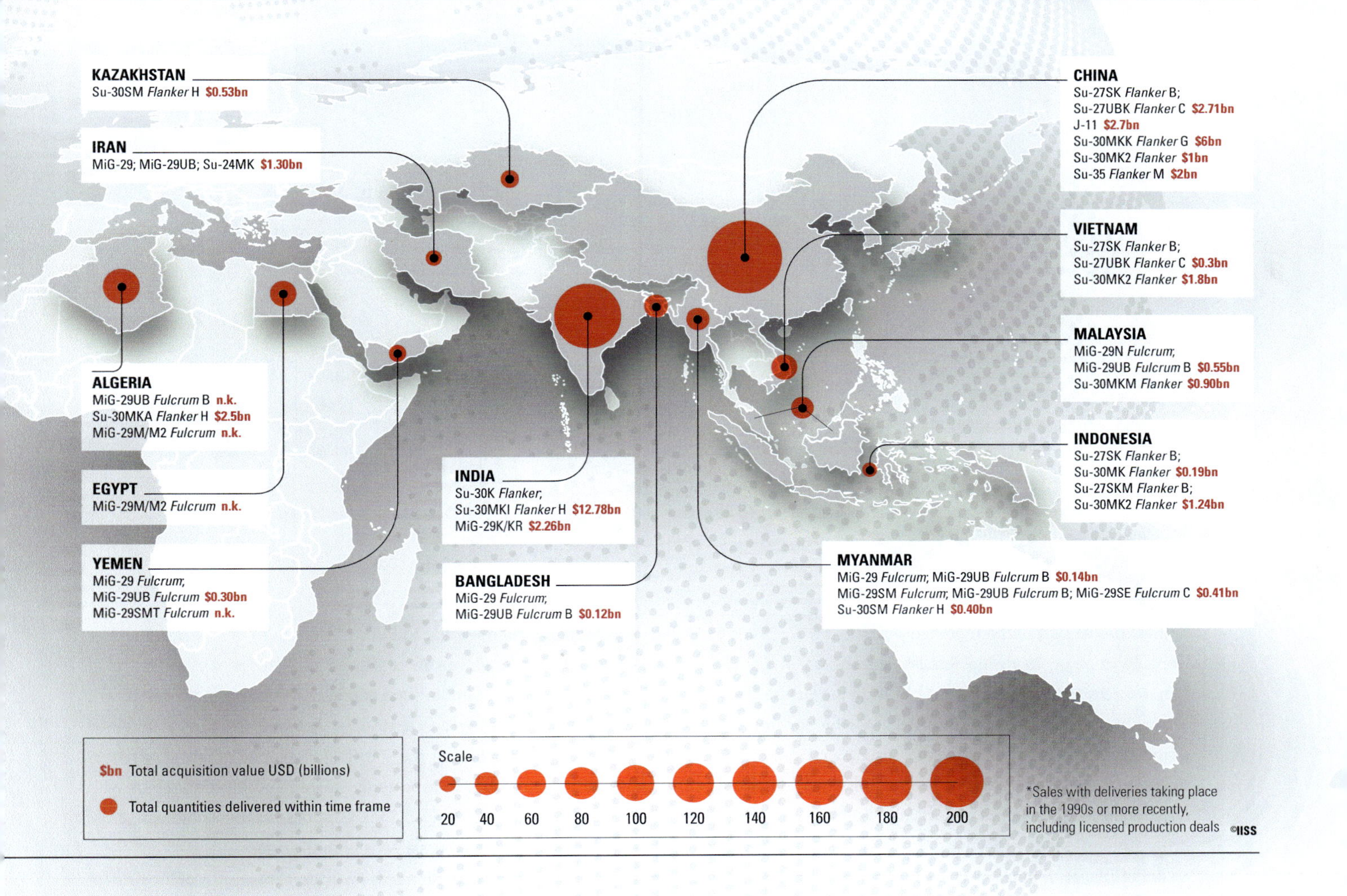

Russia is currently the world's second-largest conventional-armaments exporter, accounting for one-quarter of all global arms exports between 2000 and 2020.[1] Only the United States is more competitive across a similarly wide range of major weapons systems.[2] Russia's strength as an arms exporter stems from its broad production base, a heritage from the militarised Soviet state. Russian weapons have had a reputation of being easy to use, reliable and relatively cheap, making them popular with middle-income countries. However, it remains to be seen how far the Russian armed forces' failure to quickly overcome Ukraine, and the apparent poor performance of much of its main combat equipment, will dissuade prospective buyers. The main market for Russian arms is Asia, but in recent years Russian officials have worked hard to increase arms sales to growing markets in the Middle East and North Africa (MENA), with some success.

The strategic and economic importance of arms exports for Russia

Arms exports are both strategically and economically important to Russia. Since Russia is unlikely to be allowed, or financially able, to buy all the military equipment it desires abroad, maintaining domestic production capabilities is perceived as essential. Anatoly Serdyukov, the Russian defence minister from 2007–12, had introduced the notion of importing some military systems as part of wider reforms, with the planned purchase from France of two *Mistral*-class amphibious assault ships and the licence build of two more being the

INTERNATIONAL MILITARY TECHNICAL FORUM ARMY-2020 IN RUSSIA
A *Buk*-M3 (RS-SA-27) surface-to-air missile systems on display at the International Military Technical Forum 'Army-2020' at the Patriot Park in Kubinka, 23 August 2020.
CREDIT: Mikhail Svetlov/Getty Images.

highest-profile part of the modified policy.[3] However, Paris cancelled the sale in 2015, following Russia's annexation of Crimea and its armed forces' involvement in the fighting in the Donbas region.

By supporting defence-industrial production in areas where domestic demand is insufficient, arms exports allow Russia to maintain a wider spectrum of production lines that would otherwise be impossible.[4] Arms exports also help Russia achieve various other foreign-policy objectives, including supporting its image as a global player, maintaining an independent foreign policy, and exerting and expanding its regional influence.[5] Multiple production sites for military aircraft continue to be supported, for example, in part because they provide direct and indirect employment for whole Russian communities.[6]

When export data is compared to information on national acquisitions, it becomes clear that exports are a significant source of revenue for Russian defence manufacturers. Production for foreign markets may have accounted for up to one-third of all arms production within Russian defence industries between 2011 and 2020. The export share has increased since 2017 due to lower national investment levels and a decrease in the value of the rouble. As the modernisation of Russia's armed forces slows following a cut in defence expenditures after 2016, export revenues are likely to become even more important for the maintenance and further development of Russia's military-industrial complex in the coming years. Sustaining and building on its client base, however, could become challenging due to Putin's decision to invade Ukraine. The sale of major weapons can be viewed as an element of the return of 'great-power competition'. India, one of Moscow's main customers, will almost certainly be courted further by the US as a potential 'swing state' in at least some of its major-weapons acquisitions. New Delhi has already also reportedly slowed some programmes with Moscow, including a long-planned upgrade of the Sukhoi Su-30MKI *Flanker* H, because of Russia's war with Ukraine.[7]

Although export revenue is an important source of income for many Russian defence companies, arms sales are of limited significance to state finances. The Russian economy continues to depend heavily on revenues from the hydrocarbon sector. Arms exports only account for 4% of Russia's total exports,[8] while hydrocarbons make up a 50% share of all exports.[9] However, arms are Russia's fourth-most exported commodity and its most exported manufactured good.

Like other arms-exporting countries, Russia's arms-export policy towards a country, including the commercial terms, depends on their foreign-policy relations. Poorer members of the Collective Security Treaty Organization, a defence alliance in Eurasia, occasionally receive older Russian systems free of charge or for relatively low prices.[10] Over the last decade, Russia has also increasingly offered to finance purchases by interested customers with loans on so-called 'ideological terms'. The practice serves both economic and political purposes: Russia builds foreign-policy ties and alliances through offering military

RUSSIAN AIR FORCE AND THE CONFLICT IN SYRIA
A Russian Air Force Su-35S *Flanker* M is prepared for flight at the Russian military base of Hmeimim, located south-east of the city of Latakia in Hmeimim, Latakia Governorate, Syria, 26 September 2019. CREDIT: MAXIME POPOV/AFP via Getty Images.

equipment to countries that may not otherwise be able to afford it. At the same time, government-secured export contracts help financially support the Russian military–defence industry.[11]

Russia's presence

Although Russia has military-industrial agreements with many countries all over the world, the Russian arms industry relies mainly on relations with a few key export partners. Between 2010 and 2020, eight countries accounted for 80% of all Russian arms transfers compared to 17 countries for the US.[12] Nevertheless, Russia's customer base has become more diverse since the early 2000s, when almost all Russian arms exports went to India and China. Although Asia remains the most important market for Russian weaponry, the MENA region has grown in importance over the last 15 years.

Russia's main partners in Asia are China, India and Vietnam. Between 2010 and 2020, 53% of all Russian arms transfers went to one of these three countries.[13] China has historically been particularly interested in Russian aircraft. China began to take delivery of the Sukhoi Su-27SK *Flanker* B in 1992, with the locally assembled version known as the Shenyang J-11. As of mid-2022, the People's Liberation Army Air Force (PLAAF) had over 500 *Flanker* derivatives in its inventory,[14] most of which were built locally. In December 2016, the PLAAF took delivery from Russia of the first of 24 Su-35 *Flanker* M multi-role combat aircraft.[15] *Flanker* M aircraft began to be handed over to the Russian Air Force in February 2014, with the type now the service's most capable combat aircraft pending the eventual arrival of the Su-57 *Felon*. In the early 2000s, China was the main customer for Russian arms in the region, contributing to 56% of Russia's arms-export revenues.[16] Since 2011, however, India has become the main importer of Russian armaments. Vietnam has recently become an important market for Russian arms exports, accounting for 10% of all Russian arms-exports revenues between 2015 and 2020.[17] After nearly abandoning the import of Russian weapons between 2011 and 2015, China has returned as an important customer, accounting for 16% of Russian arms-export revenues between 2015 and 2020. Several other Asian countries, including Mongolia, Myanmar and Turkmenistan, also mainly buy armaments from Russia, but their share of the total of Russian arms exports is small. Potential future markets in Asia for the Russian defence industry include Bangladesh, Indonesia, the Philippines and Sri Lanka.[18]

The Kremlin has worked systematically to increase Russian arms trade to the MENA region since the early 2000s, and from 2005 those efforts started to pay off. Russia's strengthened presence in the region is mainly a result of sales to Algeria and Egypt. Other important markets for Russia in the region are Iraq and Syria, which along with Iran accounted for 25% of all Russian arms exports to the region between 2000 and 2020.[19] Prior to 2011, Russia also had a close relationship with Libya. According to the Federal Service of Military and Technical Cooperation (FSMTC), the fall of Muammar Gadhafi cost

Figure 5.1: **Russia: annual value of defence exports, 1994–2020**

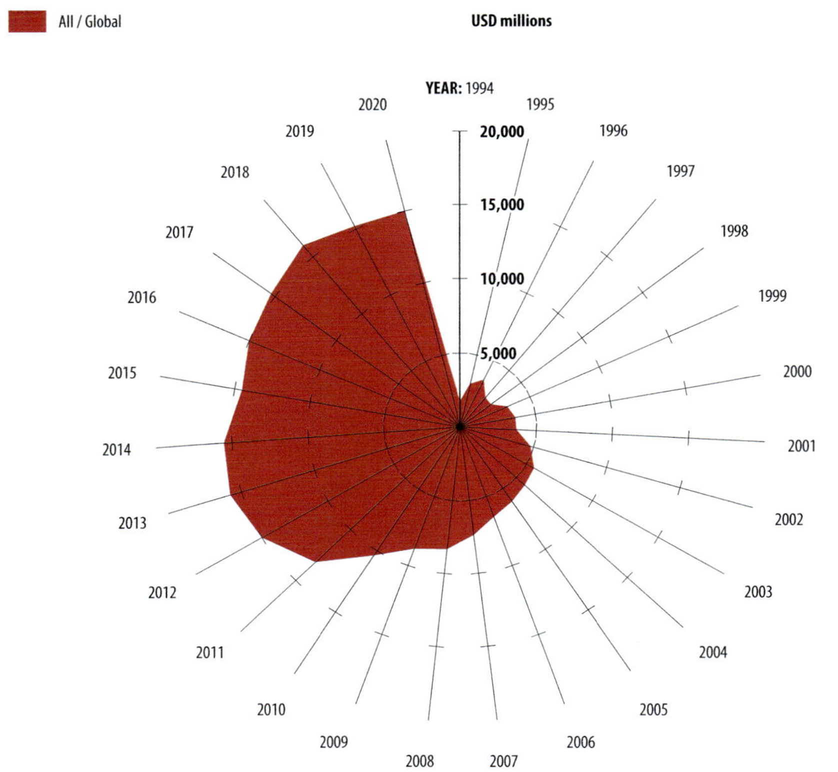

Source: FSMTC of Russia

Russia at least USD4 billion in lost arms sales.[20] In recent years Russia has aspired regionally to break into markets in Saudi Arabia and the United Arab Emirates (UAE).[21]

With the lifting of the United Nations' 13-year conventional-arms embargo on Iran in 2020, Tehran is once again able to import major weapons. To begin replacing its aged inventory, Iran will likely look to import from Russia and China. Combat aircraft are likely to be a priority for Tehran. As of September 2022, speculation continued that Iran could receive 24 Su-35s originally built for Egypt.[22] The latter country has reportedly cancelled its order for the aircraft, with suggestions that the United States' Countering America's Adversaries Through Sanctions Act (CAATSA) may have influenced Cairo's decision-making. In March 2022, meanwhile, the US indicated it was willing to release the Boeing F-15 to Egypt.[23]

So far, Russia has refrained from selling its most advanced equipment to Iran. According to one report, Russia and Israel reached a tacit deal in 2019 in which Russia refrained from deepening military ties with Iran on the condition that Israel would not sell uninhabited aerial vehicles (UAVs) to Ukraine.[24] However, how quickly Tehran begins replacing its current inventory will depend on its capacity to fund such acquisitions. The Su-35 deal is estimated to be worth USD3bn.[25] Even if a deal like this would not put Iran in the top four list of Russia's most important arms-trade partners in the next few years, it would certainly place them among the top eight.

Moscow's approach to arms sales

Since 2014, Russia's trade policy has focused on diversification of foreign trade relations in order to become less dependent upon the West.[26] Strengthening trade relations with other regional powers, in this case the other so-called BRICS countries (Brazil, India, China and South Africa), and Russia's 'pivot to Asia' are key elements of this strategy.[27] Arms exports are important in this respect, as it is one of the few sectors where Russia holds a dominant position in non-European markets. Military technologies are also among the few commodities possessed by Russia that China retains an interest in accessing, although the list is shrinking.

Russia's arms exports to China are not without ambivalence. While officially seeking cooperation and partnership, Russia and China have potentially conflicting interests that could lead to military confrontation. China's rise as a stronger rival to Russia in the global arms industry represents a more immediate challenge.

Timeline 5.1: **Selected* combat-aircraft sales to the Middle East and North Africa from Russia**

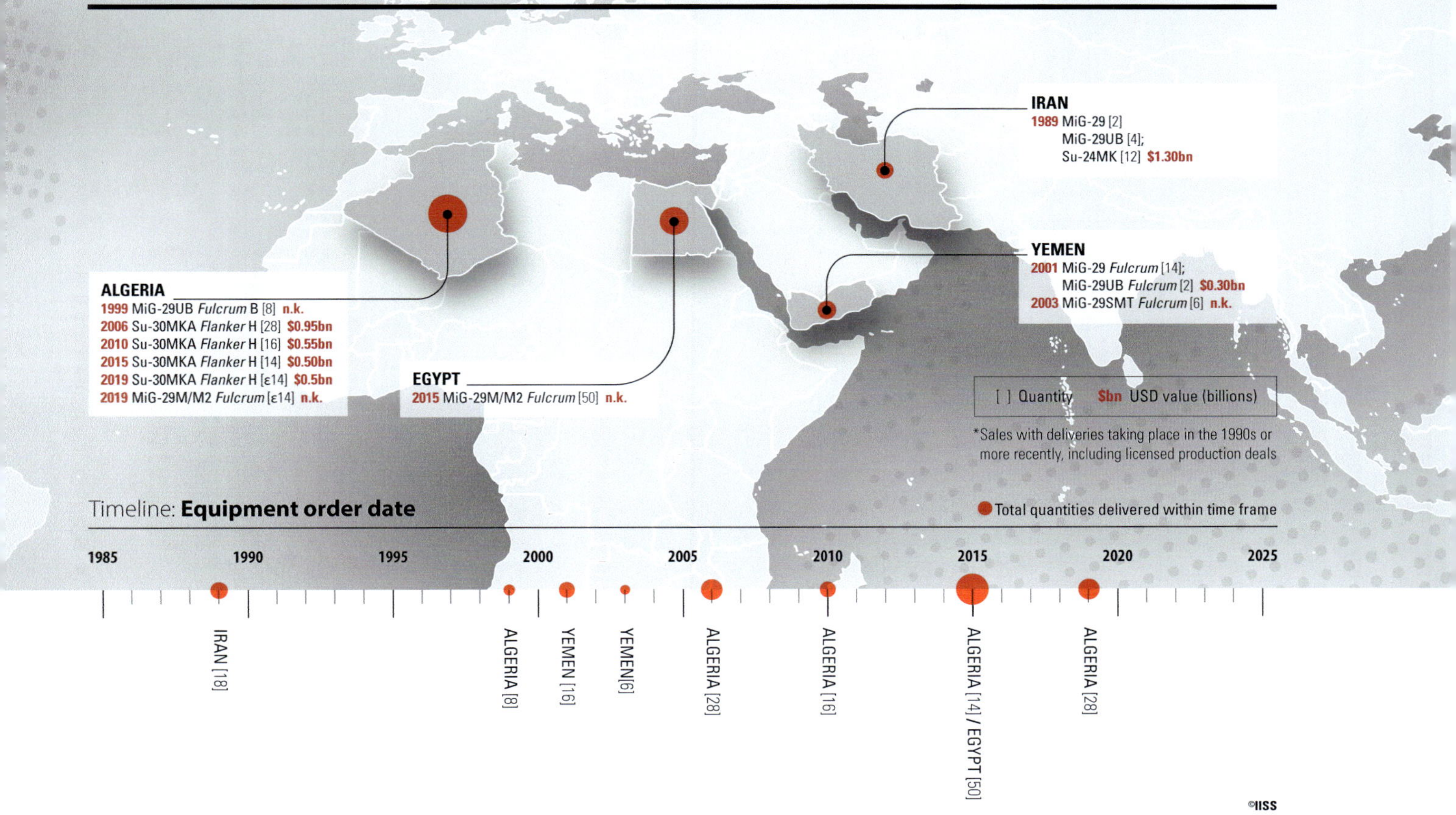

Source: IISS

In the past, China has breached intellectual-property laws and copied Russian equipment such as combat aircraft. For example, the Shenyang J-15 is an unlicensed version of the Russian Su-33 *Flanker* D carrier-borne combat aircraft.[28] While developing military cooperation with and selling arms to China, Russia has also strived to develop strong military-technological relations with other countries in China's vicinity, most importantly India and Vietnam, in an effort to balance the power in the region and maintain its own strategic flexibility.[29] Likewise, Russia's arms-export policy to the MENA reflects its desire to limit US and increasingly Chinese influence in the region while at the same time trying to balance the regional power dynamics.

In Asia, Russia has generally avoided any challenge to China's claim to influence in the region and upholds a policy of non-interference in the South China Sea.[30] In the MENA region Russia has used arms exports more actively, usually as part of larger military-cooperation agreements, to influence the political situation and secure continued access to naval facilities. Key examples of this include airspace and air bases in Syria and the signing of a preliminary deal with Egypt in 2017, thereby strengthening its presence around the Mediterranean Sea.[31]

Traditionally, Russia has been reluctant to export its latest and most advanced armaments.[32] For instance, the version of the *Kilo*-class conventional submarines sold to Algeria, China and Vietnam has a shorter range and higher acoustic signature than the more advanced Project 06363, of which Russia is the sole operator.[33] Russia is in general also hesitant to sell or transfer the technology of its more advanced offensive systems, preferring to export 'defensive' weapons such as the S-300 (RS-SA-20 *Gargoyle*) and S-400 (RS-SA-21 *Growler*) long-range surface-to-air missile systems.[34] While Moscow has exported a variety of land-attack and anti-ship cruise missiles, the ranges of such systems have been reduced to remain broadly compatible with the Missile Technology Control Regime. During the Soviet era, India relied on Russian combat aircraft for much of its airpower, with several types licence built in-country in the 1970s and 1980s. This was not the case with China. Since the collapse of the Soviet Union, Moscow has tried to ensure that New Delhi and Beijing, despite the regional rivalry between them, both continue to buy from Russia. During the 1990s, India appeared to continue to get better access to Russian systems, even if China was the first to acquire a member of the Su-27 *Flanker* family. India and Russia agreed in 1996 that the latter would develop the Su-30MKI *Flanker* H, with deliveries

Timeline 5.2: **Selected* combat-aircraft sales to Asia from Russia**

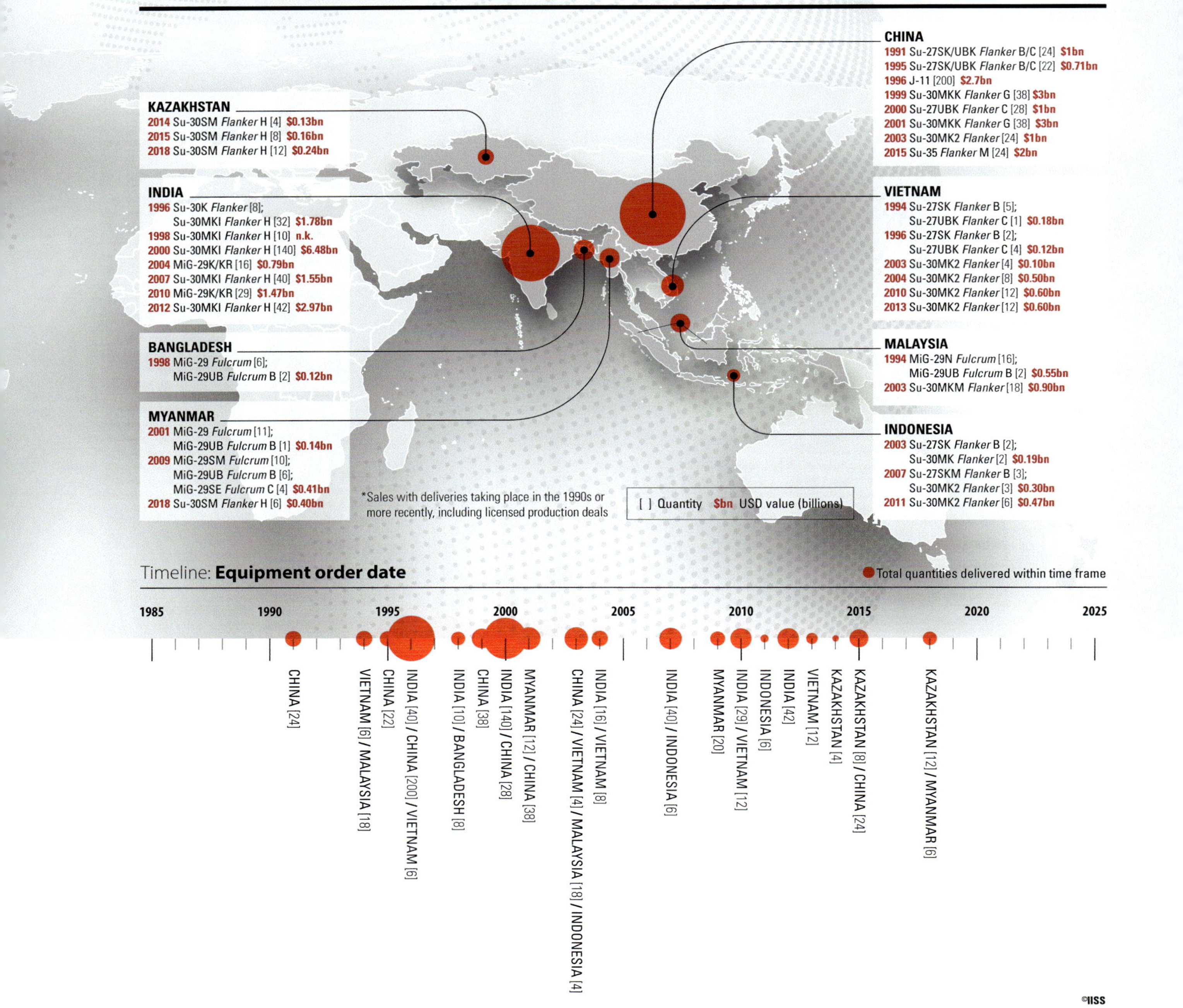

Source: IISS

to the Indian Air Force beginning in 2002. The two-seat Su-30MKI was for some time viewed as the most advanced variant of the *Flanker* family.[35] Moscow also spent years courting New Delhi as a 'development' partner in its fifth-generation fighter programme, now known as the Su-57. A preliminary agreement was struck in 2003,[36] but the project was eventually shelved in 2018.

While the prospect for Indian participation waned, and the US continued to make inroads into New Delhi's defence market, Russia was taking a more liberal approach to its arms sales to China. At the end of 2015, the two agreed the sale of the Su-35, with China the first export customer for the advanced development of the original Su-27.

Since 2015, technology transfers between Russia and China have expanded into new areas and now include cooperation in the development of weapons for land, air and naval use, a joint early-warning-system project as well as collaboration on artificial intelligence and space technology.[37] In return, Russia likely hoped to gain access to Chinese technology, including microelectronic components. In 2019 Russia and China also announced cooperation on a new Chinese missile-launch detection system.[38]

Russia's mercenary exports

Russia has a long history of using mercenaries, dating back centuries, as do other powers with global interests. What is notable, however, is the extent to which Moscow has turned to private military companies (PMCs) in recent years as a lever of foreign policy and a complement to arms sales. Over the course of the previous decade, the Russian government has increasingly sanctioned PMC operations. In 2022, Russian PMCs were operating in at least 27 countries, including in Africa, Asia, the Middle East and South America.[39] Nearly 10,000 PMC personnel have been used in Russia's war on Ukraine, according to some estimates, with substantial casualties.

The most widely known is the Wagner Group, which has experienced a rapid expansion over the last decade.[40] Unlike 'conventional' Russian PMCs, it has no defined commercial status or legal existence; it is not officially tied to any company or state. Its men are thus identified as mercenaries, mainly fighting for remuneration. Yet the organisation is state-sponsored, allowing Wagner's troops to be deployed in at least nine countries, including the Central African Republic (CAR), Libya, Syria and Ukraine. The extent to which the use of Wagner in Ukraine has forced the group to draw down on other deployments is unclear, but given the potential number fielded in the war on Ukraine, there will almost certainly have been an impact.

The resurgence of state-sponsored mercenaries

Officially, PMCs do not have direct relations with the Kremlin. Yet for some, 'even if Russia denies it, the legibility is so strong that it does not fool anyone'.[41] Their growing presence abroad is generally believed to be supported by President Vladimir Putin. He noted in April 2012 that 'a corporation of private military companies would be an effective tool for achieving national objectives without calling on the direct participation of the Russian state'.[42] Ten years on, Putin is using them as proxies as he seeks to gain geopolitical and economic influence for the Russian state.

Supporting paramilitary groups has several advantages for Russia: they cost less than regular soldiers and their operations are more discreet, meaning they do not directly implicate the Russian state. Besides, the use of PMCs benefits many parties: it is profitable for the operating company as well as its personnel. Indeed, PMC salaries are attractive to both the Russian population and former officers. Created in 2014 by a former Russian officer, Lt. Col. Dmitry Utkin, the Wagner Group is led and financed by the Russian oligarch Yevgeny Prigozhin, a businessman and restaurateur with close ties to Putin. With currently around 10,000 personnel, Wagner has become the largest Russian PMC and an unofficial sword arm of the Kremlin. Its agility allows its troops to be deployed on a near-global basis to conduct a variety of operations, including infiltration, protection and execution. Over the last eight years, Wagner has multiplied and diversified its activities and widened its presence. This is notable in Africa, where it now operates from the CAR to Mali, conducting missions that include training local forces, protecting Russian companies' interests, and alleged disinformation and electoral-interference campaigns.[43] The group also uses propaganda to legitimise Putin's moves in the continent. Wagner provides the Russian state with the capacity to use military force in the pursuit of its foreign-policy goals while providing at least a gloss of 'plausible deniability'.[44]

In 2014, Wagner's men were seen fighting in eastern Ukraine. They appeared in large numbers alongside separatists in the Luhansk region. A year later, the company is estimated[45] to have sent at least 2,500 men to Syria to support Bashar al-Assad's regime, where the group operated for almost three years, until the failed assault, in February 2018, against the Conoco oil- and gas-field installations in the Deir ez-Zor region held by American forces. In January 2019, during the presidential crisis, agents from the Wagner Group were also sent to Venezuela to reinforce the security of President Nicolás Maduro.[46] At the same time, they had already started to extend their activities in Africa, where Putin had been seeking to build political ties since the mid-2010s[47] by breaking into the African arms-sales market and operating PMCs and mercenaries.

While not officially recognised, both their structures and missions indicate PMC groups are maintaining direct or indirect relations with the Russian Ministry of Defence, especially the military intelligence service (GRU). The link between Moscow and Wagner was made public with a picture showing Putin and Wagner's commanders – including Utkin – at an official reception at the Kremlin held on 9 December 2016.[48] The relationship between Wagner and the GRU and Foreign Intelligence Service (SVR) is evidenced by the location of several Wagner Group bases in Russia.[49] It is also assumed that the organisation receives indirect funds through contracts signed between the government and some of Prigozhin's companies.[50]

In January 2020, after the Wagner Group was accused of being involved in multiple and repeated breaches of the UN arms embargo on Libya, Putin declared that any Russian nationals in Libya did not represent Moscow, nor were they paid by the state. A few months before this, he also said that 'these men do not participate in combat actions'.[51] This runs contrary to testimonies, evidence and investigations that have highlighted not only the presence of Wagner's men in Africa but also the Kremlin's support for their actions in Libya supporting General Khalifa Haftar's troops. The Russian Ministry of Defence provided indirect funds and military support, including equipment.[52]

PROTESTS IN MALI
Malians protest ECOWAS-imposed sanctions over delayed elections, January 2022. CREDIT: Florent Vergnes/AFP via Getty Images.

The African arms market and PMCs

Russia's arms-sales strategy for the African market has begun to reap modest rewards: the number of African countries buying Russian arms has increased over the last two decades. In the early 2000s, 16 African countries were recipients of Russian arms. Between 2010 and 2019, the figure went up to 21.[53] Rosoboronexport – Russia's state arms-export agency – has become the largest arms exporter to Africa, accounting for 49% of total exports to the continent in 2020.[54] In 2021, the company signed contracts worth USD1.7bn with sub-Saharan African states to sell helicopters, air-defence systems, naval products, armoured vehicles, equipment for law-enforcement agencies, airports, critical-infrastructure security equipment and small arms (including special weapons) in the region.[55]

Moscow has benefited from growing anti-Western sentiment in sub-Saharan Africa. Russia's arms-sales doctrine offers competitive advantages for local governments, its materiel is less expensive, and the country has fewer normative requirements than many Western democracies have. African governments thus welcome Russia as an appropriate partner that offers mutually beneficial agreements and is less likely to interfere in local affairs – at least officially. Russia's arms-sales activity is complemented on the continent by its PMCs.

Officially, PMCs mainly conduct regular activities such as providing site security and training foreign forces. Their reach, however, arguably goes far beyond these activities, with the goal of furthering Moscow's regional geopolitical interests.

The CAR is a notable example of this. Wagner has had an established presence in the country since 2017 and has taken advantage of the state's political, social and economic weaknesses. Initially deployed for security operations to back President Faustin-Archange Touadéra against local rebels, the PMC now has considerable political influence. Wagner has allegedly engaged in

> mass summary executions, arbitrary detentions, torture during interrogations, forced disappearances, forced displacement of the civilian population, indiscriminate targeting of civilian facilities, violations of the right to health, and increasing attacks on humanitarian actors.[56]

The Russian state, meanwhile, gains preferential access to valuable natural resources.[57] More recently, Russia has benefited from local Francophobe feeling and the withdrawal of French troops from Mali. Between 2017 and 2021, it became the largest arms supplier to the country. In October 2021, Mali's Minister of Defence and Veterans Affairs Colonel Sadio Camara announced the receipt of four Mi-171 *Hips*.[58] The next month, the construction of a new military camp to the south of base 101 of the Malian Armed Forces – next to the airstrips of Bamako airport – was identified by French surveillance satellites. Alongside enlisted Russian soldiers and officers, around a thousand mercenaries would operate in the country from those headquarters to 'protect the junta' in power in Bamako.[59] Similar to the situations in the CAR and Libya, they have been supplied by the Russian Air Force using aircraft such as the Tupolev TU-154M *Careless*.[60]

Moscow's recent use of PMCs has proven valuable. In Ukraine, PMCs have been used to supplement regular forces, with the former personnel perhaps also offering more regular and recent combat experience. Though high-profile, the concerns over arms-embargo violations and human-rights abuses means their worth should not be overstated: 'PMCs represent only one tool in a broad tool kit that Moscow utilizes … and by no means the most important.'[61]

THE *PANTSIR*-S1 (RS-SA-22)
A *Pantsir*-S1 (RS-SA-22) on display at the 2016 International Military-Technical Forum in Moscow. CREDIT: Leonid Faerberg/SOPA Images/LightRocket via Getty Images.

Russia's arms-export challenges

Russian arms exports face multiple challenges. China's and India's growing defence industries and India's and Vietnam's efforts to diversify their arms imports are reducing demand for Russian armaments in its main Asia markets. After 14 years of growth (1999–2013), Russia's budget revenues from arms exports stagnated in 2014. The financial value of Russia's arms-export portfolio peaked at USD15.7bn in 2013 and has since settled at around USD15bn annually.[62]

Russia is facing increased competition from China. In addition, the US threat to impose sanctions on third parties trading arms with Russia under CAATSA is likely pushing away some of Russia's potential customers. As well as Egypt, Indonesia and Algeria have reportedly withdrawn their plans to buy the Su-35.[63]

Despite all the money invested in military-technological development in the last decade, Russia's arms exports still mainly depend on equipment developed in the Soviet era.[64] Mapping each armament deal with the respective weapons system's development period reveals that the weighted average age of exported technology has remained relatively constant, increasing only slightly over the past ten years. The most frequently exported systems include Sukhoi and MiG combat aircraft, Yakovlev Yak-130 *Mitten* advanced jet trainers, Mil and Kamov helicopters, T-72 and T-90 tanks, BTR armoured vehicles, and Tor (RS-SA-15 *Gauntlet*), 96K6 *Pantsir* (RS-SA-22 *Greyhound*) and S-300 (RS-SA-20 *Gargoyle*) air-defence systems. China, on average, buys more newly developed technology than the other major Russian arms importers (Algeria and India). In recent years, Vietnam has also imported more modern technology. This is mainly due to imports of the improved *Kilo*-class submarines and the *Tarantul* fast patrol craft.

This is not surprising considering Russia failed to put into serial production many of the new-generation weapons systems that it initially planned to before 2020, such as the Su-57 *Felon* combat aircraft or the T-14 *Armata* main battle tank.[65] The Russian defence industry is also playing catch-up with the US and China in the development of so-called Fourth Industrial Revolution technologies such as artificial intelligence (AI), automated decision-making, autonomous and AI-enabled uninhabited systems, and intelligent robotics.[66]

Conclusion

How Russia will fare on the arms-export market in the wake of its invasion of Ukraine will only become clear over time. The performance of some of Russia's major weapons systems used in the invasion has been patchy, and there is a risk of reputational damage among potential customers. Furthermore, the extent of the effect of the wide-ranging embargo on Russia on the country's defence-industrial base has yet to become clear. Moscow is unlikely to be able to access European subsystems for inclusion in export products for some time. Additionally, the domestic defence industry may in the comparatively near term have to replenish weapons stocks and replace platforms, most notably land systems, destroyed in the war.

Putin, however, has positioned himself as an opponent of what he refers to as moral interventionism by Western leaders. According to Moscow, it should be up to each government to decide how they rule their country and people.[67] Russia's willingness to turn a blind eye to its customers' human-rights records is illustrated by the country's military support of the Assad government in Syria.

Russian armaments will remain a choice for countries prohibited from buying armaments from the US or the main European producers. Moscow, however, could find that it faces growing competition from China amongst at least some of this market. Increasingly, China is no longer hampered by the limitations of the defence technology it is able to offer. In a number of areas, not least of all in the defence-aerospace realm, Beijing's offerings are at least on a par with those of Moscow.

NOTES

1 'SIPRI Arms Transfers Database', https://www.sipri.org/databases/armstransfers. SIPRI uses *trend-indicator values (TIV)*, which does not reflect the financial values of the deals, but is rather an indicator of transfer of military resources. TIV should not be compared with, for example, defence expenditures.

2 Richard Connolly and Cecilie Sendstad, 'Russia's Role as an Arms Exporter: The Strategic and Economic Importance of Arms Exports for Russia', Chatham House, 2017, https://www.chathamhouse.org/2017/03/russias-role-arms-exporter.

3 Douglas Barrie and James Hackett, 'Russia's Military Modernisation: An Assessment', The International Institute for Strategic Studies, September 2020, p. 27.

4 *Ibid.*, pp. 3–4.

5 Stephen Blank and Edward Levitzky, 'Geostrategic aims of the Russian arms trade in East Asia and the Middle East', *Defence Studies,* vol. 15, no. 1, 2015.

6 Una Hakvåg, 'Russian defense spending after 2010: the interplay of personal, domestic, and foreign policy interests', Post-Soviet Affairs, vol. 33, no. 6, 2017.

7 'Amid Ukraine-Russia war, IAF's Rs 35,000 crore plan to upgrade Su-30 fighter fleet put on back burner', *Times of India*, 8 May 2022, https://timesofindia.indiatimes.com/india/amid-ukraine-russia-war-iafs-rs-35000-crore-plan-to-upgrade-su-30-fighter-fleet-put-on-backburner/articleshow/91417758.cms.

8 World Bank, 'World Development Indicators', https://databank.worldbank.org/source/world-development-indicators.

9 Central Bank of Russia, 'Balance of Payments of the Russian Federation (Analytical Presentation)'. https://www.cbr.ru/eng/statistics/macro_itm/svs/.

10 Julian Cooper, 'Russian Arms Exports,' in Laurence Lustgarten (ed.), *Law and Arms Trade* (Oxford: Hart, 2020), p. 309.

11 Said Aminov, 'Oruzhie v kredit: finansirovanie voenno-tekhnicheskogo sotrudnichestva Rossii c inostrannymi gosudarstvami' [Arms on credit: funding of Russia's military-technological cooperation with foreign states], *Eksport Vooruchenii*, no. 6, 2021, p. 20.

12 Based upon SIPRI-data, which uses *trend indicator values*.

13 SIPRI Arms Transfers Database.

14 IISS, *The Military Balance* (Abingdon: Routledge, 2022), p. 261.

15 Mike Yeo, 'China receives first advanced Su-35 Flankers from Russia', DefenseNews, 9 January 2017, https://www.defensenews.com/air/2017/01/09/china-receives-first-advanced-su-35-flankers-from-russia/.

16 Data from IISS Military Balance+, accessed June 2022. Percentage is based on share of total value disclosed in the IISS-dataset, which is less than half the size of the financial arms export values from FSMTC. The discrepancy of total value can be explained by the fact that the IISS-dataset only covers major deals, while FSMTC-data include transfers of a broader set of military-related goods and services, such as building of military installations, training of personnel, establishment of service centers and military aid (Cooper, Julian. 'Russian Arms Exports,' p. 305).

17 Military Balance+, accessed June 2022.

18 Mikhail Khodarenok, 'Ne to prodaem: pochemu buksuet rossiiskaia oboronka [We sell something else: Why the Russian defence industry is stalling]', *Gazeta.ru*, 3 November 2019, https://www.gazeta.ru/army/2019/11/03/12793520.shtml?updated.

19 SIPRI Arms Transfers Database.

20 'Gaddafi fall cost Russia tens of blns in arms deals', *Reuters*, 2 November 2011, https://www.reuters.com/article/russia-libya-arms-idUSL5E7M221H20111102.

21 Khodarenok, 'Ne to prodaem'.

22 'Is Iran leveraging Ukraine war to access advanced Russian arms?' Amwaj media, 8 September 2022, https://amwaj.media/media-monitor/is-iran-eyeing-closer-military-ties-with-russia.

23 See US House Armed Services Committee, 'Hearing to Receive Testimony on the Posture of United States Central Command and United States Africa Command', 15 March 2022, p. 53, https://www.armed-services.senate.gov/imo/media/doc/22-12_03-15-2022.pdf.

24 Nikola Mikovic, 'Russia keeps Iran waiting on advanced weapons', *Asia Times*, 10 January 2022, https://asiatimes.com/2022/01/russia-keeps-iran-waiting-on-advanced-weapons/.

25 Valius Venckunas, 'Reports suggest that Iran could pick up Egypt's rejected SU-35s', Aerotime, 5 January 2022, https://www.aerotime.aero/29867-iran-could-pick-up-egypts-rejected-su-35s.

26 Alexandra G. Koval and Sergei F. Sutyrin, 'Transformation of the Russian trade policy facing the geopolitical challenges', in Sergei F. Sutyrin, Olga Y. Trofimenko and Alexandra G. Koval (eds.), *Russian Trade Policy: Achievements, Challenges and Prospects*, (Abingdon: Routledge, 2020).

27 *Ibid.*, p. 35.

28 John Watts, Sofia Ledberg and Kjell Engelbrekt, 'Brothers in arms, yet again? Twenty-first century Sino-Russian strategic collaboration in the realm of defence and security', *Defence Studies*, vol. 16, no. 4, p. 434, 2016.

29 Blank and Levitzky, 'Geostrategic aims of the Russian arms trade', p. 75.

30 Sergey Lunev and Ellina Shavlay, 'Russia and India in the Indo-Pacific', *Asian Politics & Policy,* vol. 10, no. 4, 2018, 726–7.

31 Alexandra Kulimova, 'Russia's Arms Exports to the MENA Region: Trends and Drivers',

Euromesco, 2019, https://www.iemed.org/publication/russias-arms-exports-to-the-mena-region-trends-and-drivers/.

32 Cooper, 'Russian Arms Exports', p. 300.

33 Caleb Larson, 'Why Russia Just Can't Get Enough Kilo-Class Submarines', *National Interest*, 12 January 2021, https://nationalinterest.org/blog/reboot/why-russia-just-can%E2%80%99t-get-enough-kilo-class-submarines-176258.

34 Paul N. Schwartz, 'The Changing Nature and Implications of Russian Military Transfers to China', CSIS report, 21 June 2021, https://www.csis.org/analysis/changing-nature-and-implications-russian-military-transfers-china.

35 Piotr Butowski, 'Russia's Warplanes Voume 1,' Harpia Publishing, 2015, p. 65.

36 *Ibid*., p. 100.

37 Schwartz, 'The Changing Nature'.

38 Vassily Kashin, 'Tacit Alliance: Russia and China Take Military Partnership to New Level', Carnegie Moscow Center, 22 October 2019, https://carnegiemoscow.org/commentary/80136.

39 'Russia's Corporate Soldiers: The Global Expansion of Russia's Private Military Companies', Center for Strategic & International Studies, July 2021, p. 1.

40 Several sanctions have been made against the group and its founder, Evgueni Prigojine. See OpenSanctions, updated on 18 May 2022, https://www.opensanctions.org/entities/Q20850503/.

41 Jean-Yves Le Drian, https://touch.facebook.com/Cdanslairf5/videos/jean-yves-le-drian-documentaire-poutine/284542470339277/?_se_imp=2b6LrbDEyd7QWI5Rs.

42 'Путин поддержал идею создания в России частных военных компаний', [Putin supported the idea of creating private military companies in Russia], *Ria.ru*, 11 April 2012, https://ria.ru/20120411/623227984.html.

43 'Russia's Corporate Soldiers', Center for Strategic & International Studies, July 2021.

44 Emmanuel Dreyfus, 'Sociétés militaires russes. Wagner, combien de divisions ?' [Russian military companies. Wagner, how many divisions?], Orient XXI, 24 April 2020, https://orientxxi.info/magazine/societes-militaires-russes-wagner-combien-de-divisions,3804.

45 'Syria war: Who are Russia's shadowy Wagner mercenaries?', BBC News, 23 February 2018, https://www.bbc.co.uk/news/world-europe-43167697.

46 Andrew Roth, 'Russian mercenaries reportedly in Venezuela to protect Maduro', *Guardian*, 25 January 2019, https://www.theguardian.com/world/2019/jan/25/venezuela-maduro-russia-private-security-contractors.

47 Since 2015, official visits from African heads of states followed one after the other. Between 2018 and 2021, Russia welcomed several multilateral meetings with a focus on Africa, including the St. Petersburg International Economic Forum (SPIEF) 2018, whose guests of honour in 2018 was President of the Central African Republic Faustin-Archange Touadéra; the annual meeting of the African Export-Import Bank (Afreximbank), of which Russia became a shareholder two years before; a Russia-Africa interparliamentary meeting and the first Russia-Africa summit in 2019.

48 Alexandra Jousset and Ksenia Bolchakova, 'Wagner, les hommes de l'ombre de Poutine' [Wagner, Putin's shadow men] Documentary, France 5, 20 February 2022, https://www.france.tv/documentaires/politique/3140025-wagner-l-armee-de-l-ombre-de-poutine.html.

49 András Rácz, 'Band of Brothers: The Wagner Group and the Russian State', CSIS, 21 September 2020, https://www.csis.org/blogs/post-soviet-post/band-brothers-wagner-group-and-russian-state.

50 Jousset and Bolchakova, 'Wagner, les hommes de l'ombre de Poutine'.

51 Vladimir Putin answers to a journalist, Moscow, 20 June 2019 (from Alexandra Jousset, Ksenia Bolchakova, 'Wagner, les hommes de l'ombre de Poutine' [Wagner, Putin's shadow men] Documentary, France 5, 20 February 2022, https://www.france.tv/documentaires/politique/3140025-wagner-l-armee-de-l-ombre-de-poutine.html.

52 Different type of materiel would have been sent by Russia and operated by Wagner's men in Libya, including military armoured vehicles, towed artillery, air defence systems (surface-to-air missiles and UAVs) and supplies. Moreover, in 2020, Russia was reported to have flown fighter aircrafts in the Libyan sky– at least fourteen MiG-29S; Su-24M according to US Africa Command. 'The type and volume of equipment demonstrates an intent toward sustained offensive combat action capabilities, not humanitarian relief, and indicates the Russian Ministry of Defence is supporting these operations', said Marine Corps Maj. Gen. Bradford Gering, former Africom director of operations.

53 Tatiana Kondratenko, 'Russian arms exports to Africa: Moscow's long-term strategy', DW, 29 May 2020, https://www.dw.com/en/russian-arms-exports-to-africa-moscows-long-term-strategy/a-53596471.

54 SIPRI database.

55 Alexander Mikheev, Director General of Rosoboronexport, as quoted by the press service, TASS, June 2021.

56 United Nations, 'CAR: Experts alarmed by government's use of "Russian trainers", close contacts with UN peacekeepers', Press release, 31 March 2021, https://www.

ohchr.org/en/press-releases/2021/03/car-experts-alarmed-governments-use-russian-trainers-close-contacts-un?LangID=E&NewsID=26961.

57 Ghizlane Kounda, 'Avancées russes sur le continent africain: l'UE doit-elle s'en inquiéter?' [Russian progress on the African continent: should the EU be concerned?], 17 February 2022, https://www.rtbf.be/article/avancees-russes-sur-le-continent-africain-lue-doit-elle-sen-inquieter-10935681.

58 Malian Armed Forces, (@FAMa_DIRPA), Tweet, 1 October 2021, https://twitter.com/FAMa_DIRPA/status/1444030466466762752.

59 Jean-Yves Le Drian, https://touch.facebook.com/Cdanslairf5/videos/jean-yves-le-drian-documentaire-poutine/284542470339277/?_se_imp=2b6LrbDEyd7QWI5Rs.

60 Aude Dejaifve, Arthur Bamans and Poline Tchoubar, 'Des vols et des images satellites font craindre un déploiement du groupe Wagner au Mali' [Flights and satellite images raise fears of Wagner Group deployment in Mali], France 24, 4 January 2022, https://observers.france24.com/fr/afrique/20220104-mali-russie-d%C3%A9ploiement-wagner-avions-a%C3%A9roport.

61 'Russia's Corporate Soldiers', Center for Strategic & International Studies, July 2021, p. 12.

62 Federal Service of Military-Technological Cooperation (FSVTS), 'Informatsionnye i analicheskie materialy o deiatelnosti FSTVS Rossii' [Informational and analytical materials on the activities of the FSTVS of Russia], FSVTS, 2 August 2021, https://fsvts.gov.ru/informatsionnyye-i-analiticheskiye-materialy-o-deyatelnosti/1/.

63 Venckunas, 'Reports suggest that Iran could pick up Egypt's rejected SU-35s'.

64 Richard Connolly and Cecilie Sendstad, 'Russian Rearmament: An Assessment of Defense-Industrial Performance', *Problems of Post-Communism*, vol. 65, no. 3.

65 Richard Connolly and Mathieu Boulègue, 'Russia's New State Armament Programme – Implications for the Russian Armed Forces and Military Capabilities to 2027', Chatham House, 2018, https://www.chathamhouse.org/2018/05/russias-new-state-armament-programme.

66 Katarzyna Zysk, 'Defence innovation and the 4th industrial revolution in Russia', *Journal of Strategic Studies*, vol. 44, no. 4, 2021.

67 Bobo Lo, *Russia and the New World Disorder* (Washington DC: Brookings Institution Press, 2015), p. 93.

THE UNITED KINGDOM

Source: IISS

CHAPTER 6

Map 6.1: **Selected* combat-aircraft sales to the Middle East, North Africa and Asia from the UK**

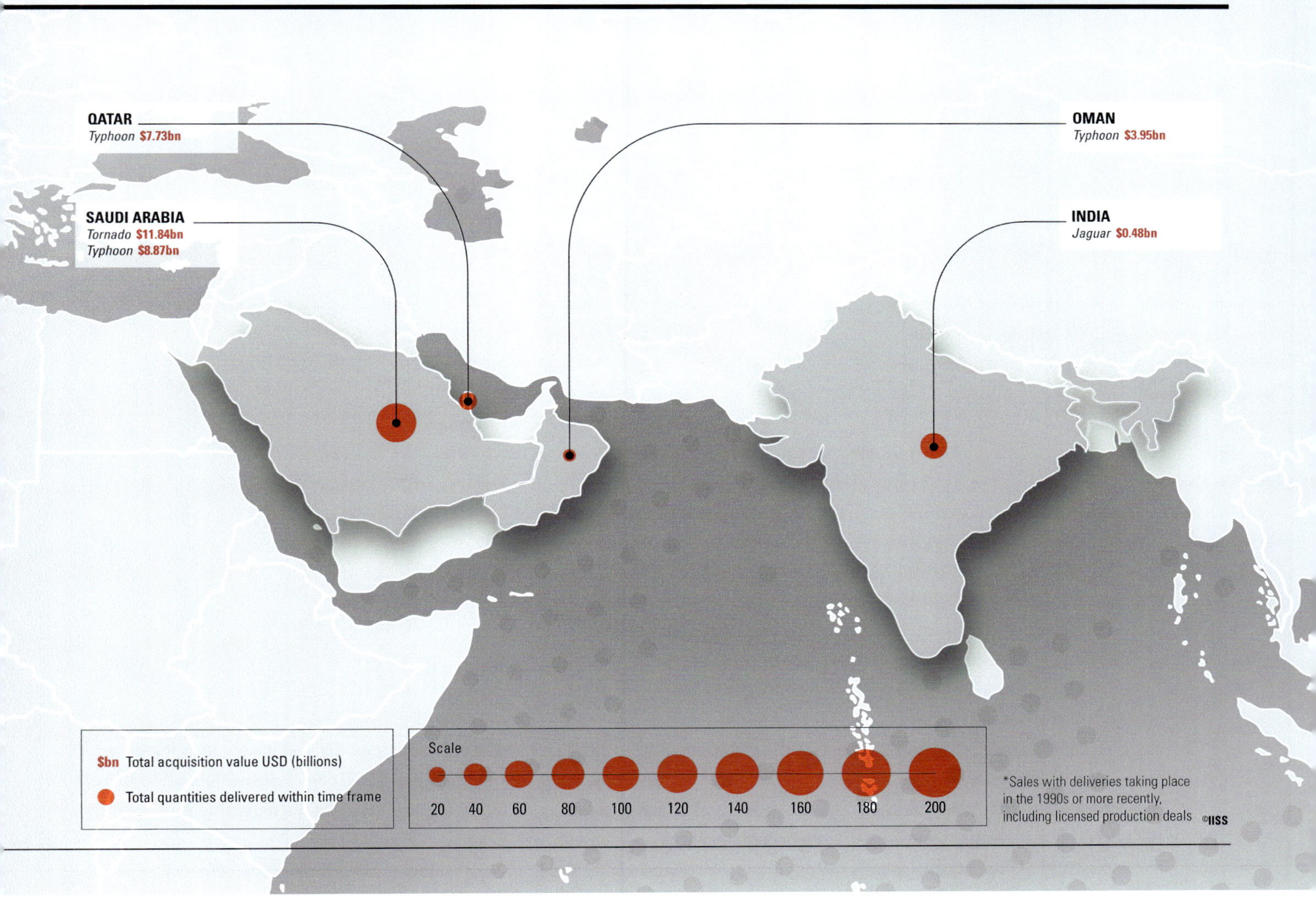

The UK's well-established and wide-ranging, albeit no longer full-spectrum, defence-industrial base has placed the country on a strong footing as a global defence exporter. Industry lobby group ADS estimated that the UK defence sector's turnover reached GBP25.3 billion (USD32.5bn) in 2020 and directly employed 133,000.[1] On a ten-year rolling basis (2011–20), the UK's Defence and Security Exports (DSE) found that the UK is the second-largest defence exporter in the world (after the United States) based on the value of orders and contracts signed.[2] In more recent years, estimates suggest the UK has fallen to a lower position (sixth), but this depends on whether contracts or deliveries are measured.[3]

This fall in global position comes despite a renewed focus on the economic benefits of defence exports during licence deliberations. The factors behind this shift include the defence industry's contribution to the UK economy, the crucial industry revenues from exports to support investment and innovation and the role defence plays in the Conservative government's prosperity and 'levelling up' agenda. The UK's 2021 Defence and Security Industrial Strategy (DSIS) explicitly linked the export of military systems with the wider economic and security aims of 'Global Britain'.[4] According to the strategy, this requires

> a sustainable defence industrial base to ensure that the UK has access to the most sensitive and operationally critical areas of capability for our national security, and that we maximise the economic potential of one of the most successful and innovative sectors of British industry.[5]

Figure 6.1: **Annual value of UK defence exports, 1983–2019**

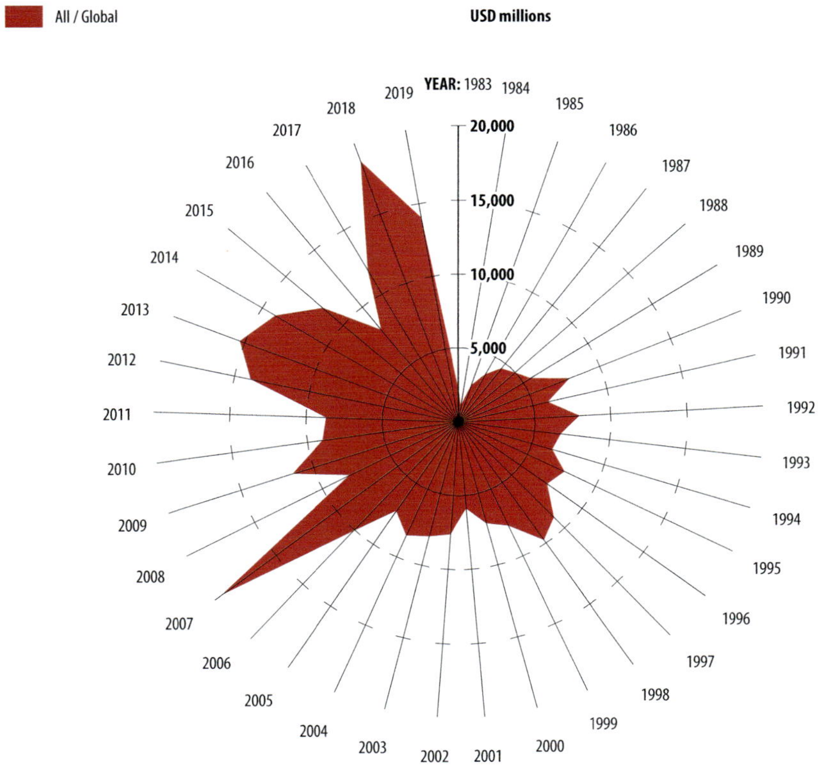

Source: UK Defence & Security Exports

It essentially argued that 'guns and butter' is a complementary rather than a binary choice. The economic worth of sustaining a defence-industrial base is sometimes questioned in terms of opportunity cost,[6] with a similar argument also made regarding purchaser states. The DSIS did not directly address the opportunity-cost question – that is, the allocation of government funds for military-related expenditure rather than for investment in the commercial sector or for more socially beneficial spending. The counter-argument is that protecting a national population and ensuring their security is a fundamental social good. The DSIS did attempt to reflect what the government considers to be the wider 'social value' of investment in defence manufacturing, raising the Type-31 frigate as an example.[7]

The national economic value of the UK's defence industry, defined broadly as companies that derive a significant element of their turnover from military-related business, was further illustrated in the DSIS by a policy shift. Despite the study being led under a Conservative government, the policy of 'global competition by default'[8] was dropped in favour of a less doctrinaire approach.[9] Couched in terms of still adopting 'competition where appropriate', it in effect allows protectionist methods to be used where an open competition would be deemed counter to national interests.[10] The UK had up to this point portrayed itself as an open defence market with the government willing to acquire major weapons systems from international suppliers if a bid was deemed to meet the requirement and provide best value.[11]

The DSIS also formalised the adoption of a coherent 'Team-UK' approach, with greater government and industry cooperation and a renewed level of cross-departmental support for the defence and security sectors, with the government taking on greater responsibility for export success through government-to-government (G2G) commercial agreements.[12] This active political engagement and support for UK defence exports perhaps moves the UK towards a more French approach in which senior political support is given to encourage sales abroad.[13]

A further economic benefit suggested by IISS interviewees[14] is the potential for exports to reduce the unit costs for material domestically through economies of scale. Interviewees were also keen to stress that arms exports are a tool for regional influence. If the UK's relationship with key export markets (e.g., Saudi Arabia) broke down, competitors would quickly move to fill the space. This is less of a problem when it is the US or European allies, but if it is China and Russia then it creates a strategic issue. There is a concern that while the West is 'distracted

DEFENCE SECRETARY OF THE UK IN QATAR
Defence secretary of the UK, Gavin Williamson, shakes hands with the minister of state for defense of Qatar, Khalid bin Mohammad Al Attiyah, after signing an agreement on the sale of Eurofighter *Typhoon* fighters jets to Qatar at a meeting in Doha, Qatar, 10 December 2017. CREDIT: Defence Ministry of Qatar – Handout/Anadolu Agency/Getty Images.

with other issues', China has rapidly moved to increase its influence in key export markets, becoming a strategic power with clearer, more focused regional ambitions than the UK. If the UK values the global community and rules-based international order in the context of great-power shifts, it should move to protect these things. An interviewee believed that to maintain the UK's position as an economic and strategic power, it is 'worth the UK selling arms for influence'.[15]

Others argue[16] that, despite ethical differences, it is better to engage with countries to encourage progress on human rights and equality issues. Otherwise, the UK loses a geopolitical 'chip' and Western influence could wane. With Western-friendly countries in the Middle East, arms sales are a pact, as they 'put you at a table that all other exports do not'.[17] Effectively, the UK needs to support strategic lynchpins in the Middle East in order to maintain both regional stability and Western influence over decisions and values.

UK defence-export policy considers the impact on human rights, internal conflict and regional stability. The 'Consolidated EU and National Arms Export Licensing Criteria',[18] or simply the Consolidated Criteria, which were developed between the UK and the European Union (EU) and last agreed in 2014, include eight criteria to assess licence applications for defence exports. The second, third and fourth of these consider human rights, internal repression and regional stability. But as ever with EU legislation, there are national-interest clauses that balance these considerations with the potential impact on the seller's economic, financial and commercial interests as well as the protection of their strategic-industrial base.[19]

Having been instrumental in developing the Consolidated Criteria, the UK continued to uphold the regulations after officially leaving the EU on 31 January 2020. However, a new policy was announced in December 2021 named the Strategic Export Licensing Criteria that replaced the Consolidated Criteria.[20] The eight criteria are largely the same but references to conforming to EU legislation – including the Common Position 2008/944/CFSP – were removed throughout. Adjustments were also made to the language of some statements, and the definition of military end use was 'enhanced to improve its effectiveness'.[21] The criteria still consider the impact on human rights, internal conflict and regional stability;[22] however, concerns have been raised that shifts in language would make it easier to export arms to countries implicated in serious human-rights abuses.[23]

The balance between foreign-policy goals, geopolitical issues, domestic industry and the regional stability surrounding the buyer is considered in export-licence decisions but it is often overridden by other priorities. Sustaining a domestic industrial base that is competitive and supportive of allies gives the UK value on the global stage, in the view of one interviewee.[24]

History

UK defence exports fluctuate according to wider trends and demand, with peaks evident in 2007[25] (Project Salam) and 2018 (*Typhoon* sales to Qatar).[26] Annual exports average USD9.8bn annually, and the 2018 surge year was a significant contributor to the DSE calculation that the UK was the second-largest defence exporter globally on a ten-year basis between 2011 and 2020.[27]

The UK steadily grew its share of global defence exports from 9% in 2016 to 19% in 2018. However, this share fell slightly to 16% in

Timeline 6.1: **Selected* combat-aircraft sales to the Middle East, North Africa and Asia from the UK**

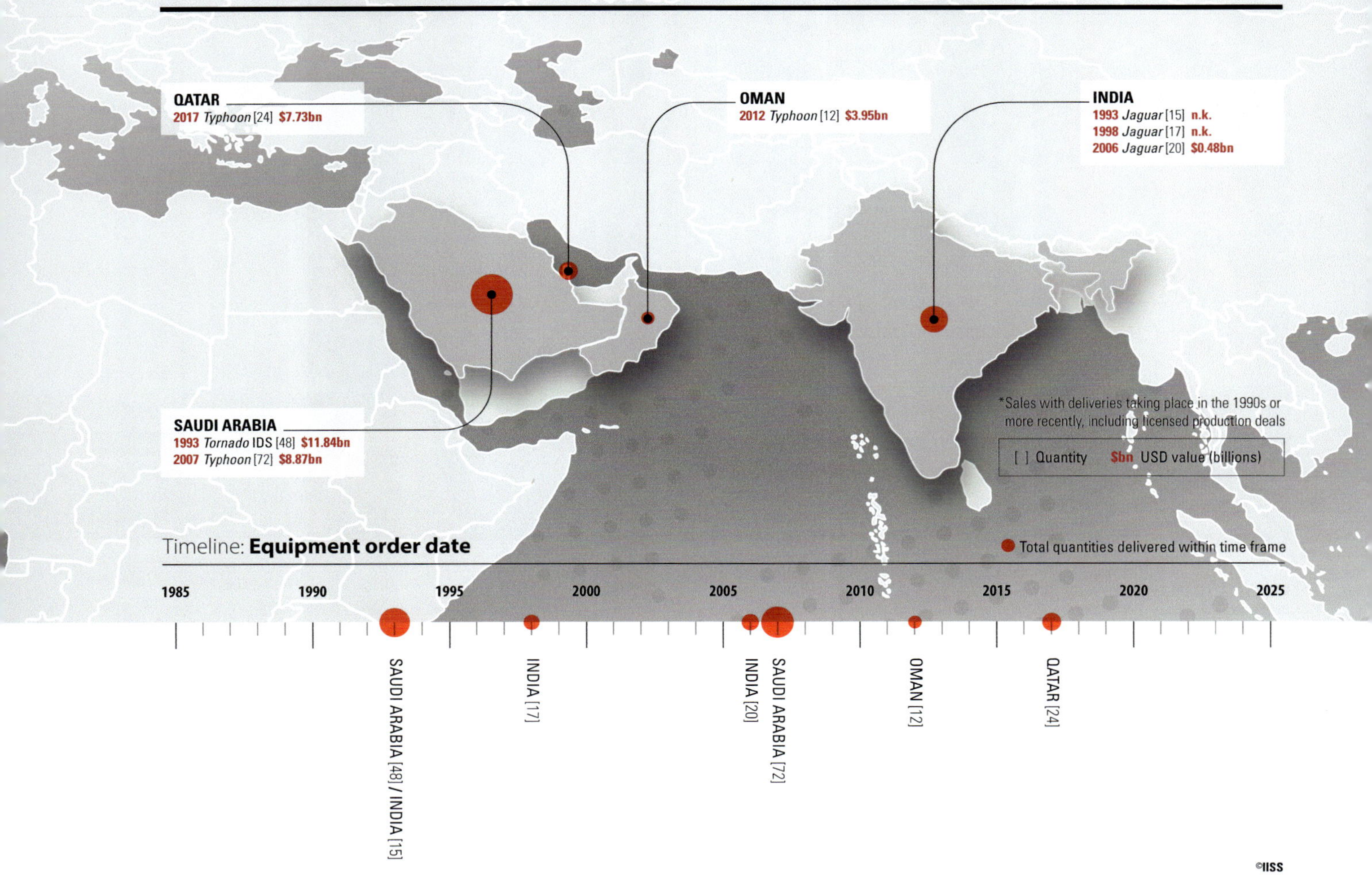

Source: IISS

2019 and much lower to just 6% in 2020. Global defence exports are estimated to have fallen slightly in 2019, which could be an indication of more constrained export markets at the time, particularly in the Middle East where oil prices were still subdued.

Partially explaining the significant drop in the UK's share in 2020 is that total global defence exports surged that year, the result of a significant USD62bn export contract from the US to Taiwan for F-16 aircraft over the next decade.[28] This surge 'skews competitor shares', but UK defence exports still fell in value terms in 2020 to GBP7.9bn (USD10.1bn), down from GBP11bn (USD14.1bn) the year before. For the UK, then, 2019 and 2020 were more constrained years, with the dependence on major aircraft exports meaning that without these deals, the UK's market share declined.

Since 2010, the US has been the dominant global arms exporter, accounting for more than 40% of the global market in most years and 68% in 2020.[29] In 2007, the UK's global share surpassed that of the US thanks to the GBP4.43bn (USD8.87bn) Project Salam contract, which comprised the supply of 72 Eurofighter *Typhoons* and *Storm Shadow* land-attack cruise missiles to Saudi Arabia.[30] However, as the UK's share of global exports has declined in recent years, focusing solely on the period 2016–20 would, according to one estimate, place the UK as the sixth-largest defence exporter globally, behind the US, Russia, France, Germany and China.[31]

Middle East importer importance

The Middle East has been the biggest market for global defence imports over the last decade, representing as much as 40% of the total over the 2011–20 period. Four of the ten biggest importers globally over the same period were in the Middle East: Saudi Arabia, Qatar, the United Arab Emirates (UAE) and Kuwait in descending order.[32] Between 2012 and 2015, defence spending in the Middle East and North Africa (MENA) grew at an average annual rate of 12% in real terms as oil prices passed USD100/barrel. However, the subsequent collapse in oil prices between 2014 and 2016 saw the region – especially the Gulf states – pursue fiscal consolidation.

In line with the poor performance of oil prices, defence spending in the MENA region contracted in real terms for the fourth consecutive year in 2021 and the regional share of global defence spending fell to 8.6% from a peak of 10.8% in 2017.[33] In recent years, the MENA region's

Figure 6.2: **Estimated total UK defence exports (based on orders/contracts signed) by region, 2004–2020**

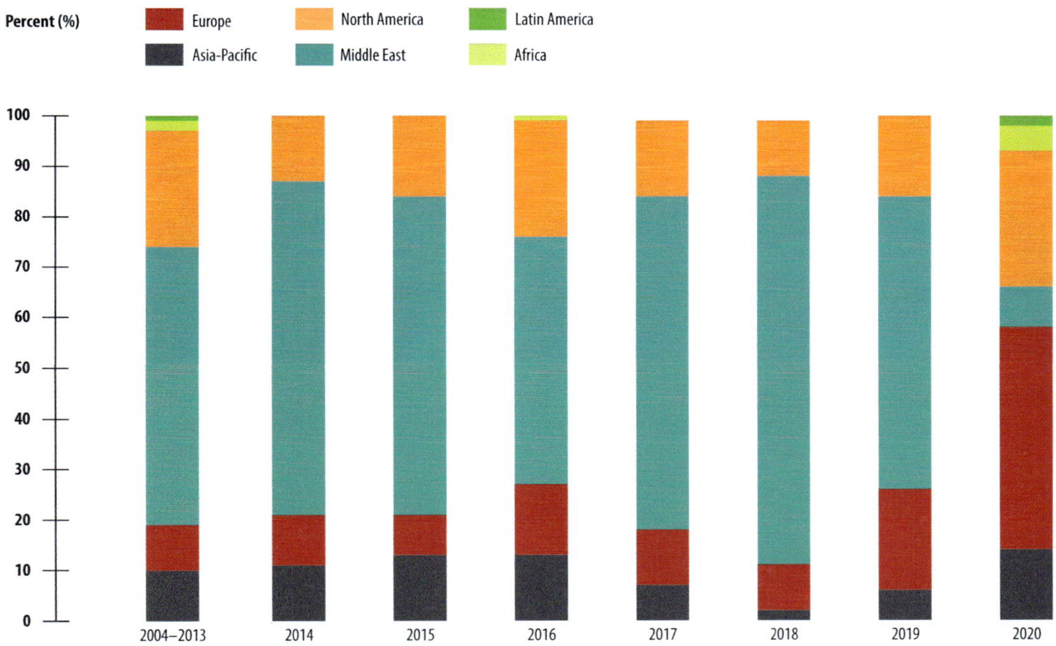

Source: UK Defence & Security Exports

share of defence imports has fallen close to 25% as a result. As the global economy recovered in 2021, oil prices strengthened and have since soared to levels in excess of USD100/barrel, as Russia's invasion of Ukraine on 24 February 2022 created a severe commodity supply shock.[34]

While the Middle East is the primary export market for the UK, accounting for 58% of UK defence exports by destination between 2011 and 2020, it is not the primary supplier to the region. As a proportion of total imports to the Middle East, the UK represented just 21% over the same time period. The US is the primary supplier, accounting for 52% of regional arms imports between 2016 and 2020, while France and Russia are the next-largest suppliers to the region.[35]

North America represents the second-highest region for UK defence exporters, accounting for 17% of total UK defence exports by customer destination between 2011 and 2020. As a proportion of imports to North America, the UK represents a significant 39%. But it should be noted that compared to the Middle East, the Asia-Pacific and, to a lesser extent, Europe, the US imports relatively few arms, the result of their high level of domestic self-sufficiency.

Beyond the Middle East and North America, Europe and the Asia-Pacific were the next most important regional markets for the UK in this period, accounting for 15% and 8% respectively. The small Asia-Pacific share of UK exports, despite the region being the second-biggest defence-export market, shows the UK's difficulty in competing with established regional suppliers US, Russia and increasingly China. Indeed, over the last ten years, the UK's share of an estimated USD230bn-worth of imports to the region was just 4%.

Europe: target market and competitor

Over the last ten years, Europe has accounted for a small percentage of UK defence exports by destination, averaging 11% annually. The European states with the most significant budgets pursue their own arms exports, with France, Germany, Italy and Spain all usually appearing in the list of top ten exporters worldwide. However, Europe's proportion of UK exports jumped in 2020 to 43% as a result of both the USD6.8bn order for 38 Eurofighter *Typhoons* for Germany[36] as well as a pause in the UK granting of licences to Saudi Arabia between July 2019 and July 2020.[37]

The Eurofighter consortium is a key example of how the UK engages with Europe (i.e., through multinational efforts that would also include companies like MBDA). Therefore, while exports to Europe have not traditionally been as significant, the UK is highly involved in the European defence industry, with companies such as BAE and Rolls Royce establishing significant footprints on the continent. This is also reciprocated with several European-owned subsidiaries based across the UK, including Leonardo, Thales, Airbus and Rheinmetall.

The UK's European competitors face the same market challenges in Asia and the Middle East. France's 2021 arms-exports report noted that the 2020 order intake had slowed, as was to be expected in light of a slowdown in trade relations and budgetary adjustments.[38] Order intake fell to EUR4.9bn (USD5.6bn) compared to EUR8.3bn (USD9.3bn) in 2019.[39] The report further stated that despite the challenges posed by the coronavirus pandemic, France continued with export-control and regulation practices, indicating

BAE SYSTEMS CELEBRATES F-35 AFT FUSELAGE DELIVERY
BAE Systems shipped the first F-35 Joint Strike Fighter aft fuselage to Lockheed Martin Aeronautics Company in Ft. Worth, June 2005. CREDIT: Business Wire via Getty Images.

that the constrained marketplace had not caused a loosening of restrictions or best practices.

Similarly, after experiencing a bumper year for defence exports in 2019 in which the value of export licences reached EUR8.0bn (USD9.0bn),[40] Germany saw exports fall back to EUR5.8bn (USD6.6bn) in 2020.[41] For Germany, the primary market for defence exports tends to be 'EU-/NATO and NATO equivalent countries', which accounted for 49.9% in 2020 and 55.9% in 2019.[42] Over the last decade, the Middle East accounted for 30% of German export licences while the Asia-Pacific was much lower, closer to 13%. Therefore, while the UK and France often target the MENA region and increasingly Asia-Pacific markets, Germany relies more on European opportunities. This might be due to the nature of defence exports by domain for each exporter, where France and the UK are more aerospace focused while Germany's licences are more diverse, with a greater dependence on land systems, naval platforms and small arms.[43]

Over the 2011–20 period, 91% of UK defence exports were in the aerospace domain compared with a much lower global average of 65%.[44] This higher proportion is understandable considering the high value of platforms in this domain. But the UK has previously expressed concerns that so much of its exports are aerospace focused while their competitors have more diversified portfolios. According to the ADS, exports generated over 90% of the UK aerospace industry's turnover in 2019.[45]

The lead times on defence equipment and the cyclical nature of key export-market procurement spending and priority programmes create an undulating trend in defence exports. This cyclical character is made more vulnerable by the predominance of aircraft in UK export figures. The UK-led future combat air development work, which also involves Italy, Japan and Sweden, will enter an increasingly contested marketplace with the Franco-German programme as well as the US, Russia and emerging competitors in Asia potentially launching programmes in the 2040s, too.

Evolution of UK policy

To understand the evolution of UK arms policy since the 1990s, it is helpful to review the key developments of the two preceding decades. Laurence Lustgarten argues that UK foreign policy and arms sales had become intertwined due to the economic difficulties of the 1970s.[46] This resulted in a series of sales to the Shah of Iran between 1971 and 1976 which included transfers of *Chieftain* tanks. As the UK halted sales to Iran, the Thatcher government continued to focus on creating economic prosperity with the controversial 1985 al-Yamamah contract with Saudi Arabia.

Countering this economic focus was the increasing influence of the anti-nuclear movement and other civil-society organisations on both the Labour Party and public policy.[47] Civil-society organisations lobbied to stop arms sales to South Africa and Chile, contributing to an embargo on the former in 1964 and the latter in 1974. The decision not to impose an embargo on Argentina following the 1976 coup was arguably because there was less public pressure in the UK and the strong advocacy network that campaigned on Chile was not as prevalent for Argentina.[48] Nonetheless, Lustgarten finds that the South African embargo was a watershed moment, as it was the first time humanitarian considerations were incorporated into official export policy.[49] While the 1980s Thatcher government continued to impose the South Africa embargo, the Chilean embargo was loosened in 1980 to refuse only sales that might be used to suppress internal disorder.[50]

'Arms-to-Iraq'

The supply of equipment to Iraq between 1984 and 1990 led to the prosecution of three directors of Matrix Churchill – a Coventry-based machine-tools manufacturer – for violating export-control regulations. The charge was that licences had been secured under the proviso that the material would be used for civilian purposes but with full knowledge that it was intended for military use in Iraq by Saddam Hussein's

LORD JUSTICE SCOTT TALKS TO REPORTERS
Lord Justice Scott talks to reporters on at a press conference in London after the publication of his report on his three-year inquiry into the arms sales to Iraq prior to the Gulf War, 15 February 1999. CREDIT: JOHNNY EGGITT/AFP via Getty Images.

regime. The prosecution collapsed at trial based on the defence that government was aware of the intended final use of the exports and following the admission from then-minister for trade Alan Clark under cross-examination that he knew the machine tools could be used to manufacture munitions and that the notes of one DTI (Department of Trade and Industry) meeting were 'economical with the actualité'.[51]

The 'Arms-to-Iraq' affair resulted in an extensive inquiry by Sir Richard Scott that was published in February 1996.[52] The Scott Inquiry (or 'Inquiry into Exports of Defence Equipment and Dual Use Goods to Iraq') aimed to establish whether government departments at the time operated in accordance with policy. The inquiry found that the government had failed to disclose to Parliament its decision to adopt a 'more liberal policy on defence sales to Iraq' in 1988.[53]

This more liberal approach refers to adjustments made to the 1984 guidelines as set forward by then-foreign secretary Sir Geoffrey Howe which included a clause prohibiting the sale of lethal equipment to Iran or Iraq that could 'significantly enhance the capability of either side to prolong or exacerbate the conflict'.[54] According to Marquand, when the Iran–Iraq War ended in 1988, the clause became defunct and the language was adjusted so that the prohibition would apply to exports 'which, in our view, would be of direct and significant assistance to either country in the conduct of offensive operations'.[55] The less restrictive language was not made known to Parliament, and the Scott Inquiry concluded that this was due to 'a fear of strong public opposition to the loosening of restrictions on the supply of defence equipment to Iraq and a consequential fear that the pressure of the opposition might be detrimental to British trading interests'.[56]

From Scott to Cook

The Scott Inquiry made a series of recommendations regarding export-control procedures, the disclosure of information to the public and ministerial accountability. Robin Cook, then Labour MP for Livingstone, was highly critical of the government's response to the Scott Inquiry[57] and when he later became foreign secretary in 1997, he pursued an 'ethical foreign policy' that 'recognises that the national interest cannot be defined only by narrow realpolitik'.

> Our foreign policy must have an ethical dimension and must support the demands of other peoples for the democratic rights on which we insist for ourselves. The Labour Government will put human rights at the heart of our foreign policy and will publish an annual report on our work in promoting human rights abroad.[58]

The tension between ethical values and the national interest still plagued the New Labour government as Cook was criticised for approving licences for *Hawk* jets to Indonesia, a country known for violently repressing East Timor's independence movement, just two months after this speech.[59] Cook argued that the deal had already been signed by the previous government and future orders were indeed blocked under new criteria,[60] but the incident undermined the credibility of the ethical message.

Realpolitik arguably thwarted Cook's ambition. By 2000, Cook's ethical language had been replaced with proposals for a 'more responsible arms trade'.[61] The criticisms of Labour's arms exports recorded over this period focused on the export of materiel to China despite the EU arms embargo, to Israel during a period of offensive operations in the Occupied Territories and war with Lebanon, and to countries where the material was either unsuitable, unnecessary or unaffordable.[62] Nonetheless, Cook did manage to enact significant improvements in institutional structures, including the establishment of a committee responsible for overseeing arms exports and a framework for more extensive annual reporting and transparency in export-licence decisions.[63] Over the course of the New Labour era, the UK also established the Export Control Act (2002), signed new criteria for the assessment of arms exports and led, with France, the effort to establish the EU's Common Position.

The Defence Export Services Organisation

Established in 1966 by then-secretary of state for defence Denis Healey, the Defence Sales Organisation – which later became (DESO) – provided government assistance to the defence industry for securing overseas orders.[64] Healey stated at the time that this was a practical step towards ensuring that the country did not 'fail to secure its rightful share of this valuable commercial market' and that sales would reduce the burden of UK military commitments by recouping foreign currency spent on overseas operations.[65]

DESO's key roles were to support company-led marketing campaigns and advise both government and industry on export-licence applications.[66] This industry support was criticised by campaign groups. Campaign Against the Arms Trade (CAAT) alleged that the increased privatisation of the defence sector meant the government was using public money to bolster the profits of private entities with no consideration of the impact on human rights, regional stability or even 'the defence of the UK'.[67] As DESO reached close to 500 civil servants in 2007, 200 of which focused on G2G projects,[68] a further criticism, this time by Saferworld, was that defence received an unfair advantage over other exports and was considered a privileged sector by the government.[69] CAAT, along with the Fellowship of Reconciliation (FoR) and Christian campaign group SPEAK, heavily campaigned for the closure of DESO and led a March 2007 petition calling for such to the Treasury which reached 10,000 signatures.[70]

UK prime minister Gordon Brown effectively closed DESO in July 2007 by integrating the promotion of defence exports into UK Trade and Investment (UKTI), the organisation responsible for supporting all UK exports.[71] The move was met with cautious approval from CAAT[72] but dismay by the UK defence industry[73] and some politicians, the latter pointing out that France was in the process of establishing a similar agency to DESO to promote their exports.[74]

The current incarnation of the organisation responsible for assisting UK defence- and security-industry overseas sales is the UK Defence and Security Exports (UKDSE). UKDSE sits within the UKTI and has 100 staff in London with a further 27 members in the Export Support Team, which comprises serving military personnel.[75] UKDSE works with the Ministry of Defence (MOD), the Home Office and the Export Control Joint Unit (ECJU), implying there is more consideration of the wider impact of arms exports given the ECJU is responsible for administering export controls and licences within the framework of the Consolidated Criteria.

Coalition tension

The difficult balance between economic interest, the protection of human rights and the preservation of regional stability appeared fraught during the 2010 Conservative–Liberal Coalition government. Foreign secretary William Hague stated in 2010 that UK foreign policy 'will always have support for human rights and poverty reduction as its irreducible core' while also reaffirming the commitment to 'prevent nuclear proliferation in the Middle East or risk the world's most unstable region from becoming festooned with the most dangerous weapons known to the world'.[76] Hague was also keen to clarify that there would be 'no downgrading of human rights' under the Coalition government.[77]

However, when prime minister David Cameron undertook a series of trips to promote UK defence exports to the Gulf[78] between 2010 and 2012, CAAT responded that because it was actively promoting arms exports to 'authoritarian regimes', the government's human-rights statements were 'empty words'.[79]

The economic agenda was a clear driver at this time, with Cameron stating in December 2012 that 'boosting exports is vital for economic growth, and that's why I'm doing all I can to promote British business ... so [it] can thrive in the global race', and 'every country in the world has a right to self-defence, and I'm determined to put Britain's first-class defence industry at the forefront of this market, supporting 300,000 jobs across the country'.[80]

Somewhat balancing this purely economic-driven agenda was the suspension of licences to countries during the Arab Spring, including Bahrain, Egypt, Libya and Tunisia, under the criteria that UK equipment would not provoke or prolong regional or internal conflicts or be used to facilitate internal repression.[81] This can be seen in the spike in Criterion 2- and 3-based (and to a lesser extent Criterion 4-based) rejections and revocations of export licences in 2011.

In its 2012 Scrutiny of Arms Exports Report, the UK Parliament's Committees on Arms Export Controls (CAEC) welcomed the revocation of 158 arms-export licences following the Arab Spring but found the high number of revocations was evidence that the initial judgements to approve the applications were flawed.[82] The government strongly disagreed with this conclusion, arguing that the revocations were a good example of the licensing system working effectively, and reiterated previous statements that there was no evidence of UK materiel being used for internal repression during the Arab Spring.[83] The issue therefore seems to be in pre-empting potential problems; if the policy is more reactive, then this risks transfer of lethal equipment to governments that are using the materiel for internal repression or to shift the balance in an emerging conflict.

Procurement reform and the prosperity agenda

Reform of the UK's procurement and acquisition has been a key trend over the last two decades, with the release of a small library of policy papers, White Papers, reviews and strategies. Labour defence secretary John Hutton commissioned Bernard Gray in 2008 to undertake an independent review of defence acquisition. The Gray report[84] published in 2009 found:

> The Ministry of Defence has a substantially overheated equipment programme, with too many types of equipment being ordered for too large a range of tasks at too high a specification. This programme is unaffordable on any likely projection of future budgets.[85]

The report recommended routine Strategic Defence Reviews to ensure periodic 'resetting' of the MOD's plans. The report also recommended a set of detailed changes to keep the Equipment Programme on track between reviews, including forming an Executive Committee of the Defence Board to be accountable for ensuring the programme's affordability.

Reforms made by the 2010–15 Coalition government were shaped by this review. The 2012 *National Security Through Technology* White Paper determined that the best way to achieve value for money, while also delivering the best equipment, was to pursue competition by default. The paper did qualify that this would be balanced against the need to protect the UK's technological advantage 'where essential for national security'.[86]

The end of the Coalition government and election of a full Conservative government in 2015 brought with it further emphasis on the prosperity agenda.[87] 'Promote our prosperity' was one of the three high-level National Security Objectives of the 2015 *Strategic Defence and Security Review* (SDSR), the other two being 'protect our people' and 'project our global influence'.[88] The SDSR stated the continued commitment to robust export-licensing procedures but also outlined greater government support for defence and security exports. This included establishing a dedicated team in UKTI to support G2G deals, making support for exports a core task of the MOD, and ensuring that exportability is factored into UK equipment-procurement decisions, with potential customers routinely invited to trials.[89]

The next paper to inform the prosperity agenda was the 2018 Phillip Dunne report, *Growing the Contribution of Defence to UK Prosperity*, which recommended more encouragement from both government and industry for a 'Team-UK' approach. The report stated that the MOD should resource its responsibility to promote prosperity more 'appropriately and effectively' as well as take into account the additional commitments to support strategic exports as stated in the SDSR.[90]

These recommendations helped shape the 2021 DSIS, which was released alongside the Defence Command Paper[91] and moved away from the 2012 policy of global competition by default towards the adoption of a more flexible and nuanced approach to defence procurement.[92] This approach would balance the required capability with both national-security considerations and the potential impact on UK 'prosperity', which would allow future procurement decision-makers to use 'competition where appropriate, but also to establish where global competition at the prime level may be ineffective or incompatible with our national security requirements'.[93]

The move to improve flexibility in procurement decisions and adopt a more protective industrial stance stems from the increasing recognition that the UK's defence industry is a strategic capability 'in its own right'. In the context of a more competitive global environment as described in the Integrated Review,[94] the DSIS argues that flexibility is needed to deliver and develop the key onshore skills, technologies and capabilities that will ensure resilience in UK defence.[95]

Political consensus

Political consensus is difficult to gauge but it was suggested to the IISS that it can be politically unpopular to restrict certain industries. Shipbuilding, for example, has a significant economic footprint in the UK but is also responsible for certain peacekeeping roles, for protecting supply lines and for providing humanitarian support.[96]

There is also widespread recognition that the arms industry creates employment and wealth and that MPs face undeniable constituent pressure to maintain key industries in their home seats.[97] Defence-industrial sites are located throughout the UK, including in socio-economically struggling areas which depend on the skilled jobs and revenues they create. Many of these locations are in Labour stronghold areas, so even if there is evidence that in the past, Conservative-led governments were more pro-arms exports than Labour, the political and economic pressure has perhaps eroded the ethical foreign-policy ambitions of Robin Cook within the Labour Party.

Countering this is a renewed effort on the part of Labour to revive some of these goals. Emily Thornberry, shadow attorney general for England and Wales, lamented in 2021 that Robin Cook's ambitions in the wake of the Scott Inquiry have been unfulfilled. Thornberry argued that efforts to impose a more ethical approach to individual decisions on arms sales 'were stymied from the outset by the commercial interests of UK weapons manufacturers and the strategic demands of our alliances overseas'.[98] Thornberry proposed that such decisions need to be made independent of political influence and that the process needs to be truly transparent.[99]

UK export process

The UK arms-export process is subject to a number of elements.

The **Export Control Act** 2002[100] was signed by the then Labour government following the review of the UK's statutory framework governing export controls. The Act gave the government new powers that included the control of transfers of military and other sensitive technology, the transfer of weapons of mass destruction

EGYPT GOES TO THE POLLS FOR PARLIAMENTARY ELECTIONS
Tahrir Square occupied by a few hundred protestors on election day, 28 November 2011. Eleven months after the fall of Hosni Mubarak, 45 million Egyptians voted in the first round of six for the upper and lower houses of parliament. CREDIT: Peter Macdiarmid/Getty Images.

(WMD)-related technology, the trafficking of controlled goods between overseas countries and the provision of technical assistance overseas. The Act aimed to increase the transparency and accountability of UK arms export controls while also formalising parliamentary scrutiny and the requirement for the government to report annually to Parliament on strategic export-licensing decisions. The specific controls of the 2002 Act are found in the secondary legislation, the Export Control Order 2008.[101]

Wassenaar Arrangement

The Wassenaar Arrangement on Export Controls for Conventional Arms and Dual-Use Goods and Technologies,[105] formally established in July 1996, is a multilateral arms-exports control regime with 42 participating states. The Arrangement aims to contribute to regional and international security and stability by promoting transparency and greater responsibility in arms transfers, thus preventing destabilising accumulations. The Arrangement maintains lists of items for which members are to apply export controls and imposes some reporting requirements on members.

The **Consolidated List** – formally, the UK Strategic Export Control Lists[102] – describes which items are controlled and therefore require a licence before export. The Consolidated List draws from both UK and EU measures as well as international regimes like the Wassenaar Arrangement.[103] Exporters must apply for a licence from the ECJU, the UK government's regulatory authority for export licensing of strategic goods. The ECJU also has the power to invoke 'end-use controls' if there are concerns about the possible use of an item in a WMD programme, even if the goods are not included in the Consolidated List.[104]

Consolidated Criteria

If an item is on the Consolidated List, then the export is considered against the **Consolidated Criteria**. The Consolidated EU and National Arms Export Licensing Criteria[106] (Consolidated Criteria for short) brought together the UK's national export-licensing criteria developed under the 1997 Labour government[107] with the EU Code of Conduct on Arms Exports (now known as the Common Position).[108] The Consolidated Criteria include eight criteria to assess licence applications for defence exports. Briefly, licence decisions consider whether the export will:

(1) contravene the UK's international commitments or obligations;
(2) be used for internal repression;
(3) provoke or prolong armed conflicts or aggravate internal tensions in the recipient country;
(4) undermine regional stability;
(5) adversely affect the national security of the UK or its allies;
(6) be sold to a country that does not respect international law;
(7) be diverted or re-exported to undesirable end users; or
(8) seriously undermine the technical and economic capacity of the buyer country.

Three government departments are relevant in the assessment of UK arms exports: the Foreign, Commonwealth and Development Office (FCDO), the Department for International Trade (DIT) and the MOD. Each department focuses on different elements of the Consolidation Criteria, for example, the FCDO is the lead advisory department for regional stability (Criterion 4), among others, while the MOD's main focus is on national security (Criterion 5). Interviews conducted by the IISS suggest that this creates a fundamental conflict of interest. The FCDO is interested in the diplomacy aspect of the discussion while the DIT is keen to promote exports where success is measured by increases in UK transfers. The different viewpoints therefore create divergences and a contradiction between promoting and preventing. The government's decisions against these criteria, as well as the annual report to Parliament regarding UK defence exports,[109] are scrutinised by CAEC.

Some suggest that there is a misplaced focus by MPs on the Consolidated Criteria because there are loopholes throughout that make it possible to bypass them.[110] Arguably, the Consolidated Criteria are largely 'for optics' as human-rights-related considerations feature more prominently than in the guidance of legislations determining other countries' exports, such as the US. The lack of official definitions for terms used throughout the document – that is, what actually constitutes a human-rights issue – is why loopholes emerge. An expert in UK arms-export law argued that the UK courts would be reluctant to intervene to define such aspects for fear of restricting UK exports and government policy.[111] The courts grant significant deference to the government on international or foreign-policy law. Therefore, while the Consolidated Criteria are useful and provide a discipline for the government to consider when making export decisions, the loose definitions create gaps through which export licences can be granted.

The fourth of these criteria considers the impact on regional stability but is not the most common reason for an export licence being rejected or revoked. By far the more common reasons over the

ANTI-ARMS TRADE GROUPS PROTEST INDUSTRY BLACK-TIE DINNER IN LONDON
Demonstrations held by activists outside the annual black-tie dinner of the Aerospace, Defence and Security Group at the Grosvenor House Hotel in London, 22 January 2020. The protest was called by CAAT and Stop The Arms Fair pressure groups, citing sales of UK-made weapons and ammunition to Saudi Arabia. CREDIT: David Cliff/NurPhoto via Getty Images.

last decade have been Criterion 1 (existing obligations) and Criterion 7 (risk of transfer to undesirable end users), while Criterion 5-based (impact on the UK and its allies' national security) rejections have increased in recent years. Over the 2010 to 2020 period, Criterion 1 rejections accounted for 44% of the total, with Criterion 7 accounting for 26%. Regional stability (Criterion 4) accounted for just 2% of the rejections over the ten-year period. The impact on human rights was considered (Criteria 2 and 3) but the lack of a complex set of regulations and definitions, and indeed the fact that it is deemed too complicated to formulate them, limits the effectiveness that these considerations can have.

As ever, there are national-interest clauses that balance these considerations with the potential impact on the UK's economic, financial and commercial interests as well as the protection of the UK's strategic-industrial base.[112] Article 10 of the EU Common Position specifies that member states may, where appropriate, also take into account the effect of proposed exports on their economic, social, commercial and industrial interests, 'but that these factors will not affect the application of the criteria in the common position'.[113]

Committees on Arms Export Controls (CAEC)

The 'Quadripartite Committee' was set up in 1999 with the responsibility of assessing UK arms exports. Renamed the Committees on Arms Export Controls in 2008, members are drawn from four separate select committees that have an interest in arms exports given the respective government departments they examine: the Foreign Affairs, Defence, International Trade and International Development committees.[114]

Since 1999, the UK has published a Strategic Export Controls Annual Report, which has been supplemented by the quarterly publication of statistical data since 2004. CAEC is tasked with scrutinising these reports along with the UK government's arms-export control procedures and legislation, individual arms-export-licence decisions, and the UK's role in international arms-control agreements.[115] CAEC examines trends in the UK's arms exports, implications of those trends, the transparency of government reporting and compliance with export controls.[116] CAEC can also pursue separate enquiries into particular topics (e.g., the ill-fated 2015–16 inquiry into UK exports to Saudi Arabia).

The unique structure of CAEC was intended to generate cross-government thinking, with members from various committees offering different perspectives and a wide range of knowledge and experience when receiving evidence and reviewing UK export reports. However, the composition from four separate committees also creates challenges, particularly as all committee members must agree before any report is published. One IISS interviewee stated that this complicates the process as the members have different viewpoints and there is a 'fundamental conflict in the priorities of defence and international development'.[117]

A further critique was that CAEC only meets once a month while most select committees meet more frequently, sometimes up to once a week. This means there is no 'rhythm, coordination or regular flow'.[118] Furthermore, not all members attend evidence sessions, which creates a sense of inertia. Unless at least two members from each committee attend, the session has to be suspended under parliamentary rules. This sense of inertia is deepened by the protracted time frame of the reports. The government's Strategic Export Controls Annual Report comes out the following year – usually in June – and CAEC usually take another year to review the report. As such, the CAEC report is usually published up to two years after the data it is analysing is released.

A further challenge is that CAEC has to be reformed after each general election, which itself depends upon the formation of the four constituent committees, the drawing of members within them

Figure 6.3: **UK and global defence-export market (based on orders/contracts signed) by sector, 2015–19**

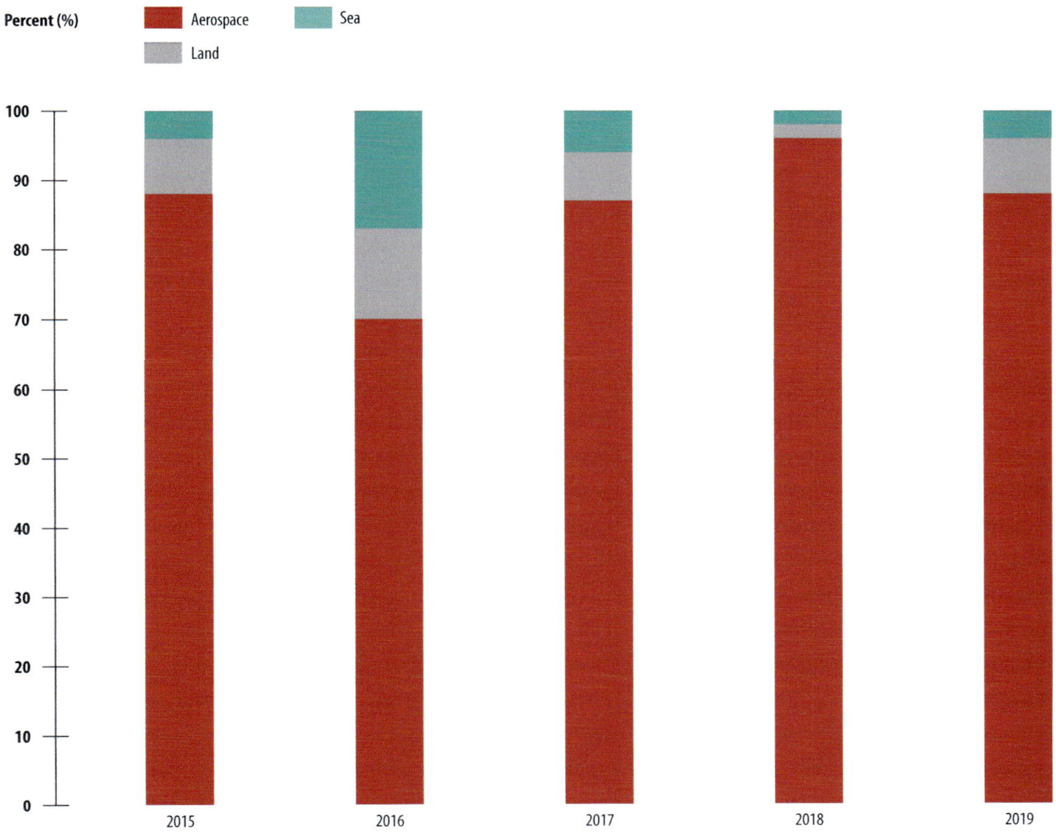

Source: UK Defence & Security Exports

for CAEC, and the agreement of a new Chair. This process was very protracted following the 2015 general election and, when combined with a lack of staff support, led to difficulties in reaching a consensus on the approval of exports to Saudi Arabia in 2016. One constituent committee, International Development, approved a draft report which the Foreign Affairs Committee rejected. The latter then produced its own, but the Defence Committee refused to consider it at all as proper protocol had not been followed.[119]

Following this, scrutiny reports were not published for two years, with the 2018 CAEC report primarily covering 2016 exports with reference to 2014 and 2015 as these years had not been subjected to scrutiny by the previous committees.[120] The 2018 report criticised the fact that neither the foreign secretary nor the secretary of state for international trade had provided oral evidence to the committee. The committee also recommended that the government give formal consideration to the creation of an additional licensing criterion relating to corruption.

In response to the suggestion that a more stringent process needs to be in place to assess exports to countries that have not signed the Arms Trade Treaty or that feature on the Foreign and Commonwealth Office's list of 'Human Rights Priority Countries', the government said:

> The Government has confidence in the ability of the UK's thorough and robust export licensing system to distinguish between exports for legitimate civilian, defence and security purposes and exports which pose unacceptable risks to human rights.[121]

Further conclusions from the 2018 CAEC report (covering 2016 exports) included the need for more effective end-use monitoring, a registration system for arms brokers and improved transparency regarding open licences. A criticism levelled at CAEC by the non-governmental organisation Saferworld was the lack of scrutiny of actual export decisions made in 2016, specifically those to parties involved in the Yemen conflict (Saudi Arabia and the UAE).[122]

The 2019 general election, administrative difficulties, delays in government reporting and the coronavirus pandemic stalled CAEC reports over 2019–20. An inquiry into UK arms exports in 2019 was launched on 9 February 2021, with a call for further evidence in July 2021 when the government published the Strategic Controls Annual Report 2020.

Despite challenges, CAEC has helped to improve the transparency of UK arms exports. Under the chairmanship of Sir John Stanley between 2010 and 2015, the greater level of detail provided in annual reports and in response to Stanley's frequent information requests made the UK one of the most transparent countries with regard to arms-trade data and policy decisions.[123] Ongoing efforts by this committee are crucial to ensuring accountability in UK defence-export decisions. Providing greater security to the committee, perhaps by assigning it the same status as a select committee, would help overcome the logistical and administrative challenges it faces.

Shift in criteria

Prior to the UK's departure from the EU, export controls were also shaped by the **2008 EU Common Position**[124] on arms exports, which set out common rules governing the control of exports. The Common Position aimed to establish a coherent approach to arms-exports control across all the EU's member states. Conversely, because of the lack of any capacity to enforce the Criteria at the transnational level, the effectiveness is challenged as all decision-making and implementation rests at the member-state level.[125] This provides considerable latitude for states to interpret the Criteria in such a way as to have the desired outcome, often in favour of a sale.

Such latitude is similar to how countries make use of exemptions to the EU Defence and Security Procurement Directive 2009/81/EC, which commands free, fair and open competition by default within the EU. Countries can apply Article 346 of the Treaty of the Functioning of the European Union – the right to not enforce free-market rules on national-security grounds.

> Any Member State may take such measures as it considers necessary for the protection of the essential interests of its security which are connected with the production of or trade in arms, munitions and war material.[126]

When the UK left the EU, most common defence-export regulations were continued. However, a new policy was announced in December 2021, named the Strategic Export Licensing Criteria, that fully replaced the Consolidated Criteria.[127] Justifying the change, then secretary of state for International Trade Anne-Marie Trevelyan stated:

> We keep our controls under regular review to ensure that they continue to properly address the threats we face, keep pace with new technologies, and adapt to changing circumstances such as our exit from the EU, while providing an efficient service which does not impose an unworkable administrative burden on the defence and security industry.[128]

The eight criteria are largely the same, but references to conforming to EU legislation – including the Common Position – were removed throughout. Criterion 4 of the new policy still considers the impact on regional stability, while Criteria 2 and 3 still assess the risk of internal repression or unrest respectively.[129]

One change in language did cause controversy: that an export would be allowed if a minister decided there was only a 'theoretical' risk that a buyer would break the rules regarding the use of weapons.[130] Within the guidance, this is exemplified by a shift in the language of Criterion 2 where 'a risk items might be used for' has been replaced with 'a clear risk that items might be used to commit or facilitate internal repression or a serious violation of international humanitarian law'. [131] One other major change was that China was added to the list of countries subject to military end-use controls.[132]

Criterion 4 was also adjusted, with 'regional' removed from the primary statement. 'Preservation of regional peace, security and stability' has been generalised to 'preservation of peace and security'. Regional stability appeared to have become only a factor in decision making rather than a primary criterion. The increase in ambiguity is unlikely to help, given how rarely this Criterion is cited to justify rejections or revocations of licences.

Wider impact of Brexit

It has been suggested that Brexit increased the variation in trade controls between the UK and its partners, and the current turbulent times make it difficult to understand how the UK differs from its partners.[133] In terms of military trade with Europe, there are no sharp divergences because of Brexit as regulations have largely remained the same and generally defence trade between the UK and EU is quite low given similar levels of capability. The UK–EU trade agreement confirmed ongoing commitments to existing obligations under international disarmament and non-proliferation treaties and established a regular dialogue on those matters.[134]

Beyond the EU regulations, post-Brexit the UK remained a member of the multilateral export-control regimes (the Wassenaar Arrangement, Missile Technology Control Regime, Australia Group, Nuclear Suppliers Group and Zangger Committee), all of which underpin the EU's export policy. As such, the underlying fundamentals remain the same and it is certainly in the UK's interest to retain a high degree of commonality with EU regulations in order to ease future trade and collaboration.

Avoiding a race to the bottom in terms of arms-exports control and any rollback of the progress achieved over the last two decades is desirable. Continued collaboration and information sharing is required to prevent exploitation of discrepancies between the UK and the EU.

UK exports to Saudi Arabia

The UK's DSIS recognised what in narrow economic terms was an overdependence on one sector, the air sector, and even more so one region.

SAUDI DEFENCE
Saudi Air Force Eurofighter *Typhoon* combat aircraft were flown in a flypast to mark the 50th anniversary of the creation of the King Faisal Air Academy at King Salman airbase in Riyadh, 25 January 2017. CREDIT: FAYEZ NURELDINE/AFP via Getty Images.

> The UK is the second biggest exporter of defence products globally (after the US) ... However, the defence sector is extremely reliant on sales of air platforms to the Middle East and is all but unrepresented in exports to 17 of the 20 largest defence importers.[135]

Implicit within the DSIS was the potential difficulty of managing the supplier–purchaser relationship where the core customer base was too narrow. The sale of major weapons can provide an element of leverage or influence concerning the purchasing state's behaviour, but this can often be overstated. Any influence, however, will only be further diluted by overdependence on the part of the supplier state on a single country.

Saudi Arabia is by far the dominant market for UK defence exports. Over the 2016–20 period, Saudi Arabia accounted for an estimated 32% of all UK arms exports, followed by Oman with 17% and then the US with 14%. The reliance is not reciprocated. Of all imports to Saudi Arabia, UK kit accounted for just 9.3% compared to the 79% share for US kit between 2016 and 2020.[136]

The strong arms-trade relationship stems from a series of high-value deals over the last three decades, including the 1985 al-Yamamah deal and its 1993 renewal, reportedly worth between USD2bn and USD4bn a year to the UK into the years that followed, which included the transfer of *Tornado* IDS and ADV aircraft, *Hawk* advanced trainers, Pilatus PC-9 trainers, Jetstream aircraft, *Black Hawk* helicopters, mine countermeasures vessels (MCMVs), and command, control, communications and intelligence systems.[137] This deal was the subject of National Audit Office scrutiny and a Serious Fraud Office investigation regarding payments to consultants. The investigation was halted in 2006 on the grounds of needing to 'safeguard national and international security'. This was after the government of Saudi Arabia had expressed a clear view that continuing the investigation would seriously damage UK–Saudi security, intelligence and diplomatic cooperation, which, it was argued, would then have seriously negative consequences for UK national-security and foreign-policy objectives in the Middle East. Upon announcing the end of the investigation, attorney general Lord Goldsmith stated: 'It has been necessary to balance the need to maintain the rule of law against the wider public interest. No weight has been given to commercial interests or to the national economic interest.'[138]

Nonetheless, the following year, the GBP4.43bn (USD8.87bn at the 2007 exchange rate) Project Salam deal, which involved the transfer of 72 Eurofighter *Typhoons* and *Storm Shadow* land-attack cruise missiles to Saudi Arabia, signified the ongoing relationship and saw the UK's share of arms exports exceed that of the US globally.[139]

The risks of overdependence on one country include shifts in recipient defence spending and political preferences. A competitor may be more willing to engage in technology transfer and agree to demands for industrial participation. Sales are also subject to domestic policy if the country is suddenly subject to UK export restrictions on the grounds of any of the eight Consolidated Criteria.

Defenders of the relationship suggest it is worthwhile to maintain ties with Saudi Arabia even through the export of arms in order to retain influence over defence and security policy. This relationship, it is argued, can lead to more measured decisions about targeted strikes and regional engagements where other suppliers, such as Russia, are less likely to make these recommendations. Furthermore, the export of precision weapons with smaller conventional warheads should also reduce any wider casualties should a strike against an enemy combatant be made. Concerns have been raised that the UK is perhaps not using this influence to best effect, and that London could be stronger in its admonishment of any human-rights abuses, but any influence is better than none.

UK weapons sales to Saudi Arabia resulted in a long-running court case in the UK brought by CAAT against the British government. CAAT contested that despite 'overwhelming evidence of violations of International Humanitarian Law'[140] the UK continued to support the Royal Saudi Air Force (RSAF), including with the delivery of weapons that could be used in Yemen. That the RSAF had struck civilian targets was not disputed; rather, the CAAT case was based on Criterion 2c of the EU's Common Position policy (i.e., the policy the UK used to adhere to). This is where a proposed export represented a 'clear risk the items might be used in the commission of a serious violation of International Humanitarian Law'.[141] A ruling in June 2019 found in favour of CAAT in that the judgment determined that the UK government 'had not met its legal obligation … to make a systemic assessment of past possible violations' before it continued to grant arms-export licences to Saudi Arabia.[142]

In response, the UK government re-examined airstrikes that were identified as potentially causing civilian deaths. Following this review, it said it had found there were not 'any patterns of non-compliance' but rather that the civilian deaths were the result of 'isolated incidents'.[143] In the government's view, Saudi Arabia had a 'genuine intent'[144] to comply with international humanitarian law (IHL). Then-secretary of state for foreign, Commonwealth and development affairs Liz Truss said there was a not a 'clear risk'[145] that the continued supply of UK weapons to Saudi Arabia would result in a 'serious violation'[146] of IHL, which was not quite the same as saying there was no risk. Given the value of Saudi Arabia in terms of defence exports, and the wider security relationship, it appeared to be a risk the UK government was willing to accept. Despite the results of the review, CAAT's legal challenge will proceed to the High Court in January 2023.

Conclusion

The evolution of the UK's arms-export policy has been turbulent, with a chequered history regarding the extent to which human rights, internal repression and regional stability are considered seriously in licensing decisions. Various governments have enacted measures to improve the transparency and accountability of the policy, but the high ambitions of Robin Cook remain unfulfilled in deference to an economic prerogative. Arguably, the level of political influence over export decisions is too high to ensure an independent decision that adheres to the ultimate aims of the policy rather than an interpretation of language to suit foreign-policy or prosperity goals. The flaws in the fundamental set-up of CAEC also make holding government decisions to account challenging.

Regionally, the absence of a consolidated European market, one that potentially has the volume demand to reduce the need for extra-European sales, underscores the continuing importance of defence exports for countries where domestic requirements alone are economically prohibitive. In the case of the UK, this has been compounded by the 2016 decision to leave the EU and the wider economic impact of the withdrawal. Defence exports have, if anything, taken on even greater economic importance for the UK government.

Both the UK and the EU criteria for assessment of export decisions include a consideration of the impact on regional stability among seven other factors of concern. However, over the last decade, this consideration has only been cited in 2% of the total refusals or revocations of export licences. By far the more prohibitive factors are those international obligations the UK already adheres to and the risk of future transfer to undesirable end users. There are flaws in the criteria where the definitions are loose and open to interpretation. The language of the criteria has shifted in the wake of Brexit, making export decisions less restrictive, particularly if only a theoretical violation of rules by the buyer is perceived.

This shift arguably has its roots in the promotion of the prosperity agenda in the UK and the renewed support for arms exports seen under David Cameron's leadership, when the economic benefits of arms exports (and indeed a thriving defence industry as a result) – including more jobs, and higher-skilled and better-paid labour – were key drivers of policy. Furthermore, such benefits are also conducive to the 'levelling up' agenda, with profits spread across the UK owing to the various centres of industrial focus.

In the case of Saudi Arabia, while the argument holds firm that it is better to influence as an ally than to condemn as a critic – and lose a geopolitical chip in the process – this influence is currently not being used effectively. The benefits to the UK in terms of information sharing are also crucial to maintaining a presence in the Gulf.

Furthermore, the UK's position of influence will only last as long as domestic equipment remains competitive or desirable, which itself requires the requisite investment and becomes all the more challenging as market entrants enhance their offerings. The desire to support domestic industry and use export revenue to fund innovation may result in a race to the bottom, particularly if countries in the EU perceive that the UK has loosened its version of the Consolidated Criteria too much. The UK should hold firm on the ethical dimension and only take the economic argument so far. However, the revocations during the Arab Spring show that licensing policy is not forward-looking enough and needs to be more pre-emptive rather than reactive.

NOTES

1 ADS Group, 'Facts and Figures', https://www.adsgroup.org.uk/industry-issues/facts-figures/.

2 UK Defence and Security Exports, 'UK defence and security export statistics: 2020', October 2021, https://www.gov.uk/government/statistics/uk-defence-and-security-exports-for-2020/uk-defence-and-security-export-statistics-for-2020.

3 SIPRI, 'Trends in International Arms Transfers', 2020, https://sipri.org/sites/default/files/2021-03/fs_2103_at_2020.pdf.

4 HM Government, 'Defence and Security Industrial Strategy: A strategic approach to the UK's defence and security industrial sectors' CP410, March 2021, p. 3, https://assets.publishing.service.gov.uk/government/uploads/system/uploads/attachment_data/file/971983/Defence_and_Security_Industrial_Strategy_-_FINAL.pdf.

5 *Ibid.*, p. 4.

6 Sam Perlo-Freeman, 'The opportunity cost of world military spending', SIPRI, 5 April 2016, https://www.sipri.org/commentary/blog/2016/opportunity-cost-world-military-spending.

7 HM Government, 'Defence and Security Industrial Strategy: A strategic approach to the UK's defence and security industrial sectors' CP410, March 2021, p. 42, https://assets.publishing.service.gov.uk/government/uploads/system/uploads/attachment_data/file/971983/Defence_and_Security_Industrial_Strategy_-_FINAL.pdf.

8 *Ibid.*, p. 24.

9 *Ibid.*

10 *Ibid.*

11 Louisa Brooke-Holland, 'An Introduction to Defence Procurement', House of Commons Library CBP08486, 28 January 2019, p. 9, https://researchbriefings.files.parliament.uk/documents/CBP-8486/CBP-8486.pdf.

12 HM Government, 'Defence and Security Industrial Strategy: A strategic approach to the UK's defence and security industrial sectors' CP410, March 2021, p. 18, https://assets.publishing.service.gov.uk/government/uploads/system/uploads/attachment_data/file/971983/Defence_and_Security_Industrial_Strategy_-_FINAL.pdf.

13 IISS interviews with government and industry, 2021 and 2022.

14 *Ibid.*

15 *Ibid.*

16 *Ibid.*

17 *Ibid.*

18 Hansard, 'Consolidated EU and National Arms Export Licensing Criteria', March 2014, https://hansard.parliament.uk/commons/2014-03-25/debates/14032566000018/ConsolidatedEUAndNationalArmsExportLicensingCriteria.

19 *Ibid.*

20 UK Parliament, 'Trade Policy Update', Statement by Anne-Marie Trevelyan, Secretary of State for International Trade, 8 December 2021, https://questions-statements.parliament.uk/written-statements/detail/2021-12-08/HCWS449.

21 HM Government, 'NTE 2021/14: updates to the export control regime', 8 December 2021, https://www.gov.uk/government/publications/notice-to-exporters-202114-updates-to-the-export-control-regime/nte-202114-updates-to-the-export-control-regime.

22 House of Commons Library, 'UK amends its criteria for arms exports', March 2022, https://researchbriefings.files.parliament.uk/documents/CBP-9494/CBP-9494.pdf.

23 Emma Graham-Harrison, 'New rules on UK arms trade make it "easier" to sideline human rights', *Guardian*, 12 December 2021, https://www.theguardian.com/world/2021/dec/12/new-rules-on-uk-arms-trade-make-it-easier-to-sideline-human-rights.

24 IISS interviews, 2021 and 2022.

25 UK DSE values are based on when contracts are signed (not won as in IISS data) and reflect the value of orders won by UK companies for not only export of defence equipment but also services and support.

26 UK Department for International Trade (DIT), Defence & Security Organisation (DSO), 'UK defence and security export statistics for 2018', 30 July 2019, https://www.gov.uk/government/publications/uk-defence-and-security-exports-for-2018/uk-defence-and-security-export-statistics-for-2018.

27 UK Defence and Security Exports, 'UK defence and security export statistics: 2020', 26 October 2021, https://www.gov.uk/government/statistics/uk-defence-and-security-exports-for-2020/uk-defence-and-security-export-statistics-for-2020.

28 UK Defence and Security Exports, 'UK defence and security export statistics: 2020', 26 October 2021, https://www.gov.uk/government/statistics/uk-defence-and-security-exports-for-2020/uk-defence-and-security-export-statistics-for-2020; and House of Commons Library, 'UK Arms Exports Statistics', 1 December 2021, p. 6, https://researchbriefings.files.parliament.uk/documents/CBP-8310/CBP-8310.pdf.

29 UK Defence and Security Exports, 'UK defence and security export statistics: 2020', 26 October 2021, https://www.gov.uk/government/statistics/uk-defence-and-security-exports-for-2020/uk-defence-and-security-export-statistics-for-2020.

30 UK Department for International Trade (DIT), Defence & Security Organisation (DSO), 'UK defence and security export statistics for 2013', 8 July 2014, https://webarchive.nationalarchives.gov.uk/

ukgwa/20190802104341/https://www.gov.uk/government/statistics/uk-defence-and-security-export-figures-2013.

31 SIPRI, 'Trends in International Arms Transfers, 2020,' SIPRI Fact Sheet, March 2021 https://sipri.org/sites/default/files/2021-03/fs_2103_at_2020.pdf.

32 UK Defence and Security Exports, 'UK defence and security export statistics: 2020', 26 October 2021, https://www.gov.uk/government/statistics/uk-defence-and-security-exports-for-2020/uk-defence-and-security-export-statistics-for-2020.

33 Military Balance+, accessed June 2022.

34 US Energy Information Administration, 'Short Term Energy Outlook', 10 May 2022, https://www.eia.gov/outlooks/steo/pdf/steo_full.pdf.

35 SIPRI, Trends in International Arms Transfers, 2020, https://sipri.org/sites/default/files/2021-03/fs_2103_at_2020.pdf.

36 Military Balance+, accessed June 2022.

37 House of Commons Library, 'UK Arms Exports Statistics', 1 December 2021, p. 7, https://researchbriefings.files.parliament.uk/documents/CBP-8310/CBP-8310.pdf.

38 Ministry of the Armed Forces, 'Rapport au Parlement sur les exportations d'armement de la France 2021', [Report to Parliament on French arms exports 2021], 2 June 2021, https://www.vie-publique.fr/sites/default/files/rapport/pdf/280174.pdf.

39 Ministry of the Armed Forces, 'Rapport au Parlement sur les exportations d'armement de la France 2020', [Report to Parliament on French arms exports 2020], 2 June 2020, https://www.vie-publique.fr/sites/default/files/rapport/pdf/274475.pdf.

40 Federal Government, 'Bericht der Bundesregierung über ihre Exportpolitik für konventionelle Rüstungsgüter im Jahre 2019' [Report of the federal government on its export policy for conventional armaments in 2019], 20 June 2020, p. 9, https://www.bmwk.de/Redaktion/DE/Publikationen/Aussenwirtschaft/ruestungsexportbericht-2019.pdf?__blob=publicationFile&v=12.

41 Federal Government, 'Bericht der Bundesregierung über ihre Exportpolitik für konventionelle Rüstungsgüter im Jahre 2020' [Report of the federal government on its export policy for conventional armaments in 2020], 30 June 2021, p. 9, https://www.bmwk.de/Redaktion/DE/Downloads/B/bericht-der-bundesregierung-ueber-ihre-exportpolitik-fuer-konventionelle-ruestungsgueter-im-jahre-2020.pdf?__blob=publicationFile&v=6.

42 *Ibid.*, p. 9.

43 *Ibid.*, p. 28.

44 UK Defence and Security Exports, 'UK defence and security export statistics: 2020', 26 October 2021, https://www.gov.uk/government/statistics/uk-defence-and-security-exports-for-2020/uk-defence-and-security-export-statistics-for-2020.

45 ADS Group, 'Facts and Figures', https://www.adsgroup.org.uk/industry-issues/facts-figures/.

46 Laurence Lustgarten, *Law and the Arms Trade: Weapons, Blood and Rules* (Oxford: Hart Publishing, 2020), p. 107.

47 *Ibid.*

48 Rodrigo Fracalossi de Moraes, 'Arming a few dictators but not others: The politics of UK arms sales to Chile (1973–1989) and Argentina (1976–1983)', *The British Journal of Politics and International Relations*, vol. 24, no. 2, 324-342. https://journals.sagepub.com/doi/abs/10.1177/13691481211033192.

49 Lustgarten, *Law and the Arms Trade: Weapons, Blood and Rules*, p. 108.

50 'UK lifts ban on arms sales to Chile', *Guardian*, 23 July 1980, https://www.theguardian.com/world/2014/jul/23/pinochet-chile-thatcher-arms-sales.

51 'Q&A: The Scott Report', BBC, 27 April 2004, https://web.archive.org/web/20110715132532/http://news.bbc.co.uk/2/hi/programmes/bbc_parliament/3631539.stm.

52 The National Archives, 'Records of the Inquiry into Exports of Defence Equipment and Dual-Use Goods to Iraq and Related Prosecutions (Scott Inquiry)', 1996, https://discovery.nationalarchives.gov.uk/details/r/C188.

53 Hansard, 'Scott Report', House of Commons Debate, 15 February 1996, https://api.parliament.uk/historic-hansard/commons/1996/feb/15/scott-report.

54 David Marquand, 'Decline of the Public: The Hollowing Out of Citizenship', Ch. 1. Economical with the Actualité, p. 10, 20 January 2004, https://www.blackwellpublishing.com/content/BPL_Images/Content_Store/Sample_Chapter/0745629105/Marquand_001.pdf.

55 *Ibid.*, p. 10.

56 Hansard, 'Scott Report', House of Commons Debate, 15 February 1996, https://api.parliament.uk/historic-hansard/commons/1996/feb/15/scott-report.

57 *Ibid.*

58 'Robin Cook's speech on the government's ethical foreign policy', *Guardian*, 12 May 1997, https://www.theguardian.com/world/1997/may/12/indonesia.ethicalforeignpolicy.

59 Stephen Castle, 'Hawk jets sold to Indonesia,' *Independent*, 12 July 1997, https://www.independent.co.uk/news/hawk-jets-sold-to-indonesia-1250415.html.

60 'Examination of Witnesses (Questions 39–59)', Minutes of Evidence, Select Committee on Trade and Industry, 3 November 1999, https://publications.parliament.uk/pa/cm199899/cmselect/cmtrdind/541/9110302.htm.

61 Vikram Dodd and Ewen MacAskill, 'Labour drops "ethical" tag', *Guardian*, 4 September 2000, https://www.theguardian.com/politics/2000/sep/04/ethicalforeignpolicy.economy.

62 Saferworld, 'The Good, the Bad and the Ugly: A decade of Labour's arms exports', May 2007, pp.4–5, https://www.files.ethz.ch/isn/39520/The_Good_the_Bad_and_the_Ugly_rev.pdf.

63 Lustgarten, pp. 109, 111.

64 Defence Export and Services Organisation, 'Origin of DESO', 3 February 2007, https://web.archive.org/web/20070203204900/http://www.deso.mod.uk/origin.htm.

65 Hansard, 'Defence Equipment – Overseas Sales', 25 January 1966, https://api.parliament.uk/historic-hansard/commons/1966/jan/25/

defence-equipment-overseas-sales#S5CV0723P0_19660125_HOC_332.

66 Defence Export and Services Organisation, 'Our Mission, Vision and Role', 3 February 2007, https://web.archive.org/web/20070203123434/http://www.deso.mod.uk/about.htm.

67 Campaign Against Arms Trade, 'Call the Shots. DESO Campaign briefing', 3 February 2007, https://web.archive.org/web/20070203013500/http://www.caat.org.uk/publications/government/desobriefing0106.php#refer.

68 Defence Export and Services Organisation, 'DESO Facts', 3 February 2007, https://webarchive.nationalarchives.gov.uk/ukgwa/20080331131205/http://www.deso.mod.uk/fact.htm.

69 Select Committee on Defence, Written Evidence, 'Memorandum from Saferworld', 17 July 2008, https://publications.parliament.uk/pa/cm200708/cmselect/cmdfence/254/254we21.htm.

70 Campaign Against Arms Trade, 'Thousands Call for Closure of Arms Marketing Unit', 7 March 2007, https://caat.org.uk/news/2007-03-07-2/.

71 Hansard, 'Machinery of Government: Defence Trade Promotion,' 25 July 2007, https://publications.parliament.uk/pa/cm200607/cmhansrd/cm070725/wmstext/70725m0005.htm.

72 Campaign Against Arms Trade, 'Government announces closure of arms marketing unit after public campaign', https://caat.org.uk/news/2007-07-26-2/.

73 Rob Evans, 'Export department closure leaves defence firms out in the cold', *Guardian* 26 July 2007, https://www.theguardian.com/business/2007/jul/26/1.

74 Hansard, 'Foreign Affairs and Defence Volume 467', 12 November 2007 https://hansard.parliament.uk/commons/2007-11-12/debates/0711122000001/ForeignAffairsAndDefence.

75 UK Defence and Security Exports, 'About us', https://www.gov.uk/government/organisations/uk-defence-and-security-exports/about.

76 UK Foreign and Commonwealth Office, 'Britain's Foreign Policy in a Networked World', 1 July 2010, https://www.gov.uk/government/speeches/britain-s-foreign-policy-in-a-networked-world--2.

77 UK Foreign and Commonwealth Office, '"There will be no downgrading of human rights under this Government"', 31 March 2011, https://www.gov.uk/government/speeches/there-will-be-no-downgrading-of-human-rights-under-this-government.

78 Ian Black, 'David Cameron: UK arms sales to Gulf countries "legitimate"', *Guardian*, 6 November 2012, https://www.theguardian.com/politics/2012/nov/05/david-cameron-arms-sales-gulf.

79 'Cameron in Middle East Arms Tour Hypocrisy', Campaign Against Arms Trade (CAAT), 5 November 2012, https://caat.org.uk/news/2012-11-05-2/.

80 Prime Minister's Office, 'Prime Minister visits Oman', 21 December 2012, https://www.gov.uk/government/news/prime-minister-visits-oman.

81 UK Foreign and Commonwealth Office, 'Foreign Office Minister comments on review of arms exports', 18 February 2011, https://www.gov.uk/government/news/foreign-office-minister-comments-on-review-of-arms-exports; and UK Quadripartite Committee, 'Committees on Arms Export Controls – First Joint Report Scrutiny of Arms Exports (2012): UK Strategic Export Controls Annual Report 2010, Quarterly Reports for July to December 2010 and January to September 2011, the Government's Review of arms exports to the Middle East and North Africa, and wider arms control issues', p. 8. Arms Export Control Policies, 2 July 2012, pp. 21, 114, https://publications.parliament.uk/pa/cm201213/cmselect/cmquad/419/419.pdf pp. 21, 114.

82 House of Commons, 'Scrutiny of Arms Exports (2012)', Conclusions and Recommendations, pp. 21–2, 2 July 2012.

83 UK Foreign and Commonwealth Office, 'Response to Parliamentary Committee report on Arms Export Controls', 12 October 2012, https://www.gov.uk/government/news/response-to-parliamentary-committee-report-on-arms-export-controls.

84 Bernard Gray, 'Review of Acquisition for the Secretary of State for Defence An independent report by Bernard Gray', October 2009, https://delta.bipsolutions.com/docstore/ReviewAcquisitionGrayreport.pdf.

85 *Ibid.*, p. 6.

86 Ministry of Defence, 'National Security Through Technology: Technology, Equipment, and Support for UK Defence and Security', February 2012, p. 19, https://assets.publishing.service.gov.uk/government/uploads/system/uploads/attachment_data/file/27390/cm8278.pdf.

87 Lustgarten, p. 112.

88 HM Government, 'National Security Strategy and Strategic Defence and Security Review 2015 A Secure and Prosperous United Kingdom', November 2015, pp. 11–12, https://assets.publishing.service.gov.uk/government/uploads/system/uploads/attachment_data/file/555607/2015_Strategic_Defence_and_Security_Review.pdf.

89 HM Government, 'National Security Strategy and Strategic Defence and Security Review 2015: A Secure and Prosperous United Kingdom', November 2015, pp. 77–78, https://assets.publishing.service.gov.uk/government/uploads/system/uploads/attachment_data/file/555607/2015_Strategic_Defence_and_Security_Review.pdf.

90 Phillip Dunne, 'Growing the Contribution of Defence to UK Prosperity', July 2018, p. 57, https://assets.publishing.service.gov.uk/government/uploads/system/uploads/attachment_data/file/723679/20180709_MOD_Philip_Dunne_Review_FOR_WEB_PUB.pdf.

91 UK Ministry of Defence, 'Defence in a Competitive Age' CP 411, March 2021, https://assets.publishing.service.gov.uk/government/uploads/system/uploads/attachment_data/file/974661/CP411_-Defence_Command_Plan.pdf.

92 HM Government, 'Defence and Security Industrial Strategy: A strategic approach to the UK's defence and security industrial sectors', March 2021, p. 6, https://assets.publishing.service.gov.uk/government/uploads/system/uploads/attachment_data/file/971983/Defence_and_Security_Industrial_Strategy_-_FINAL.pdf.

93 *Ibid.*

94 HM Government, 'Global Britain in a competitive age: The Integrated Review of Security, Defence, Development and Foreign Policy', March 2021, https://assets.publishing.service.gov.uk/government/uploads/system/uploads/attachment_data/file/975077/Global_Britain_in_a_Competitive_Age-_the_Integrated_Review_of_Security__Defence__Development_and_Foreign_Policy.pdf.

95 HM Government, 'Defence and Security Industrial Strategy: A strategic approach to the UK's defence and security industrial sectors.' March 2021, p. 6, https://assets.publishing.service.gov.uk/government/uploads/system/uploads/attachment_data/file/971983/Defence_and_Security_Industrial_Strategy_-_FINAL.pdf.

96 IISS interviews with government and industry, 2021 and 2022.

97 *Ibid.*

98 Emily Thornberry, 'To honour Robin Cook's legacy we must end the scandal of secretive UK arms sales', *New Statesman*, 15 February 2021, https://www.newstatesman.com/politics/uk-politics/2021/02/honour-robin-cook-s-legacy-we-must-end-scandal-secretive-uk-arms-sales.

99 *Ibid.*

100 HM Government, 'Export Control Act', 2002, https://www.legislation.gov.uk/ukpga/2002/28/pdfs/ukpga_20020028_en.pdf.

101 HM Government, 'The Export Control Order', 2008, https://www.legislation.gov.uk/uksi/2008/3231/contents/made.

102 Department for International Trade, 'UK Strategic Export Control Lists', June 2021, https://assets.publishing.service.gov.uk/government/uploads/system/uploads/attachment_data/file/1052560/uk-strategic-export-control-lists.pdf.

103 'Wassenaar Arrangement on Export Controls for Conventional Arms and Dual-Use Goods and Technologies. List of Dual-Use Goods and Technologies and Munitions List', December 2021, https://www.wassenaar.org/app/uploads/2021/12/Public-Docs-Vol-II-2021-List-of-DU-Goods-and-Technologies-and-Munitions-List-Dec-2021.pdf.

104 Department for International Trade and Export Control Join Unit, 'UK Strategic Export Control Lists', 3 August 2012 (updated 23 February 2017), https://www.gov.uk/guidance/uk-strategic-export-control-lists-the-consolidated-list-of-strategic-military-and-dual-use-items.

105 'Wassenaar Arrangement on Export Controls for Conventional Arms and Dual-Use Goods and Technologies' Public Documents, December 2019 (update), https://www.wassenaar.org/app/uploads/2019/12/WA-DOC-19-Public-Docs-Vol-I-Founding-Documents.pdf.

106 Hansard, 'Consolidated EU and National Arms Export Licensing Criteria', March 2014, https://hansard.parliament.uk/commons/2014-03-25/debates/14032566000018/ConsolidatedEUAndNationalArmsExportLicensingCriteria.

107 Hansard, 'Defence Exports', 28 July 1997, https://hansard.parliament.uk/commons/1997-07-28/debates/4451d964-73fa-4218-8bba-cc3c48bb40de/DefenceExports#contribution-0182fe25-f60c-4c60-8147-10d07addb6b2.

108 European Parliament, 'EU rules on control of arms exports', November 2018, https://www.europarl.europa.eu/RegData/etudes/ATAG/2018/628317/EPRS_ATA(2018)628317_EN.pdf; and Eur-Lex, 'Council Common Position 2008/944/CFSP of 8 December 2008 defining common rules governing control of exports of military technology and equipment', 8 December 2008, https://eur-lex.europa.eu/legal-content/EN/TXT/?uri=CELEX%3A32008E0944.

109 Export Control Joint Unit and Department for International Trade, 'Strategic export controls: licensing data annual reports', 12 April 2022, https://www.gov.uk/government/collections/strategic-export-controls-licensing-data-annual-reports.

110 IISS interviews with government and industry, 2021 and 2022.

111 *Ibid.*

112 Hansard, 'Consolidated EU and National Arms Export Licensing Criteria', March 2014, https://hansard.parliament.uk/commons/2014-03-25/debates/14032566000018/ConsolidatedEUAndNationalArmsExportLicensingCriteria.

113 Hansard, 'Consolidated EU and National Arms Export Licensing Criteria', March 2014, https://hansard.parliament.uk/commons/2014-03-25/debates/14032566000018/ConsolidatedEUAndNationalArmsExportLicensingCriteria.

114 UK Parliament, 'Role – Committees on Arms Exports Control', https://committees.parliament.uk/committee/15/committees-on-arms-export-controls/role/.

115 House of Commons Library, 'An Introduction to UK Arms Exports', 16 May 2018, p. 24, https://researchbriefings.files.parliament.uk/documents/CBP-8312/CBP-8312.pdf.

116 UK Parliament, 'UK arms exports in 2019 inquiry launched', 9 February 2021, https://committees.parliament.uk/committee/15/committees-on-arms-export-controls/news/139111/uk-arms-exports-in-2019-inquiry-launched/.

117 IISS interview.

118 *Ibid.*

119 Lustgarten, p. 119.

120 House of Commons Committees on Arms Export Controls, 'UK arms exports during 2016', 11 July 2018, p. 6, https://publications.parliament.uk/pa/cm201719/cmselect/cmquad/666/666.pdf.

121 House of Commons Committees on Arms Export Controls, 'UK arms exports during 2016: Government Response to the Committees' First Joint Report', 27 November 2018, https://publications.parliament.uk/pa/cm201719/cmselect/cmquad/1789/1789.pdf.

122 Saferworld, 'Saferworld statement on UK arms exports report by the Committees on Arms Export Controls (CAEC)', 19 July 2018, https://www.saferworld.org.uk/resources/news-and-analysis/post/783-saferworld-statement-on-the-report-on-uk-arms-exports-during-2016-by-the-committees-on-arms-export-controls-caec.

123 Lustgarten, p. 121.

124 European Union, 'Council Common Position 2008/944/CFSP of 8 December 2008 defining common rules governing control of exports of military technology and equipment', https://eur-lex.europa.eu/legal-content/EN/TXT/?uri=CELEX%3A32008E0944.

125 *Ibid.*

126 Eur-Lex, 'Consolidated version of the Treaty on the Functioning of the European Union PART SEVEN – GENERAL AND FINAL PROVISIONS Article 346 (ex Article 296 TEC)', 7 July 2016, https://eur-lex.europa.eu/legal-content/EN/TXT/HTML/?uri=CELEX:12016E346&from=EN.

127 UK Parliament, 'Trade Policy Update', Statement by Anne-Marie Trevelyan, Secretary of State for International Trade, 8 December 2021, https://questions-statements.parliament.uk/written-statements/detail/2021-12-08/HCWS449.

128 *Ibid.*

129 House of Commons Library, 'UK amends its criteria for arms exports', March 2022, https://researchbriefings.files.parliament.uk/documents/CBP-9494/CBP-9494.pdf.

130 *Ibid.*

131 Emma Graham-Harrison, 'New rules on UK arms trade make it "easier" to sideline human rights', *Guardian*, 12 December 2021, https://www.theguardian.com/world/2021/dec/12/new-rules-on-uk-arms-trade-make-it-easier-to-sideline-human-rights.

132 *Ibid.*

133 IISS interviews with government and industry, 2021 and 2022.

134 Eur-Lex, 'Trade and Cooperation Agreement between the European Union and the European Atomic Energy Community, of the one part, and the United Kingdom of Great Britain and Northern Ireland, of the other part', 30 April 2021, https://eur-lex.europa.eu/legal-content/EN/TXT/?uri=uriserv:OJ.L_.2021.149.01.0010.01.ENG.

135 HM Government, 'Defence and Security Industrial Strategy: A strategic approach to the UK's defence and security industrial sectors' CP410, March 2021, p. 75, https://assets.publishing.service.gov.uk/government/uploads/system/uploads/attachment_data/file/971983/Defence_and_Security_Industrial_Strategy_-_FINAL.pdf.

136 SIPRI, Trends in International Arms Transfers, 2020, https://sipri.org/sites/default/files/2021-03/fs_2103_at_2020.pdf.

137 'The Complete Package', Janes, 28 March 1992, https://customer.janes.com/Janes/Display/jdw00718-jdw-1992; and David Pallister, 'The arms deal they called the dove: how Britain grasped the biggest prize', *Guardian*, 15 December 2006, https://www.theguardian.com/world/2006/dec/15/bae.saudiarabia.

138 Hansard, 'BAE Systems: Al Yamamah Contract', 14 December 2006, https://hansard.parliament.uk/lords/2006-12-14/debates/06121476000003/BAESystemsAlYamamahContract.

139 Military Balance+, accessed June 2022.

140 Campaign Against Arms Trade, 'CAAT's Legal Challenge', https://caat.org.uk/homepage/stop-arming-saudi-arabia/caats-legal-challenge/.

141 Eur-Lex, 'Council Common Position 2008/944/CFSP of 8 December defining common rules governing control of exports of military technology and equipment', https://eur-lex.europa.eu/legal-content/EN/TXT/?uri=CELEX%3A32008E0944.

142 Louisa Brooke-Holland and Ben Smith, 'UK arms exports to Saudi Arabia: Q&A' House of Commons Library Briefing Paper, 29 January 2021, p. 14, https://researchbriefings.files.parliament.uk/documents/CBP-8425/CBP-8425.pdf.

143 Elizabeth Truss, Secretary of State for International Trade, 'UK Parliament statement', 7 July 2021, https://questions-statements.parliament.uk/written-statements/detail/2020-07-07/HCWS339.

144 *Ibid.*

145 *Ibid.*

146 *Ibid.*

FRANCE AND GERMANY

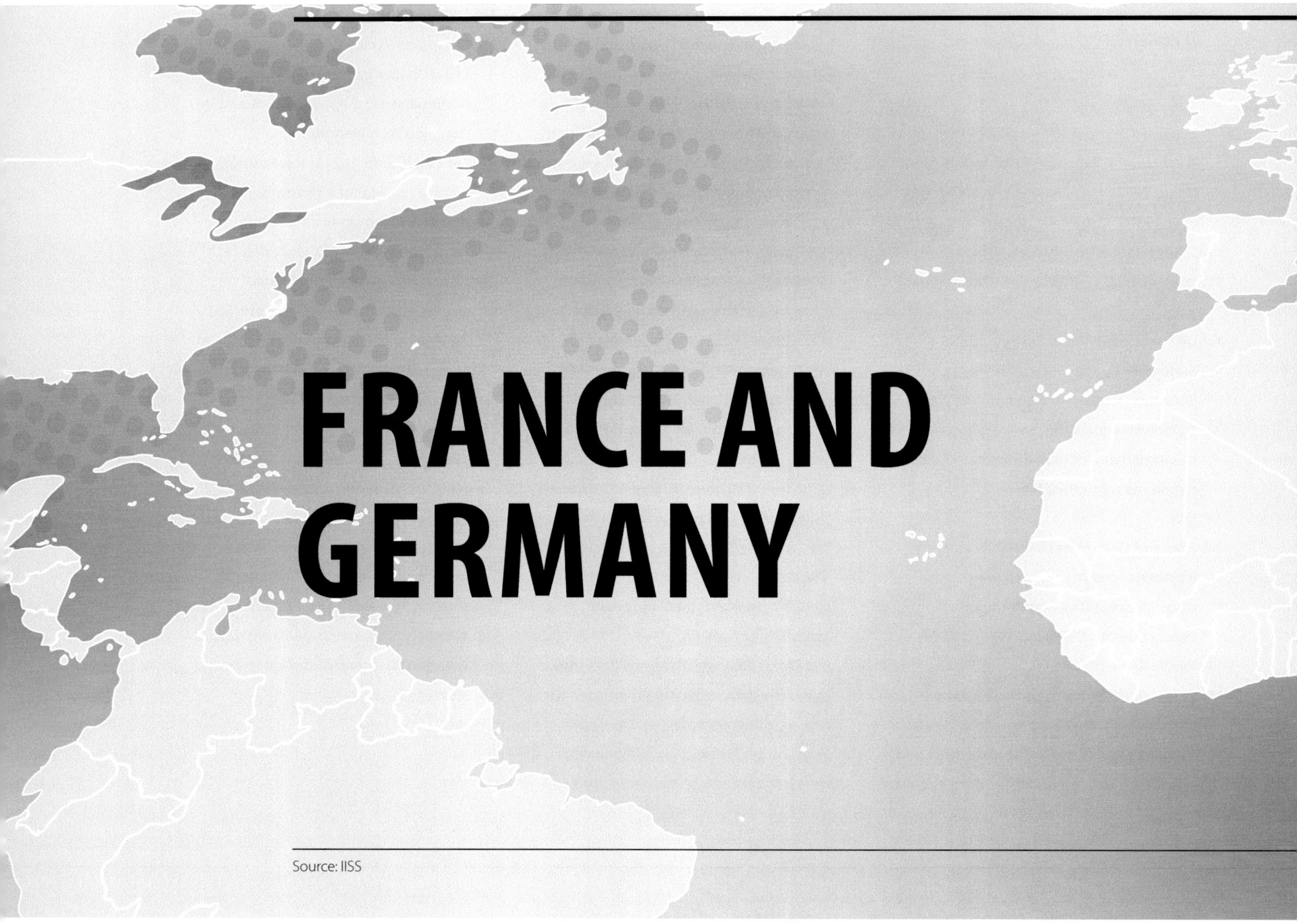

Source: IISS

CHAPTER 7

Map 7.1: **Selected* combat-aircraft sales to the Middle East, North Africa and Asia from France**

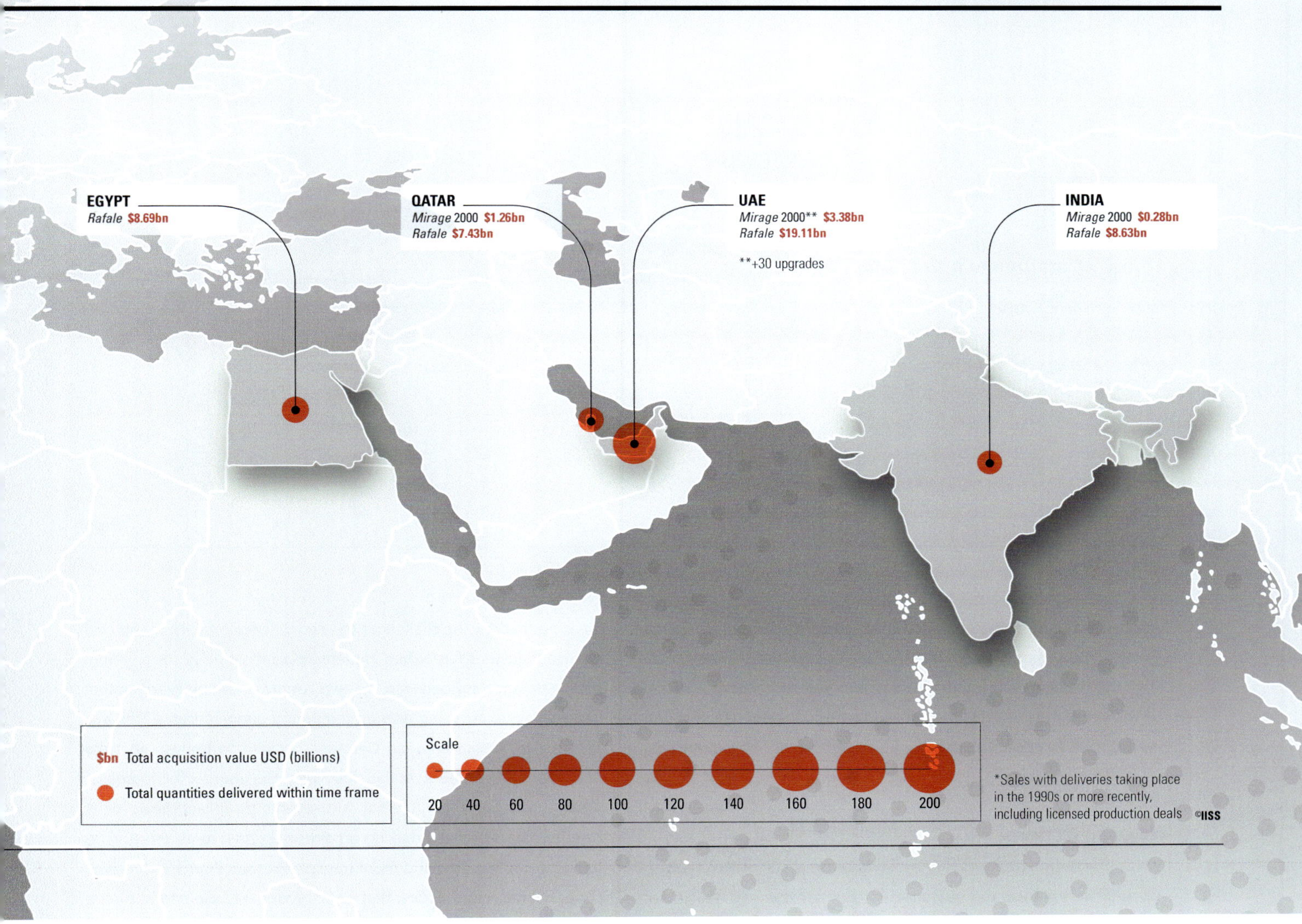

At first glance, the European Union's (EU) two largest exporters of major weapons, France and Germany, have markedly different arms-export policies. These differences are exemplified by the disagreements between the two over the course of the past decade, with Germany blocking exports of joint programmes or slowing down or denying the approval of licences for sub-components supplied to France.[1] While clear divergences exist, they should not be overemphasised, and irrespective of the differences, both countries' national decision-making processes on arms exports can on occasion deliver surprisingly similar outcomes.

For most of the twenty-first century, Germany was led by Angela Merkel, whose tenure as chancellor lasted from 2005 to 2021. While France arguably experienced more political upheaval than Germany during this period, Paris's arms-export policy has been more consistent than Berlin's.

Germany's Bundestag has greater oversight of arms-export policy than the Assemblée Nationale has in France. As the issue is more politicised in Berlin than it is in Paris, with some political parties opposing arms sales and arguing for a more restrictive approach, German decision-makers in this area are more constrained.[2] One explanation for the greater politicisation in Germany may be the higher sensitivity of its citizens to the topic of the arms trade. A 2021 study, surveying over 6,600 citizens in France and Germany on their views on the arms trade, found that 'German respondents are more caring for the moral consequences of arms trade, react less positively to its economic benefits, and that a larger share of German respondents is in

Timeline 7.1: Selected* combat-aircraft sales to the Middle East, North Africa and Asia from France

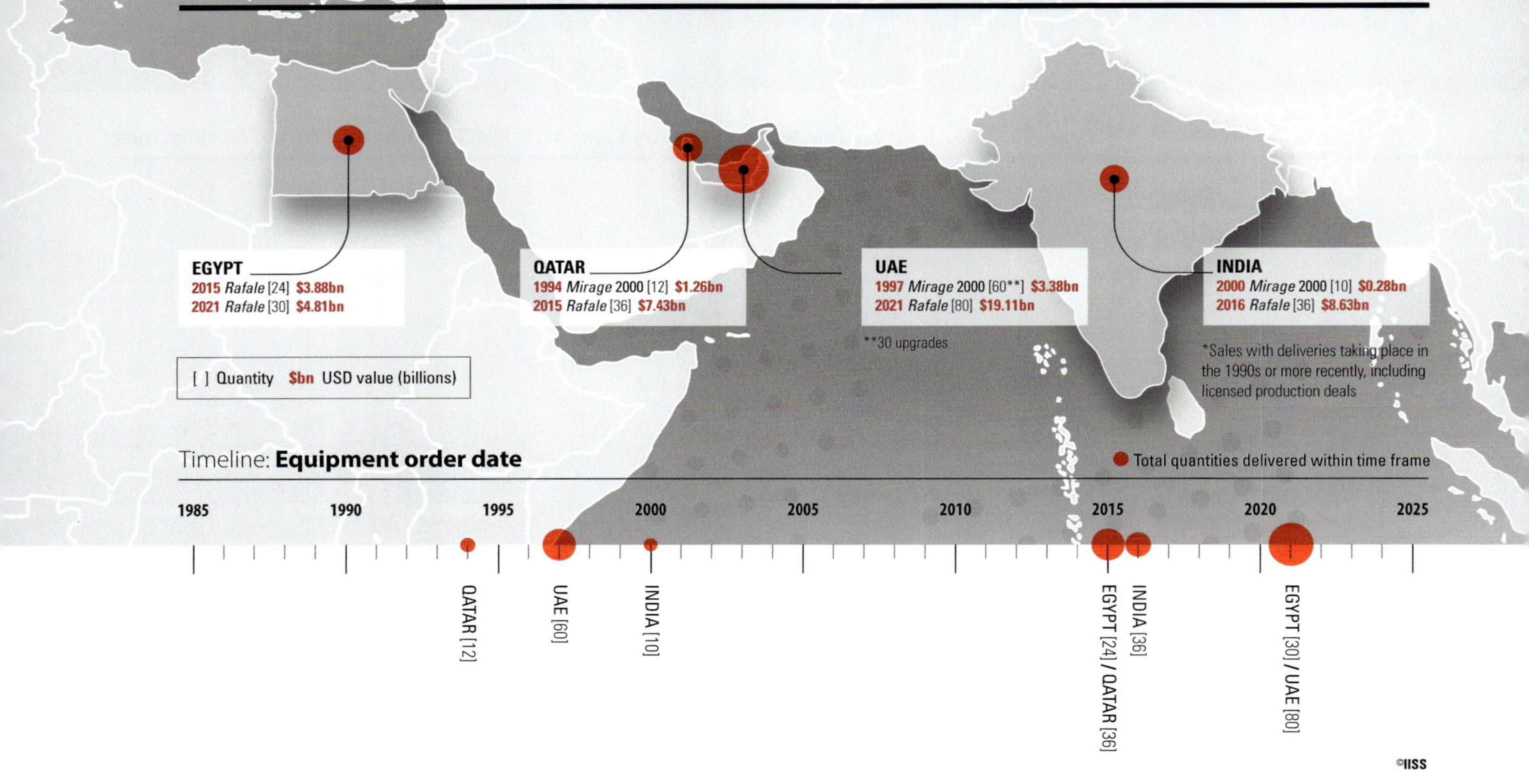

Source: IISS

fundamental opposition compared to French respondents'.[3] German society appears to have a generally negative view of the arms industry.[4] The German government, however, in September 2022 indicated it wished to pursue a less restrictive export policy where the country was involved as a partner in wider European defence programmes.[5]

Different yet similar

While the two neighbours vary widely in terms of political context and societal acceptance, the outcomes of their arms-export policies are not too dissimilar. France and Germany have been among the world's five largest arms suppliers for several decades.[6] Both countries have an advanced defence technological and industrial base (DTIB), ranking among the world's largest arms manufacturers in all domains.[7] In 2014, according to the latest available data on the industry association's website, Germany's defence and security sector accounted for 135,700 direct and 273,400 indirect jobs.[8] In France, according to the Ministry of Armed Forces, the industry generates around 200,000 jobs.[9] France and Germany also already export common weapons programmes, as the two governments jointly hold, alongside Spain, 25.9% of Airbus.[10] Airbus is involved in most of Germany's military fixed-wing-aircraft sales.[11] For both France and Germany, Middle Eastern countries are among their most important customers.[12]

When examining policies rather than politics, French and German arms exports may therefore be more similar than first meets the eye. This is not to deny the challenges the two defence establishments and defence industries face when implementing day-to-day cooperation. But the antagonism between the two countries can be exaggerated, especially when focusing only on temporary disagreements. This was the case, for instance, when Germany decided to impose an arms embargo against Saudi Arabia following the murder of journalist Jamal Khashoggi in 2018. What such events do reflect, however, is that Germany's decision-making on arms exports is more sensitive to domestic politicisation and more transparent than France's. However, it does not necessarily follow that Berlin has more concern for the issue of regional stability in the context of military sales than Paris does.

The export processes

The French arms-export control system rests on a principle of prohibition: companies cannot export war materials to non-member states of the EU or to territories excluded from the customs territory of the EU, unless a licence is granted. All licences are examined via an inter-ministerial process. The key institutions involved are the Ministry of Defence, the Ministry of Foreign Affairs, the Ministry of Economy and the Secrétariat général de la défense et de la sécurité nationale (SGDSN, the defence and foreign-policy office of the prime minister).

Firms must apply for export licences. Applications are processed using the export-licence information, management and administration system (système d'information, de gestion et d'administration des

THE REICHSTAG BUILDING
The Reichstag building which houses Germany's lower house of parliament (Bundestag). CREDIT: JOHN MACDOUGALL/AFP via Getty Images.

licences d'exportation, SIGALE). On this platform, companies declare their intention to use a licence and submit their applications. The various ministerial departments also use the SIGALE system to examine the applications and, where appropriate, issue export licences.

Once the Ministry of the Armed Forces' Direction générale de l'armement (DGA) has verified the admissibility of the application, the inter-ministerial procedure begins. Representatives of the Ministry of Defence, the Ministry for Foreign Affairs and the Ministry of the Economy[13] each evaluate the licence applications according to their own assessment criteria and issue an opinion (favourable, favourable with conditions or unfavourable).

The Ministry of Defence's assessment is based on strategic, industrial and technological issues. It also considers the potential operational impact that these exports could have on the French forces and their allies and assesses the risks. The Ministry of Foreign Affairs evaluates the geopolitical impact of the sales and the adequacy of the requests with the orientations of France's foreign policy and international commitments. The Ministry of the Economy assesses the projects by considering the client's financial resources. It also considers the industrial dimension, especially the interest that such an export may represent for the preservation, or even survival, of an industrial sector.[14] Apart from these criteria, ministerial instructions are also based on the antecedents (agreements or refusals) formulated at the national level or by other EU member states, and on the evolutions (technical, political) likely to change these former decisions.[15]

The length of this ministerial-examination phase varies depending on both the department and the issues raised by each request. In most cases, opinions are delivered electronically. Nevertheless, if the request is the subject of disagreements between the numerous ministries, it is submitted to a specific body, the Commission interministérielle pour l'étude des exportations de matériels de guerre (CIEEMG, Interministerial commission for the study of war materials exports).

The CIEEMG is composed of representatives of the Ministry of Defence, the Ministry of Foreign Affairs and the Ministry of the Economy, as well as from the SGDSN. It meets once a month (except in August) in a plenary session chaired by the SGDSN. The CIEEMG issues an opinion to the attention of the prime minister of France, who is formally responsible for the final decision. However, the president of the Republic has the final say on politically, diplomatically or economically sensitive cases. Once the decision is made, the SGDSN notifies customs, who issue the licence.

Since 2012, agents of the DGA and the Armed Forces Inspectorate (Contrôleur général des armées, CGA) have carried out *a posteriori* controls of arms exports. This monitoring takes the form of off-site checks and on-site inspections at the companies' premises. It aims to verify all the obligations with which the industrials are required to comply when exporting war materials and similar materiel. It is not equivalent to the post-shipment controls, conducted in the recipient country, that Germany has implemented since 2015.

The on-site inspection involves officials reviewing each commercial, technical, managerial and legal document related to the licence and contract. The officials also have the right to inspect the company's accounts and to audit its processes to ensure compliance with export-control legislation. Following the inspection, an official report is issued, to which the company has ten days to respond. The report and the response are then submitted to the Comité ministériel du contrôle a posteriori (CMCAP, Ministerial committee for a posteriori control). This committee, chaired by a member of the CGA, meets once a month to examine the results of the various inspections and decides on the appropriate follow-up action. Significant or repetitive non-compliance can lead to sanctions.[16]

In Germany, the export-control system distinguishes between two categories of defence-related products: 'weapons of war' (*Kriegswaffen*) and 'other military equipment' (*sonstige Rüstungsgüter*). 'Weapons of war' include major weapons such as combat aircraft or naval vessels, while 'other military equipment' encompasses weapon categories such as small arms and light weapons, electronic-warfare equipment and explosive substances.[17]

As in France, different ministerial departments or agencies in Germany scrutinise export licences, and elected officials eventually decide on sensitive export-licence applications. The Ministry for Economic Affairs and Climate Action (Bundesministerium für Wirtschaft und Klimaschutz, BMWK)[18] oversees the licencing process for both categories of defence product, but it obtains input from the

ISRAELI MILITARY EXERCISE
A German Luftwaffe Eurofighter *Typhoon* lands during the 'Blue Flag' multinational air-defence exercise at the Ovda air force base, north of the Israeli city of Eilat, 24 October 2021.
CREDIT: JACK GUEZ/AFP via Getty Images.

ministries of defence, foreign affairs, finance and interior. BMWK is the parent agency for the Federal Office for Economic Affairs and Export Control (Bundesamt für Wirtschaft und Ausfuhrkontrolle, BAFA), the central licensing authority for both military equipment and dual-use goods.

The bureaucratic route that licence applications take depends on whether the products under consideration for the licence are 'war weapons' or 'other military equipment'. Exports of war weapons are, in the first instance, presumed to be prohibited, while 'other military equipment' products are considered free-trade goods and presumed to be exportable. For this second category, BAFA assesses the potential export. BAFA can only opt to deny the licence if there are clear grounds for doing so.

The licensing process for 'weapons of war' is more restrictive than it is for 'other military equipment'. Firms submit their licence applications to BAFA, but they are forwarded to BMWK. BMWK consults with the Ministry of Foreign Affairs and sometimes the Ministry of Defence if there are no precedent cases.[19] If disagreements emerge within or between the BMWK and BAFA, licence requests are sent up to the state secretaries, the second-highest-ranking ministerial officials. If the proposed export is especially sensitive or complex and they cannot agree, the Federal Security Council (Bundessicherheitsrat, BSR) is asked to settle the matter. However, the BSR comprises the ministers of foreign affairs, defence and finance, among others, with the chancellor presiding.[20]

The French and German export systems have similarities, such as an inter-ministerial process, and the fact that the final decision rests with political leadership, but they also differ. In Germany, dual-use-goods licences are also considered by BAFA, whereas in France dual-use-goods exports follow a different bureaucratic route than 'war materials'.[21] Another difference is the 'advance inquiry' process that BAFA implements with the firms. This allows for companies to consult the administration on the potential outcome of the licence assessment. The answer to the advance inquiries is not binding and cannot be substituted for a licence.[22]

Since 2015, Germany has exercised post-shipment export controls with on-site inspections. This concerns all types of 'weapons of war' and specific types of small arms (pistols, revolvers and sniper rifles).[23] This new type of exports control was introduced as part of a broader effort to implement a more restrictive approach. The first on-site inspections started in 2017.[24]

Considering regional impacts

By their very nature, French and German bureaucratic processes alone provide little insight into how a prospective customer state is evaluated in its regional context. For a better understanding of a country's export policy, one needs to further explore how political assessments are reached.

In France, all licences are assessed based on the criteria defined in the framework of international agreements, including the European Union Common Position defining common rules governing the control of exports of military technology and equipment (2008/944/CFSP) and the Arms Trade Treaty (ATT). However, unlike other EU member states, France did not transpose the Common Position in its legislation. The political criteria applied instead are not disclosed, rather they are included under the 'high level government directives' (*directives de haut niveau*, DHN), which are classified.[25]

The political-assessment criteria were divulged only once, in a 2000 parliamentary report. It is most likely that these have evolved over the past 20 years. But in 2000 the list included internal repression; not provoking or prolonging armed conflicts or aggravating tensions either internally or regionally; the possibility of the exported arms being used against French armed forces or allied forces; risks of diversion; and unwanted technology transfer. Those criteria were all referring to the European Code of Conduct (predecessor to the EU Common Position). Other criteria not related to the

EGYPT–FRANCE WEAPONS DIPLOMACY
Three French *Rafale* fighter jets flown over Cairo with other Egyptian Air Force warplanes (unseen), 21 July 2015. Egypt took delivery of three *Rafale* fighter jets from France, the first of 24 warplanes sold in a EUR5.2 bn deal. CREDIT: KHALED DESOUKI/AFP via Getty Images.

Code of Conduct included any 'request ill-adapted to the estimated need of the buyer country'.[26]

Jacques Maire and Michèle Tabarot, authors of a 2020 parliamentary report on arms exports, were unable to access the content of the DHN. But the authors argued that some DHN are specific to a country and determine whether the risks are great enough to justify not exporting particular military equipment. Other DHN are specific to a certain type of equipment and categorise countries depending on the level of performance to which they can be granted access. The DHN are not binding, meaning the decision-makers in the CIEEMG can assess every licence on a case-by-case basis. These documents are revised every two to three years.[27]

According to individuals previously involved in the export-control process who were interviewed for this dossier, CIEEMG members, including those in the Ministry of Armed Forces, carefully consider regional stability as a criterion. Paris, like Washington, the interviewees suggested, is also generally unwilling to introduce a military capability into a region where it is not already present. Moreover, they asserted that industrial considerations are not allowed to trump concerns over regional stability. The recipient country's human-rights record is also taken into consideration.[28] Irrespective of these hurdles, France continues to remain in the top five major arms-exporting states.

Such considerations sometimes emerge in the public debate. For instance, Maire and Tabarot noted that France suspended export licences to Turkey following Ankara's intervention in northeastern Syria in October 2019.[29] But there have also been cases where the criterion of regional stability did not sway the decision. For example, when France decided to sell the *Mistral*-class amphibious assault ship to Russia in 2010, 'it was borderline in terms of the risk of destabilization at the regional level', according to one French arms-export specialist. They said that the director for strategic affairs at the French Ministry of Foreign Affairs at the time was opposed to the sale.[30]

The weight, or otherwise, given to certain criteria is not always clear. For instance, France sold *Sherpa* armoured vehicles to Egypt, which the country then used for internal repression.[31] While in the French assessment of export licences regional stability is discussed, it is not the most important factor when deciding to grant or deny a licence.

Unlike France, Germany's decision-making criteria are available. The key document is the 'Political Principles Adopted by the Government of the Federal Republic of Germany for the Export of Weapons of War and Other Military Equipment'.[32] The Political Principles incorporate the EU Common Position 2008/944/CFSP licensing criteria. Notably, the domestic criteria take precedence if they are more restrictive.[33] German authorities claim that this is the case when it comes to assessing the risk of misuse of weapons for internal repression or human-rights violations. The Political Principles prohibit the export when there is 'sufficient suspicion' of such misuse, whereas the EU Common Position criteria deny the export if there is a 'clear risk' and the ATT when an 'overriding risk' exists.[34]

The Political Principles apply differently to EU and NATO members, and to 'NATO-equivalent countries' (Australia, Japan, New Zealand and Switzerland), on the one hand, and 'third countries' on the other. The former enjoy a presumption of licence approval, while the latter face a presumption of denial. Accordingly, for arms exports to third countries, a licence must be justified by 'particular German foreign policy or security-policy interests'.[35] Exceptions to the prohibition rule for licences to 'third countries' must be justified on a case-by-case basis.[36]

For 'third countries', the Political Principles state that the licence will not be approved if there is an internal armed conflict and if there is 'sufficient suspicion of abuse of internal repression and systematic human rights violations'.[37] When it comes to regional stability, the licence will not be approved if the recipient state is involved in an armed conflict or where there is a threat of conflict, or where the export of weapons may trigger, maintain or exacerbate the outbreak of an armed conflict. As a matter of principle, deliveries to countries that are involved in external armed conflict or where there is a risk of such conflict breaking out are therefore ruled out.[38]

Despite this seemingly strong statement on the importance of regional stability in assessing export licences, there are claims it has not always been strictly implemented in practice. According to a January 2021 report, a more important criterion for denying licences was a poor human-rights record, rather than regional stability. The report raises the examples of civilian massacres following the military takeover in Egypt 2013 and the murder of the Saudi dissident and *Washington Post* journalist Jamal Khashoggi in 2018.[39]

The Political Principles were updated in June 2019 and were stricter than the previous version adopted in 2000. The added restrictions were threefold. Firstly, small-arms exports to third countries were no longer permitted in principle. Secondly, the political guidelines were revised to emphasise the support for armament cooperation at the EU level; Permanent Structured Cooperation and the European Defence Fund are now taken into consideration when assessing export licences. Thirdly, the principles were updated to integrate changes in international export-control regimes such as the inclusion of the Arms Trade Treaty.[40] Further revisions of Germany's arms-export regulation are expected at the end of 2022. As of October 2022, the coalition government was still trying to reconcile a desire to adopt a more restrictive position in general, with pressure to ensure compatibility with the objectives of other European partners to lower obstacles for exports of jointly developed and produced systems and with the need – highlighted by the war in Ukraine – to be able to support the right to self-defence of countries under the UN Charter.[41]

An outline that was circulated in October suggested that the criteria for export decisions will in future be defined in law rather than as political guidance. Furthermore, human rights concerns and the implications of European armaments cooperation are expected to feature prominently. The list of NATO equivalent countries is likely to expand and Chile, the Republic of Korea, Singapore, and Uruguay were muted as candidates. Post-shipment controls are likely to expand. The issue of regional stability is not explicitly mentioned. The published outline had yet to be discussed among ministries and elements of it might thus be adopted before new legislation is passed on to parliament for consideration.

Accounting for French interests

As previously discussed, there is no universal definition of what constitutes regional stability, nor indeed an agreed approach to assess this in any specific context as part of a major-weapons export process. What is clear is that the export of major conventional weapons has a foreign-policy strand and that sales can often attract wider attention.

In France, there is a close link between foreign policy and arms exports regarding industrial and strategic considerations. The logic is as follows:

> for France to be able to act independently in the defence and foreign-policy domains, which means not having to depend on other states when it wishes to use force, it requires its own weapons-manufacturing capacity. However, the French defence industry cannot survive on domestic orders alone: it also needs to export.[42]

This rationale 'is perceived, not always real and sometimes fantasized'.[43] But it is nonetheless the main issue in any official discussion and the justification for the French arms-export policy, and it can be found repeatedly in French public debate. Defence ministers under Nicolas Sarkozy,[44] François Hollande[45] and Emmanuel Macron[46] all subscribed to it. Most of those within the French defence establishment employ this rationale.[47] Furthermore, the question of 'sovereignty' was central to arms-export decision-making and was taken into account by the DGA within the CIEEMG process.[48] For one French arms-export specialist, the key motivation for arms exports is not economics, but rather 'strategic autonomy'. Without sales, technological development will slow down, and competence will thus dry out, compromising strategic autonomy.[49]

In this regard, arms sales are seen as both an expression and a fundamental component of France's sovereignty. This is anchored in General Charles de Gaulle's foreign-policy vision – still arguably the point of reference for the French political establishment[50] – which entailed the development of an independent defence design, development and manufacturing capacity. The rationale for supporting arms exports was sustained during the Cold War by the belief that French arms sales helped recipient countries to gain some distance from the United States or the Soviet Union.[51] Taken together, these factors meant successive French political leaders and the wider defence community placed arms-export policy within the framework of foreign-policy aims. As such, securing major-weapons sales can be viewed as an objective of France's foreign policy. This is evident in Paris's reaction to Australia's cancellation, in September 2021, of the submarine government to government agreement signed earlier in 2016. The impact of the cancellation in preference of pursuing a US–UK alliance was not only a commercial setback; it also damaged strategic relations between Canberra and Paris.[52]

A Berlin perspective

In Germany, arms sales and foreign policy take a different approach, with greater emphasis placed on export control rather than export promotion. Berlin's foreign-policy goals appear to be less focused on defence and military issues than France's. According to Bastian Giegerich and Maximilian Terhalle, Germany failed to significantly develop a coherent strategic vision for its defence and security policy during Merkel's 16-year tenure.[53] For these authors, despite the emergence of the 'Munich consensus' in 2014 – when federal president Joachim Gauck, minister of foreign affairs Frank-Walter Steinmeier and minister of defence Ursula von der Leyen indicated that Germany

FRANCE–UAE DIPLOMACY
(l–r) French Minister of the Armed Forces Sébastien Lecornu, UAE President Mohammed bin Zayed Al-Nahyan, and Paris military governor General Christophe Abad, walk in the courtyard of Les Invalides during a welcoming ceremony in Paris, 18 July 2022. CREDIT: THOMAS PADILLA/POOL/AFP via Getty Images.

was willing to shoulder 'more responsibility' on the global stage – Germany's foreign policy remained characterised by its self-perception as a civilian power.[54] This 'civilian self-image (*Zivilmacht*) survived the end of the Cold War and German reunification'.[55] Kristina Kausch further argues that 'since reunification, Germany's foreign policy has focused largely on securing commercial interests to support the country's export-oriented economy'.[56] This has led scholars and observers to qualify Germany as a 'geo-economic power'.[57]

This broader conception of a 'civilian power' in part explains the difference between the German leadership's view of its domestic defence-manufacturing sector and the French one. The arms industry is not seen as a core element of Germany's power, which is mostly perceived as economic rather than military. As mentioned in this chapter's introduction, the sector represents more than 400,000 direct and indirect jobs,[58] less than half as many as the automotive sector (820,000 in 2018).[59] Hence, contrary to France, the linkage between the industry, exports and state sovereignty is not part of the rationale for arms sales. The defence-manufacturing base is an economic and industrial issue, not a strategic or foreign-policy one, and defence companies themselves are considered to be economic rather than security actors.[60]

The relationship between the state and the arms industry in Germany is more distant than it is in France. Except for commercial- and military-aircraft manufacturer Airbus and European guided-weapons company MBDA, German defence companies are privately owned. This is not the case in France; additionally, the industry has a worse reputation in the former.[61] As a result, there are fewer connections between the state and the industry. The German economic model also supposes less state intervention.[62]

Subsequently, in Germany arms-export promotion is not as intertwined with foreign and defence policy when compared to France. It was only in 2015 that the government published a defence industry strategy, 'Strategy Paper of the Federal Government to Strengthen the Defence Industry in Germany' (*Strategiepapier der Bundesregierung zur Stärkung der Verteidigungsindustrie in Deutschland*). It was updated in 2020, becoming the 'Strategy Paper of the Federal Government on Strengthening the Security and Defence Industry' (*Strategiepapier der Bundesregierung zur Stärkung der Sicherheits- und Verteidigungsindustrie*).[63] This publication lists several goals for supporting the arms industry: strengthening research, development and innovation; creating the 'basic conditions' for efficient production; and optimising the arms-procurement system (responsible export control is also listed under the goals for strengthening the arms industry). The document further notes that weapons exports serve Germany's interests as they reduce procurement costs, increase inter-operability with allies and promote jobs and technological development. However, as Giegerich and Terhalle note, absent in the strategy is any argument, like in the French one, in which arms exports are seen as a tool of foreign policy.[64]

This is unsurprising given the that German government officials do not figure in an advocacy role in weapons exports in the same way as their French counterparts. Rather, it is more junior officials who often support German defence firms on foreign markets, while the German armed forces have only a modest presence, if any, in international arms exhibitions.[65] The 2020 defence-industry strategy paper nonetheless indicates that the coordination of arms-export promotion will be formalised in a permanent steering committee.[66]

Overall, the link between Germany's arms-export policy and its foreign policy is less direct than in France. Whereas arms exports are integral to France's foreign-policy objectives, the connection is more subtle in Germany. It could be argued that only in the case of export denials – for example, when Germany decided not to export to Saudi Arabia following Khashoggi's murder in 2018 – that the link is made. Denying a sale, then, is an expression of German foreign policy, whereas in France the link manifests itself in export promotion: making the sale is the expression of French foreign policy.

Regional approaches

France

France has long-standing relations with several Middle Eastern countries – including Israel – and countries where the French presence dates back to its colonial era such as Egypt, Lebanon and Syria. Strategic partnerships were established with Saudi Arabia in 1996 and the United Arab Emirates (UAE) in 1997. A French military base was built in Abu Dhabi in 2009.[67] These relationships are based on economic and military dimensions: Paris is securing its oil supply while Riyadh, Abu Dhabi and Doha are strengthening their defences – including French arms-export deals.

Defence cooperation has taken centre stage in relationships between France and the Gulf countries relatively quickly. This deepened in the early part of the 2010s as tensions in the region grew as a result of the fallout of the Arab Spring uprisings, the Syrian and Yemeni conflicts, the Gulf Cooperation Council (GCC) crisis, and negotiations with Iran on its nuclear facilities. During this decade, relations between the United States and several regional powers had reached a low point. In 2012–13, Washington recognised the Muslim Brotherhood government in Egypt, and in 2014 it condemned the coup by Abdel Fattah Al-Sisi. In 2013, the United States decided not to intervene in Syria, despite the evidence of chemical-weapons use by Bashar al-Assad's regime.[68] The deal brokered by the administration of president Barack Obama regarding Iran's nuclear programme, irrespective of the concern of the Gulf states, also strained the relationship with Washington.[69] In this context, France was seen increasingly as an alternative security guarantor: the term 'honeymoon' was used to describe Franco-Saudi relations under the presidency of Hollande (2012–17), the first foreign head of state to be invited to a GCC summit.[70]

Subsequently, Paris has secured several export sales, most notably high-value orders for the Dassault *Rafale* fighter ground-attack aircraft to Qatar in 2015 and the UAE in 2021. Over the 2011–20 period, Qatar held the second position in the ranking of orders from France, followed by Saudi Arabia, Egypt and the UAE.[71] As mentioned, France views these exports as an integral instrument of foreign policy and believes they contribute to the maintenance of regional stability and to the fight against terrorism. This was stated by the minister for armed forces as well as the ministry's spokesperson regarding the UAE's order of 80 *Rafales*.[72] France's three priorities in the region remain 'regional stability, [the] fight against radical Islamism, [and] promotion of France's attractiveness', as Macron reaffirmed on 3 December 2021 while on an official tour of the UAE, Qatar and Saudi Arabia.[73]

Following the end of the Cold War, French engagement in the Indo-Pacific declined. This, however, changed at the start of the 2010s as the regional security environment deteriorated. The emergence of an assertive China underpinned the release of France's first Indo-Pacific strategy in 2018.[74] The region is now a focus of France's foreign policy.[75] Paris defined its ambition to 'offer an alternative: a stable multipolar order based on right and free movement and a fair, effective and inclusive multilateralism'.[76] France's decision to place the Indo-Pacific zone at the heart of its strategy has several drivers, including protecting French economic interests (93% of the French exclusive economic zone being in the Indian and Pacific oceans).[77] In the defence realm, the French Indo-Pacific strategy has two main objectives: 'to ensure the protection of its nationals and the integrity of its sovereignty, just as it must contribute to regional and international security and stability'.[78]

As in the Gulf, 'regional stability' is one of the key objectives of French foreign policy for the Indo-Pacific. Several Asian countries are among France's top arms-export customers, in terms of orders, with India being the number-one customer during 2011–20, then Singapore (eighth) and South Korea (tenth).[79]

The Indo-Pacific has acquired more and more advanced weapons in recent years, as shown by the volume of arms imports, especially since the beginning of the 2010s. Between the two periods 2006–10 and 2011–15, such imports by states in Asia and Oceania increased by 26%, according to the Stockholm International Peace Research Institute (SIPRI). Over the period 2015–19, they maintained this position of leading arms-importing regions by recording together 41% of world imports of conventional arms by volume. During 2011–20, India occupied second place in the ranking of order intake from France. In total, seven countries in Asia and Oceania were among France's top 20 customers over the same period.[80]

In the Indo-Pacific, France originally chose to strengthen its partnership with Australia and make it one of the main strands of its regional strategy. The 'deal of the century' – concluded in 2016 between France and Australia for the construction of 12 diesel-powered submarines, with a total value of EUR34.5 billion (USD38.2bn) – reflected the French intent to commit further to the region. In September 2021, Canberra's decision to break this contract and turn instead to the United States and the United Kingdom to acquire a fleet of nuclear-powered submarines was viewed as 'a stab in the back' by the French authorities.[81] With the Australian reversal, France may look to further strengthen other partnerships in the region, likely with India and Indonesia.[82]

Germany

Strong support for Israel has been a constant in Germany's Middle East foreign policy.[83] In 2008, Merkel summarised this relationship in a speech to the Knesset: for her, Germany holds a special

FRANCE–QATAR DEFENCE
Qatar Minister of Defence Khalid bin Mohamed Al Attiyah delivers a speech during a ceremony for the delivery to Qatar of the first of 36 *Rafale* combat aircraft in Merignac, southwestern France, 6 February 2019. CREDIT: GEORGES GOBET/AFP via Getty Images.

responsibility for Israel's security, and this is part of Germany's '*raison d'être*'.[84] Similarly, in 2021 former foreign minister Heiko Maas said that 'solidarity with Israel is a cornerstone of our policy'.[85] This is manifest in Germany's arms exports, with continued supply to Israel.[86] Between 2000 and 2020, Israel accounted for 4% of all German arms exports, making it the eighth-largest recipient of German major conventional weapons.[87] Conversely, any sales to Middle Eastern countries, including the Gulf states, that might jeopardise Israel's security are likely to be carefully considered by the German licensing authorities.[88]

Beyond the relationship with Israel, Germany's foreign and security policy towards the Middle East has focused on economic interests.[89] Following the September 2001 terrorist attacks on the US, there was a noticeable policy shift. The policy development, for example, led to the UAE and Germany signing a strategic partnership in 2004.[90] Germany's interest in the region grew further following the Arab Spring in 2011.[91] Berlin's foreign policy called for more dialogue with Islamist parties – including the Muslim Brotherhood – in Egypt and Tunisia, following the regime changes in these countries.[92] More broadly, the Arab Spring placed the Middle East higher on Germany's diplomatic agenda. Germany was an important donor of humanitarian aid to Syria.[93] It also contributed militarily to the anti-Islamic State (ISIS/ISIL) coalition in Iraq and Syria, and to the NATO Mission in Iraq.[94] Germany refused, however, to join France, the UK and the US in retaliatory strikes against Syria in 2018.[95] Germany's greater involvement in the region was arguably also reflected by the sales of small arms, light weapons and transport vehicles to the Kurds fighting against the Islamic State in Iraq.[96]

It appears that Germany's growing interest in the Middle East was accompanied by an increase in arms exports to the region. Qatar, Saudi Arabia and the UAE have been among the Gulf states receiving the most German export permits for 'weapons of war' in recent years.[97] North African states became some of the largest German arms-export recipients, Algeria being the second-largest during 2016–20 and Egypt the third. Qatar was the sixth and Saudi Arabia the eighth in the same time frame. Germany's willingness to export military equipment to the region markedly increased after 2012–13.[98] Germany agreed to sell 62 *Leopard* 2A7 tanks to Qatar in 2013 and 2 MEKO-A200 frigates to Algeria in 2012.[99] Some observers even discussed a 'paradigm shift' for German arms exports. Weekly magazine *Der Spiegel* termed it 'the Merkel doctrine'. According to *Der Spiegel*, from 2011 onwards the German government was more willing to export arms to help partner countries, even in conflict, to avoid sending troops on the ground.[100] This period corresponded to a Christian Democratic Union (CDU)–Free Democratic Party coalition. The policy became more restrictive again once a CDU–Social Democratic Party (SPD) coalition came to power in 2013, as evidenced by the coalition agreement.[101] The SPD's Sigmar Gabriel, who later became foreign minister, blocked the sale of *Leopard* tanks to Saudi Arabia.[102] Arms-sales policy was a cause of tension throughout the CDU–SPD coalition's time in office.

Germany's Indo-Pacific diplomacy has also grown beyond narrow commercial interests. In 2020, Germany released its 'policy guidelines for the Indo-Pacific region'.[103] These reflected Berlin's interest in maintaining the rules-based order in the region, including the rule of international law, free trade and peaceful resolution of conflicts.[104] The document also reflected concerns over the rise of China.[105] Despite this apprehension, the guidelines did not include any military dimension.[106] Nonetheless, Germany's stance is evolving. The German frigate *Bayern* was deployed to the region for seven months from August 2021 to February 2022.[107] The Chief of Navy announced in late 2021 that Germany's military engagements in the Indo-Pacific would develop further in the coming years and also involve the air force. He said he would consider sending ships through the Taiwan Strait.[108] In August 2022, Germany deployed

Figure 7.1: **France: annual values of delivered material to the MENA, Asia and the rest of the world, 1991–2020**

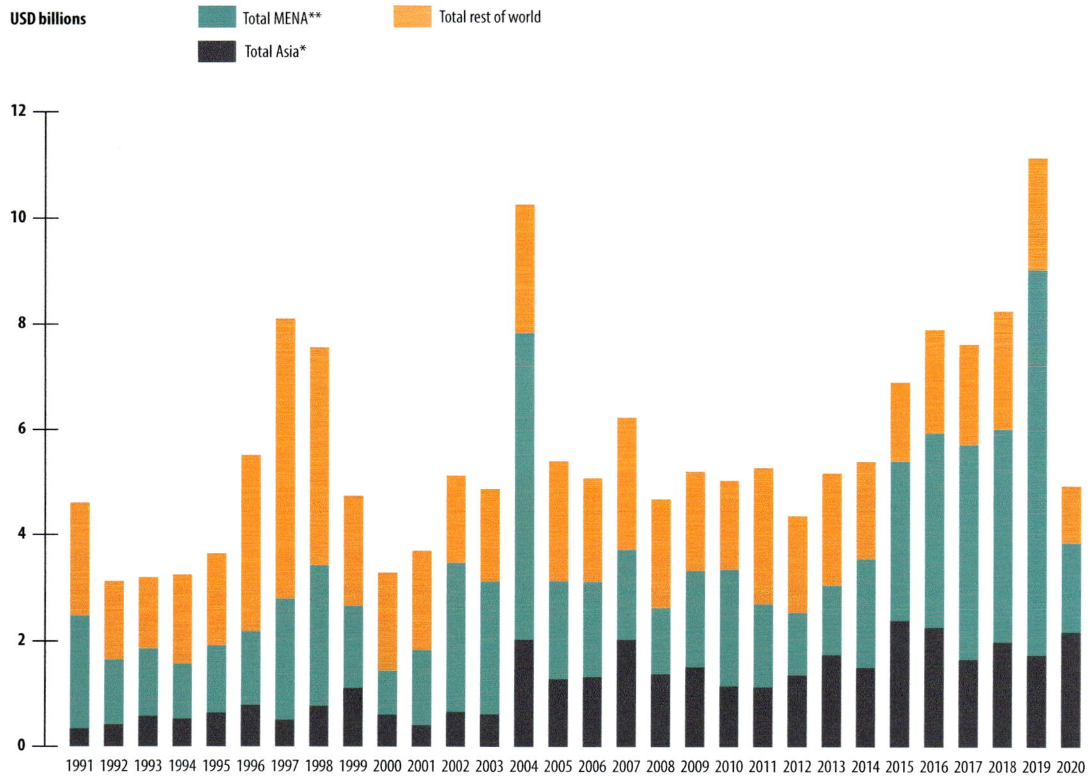

*Afghanistan, Australia, Bangladesh, Brunei, Cambodia, China, Fiji, India, Indonesia, Japan, Korea (South), Laos, Malaysia, Mongolia, Nepal, New Zealand, Pakistan, Philippines, Singapore, Sri Lanka, Taiwan, Thailand, Timor Leste, Vietnam. **Algeria, Bahrain, Egypt, Iran, Iraq, Israel, Jordan, Kuwait, Lebanon, Libya, Morocco, Oman, Qatar, Saudi Arabia, Syria, Tunisia, UAE, Yemen

Source: The Military Balance+

six Eurofighter *Typhoons*, four A400m transport aircraft and three A330 Multi Role Tanker Transport aircraft to participate in Australia's *Pitch Black* air-combat and the navy-led *Kakadu* exercise. Additional engagements with Japan, Singapore and South Korea were planned in the framework of this deployment.

In terms of arms exports, South Korea was the top customer for Germany, accounting for almost a quarter of its total arms transfers from 2016–20. India and Indonesia were respectively Germany's ninth- and tenth-largest arms recipients over the same period, accounting for 3% each of the total volume of weapons exported.[109]

Assessing stability or instability

The respective responses of Berlin and Paris to the Arab Spring and the Saudi-led intervention in the civil war in Yemen are notable when examining the extent of their wider considerations regarding regional stability and the implications of major-weapons sales. The Arab Spring involved a series of anti-government protests and uprisings in the Middle East and North Africa that started at the end of 2010 and early 2011. The events sparked debate in European countries regarding arms transfers and led some European exporters to reconsider their policies, at least temporarily.

Defence companies were asked by the German government not to use their licences for countries in the region until further review. Even prior to the outbreak of the civil war in Libya, Germany had opposed the potential sale of the Eurofighter *Typhoon* combat aircraft, jointly produced with Italy, Spain and the UK, and of the Franco-German *Tiger* attack helicopter. For Libya specifically, the United Nations and the EU imposed arms embargoes in 2011, and Germany stopped any arms exports to the country. After the end of the embargo, Germany authorised very few licences to Libya.[110] Licences to Tunisia and Bahrain were also reviewed; however, the UK government started negotiating the sale of *Typhoon* aircraft with Bahrain in 2013, implying that Germany did not veto the marketing campaign as it had done for Libya. Regarding Egypt, Germany temporarily stopped issuing licences – first in 2011 and again in 2013 – for components of the *Fahd* armoured vehicles, which had been used in repression against protesters.[111]

Figure 7.2: **Germany: annual value of export licences to the Middle East, North Africa, Asia and the rest of the world, 1999–2020**

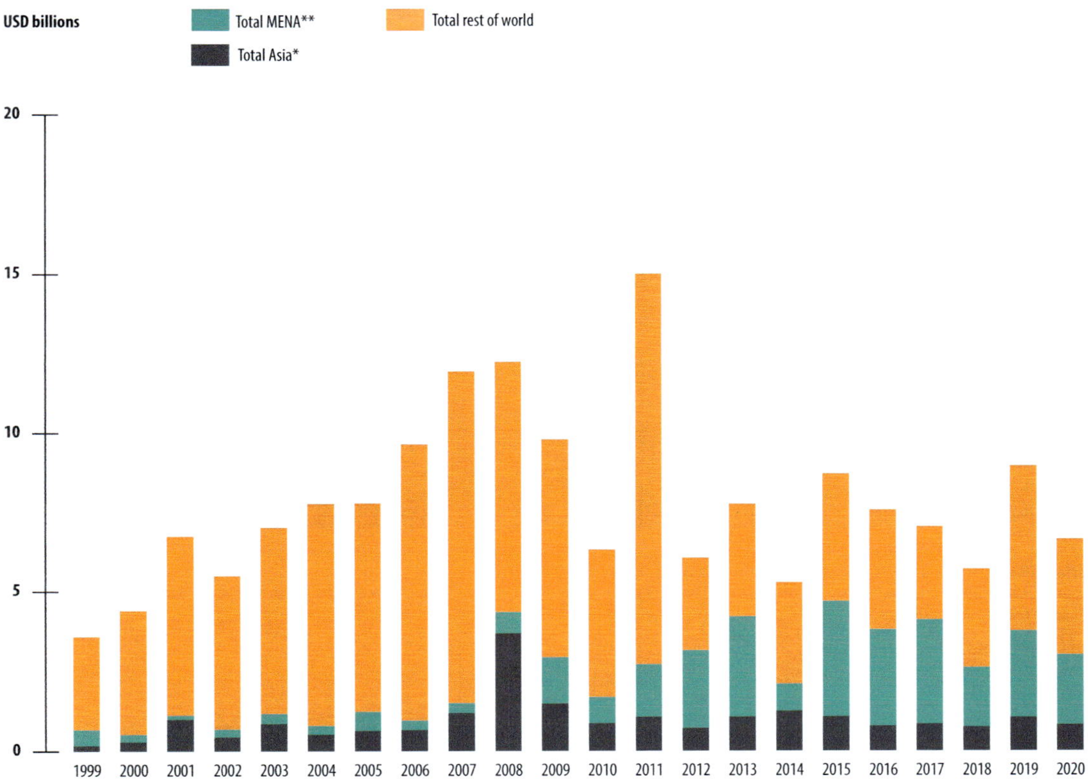

*Afghanistan, Australia, Bangladesh, Brunei, Cambodia, China, Fiji, India, Indonesia, Japan, Korea (South), Laos, Malaysia, Mongolia, Nepal, New Zealand, Pakistan, Philippines, Singapore, Sri Lanka, Taiwan, Thailand, Timor Leste, Vietnam. **Algeria, Bahrain, Egypt, Iran, Iraq, Israel, Jordan, Kuwait, Lebanon, Libya, Morocco, Oman, Qatar, Saudi Arabia, Syria, Tunisia, UAE, YemenSource: FSMTC of Russia

Source: FSMTC of Russia

France also provisionally suspended some export licences after the violent repression of protests in several states. Paris suspended export authorisations to Syria and Yemen in 2011.[112] When it came to Tunisia and Bahrain, it blocked the export of anti-riot equipment.[113] In Libya, Paris shifted from having attempted to sell the *Rafale* to the Gadhafi regime,[114] to arming rebel forces during the civil war.[115] Regarding Egypt, France suspended the authorisation of export licences early in 2011, but these were granted again before the end of the year. Egypt bought *Sherpa* armoured vehicles from Arquus (then Renault Trucks Defense).[116] These were employed by the Egyptian forces to help repress civil protests in August 2013.[117]

France and Germany suspended licences and modified their export policies – if only temporarily – after the outbreak of violent events, rather than before. Furthermore, the types of exports that were suspended or where the licences were revoked dealt with specific categories of equipment (armoured vehicles, anti-riot equipment) directly used by the recipient government. Short-term concerns over internal repression rather than regional-stability criteria underpinned the French and German responses to the Arab Spring.

The Yemeni civil war

A tragic outcome of the Arab Spring has been the prolonged civil war in Yemen and the ill-starred Saudi-led intervention. In 2015, Saudi Arabia led a coalition of regional states, including Egypt and the UAE, against the Iranian-backed Houthi rebellion.[118]

The 2018 coalition agreement between the CDU/Christian Social Union (CSU) and the SPD stated that Germany would halt licences to states involved in the war in Yemen.[119] However, the 2020 arms-export report shows that licences were still delivered after this announcement.[120] A clearer immediate response was provoked by the murder of Khashoggi in October 2018 in which Saudi security personnel were implicated.[121] European External Action Service (EEAS) figures illustrate export licences granted to Saudi Arabia fell from 15 in 2018 to only two in 2019. In 2020, this figure stood at 53, but their value was comparatively small.[122]

Concerning the UAE, the 2018 licensing policy did not appear to make any significant difference compared to previous years.[123] According to *Der Spiegel*, the licences authorised exports of artillery-positioning systems to Saudi Arabia, and of warheads and missiles to the UAE.[124]

GERMAN FOREIGN MINISTER SIGMAR GABRIEL VISITS SEVERAL COUNTRIES IN THE MIDDLE EAST
German foreign minister and vice chancellor Sigmar Gabriel and Adel bin Ahmed al Jubeir, foreign minister of Saudi Arabia, at the airport in Jeddah, Saudi Arabia, 3 July 2017. CREDIT: Michael Gottschalk/Photothek via Getty Images.

Irrespective of the Saudi-led intervention in Yemen, successive French governments continued to authorise sales to Saudi Arabia and the UAE.[125] The French minister of defence justified the continuation of the sales on the grounds that the weapons 'were not supposed to be used' in a war such as in Yemen.[126] The same year, President Macron clashed with Chancellor Merkel over Berlin's decision to halt exports to Riyadh after the murder of Khashoggi.[127]

Even though in 2019 a leaked report from the French military-intelligence services indicated that some weapons sold to Saudi Arabia and the UAE were being used in Yemen,[128] licences continued to be granted, as can be seen from the EEAS database.[129] But in the case of Saudi Arabia the number of licences dropped from over 200 in the years prior to 2015, down to 98 licences in 2020. For the UAE, the number of licences granted reached 'only' 140 in 2020, against 255 in 2015. However, the value of exports remained close to EUR200 million (USD228m) in the last five years for which data was available (2016–20).[130]

While licences for the export of weapons that risked being used in the Yemeni conflict were more closely scrutinised, Claire Landais, then head of the SGDSN, indicated that 'strategic partnerships' in the fight against terrorism weighed in favour of granting licences.[131] It is evident that there was a clear policy divide between France and Germany, particularly concerning Saudi Arabia. Even here, however, some arms-export licences continued to be approved by Berlin. Moreover, Germany's restrictive approach was not prompted by worries over regional stability, but rather by concerns over human rights and possible state involvement in the murder of Khashoggi. In the case of Paris, sustaining key relationships trumped any concern regarding regional stability.

Regional stability: the views from Berlin and Paris

That the sale of an advanced weapons system could affect regional stability is not in question. It is, after all, a criterion against which possible arms exports are considered. The effect could be either stabilising or destabilising. On the one hand, transfers can be seen as a means of reinforcing a partner state, contributing to its conventional capacity to deter attacks from rival states. On the other hand, suppliers, including France and Germany, do not necessarily always refrain from arming conceivable adversaries. In addition, weapons can be used aggressively by recipient states in their own conflicts, and not just for self-defence.[132] In any arms-export decision there is a risk that the recipient country at some point may use the weapons in a manner counter to that intended when approved. Given the longevity of some of the weapons in question, three decades or more in the case of a combat aircraft, the risk is not always inconsiderable. Industrial or strategic considerations inevitably influence decision-makers' willingness to accept some risk in any decision-making process, and risk appetite differs on a case-by-case basis.

The EEAS publishes a User's Guide to support licensing officers in EU member states in the implementation of the Common Position on weapons exports.[133] Endorsed by the EU Council, the guide explains how to implement the Common Position's criteria for assessing arms-export licences, including Criterion 4 on 'regional stability'. According to this criterion, 'member states shall deny an export licence if there is a clear risk that the intended recipient would use the military technology or equipment to be exported aggressively against another country or to assert by force a territorial claim'.[134]

CHANCELLOR ANGELA MERKEL AND FRENCH PRESIDENT EMMANUEL MACRON
German Chancellor Angela Merkel and French President Emmanuel Macron during a joint press conference at the Federal Chancellery, August 2020. CREDIT: Simone Kuhlmey/Pacific Press/LightRocket via Getty Images.

The User's Guide highlights several key dimensions to consider when coming to a judgement on this 'clear risk'. The objective of this criterion is 'to ensure that any export does not encourage, aggravate, provoke or prolong conflicts or tensions in the region of the intended recipient country'. [135]

The most important aspect that the guide highlights is the *intention* of the recipient country: whether the equipment is likely to be used for aggressive or defensive purposes. Licensing officers should come to a judgement on whether there are indications that the recipient state intends to use the exported equipment to 'attack or threaten to attack' another state. For this, licensing officers are encouraged to consider the situation of the country, whether it is involved, or has been in the past, in an armed conflict, and in the wider context of any regional tensions.

According to the User's Guide, another aspect is the type of equipment. In language that echoes the US Defense Security Cooperation Agency notification boilerplate, the guide asks: does the equipment alter the regional balance of power? Does it provide new military capabilities to the recipient country that would then prompt neighbouring or rival states to feel threatened or to acquire the same capability? Additionally, an important aspect for licensing officers is the existence of a 'clear risk that this equipment will prolong an existing conflict or bring simmering tensions into armed conflict'.[136] Finally, licensing officers should consider the existence of territorial claims on the part of the recipient country. If the prospective customer has an ongoing claim against the territory of another state, licensing officers should consider if it has tried in the past to claim this territory by force or threatened to do so.

Considering Berlin's and Paris's approach to defence-aerospace exports, including combat aircraft and uninhabited aerial vehicles (UAVs), in the context of regional stability shows both continuities and differences between the two regarding the Middle East and the Indo-Pacific. As per the EU guide, the key elements to consider in assessing an arms transfer's impact on regional stability are:

- indications that the recipient intends to use the equipment for aggression;
- the existence of regional tensions;
- the fact that the recipient pursues territorial claims; and
- the regional balance of power and the equipment's impact on military capabilities.

The following examples consider weapons-export decisions against the EU's criteria. Licensing officers, however, will look at more than these four basic aspects and in more detail, also with access to information from intelligence services, whereas the following relies on open-source information.

A question of stability: the views from Paris and Berlin

While export policy regarding armed UAVs has been a vexing issue for Washington, this has not been the case for France, nor indeed Germany, simply because neither has a comparable product to the RQ-1 *Predator* or MQ-9 *Reaper* to offer. Combat-aircraft sales, however, have and continue to be key, along with the associated air-launched-weapons packages.

After struggling initially to secure export orders for the *Rafale*, in recent years France has racked up considerable success. Since 2015 it

GERMANY AND THE EUROFIGHTER
A Eurofighter under construction destined for the German Air Force is seen at the production line of the EADS company Cassidian in Manching, southern Germany, 23 February 2013.
CREDIT: GUENTER SCHIFFMANN/AFP via Getty Images.

has secured orders from Egypt (2015), Qatar (2015 and 2017), India (2016), Greece (2021), Croatia (2021), the UAE (2022) and Indonesia (2022). If all these deals are completed, it will have added a further 278 aircraft to the *Rafale* order book.

It is instructive to consider French decision-making regarding *Rafale* sales and the extent to which issues of regional stability could – or should – play a role in policy deliberations using two examples from the Middle East and one from the Indo-Pacific.

As previously mentioned, the longevity of a major weapons system once purchased makes quantifying risk a complicated affair. Even the time taken, however, to negotiate a sale poses its own challenge, and cancelling a deal post-contract signature is not impossible, but it can be costly. It took five years, for example, from Qatar's release of request for proposals[137] for a contract to be signed. At that time, Qatar's record in terms of conflict involvement was nil, according to the Uppsala Conflict Data Program.[138] Furthermore, in 2010–15 Qatar had no known territorial claims. Its dispute with Bahrain was resolved in 2001.[139]

By the time of contract signature, however, in May 2015, Qatar was part of the Saudi-led coalition against the Houthis in Yemen. Delivery of the aircraft began in February 2019,[140] while Qatar was involved in fighting in Yemen. Meanwhile, a second batch order was concluded in December 2017,[141] at a time when Qatar was embroiled in a diplomatic crisis with its GCC neighbours that started in June that year. This crisis had some military components, as there were mutual accusations of airspace violations.[142] The country also accused Saudi Arabia and the UAE of intending to invade.[143] During this crisis, Bahrain also threatened to revive its territorial dispute with Qatar.[144] While volatile, the internal dispute within the GCC was unlikely to have resulted in hostilities. But despite being remote, the risk remained.

The *Rafale* acquisition marked the beginning of both a recapitalisation and an expansion of Qatar's combat air capability, which since then has seen it order the Eurofighter *Typhoon* and the Boeing F-15QA. While the air force will more than quadruple in size once deliveries are complete, this will not fundamentally shift the regional balance of power, and certainly not with regard to either Iran or Israel.

In December 2021, the UAE signed a contract to buy 80 *Rafale* F4 combat aircraft from Dassault.[145] The *Rafale* will replace the UAE's fleet of *Mirage*-2000s.[146] The first discussions on such a purchase, which at the time was said to be about 60 aircraft, had already begun in 2008–09.[147] The UAE, like Qatar, has had territorial issues with neighbouring states, including an unresolved border dispute with Saudi Arabia. The UAE and Saudi Arabia previously tried to solve their disagreement with the 1974 Treaty of Jeddah, rather than threaten to claim it by force, which comes into consideration in assessing a country's intention on using imported weapons. The UAE also has claims on several islands close to the Strait of Hormuz – Greater Tunb, Lesser Tunb and Abu Musa – which are currently part of Iran's territory. The UAE has prioritised using international law to solve the dispute rather than military force.[148] Nonetheless, regional tensions are high in the Gulf, and like Saudi Arabia, the UAE has had a strained relationship with Iran.

The UAE has also become more extrovert in the use of its military. A small detachment from the air force took part in operations in Afghanistan from 2012,[149] while in 2011 the UAE sent troops, also in conjunction with Saudi Arabia, after the Arab Spring protests in Manama in Bahrain.[150] In 2014,[151] the UAE carried out airstrikes on targets in Libya using air bases in Egypt, and in 2015 it joined Saudi Arabia's coalition in Yemen, also conducting airstrikes.[152]

The UAE will take delivery of the *Rafale* F4 between 2026 and 2031,[153] with the aircraft reportedly replacing the *Mirage*-2000-9, 59 of which are in the inventory. In terms of affecting regional stability and the local balance of power, the UAE will likely remain somewhat smaller in combat-aircraft numbers than the Royal Saudi Air Force, which will remain the largest of the GCC air powers. It will, however, almost certainly continue to overmatch Iran. As of 2022, Tehran continues to have to rely on an increasingly ageing combat-aircraft fleet.[154] A direct comparison between a recapitalised UAE air force and Iran's air arm would suggest a shift in the balance of power between the two, with implications for regional stability. Any comparison, however, must also consider the argument that UAE airpower is part of the conventional deterrent to Iran's ballistic-missile arsenal, an inventory capability that Iran continues to improve, and for which the UAE has no equivalent. The *Rafale* acquisition process ran in parallel to discussions between the UAE and Washington regarding the purchase of the Lockheed Martin F-35A *Lightning* II. The latter talks, however, fell into abeyance amid US concern over the UAE's growing relationship with China, and the UAE's discomfort with the security requirements that the acquisition of the low-observable F-35 would have entailed. It is likely that the French party did not have similar conditions regarding the sale of the *Rafale*.[155]

The 2017 sale of the *Rafale* to India also illustrates the importance of regional-stability issues, particularly the extent to which it is considered and the degree to which other factors take precedence in the export of a major weapons system. India ordered 36 of the *Rafale* in 2017, in effect bringing to a close a more than decade-long sales campaign on the part of France that included changing the type of aircraft on offer.

The *Rafale* purchase emerged in the wake of India's Medium Multi-role Combat Aircraft (MMRCA) programme, which can be traced back to 2002–03, when India and France negotiated the purchase of 126 *Mirage*-2000-5s.[156] However, in 2004, India decided to open a competition, issuing a request for information to the other main combat-aircraft suppliers.[157] While France initially proposed the *Mirage*-2000-5 for the requirement, it was superseded by the *Rafale* as the tender continued.[158] In 2012, the *Rafale* was selected for 'exclusive negotiations' for the 126 aircraft requirement.[159] However, in 2015, during a visit to Paris, Indian Prime Minister Narendra Modi announced that India would instead only procure 36 *Rafale* combat aircraft directly from France.[160] The actual contract was signed only in September 2016, after more negotiations on the details of the deal.[161]

India's regional security environment has changed over the roughly 15 years that these negotiations lasted. However, India's territorial disputes continued at the time of the contract signature in 2016. The two most acute are with Pakistan over the region of Indian-controlled Kashmir and the border with China. Since the Sino-Indian war in 1962, India and China have maintained bilateral dialogue over their border dispute. Several agreements have been signed, such as the Border Peace and Tranquility Agreement (BPTA) in 1993, and the agreement on confidence-building measures along the Line of Actual Control (LAC) in 1996. In 1998, China and India established a Joint Working Group to foster dialogue around the border tensions. Between 2007 and 2015, the two countries held an annual defence dialogue. Nonetheless, there were frequent military stand-offs in the years preceding the *Rafale* deal, for instance, in the Depsang valley in 2013 and Chumur village in 2014.[162] Clashes in June 2020 resulted in the deaths of Indian and Chinese soldiers.[163] Only a month later the first five *Rafale* aircraft were delivered to Delhi, a delivery that was touted by Modi and noted in some of the regional press.[164]

India's relations with Pakistan are even more strained, with regular flare-ups. The last prolonged fighting between the two was the 1999 Kargil War.[165] Although attempts were made to improve the relationship in 2003, the Mumbai attacks in 2008 undermined them.[166] Border skirmishes continued, including during the *Rafale* deal negotiations. For instance, in 2008, after the Mumbai attacks, a military stand-off occurred between the two countries, during which Indian military combat aircraft reportedly violated Pakistan's airspace.[167] In late September 2016, around the time of the *Rafale* contract signature, India conducted strikes in Pakistani territory, although this was denied by Islamabad.[168] This led to further border skirmishes.

The pre-existing regional tensions in India's neighbourhood are even more serious because they involve nuclear powers. Looking at the gap in fighter ground-attack aircraft fleets between China–India on the one hand, and India–Pakistan on the other, the addition of the 36 *Rafale* combat aircraft will not make a significant difference. At the time of the contract signature in 2016, China possessed 642 such aircraft, and India 551. However, the Chinese fleet expanded significantly over the period 2016–21, reaching over 1,140. By comparison, India's fighter ground-attack aircraft numbers went below 500. Meanwhile, Pakistan's fleet oscillated around 200 in the same time frame. While numbers are not necessarily the best indicator of military capabilities, it is notable that China's air force is now the third largest in the world, according to the US Department of Defense.[169] In this case, the addition of India's 36 *Rafale* combat aircraft is hardly sufficient to upset the balance of power with China.

Germany's combat-aircraft exports relate to sales of the Eurofighter *Typhoon*. This aircraft is built in cooperation with Italy, Spain and the UK. Different nations have taken the lead for the different exports, depending on the customers. For instance, the UK sold the *Typhoon* to Oman, Qatar and Saudi Arabia. Italy has taken over the campaign to Kuwait. Germany, for its part, oversaw the sale to Austria.

Germany has a key role in building this multinational weapons programme. Airbus Defence and Space in Germany builds the main centre fuselage for the aircraft.[170] Hensoldt, a spin-off company from Airbus, supplies sensors and jamming equipment.[171] Under German legislation, once the components have been integrated into a military platform in a country with which the programme is developed in cooperation, the country exporting the integrated weapons system can apply its own export rules. The exceptions to this principle are if the licensing authority adds a condition to the licence, compelling the company to reapply for a licence before the final goods are exported, and the government of Germany can seek to influence its partners' export-policy decisions.[172]

Berlin responded to the murder of Khashoggi by imposing an arms embargo on Saudi Arabia in October 2018, and in 2019 it renewed it initially for a further six months. As of June 2022, it remained in place but at the end of September 2022, Berlin approved the sale of elements of a *Eurofighter* and *Tornado* support package.[173] The German position has caused tension among the Eurofighter partners, and within European missile house MBDA, which includes a German subsidiary. MBDA weapons are central to the weapons package associated with the Saudi *Typhoon* aircraft.

MBDA Deutschland has, like the company's other business units, become a supplier of air-launched land-attack cruise missiles (LACMs). In the case of the German subsidiary, the weapon is not the Franco-British SCALP EG/*Storm Shadow* but the *Taurus* KEPD 350. The *Taurus* has been exported to the Republic of Korea and Spain. South Korea is Germany's most important customer in Asia. Missiles accounted for 17% of total deliveries between 2011 and 2020, the second-largest share of Germany's supplies to South Korea after submarines (72%).[174] This included the sale of over 200 *Taurus* KEPD-350 LACMs in 2013.

The Republic of Korea is embroiled in a decades-long unresolved conflict with the Democratic People's Republic of Korea (DPRK, North Korea). Since the Korean War ended in 1953, no peace treaty has been signed, and both regimes claim to be the legitimate government of the entire Korean Peninsula. There are frequent military stand-offs and skirmishes between the two states. South Korea also has ongoing territorial disputes with Japan over the Dokdo/Takeshima islands and with China in the Yellow Sea.[175] Existing regional tensions at the time of the export authorisation were already running high.

The *Taurus* missile is jointly produced by MBDA Deutschland GmbH (previously LFK-Lenkflugkörpersysteme) and Saab. MBDA has the largest share in the joint venture (67%), and Germany is the lead nation for export campaigns.[176] MBDA describes the *Taurus* as a stand-off missile system with a 500-kilometre range, 'designed to penetrate dense air defences' to aim at 'high value stationary targets'.[177]

South Korea ordered this missile system in 2013 for its F-15K combat aircraft. Seoul was originally looking to procure a US system, the AGM-158 Joint Air-to-Surface Standoff Missile (JASSM). However, the United States declined to export the AGM-158 to South Korea, which prompted Seoul to turn to the *Taurus* instead.[178] There is limited open-source information on why the United States refused, though reports cited 'strategic reasons'.[179] Such reasons could include reluctance to sell weapons systems that would exceed the Missile Technology Control Regime (MTCR) threshold of 300km, but also US relations with Japan, as South Korean–Japanese relations can sometimes be abrasive. At the time, another reason may have been to not create a precedent for other US allies to request the JASSM.[180]

It is unclear how much of the US refusal to proceed with a sale was due to a desire to avoid being the first to introduce such a capability into the region, as well as the potential impact on the regional balance. This, however, would depend on not considering China as part of the region, since by 2014 it was fielding ground and air-launched LACMs. China aside, the provision of *Taurus* could be viewed as introducing a new capability with a potential effect on the regional power balance.

This could be mitigated to some extent by taking into consideration South Korea's military doctrine – as the EU Users' Guide for assessing risks to regional stability recommends. South Korea's purchase of the *Taurus* is part of its 'Kill Chain' pre-emptive deterrence strategy,[181] today called the 'strategic strike system'.[182] This doctrine is focused on responding immediately to a detected threat of nuclear-weapons launch by North Korea. It is not, however, intended as an offensive doctrine where South Korea would launch the first attack.[183] This aspect of the weapons procurement should also be considered when looking at the exports' impact on regional stability.

The future of Franco-German cooperation

France and Germany differ in their understandings of the relationship between arms exports and foreign policy. In France, the two dimensions interact at the promotion/contract level of the arms-export decision, while in Germany this interaction occurs more when a decision is made to deny a sale or to implement an embargo. Furthermore, arms exports are more politicised in the German public debate than in France, with clear-cut positions from one or more political parties against arms sales, which is not the case in the French political landscape.

However, beyond the politics, there may be greater similarities when it comes to actual policy implementation than first thought. Firstly, the bureaucratic process is similar, with involvement of the different ministries and political leadership in decisions on the most significant contracts. Secondly, looking at outcomes, the approach and decisions appear similar when it comes to selling weapons systems to the Middle East and Indo-Pacific. The main difference was Germany's imposition of an arms embargo on Saudi Arabia following the murder of Khashoggi – but this decision was not related to regional-stability issues. Overall, regional stability does not appear to be a key factor in export-licensing decisions in either country.

France and Germany maintain close cooperation in the armaments sector, the Main Ground Combat System (MGCS)[184] and the Future Combat Air System (FCAS) being two of the most significant examples.[185] The tensions, however, are self-evident, and Berlin has already blocked exports of jointly developed systems to sensitive countries with which France had already signed contracts.[186] In this context, both countries agreed that a joint approach to arms exports was necessary to step up joint defence programmes and to strengthen European defence. This resulted in the 23 October 2019 signature of a Franco-German agreement on export controls in the field of defence.[187] The agreement establishes a common position on arms exports regarding joint projects, in accordance with the implementation of the Treaty of Aachen signed by Macron and Merkel on 22 January 2019.

The Franco-German agreement sets down the rules and procedures for export controls on defence products in three cases:

intergovernmental programmes, industrial cooperation and products for integration that are developed outside such cooperation. It also includes a more specific '*de minimis*' rule to facilitate transfers of items from one manufacturer to another, applicable below a threshold of 20% and accompanied by simplified licence-issuance methods.[188] In practice, this means that France can sell jointly developed materiel without German approval or control, if less than 20% of the given materiel comprises German components (and vice versa). This agreement was later extended to include Spain.[189]

Within the French defence establishment, the Franco-German agreement is viewed positively. In fact, in the context of recent developments for European defence – and especially since the creation of the European Defence Fund (EDF) – many institutional actors argue that Paris should replicate this Franco-German agreement to regulate the joint European projects. Yet some industry representatives are growing sceptical since the agreement has also already shown certain limits. It is more specifically the *de minimis* clause that is subject to discussion. It is seen as advantageous for some but too restrictive for others, depending on the programme. Obviously, a company like NEXTER benefits from such an agreement and from making Franco-German cooperation the core of European cooperation. But for a company like MBDA, which is more dependent on German components, the *de minimis* clause should be 'rationalized'[190] and clarification is expected, including in regard to the FCAS programme.

In case of strong political disagreements on export controls, it is unclear whether the Aachen Treaty's provisions will be sufficient to ensure the continuation of Franco-German exports. In the event of new disagreements on the issue of whether to sell arms to some specific countries, or if France or Germany takes the unilateral decision to cut arms sales to such countries,[191] the question will also be raised of whether (and how) a unilateral decision can affect the sales of common products.

Conclusion

Paris and Berlin have sometimes been more aligned than is immediately apparent in terms of arms exports, but there remain tensions. What impact Germany's new coalition government will have, and the extent to which Russia's war against Ukraine influences thinking in Berlin, had yet to become clear as of November 2022. Shortly after coming to power, Chancellor Olaf Scholz's coalition said it would work on revising arms-export policy, and a first meeting to discuss this was held in April 2022. Russia's invasion of Ukraine, however, has exposed tensions within the coalition over arms exports, even though Berlin did reverse its long-standing position on not providing weapons in an ongoing conflict.[192] Differing views continued to be apparent regarding the types of weapons Germany should be willing to provide to Ukraine to allow it to defend itself against Russia's aggression.[193] Germany's Ministry of the Economy in June 2022 suggested a 'Key Points' discussion paper was pending on the German arms review which was finally released in October.

Within mainstream French politics, the export of major weapons is far less contentious, and will likely remain so. How France and Germany will fair in attempting to agree in practice, rather than in principle, on the export of collaborative programmes now in development remains in question.

NOTES

1 Anne-Marie Descôtes, 'Vom "German-free" zum gegenseitigen Vertrauen, Bundesakademie für Sicherheitspolitik (BAKS)' [From "German-free" to mutual trust], July 2019, https://www.baks.bund.de/de/arbeitspapiere/2019/vom-german-free-zum-gegenseitigen-vertrauen.

2 Lucie Béraud-Sudreau, 'Building Franco-German Consensus on Arms Exports', *Survival*, vol. 61, no. 4, August–September 2019, pp. 86–7; Lucie Béraud-Sudreau, Samuel B. H. Faure and Michael Sladeczek, 'Réguler le commerce des armes par le Parlement et l'opinion publique. Comparaison du contrôle des exportations d'armement en Allemagne, France, Royaume-Uni et Suède' [Regulate the arms trade through Parliament and public opinion. Comparison of arms export controls in Germany, France, United Kingdom and Sweden], *Politique européenne*, 2015/2 (N° 48), pp. 82–121.

3 Lukas Rudolph, Markus Freitag and Paul Thurner, 'Deontological and Consequentialist Preferences Towards Arms Exports – A Comparative Conjoint Experiment in France and Germany', SocArXiv, April 2021, p. 30, https://osf.io/preprints/socarxiv/r73pv/.

4 Gaëlle Winter, 'La politique industrielle de défense de l'Allemagne : l'Etat pris dans un jeu de perles de verre' [Germany's industrial defense policy: the state caught in a game of glass beads], *Fondation pour la recherche stratégique* (FRS), Note no. 18/19, 16 September 2019, p. 5, https://www.frstrategie.org/sites/default/files/documents/publications/notes/2019/201918.pdf.

5 Sebastian Sprenger, 'Germany vows to relax its caveats on European arms exports,' *Defense News*, 12 September 2022, https://www.defensenews.com/global/europe/2022/09/12/germany-vows-to-relax-its-caveats-on-european-arms-exports/.

6 SIPRI Arms Transfers Database, 'Top list TIV Tables', https://armstrade.sipri.org/armstrade/page/toplist.php, accessed December 2021.

7 Alexandra Marksteiner et al., 'The SIPRI Top 100 Arms-producing and Military Services Companies, 2020', SIPRI Fact Sheet, December 2021, https://doi.org/10.55163/WDQZ7897.

8 BDSV, 'Die deutsche Sicherheits- und Verteidigungsindustrie in Zahlen' [The German security and defence industry in numbers], https://www.bdsv.eu/themen/die-industrie/articles/wifor.html.

9 France, Ministère des Armées, Direction générale de l'armement, 'Industrie', 10 January 2020, https://www.defense.gouv.fr/dga/industrie2/industrie.

10 Airbus, 'Investors / Share Price & Information', https://www.airbus.com/en/investors/share-price-and-information.

11 IISS Military Balance+, accessed December 2021, https://milbalplus.iiss.org/.

12 Pieter D. Wezeman, Alexandra Kuimova and Siemon T. Wezeman, 'Trends in International Transfers, 2020', SIPRI Fact Sheet, March 2021, p. 2, https://www.sipri.org/sites/default/files/2021-03/fs_2103_at_2020_v2.pdf.

13 The names of the French ministries change regularly. As of December 2021, those three ministries are known as the Ministry of the Armed Forces, the Ministry for Europe and Foreign Affairs and the Ministry of the Economy and Finance. For the sake of consistency, they will be referred to as the Ministry of Defence, the Ministry of Foreign Affairs and the Ministry of the Economy.

14 France, Ministère des Armées, 'Rapport au Parlement sur les exportations d'armement de la France 2021' [Report to Parliament on French arms exports 2021], June 2021, p. 29, https://www.vie-publique.fr/sites/default/files/rapport/pdf/280174.pdf.

15 Interview with member the EU Working Party on Conventional Arms Exports, 23 September 2021.

16 Code de la Défense, article R2339-3, https://www.legifrance.gouv.fr/codes/article_lc/LEGIARTI000037908185/.

17 Germany, Federal Ministry for Economic Affairs and Climate Action, 'FAQs on exports of military equipment', https://www.bmwi.de/Redaktion/EN/FAQ/Export-controls-on-military/faq-export-control-for-military-equipment.html.

18 The name of the ministry has changed over time. Between 2005 and 2013, it was the Ministry of Economics and Technology, and between 2013 and 2023 it was the Ministry of Economic Affairs and Energy.

19 Ian Davis, 'The regulation of arms and dual-use exports', SIPRI, 2002, pp. 175–6, https://www.sipri.org/sites/default/files/2018-10/sipri02davis.pdf.

20 Lucie Béraud-Sudreau, 'Building Franco-German Consensus on Arms Exports', *Survival*, vol. 61, no. 4, August–September 2019, p. 83.

21 Ongoing reform process in France may modify this in the short to medium term (https://www.vie-publique.fr/discours/280756-services-du-premier-ministre-21062021-autorisations-vente-armes).

22 Germany, Federal Ministry for Economic Affairs and Energy, 'Report by the Government of the Federal Republic of Germany on Its Policy on Exports of Conventional Military Equipment in 2018', June 2019, p. 12, https://www.bmwi.de/Redaktion/EN/Publikationen/Aussenwirtschaft/report-on-the-exports-of-conventional-military-equipment-in-2018.pdf?__blob=publicationFile&v=7.

23 Germany, Federal Ministry for Economic Affairs and Energy, 'Key points for the introduction of post-shipment controls for German arms exports', https://www.

bmwi.de/Redaktion/EN/Downloads/eckpunkte-einfuehrung-post-shipment-kontrollen-deutsche-ruestungsexporte.pdf?__blob=publicationFile&v=2.

24 Andrea Edoardo Varisco, Kolja Brockmann and Lucile Robin, 'Post-shipment control measures: European approaches to on-site inspections of exported military materiel', SIPRI Background Paper, December 2020, p. 14, https://sipri.org/sites/default/files/2020-12/bp_2012_post-shipment_controls.pdf.

25 Table C. Member States' implementing legislation or administrative rules for Common Positions 2003/468/CFSP and 2008/944/CFSP, p. 59, https://data.consilium.europa.eu/doc/document/ST-12189-2021-INIT/en/pdf.

26 France, Assemblée Nationale, 'Rapport d'information n°2334, déposé par la Mission d'information de la Commission de la Défense nationale et des forces armées sur le contrôle des exportations d'armement' [Information Report No. 2334, filed by the Information Mission of the National Defence and Armed Forces Commission on arms export control], Députés MM. Jean-Claude Sandrier, Christian Martin et Alain Veyret, 25 April 2000, pp. 90–1, https://www.assemblee-nationale.fr/legislatures/11/pdf/rap-info/i2334.pdf.

27 France, Assemblée Nationale, 'Rapport d'information n°3581, déposé par la Mission d'information de la Commission des Affaires étrangères sur le contrôle des exportations d'armement' [Information Report No. 3581, filed by the Information Mission of the Foreign Affairs Committee on the control of arms exports], Députés M. Jacques Maire et Mme Michèle Tabarot, 18 November 2020, p. 42, https://www.assemblee-nationale.fr/dyn/15/rapports/cion_afetr/l15b3581_rapport-information.pdf.

28 Interview with a former DGA high civil servant, Paris, 16 and 29 September 2021.

29 France, Assemblée Nationale, 'Rapport d'information n°3581, déposé par la Mission d'information de la Commission des Affaires étrangères sur le contrôle des exportations d'armement' [Information Report No. 3581, filed by the Information Mission of the Foreign Affairs Committee on the control of arms exports], Députés M. Jacques Maire et Mme Michèle Tabarot, 18 November 2020, pp. 43–4, https://www.assemblee-nationale.fr/dyn/15/rapports/cion_afetr/l15b3581_rapport-information.pdf.

30 Interview with academic expert in French arms exports, 29 September 2021.

31 Interview with former high civil servant from the SGDSN, Paris, 7 September 2021.

32 Germany, Die Bundesregierung, 'Strategy Paper of the Federal Government on Strengthening the Security and Defence Industry', p. 7, https://www.bmwi.de/Redaktion/DE/Downloads/S-T/strategiepapier-staerkung-sicherits-und-verteidigungsindustrie-en.pdf?__blob=publicationFile&v=4.

33 Dirk Hanschel, 'Chapter 6. The German Control Regime on Arms Exports', in Laurence Lustgarten (ed.), *Law and the Arms Trade: Weapons, Blood and Rules* (Bloomsbury Publishing, 2020) p. 167.

34 Federal Republic of Germany, 'Initial report on measures undertaken to implement the Arms Trade Treaty in accordance with its Article 13(1)', p. 9, https://thearmstradetreaty.org/download/b53fdb98-7912-39df-92d7-259131de677e.

35 Germany Federal Foreign Office, 'The Federal Government's Political Principles Governing Arms Exports', https://www.auswaertiges-amt.de/en/aussenpolitik/themen/aussenwirtschaft/-/231416#content_1.

36 Federal Republic of Germany, 'Initial report on measures undertaken to implement the Arms Trade Treaty in accordance with its Article 13(1)', p. 9, https://thearmstradetreaty.org/download/b53fdb98-7912-39df-92d7-259131de677e.

37 Bundesministerium für Wirtschaft und Klimaschutz (BMWI), ,Politische Grundsätze der Bundesregierung für den Export von Kriegswaffen und sonstigen Rüstungsgütern' [Political principles of the federal government for the export of war weapons and other armaments], p. 7, https://www.bmwi.de/Redaktion/DE/Downloads/P-R/politische-grundsaetze-fuer-den-export-von-kriegswaffen-und-sonstigen-ruestungsguetern.pdf?__blob=publicationFile&v=4.

38 *Ibid.*

39 Yannik Hüllinghorst and Stephan Roll, 'German Arms Exports and the Militarisation of Arab States' Foreign Policies', Stiftung Wissenschaft und Politik (SWP) Comment no. 6, January 2021, p. 4, https://www.swp-berlin.org/10.18449/2021C06/.

40 Bundesministerium für Wirtschaft und Klimaschutz (BMWI), 'Bundesregierung beschließt Politische Grundsätze für Rüstungsexporte' [Political principles for arms exports], 26 June 2019, https://www.bmwi.de/Redaktion/DE/Pressemitteilungen/2019/20190626-bundesregierung-beschliesst-politische-grundsaetze-fuer-ruestungsexporte.html.

41 Bundesministerium für Wirtschaft und Klimaschutz (2022): Entwurf: Eckpunkte für das Rüstungskontrollgesetz, Oktober 2022, https://augengeradeaus.net/wp-content/uploads/2022/10/20221013_eckpunkte-ruestungsexportkontrollgesetz-entwurf.pdf.

42 Lucie Béraud-Sudreau, 'French Arms Exports: The Business of Sovereignty', Adelphi vol. 475-476, March 2020, pp. 11–12.

43 Interview with French diplomat, Paris, 8 October 2021.

44 Déclaration de Hervé Morin, ministre de la Défense, sur les défis et priorités de la politique de défense [Statement by Hervé Morin, French Minister of Defence, on the challenges and priorities of defense policy], Toulouse, 11 September 2007 : *'L'enjeu est bien, pour la France, de disposer durablement des compétences clés qui nous permettront de satisfaire les besoins futurs de nos forces, avec le degré d'autonomie nécessaire.'* [The challenge is, for France, to have the key skills that will allow us to meet the future needs of our forces, with the necessary degree of autonomy], https://www.vie-publique.fr/discours/167655-declaration-de-m-herve-morin-ministre-de-la-defense-sur-les-defis-et.

45 Déclaration de Jean-Yves Le Drian, ministre de la Défense, sur les exportations d›armement [Statement by Jean-Yves Le Drian, Minister of Defence, on arms exports], Paris, 22 November 2012: *'le geste d'exporter est une condition pour conserver notre autonomie stratégique. Le maintien en France d'une industrie de défense robuste conditionne dans une très grande mesure notre capacité, celle de l'État, à orienter les choix futurs de cette industrie et donc permettre l'adéquation de ceux-ci avec les besoins de nos forces'* [the gesture of exporting is a condition for maintaining our strategic autonomy. The maintenance in France of a robust defense industry conditions to a very large extent our capacity, that of the State, to guide the future choices of this industry and therefore allow the adequacy of these with the needs of our forces], https://www.vie-publique.fr/discours/186495-declaration-de-m-jean-yves-le-drian-ministre-de-la-defense-sur-les-ex.

46 'Transformation de la DGA' [Transformation of DGA], Discours de Florence Parly, ministre des Armées, Paris, 5 July 2018: *'Je rappelais hier à la commission de défense de l'assemblée nationale que « les exportations d'armement sont le business model de notre souveraineté. » Ces exportations sont vitales pour que notre tissu industriel garde sa capacité à couvrir tout le spectre des technologies dont nous avons besoin pour préserver un modèle d'armée complet.'* [I reminded the Defense Committee of the National Assembly yesterday that "arms exports are the business model of our sovereignty. These exports are vital for our industrial fabric to maintain its ability to cover the full spectrum of technologies we need to preserve a complete army model], https://www.defense.gouv.fr/salle-de-presse/discours/discours-de-florence-parly/discours_balard_05-07-2018_transformation_dga.

47 Emma Soubrier, 'Weaponized storytelling à la française: Demystifying France's narratives around its arms export policies', World Peace Foundation/Tufts University, April 2022, https://sites.tufts.edu/wpf/files/2022/03/Weaponized-storytelling-a-la-Francaise.pdf.

48 Interview with former DGA personnel and defence attaché, 8 September 2021.

49 Interview with expert on France's defence and security market, arms industry and arms trade, 29 September 2021.

50 See https://www.lefigaro.fr/vox/histoire/jean-garrigues-pourquoi-les-francais-aiment-tant-charles-de-gaulle-20201109. This is true for the far right (https://www.la-croix.com/France/Politique/Le-RN-continuite-idees-Gaulle-assure-Marine-Le-Pen-2020-06-05-1301097806); the far left (https://melenchon.fr/2020/06/17/de-gaulle-etait-il-un-insoumis-grand-entretien-avec-jean-luc-melenchon/); and Emmanuel Macron's government, among others (https://www.leparisien.fr/politique/l-elysee-ajoute-une-croix-de-lorraine-a-son-embleme-14-09-2018-7888353.php).

51 Béraud-Sudreau, 'French Arms Exports: The Business of Sovereignty', p. 25.

52 Interview with French diplomat, Paris, 8 October 2021.

53 Bastian Giegerich and Maximilian Terhalle, 'The Responsibility to Defend: Rethinking Germany's Strategic Culture', IISS Adelphi Series, June 2021, pp. 15–17 (pdf version).

54 Federal President Joachim Gauck, 'Germany's role in the world: Reflections on responsibility, norms and alliances', Speech to open 50th Munich Security Conference, Munich, 31 January 2014, https://www.bundespraesident.de/SharedDocs/Reden/EN/JoachimGauck/Reden/2014/140131-Munich-Security-Conference.html; and Munich Security Conference, Special Edition of the Munich Security Report on German Foreign and Security Policy, https://securityconference.org/en/publications/msr-special-editions/germany-2020/.

55 Giegerich and Terhalle, 'The Responsibility to Defend', Chapter 1, p. 28.

56 Kristina Kausch, 'Enabling or evading? Germany in the Middle East', FRIDE Policy Brief, no. 191, January 2015, p. 2, https://www.files.ethz.ch/isn/187451/Germany_in_the_Middle_East.pdf.

57 See, for example, Hans Kundnani, 'Germany as a Geo-economic Power', *Washington Quarterly*, vol. 34, no. 3, 2011, pp. 31–45, https://www.tandfonline.com/doi/abs/10.1080/0163660X.2011.587950; Dieter Dettke, 'Germany: The Geopolitical Uncertainties of a Geo-Economic Power', American Institute for Contemporary German Studies, 20 October 2014, https://www.aicgs.org/2014/10/germany-the-geopolitical-uncertainties-of-a-geo-economic-power/.

58 Based on 2014 data (latest available): https://www.bdsv.eu/themen/die-industrie.html.

59 Verband der Automobilindustrie (VDA), 'Facts and Figures – Overview', https://en.vda.de/en/services/facts-and-figures/facts-and-figures-overview.html.

60 Claudia Major, Annual Conference of the Chaire Economie de Defense, IHEDN, 15 December 2021, https://www.youtube.com/watch?v=wFH4B859VXc&list=PLzMFMsSJpwt_WooTi9fP1AHV2-OhXHNmK&index=3&ab_channel=Chaire%C3%89conomieded%C3%A9fense-IHEDN; and Barbara Kunz, 'Defending Europe? A Stocktaking of French and German Visions for European Defense', IRSEM, Étude n° 41, September 2015, p. 95, https://www.irsem.fr/data/files/irsem/documents/document/file/1121/Etude_IRSEM_n41.pdf.

61 Claudia Major, 'Annual Conference of the Chaire Economie de Defense', *IHEDN*, 15 December 2021, https://www.youtube.com/watch?v=wFH4B859VXc&list=PLzMFMsSJpwt_WooTi9fP1AHV2-OhXHNmK&index=3&ab_channel=Chaire%C3%89conomieded%C3%A9fense-IHEDN.

62 Gaëlle Winter, 'La politique industrielle de défense de l'Allemagne : l'Etat pris dans un

jeu de perles de verre' [Germany's industrial defense policy: the state caught in a game of glass beads], Fondation pour la recherche stratégique (FRS), Note n°18/2019, 16 September 2019, p. 3, https://www.frstrategie.org/publications/notes/politique-industrielle-defense-allemagne-etat-pris-dans-un-jeu-perles-verre-2019.

63 Cabinet of Germany (Bundesregierung), 'Strategy Paper of the Federal Government on Strengthening the Security and Defence Industry', 2020, pp. 6–7, https://www.bmwi.de/Redaktion/DE/Downloads/S-T/strategiepapier-staerkung-sicherits-und-verteidigungsindustrie-en.pdf?__blob=publicationFile&v=4.

64 Bastian Giegerich and Maximilian Terhalle, 'The Responsibility to Defend: Rethinking Germany's Strategic Culture', *Adelphi*, no. 477, June 2021, Chapter 3, p. 82.

65 Gaëlle Winter, 'La politique industrielle de défense de l'Allemagne: l'Etat pris dans un jeu de perles de verre' [Germany's industrial defense policy: the state caught in a game of glass beads], Fondation pour la recherche stratégique (FRS), Note n°18/2019, 16 September 2019, p. 10, https://www.frstrategie.org/publications/notes/politique-industrielle-defense-allemagne-etat-pris-dans-un-jeu-perles-verre-2019.

66 Cabinet of Germany (Bundesregierung), 'Strategy Paper of the Federal Government on Strengthening the Security and Defence Industry', 2020, p. 8, https://www.bmwi.de/Redaktion/DE/Downloads/S-T/strategiepapier-staerkung-sicherits-und-verteidigungsindustrie-en.pdf?__blob=publicationFile&v=4.

67 France, Sénat, 'Rapport d'information n°630, déposé par la commission des affaires étrangères sur le Moyen-Orient à l'heure nucléaire' [Information Report no. 630, tabled by the Foreign Affairs Committee on the Middle East in the nuclear age], Sénateurs M. Jean-Francois Poncet et Mme Monique Cerisier-Ben Guiga, 25 September 2009, https://www.senat.fr/rap/r08-630/r08-63065.html.

68 Ben Rhodes, 'Inside the White House during the Syrian "Red Line" Crisis', *Atlantic*, 3 June 2018, https://www.theatlantic.com/international/archive/2018/06/inside-the-white-house-during-the-syrian-red-line-crisis/561887/.

69 Lucie Béraud-Sudreau, 'La politique française de soutien à l'export de défense, Raisons et limites d'un succès' [The French defence export support policy, Reasons and limits of a success], IFRI *Focus stratégique*, June 2017, p. 32, https://www.ifri.org/sites/default/files/atoms/files/beraud-sudreau_politique_francaise_soutien_export_defense_2017.pdf.

70 Clarence Rodriguez, 'L'Arabie saoudite et la France poursuivent leur lune de miel à Paris' [Saudi Arabia and France continue their honeymoon in Paris], *RFI*, 24 June 2015, https://www.rfi.fr/fr/france/20150623-prince-saoudien-ben-salmane-paris-visite-contrats-droits-homme; and Marc Semo, 'François Hollande en pleine lune de miel saoudienne' [François Hollande on his Saudi honeymoon], *Libération*, 4 May 2015, https://www.liberation.fr/planete/2015/05/04/francois-hollande-en-pleine-lune-de-miel-saoudienne_1287235/.

71 France, Ministère des Armées, 'Rapport au Parlement sur les exportations d'armement de la France 2021' [Report to Parliament on French arms exports 2021], June 2021, p. 113, https://www.vie-publique.fr/rapport/280174-rapport-au-parlement-2021-sur-les-exportations-darmement-de-la-france.

72 'La France vend 80 Rafale aux Émirats arabes unis, un contrat historique à 16 milliards d'euros' [France sells 80 Rafale to the United Arab Emirates, a historic contract worth 16 billion euros], LCI, 3 December 2021, https://www.lci.fr/economie/vente-historique-la-france-vend-80-rafale-aux-emirats-arabes-unis-un-contrat-a-16-milliards-d-euros-2203613.html; 'Ventes de Rafale aux Emirats arabes unis : «Ces avions ont une vocation de lutte contre le terrorisme», affirme un porte-parole du ministère des Armées' [Rafale sales in the United Arab Emirates: 'These planes are intended to fight against terrorism', says a spokesperson for the Ministry of the Armed Forces], *Franceinfo*, 3 December 2021, https://www.francetvinfo.fr/economie/aeronautique/rafale/ventes-de-rafale-aux-emirats-arabes-unis-ces-avions-ont-une-vocation-de-lutte-contre-le-terrorisme-affirme-un-porte-parole-du-ministere-des-armees_4868343.html.

73 Emmanuel Macron (@EmmanuelMacron), Président de la République française, Tweet, 3 December 2021, https://twitter.com/EmmanuelMacron/status/146666559987712259?s=20.

74 Hugo Meijer, 'Pulled East. The rise of China, Europe and French security policy in the Asia-Pacific', *Journal of Strategic Studies*, 7 September 2021, https://doi.org/10.1080/01402390.2021.1935251.

75 France, Ministère des Armées, 'France and Security in the Indo-Pacific', 2018 (updated May 2019), https://www.defense.gouv.fr/layout/set/print/content/download/532754/9176250/version/3/file/France+and+Security+in+the+Indo-Pacific+-+2019.pdf.

76 France, Ministère de l'Europe et des Affaires étrangères, 'L'espace indopacifique: une priorité pour la France' [The Indo-Pacific space: a priority for France], July 2021, https://www.diplomatie.gouv.fr/fr/dossiers-pays/asie-oceanie/l-espace-indo-pacifique-une-priorite-pour-la-france/.

77 France, Ambassade de France en Inde, 'La zone indopacifique : une priorité pour la France' [The Indo-Pacific space: a priority for France], 31 July 2019, https://in.ambafrance.org/La-zone-indopacifique-une-priorite-pour-la-France.

78 France, Ministère des Armées, 'La stratégie de défense française en Indopacifique' [French defense strategy in the Indo-Pacific], 24 June 2020, https://www.defense.gouv.fr/dgris/action-internationale/enjeux-regionaux/la-strategie-de-defense-francaise-en-indopacifique2.

79 France, Ministère des Armées, 'Rapport au Parlement sur les exportations d'armement de la France 2021' [Report to Parliament on French arms exports 2021], June 2021, p. 113, https://www.vie-publique.fr/rapport/280174-rapport-au-parlement-2021-sur-les-exportations-darmement-de-la-france.

80 *Ibid.*

81 'Jean-Yves Le Drian dénonce «un coup dans le dos» après la rupture du contrat des sous-marins par l'Australie ' [Jean-Yves Le Drian denounces «a blow in the back» after the breach of the contract of the submarines by Australia], *Franceinfo*, 16 September 2021, https://www.francetvinfo.fr/economie/emploi/metiers/armee-et-securite/rupture-du-contrat-des-sous-marins-par-l-australie-c-est-un-coup-dans-le-dos-denonce-jean-yves-ledrian_4770743.html.

82 Elise Vincent and Bruno Philip, 'La vente d'avions Rafale replace l'Indonésie au cœur de la stratégie française en Indo-Pacifique'[The sale of Rafale aircraft puts Indonesia back at the heart of French strategy in the Indo-Pacific], *Le Monde*, 11 February 2022, https://www.lemonde.fr/international/article/2022/02/11/la-vente-d-avions-rafale-replace-l-indonesie-au-c-ur-de-la-strategie-francaise-en-indo-pacifique_6113251_3210.html.

83 Kristina Kausch, 'Enabling or evading? Germany in the Middle East', https://www.files.ethz.ch/isn/187451/Germany_in_the_Middle_East.pdf.

84 Angela Merkel, Federal Chancellor, 'Speech to the Knesset in Jerusalem', 18 March 2008, https://www.knesset.gov.il/description/eng/doc/speech_merkel_2008_eng.pdf.

85 Heiko Maas, Foreign Minister, Jüdische Allgemeine', German Federal Foreign Office, 27 May 2021, https://www.auswaertiges-amt.de/en/newsroom/news/maas-juedische-allgemeine/2463340.

86 'A special case: the German-Israeli security cooperation', DW, https://www.dw.com/en/a-special-case-the-german-israeli-security-cooperation/a-18444585.

87 SIPRI Arms Transfers Database, TIV tables, https://armstrade.sipri.org/armstrade/page/values.php, accessed December 2021.

88 Nils Duquet, 'Business as usual? Assessing the impact of the Arab Spring on European arms export control policies', Flemish Peace Institute, 24 March 2014, p. 53; Kristina Kausch, 'Enabling or evading? Germany in the Middle East', no. 191, January 2015, p. 5, https://www.files.ethz.ch/isn/187451/Germany_in_the_Middle_East.pdf.

89 Kausch, 'Enabling or evading? Germany in the Middle East'.

90 Germany, Federal Foreign Office, 'Germany and United Arab Emirates: Bilateral relations', 19 May 2021, https://www.auswaertiges-amt.de/en/aussenpolitik/laenderinformationen/vae-node/unitedarabemirates/228542.

91 Jeremias Kettner, 'Germany and the Qatar Crisis', Ifimes, 24 June 2017, https://www.ifimes.org/en/researches/germany-and-the-qatar-crisis/4187.

92 Timo Behr, 'Germany and the Arab Spring', IFRI, 13 October 2012, p. 3, https://www.ifri.org/sites/default/files/atoms/files/actuellebehr131012.pdf.

93 Germany, Federal Foreign Office, 'Humanitarian aid in Syria', 4 February 2020, https://www.auswaertiges-amt.de/en/aussenpolitik/laenderinformationen/syrien-node/humanitarian-aid-syria/2303604.

94 Aljoscha Albrecht and Sarah Henkel, 'A Hint of Change: Prospects for a German Middle East Policy', *Manara Magazine*, 31 October 2021, manaramagazine.org /2021/10/31/a-hint-of-change-prospects-for-a-german-middle-east-policy/.

95 'Germany's Merkel backs air strikes on Syria as "necessary and appropriate"', Reuters, 14 April 2018, https://www.reuters.com/article/us-mideast-crisis-syria-germany-idUSKBN1HL0H6.

96 'Germany to supply arms to Kurds fighting IS in Iraq', BBC News, 1 September 2014, https://www.bbc.com/news/world-europe-29012159.

97 SIPRI National reports on arms exports (database), 'Germany, 2015–2020', https://www.sipri.org/databases/national-reports/Germany.

98 SIPRI Arms Transfers Database, 'TIV tables', https://armstrade.sipri.org/armstrade/page/values.php.

99 SIPRI Arms Transfers Database, 'Trade registers', https://armstrade.sipri.org/armstrade/page/trade_register.php.

100 Konstantin Von Hammerstein et al., 'How the Merkel Doctrine Is Changing Berlin Policy', *Spiegel International*, 3 December 2012, https://www.spiegel.de/international/germany/german-weapons-exports-on-the-rise-as-merkel-doctrine-takes-hold-a-870596.html; Von Ulrike Demmer, Ralf Neukirch and Holger Stark, 'Merkel's Risky Weapons Exports', *Spiegel International*, 30 July 2012, https://www.spiegel.de/international/germany/merkel-s-risky-weapons-sales-signal-change-in-german-foreign-policy-a-847137.html ; Holger Stark, 'Tank Exports to Saudi Arabia Signal German Policy Shift', *Spiegel International*, 14 October 2011, https://www.spiegel.de/international/world/the-merkel-doctrine-tank-exports-to-saudi-arabian-signal-german-policy-shift-a-791380.html; and 'Merkel Seeks to Ease German Arms Exports', *Spiegel International*, 8 November 2011, https://www.spiegel.de/international/germany/letter-to-brussels-merkel-seeks-to-ease-german-arms-exports-a-796541.html.

101 CDU, CSU and SPD, 'Deutschlands Zukunft gestalten, Koalitionsvertrag zwischen CDU, CSU und SPD' [Shaping Germany's future Coalition agreement between the CDU, CSU and SPD], Bundestag, 27 November 2013, https://archiv.cdu.de/sites/default/files/media/dokumente/koalitionsvertrag.pdf.

102 'German tank sale to Saudi Arabia likely to be cancelled: newspaper', Reuters, 14 April 2014, https://www.reuters.com/article/us-germany-saudi-arms-idUSBREA3C07E20140413.

103 Germany, Federal Government, 'Policy guidelines for the Indo-Pacific, Germany – Europe – Asia, Shaping the 21st Century together', last updated August 2020, https://www.auswaertiges-amt.de/blob/2380514/f9784f7e3b3fa1bd7c5446d274a4169e/200901-indo-pazifik-leitlinien--1--data.pdf.

104 Alexandra Sakaki, Gudrun Wacker and Christian Wagner, 'German Foreign Policy in Transition', *SWP Research Paper*, 2021/RP, 13 December 2021, p. 120, https://www.swp-berlin.org/en/publication/german-foreign-policy-in-transition.

105 Frédéric Grare, 'Germany's New Approach to the Indo-Pacific', Carnegie, 15 October 2020, https://carnegieendowment.org/2020/10/15/germany-s-new-approach-to-indo-pacific-pub-82978.

106 Giegerich and Terhalle, 'The Responsibility to Defend:', p. 13.

107 Germany, Foreign Federal Office, 'German engagement in the Indo-Pacific: Frigate "Bayern" crosses the South China Sea', 16 December 2021, https://www.auswaertiges-amt.de/en/aussenpolitik/regionaleschwerpunkte/asien/frigate-bayern/2502176.

108 'The Future of Indo-Pacific Maritime Security', 42nd IISS Fullerton Lecture, 21 December 2021, https://www.iiss.org/events/2021/12/42nd-iiss-fullerton-lecture.

109 SIPRI Arms Transfers Database.

110 Niels Duquet, 'Business as usual? Assessing the impact of the Arab Spring on European arms export control policies', *Flemish Peace Institute*, 24 March 2014, pp. 56-59, https://vlaamsvredesinstituut.eu/en/report/business-as-usual/; Mark Bromley, 'The review of the EU Common Position on Arms Exports: Propsects for Strengthened Controls', EU Non-Proliferation Consortium, Non-Proliferation Papers, No. 7, Jan. 2012, p. 13, https://www.sipri.org/sites/default/files/Nonproliferation7.pdf; 'Germany and France at Loggerheads over Arms Deal with Libya', *Spiegel international*, 19 April 2008, https://www.spiegel.de/international/europe/tiger-tensions-germany-and-france-at-loggerheads-over-arms-deal-with-libya-a-548459.html.

111 Niels Duquet, 'Business as usual?', pp. 59–61; Gerald Traufetter, 'Berlin Under Fire for Tank Deal with Cairo', *Spiegel international*, 27 May 2013, https://www.spiegel.de/international/world/berlin-made-dubious-tank-deal-with-cairo-a-902143.html.

112 Philippe Lesaffre, 'La France, quatrième exportateur d'armes' [France, fourth arms exporter], *L'Express*, 27 October 2011, https://www.lexpress.fr/actualite/monde/la-france-quatrieme-exportateur-d-armes_1045379.html.

113 'Paris blocked riot equipment export as Ben Ali prepared to flee', RFI, 19 January 2011, http://www.english.rfi.fr/africa/20110119-paris-blocked-riot-equipment-export-ben-ali-prepared-flee France, Assemblée Nationale, 'Question écrite N°17880 de M. François Loncle' [Written question no. 17880 from Mr François Loncle], 12 February 2013, https://questions.assemblee-nationale.fr/q14/14-17880QE.htm.

114 France, Assemblée Nationale, 'Rapport N°622 déposé au nom de la Commission d'enquête sur les conditions de libération des infirmières et du médecin bulgares détenus en Libye et sur les récents accords franco-libyens' [Report no. 622 submitted on behalf of the Commission of Inquiry into the conditions of release of the Bulgarian nurses and doctors detained in Libya and the recent Franco-Libyan agreements], Députés MM. Pierre Moscovici (Président) et Axel Poniatowski (Rapporteur), 22 January 2008, p. 227, https://www.assemblee-nationale.fr/13/pdf/rap-enq/r0622.pdf.

115 Louis Charbonneau, 'Arming rebels doesn't violate U.N. sanctions: France', Reuters, 29 June 2011, https://www.reuters.com/article/us-libya-un-france-idUSTRE75S7XR20110629.

116 Michel Cabirol, 'Renault Truck Defense cartonne en Egypte', *La Tribune*, 18 October 2012, http://www.latribune.fr/entreprises finance/industrie/aeronautique-defense/20121018trib000725713/defense-renault-truck-defense-cartonne-en-egypte.html.

117 Dominique Lewis, 'Des analyses vidéo font la lumière sur l'utilisation de blindés français en Égypte' [Video analyses shed light on the use of French armor in Egypt], Amnesty international, 9 December 2018, https://www.amnesty.fr/controle-des-armes/actualites/making-of.

118 'Yemen crisis: Why is there a war?', BBC, 2 November 2021, https://www.bbc.com/news/world-middle-east-29319423; Council on Foreign Relations, Global conflict Tracker, https://www.cfr.org/global-conflict-tracker/conflict/war-yemen.

119 Koalitionsvertrag zwischen CDU, CSU und SPD, 'Ein neuer Aufbruch für Europa, Eine neue Dynamik für Deutschland, Ein neuer Zusammenhalt für unser Land' [A new beginning for Europe, a new dynamic for Germany, a new cohesion for our country], 12 March 2018, p. 149, https://www.cdu.de/system/tdf/media/dokumente/koalitions-vertrag_2018.pdf?file=1.

120 Germany Bundesministerium für Wirtschaft und Klimaschutz: BMWK, 'Report of the federal government on its export policy for conventional armaments in 2020 - Arms export report 2020', https://www.bmwk.de/Redaktion/DE/Publikationen/Aussenwirtschaft/ruestungsexporte-bmwi-070221.pdf?__blob=publicationFile&v=12.

121 Axel Höpner, Martin Murphy, Torsten Riecke and Donata Riedel, 'Germany bans all arms exports to Saudi Arabia amid Khashoggi uproar', Handelsblatt, 20 November 2018, https://www.handelsblatt.com/english/politics/arabian-arms-germany-bans-all-arms-exports-to-saudi-arabia-amid-khashoggi-uproar/23694972.html?ticket=ST-11837930-RSdq3DGwMr WqbThI5G9b-cas01.example.org ; 'Merkel: No German arms exports to Saudi until killing cleared up', Reuters, 22 October 2018, https://www.reuters.com/article/us-saudi-khashoggi-germany-merkel-idUSKCN1MW2LT.

122 EEAS database, https://webgate.ec.europa.eu/eeasqap/sense/app/75fd8e6e-68ac-42dd-a078-f616633118bb/overview.

123 Working Party on Non-Proliferation and Arms Exports, conventional arms exports subgroup (COARM) Public v2.0 database, https://webgate.ec.europa.eu/eeasqap/sense/app/75fd8e6e-68ac-42dd-a078-f616633118bb/overview.

124 Matthias Gebauer and Gerald Traufetter, 'Regierung genehmigt neue Waffendeals mit Saudi-Arabien' [Government approves new arms deals with Saudi Arabia], 19 September 2018, https://www.spiegel.de/politik/deutschland/ruestung-bundesregierung-genehmigt-neue-waffen-deals-mit-saudi-arabien-a-1229003.html.

125 Jean Guisnel, 'Armement : la France, supermarché de l'Arabie saoudite' [Armament: France, supermarket of Saudi Arabia], *Le Point*, 20 March 2017, https://www.lepoint.fr/editos-du-point/jean-guisnel/armement-la-france-supermarche-de-l-arabie-saoudite-20-03-2017-2113291_53.php; 'Comment Macron soutient les ventes d'armes à l'Arabie saoudite' [How Macron supports arms sales to Saudi

Arabia], *Challenges*, 22 February 2018, https://www.challenges.fr/economie/comment-macron-soutient-les-ventes-d-armes-a-l-arabie-saoudite_569274.

126 See 'Yémen : les armes françaises servent au Moyen-Orient' [Yemen: French weapons are used in the Middle East], *Franceinfo*, 9 February 2018, https://www.francetvinfo.fr/monde/proche-orient/yemen/yemen-les-armes-francaises-servent-au-moyen-orient_2603056.html.

127 'Macron accuse implicitement Merkel de « démagogie » sur les livraisons d'armes à Ryad' [Macron implicitly accuses Merkel of 'demagogy' on arms deliveries to Riyadh], *Le Point*, 26 October 2018, https://www.lepoint.fr/politique/macron-accuse-implicitement-merkel-de-demagogie-sur-les-livraisons-d-armes-a-ryad-26-10-2018-2266348_20.php.

128 'Made in France', *Disclose*, 15 April 2019, https://disclose.ngo/fr/investigations/made-in-france.

129 EEAS database, https://webgate.ec.europa.eu/eeasqap/sense/app/75fd8e6e-68ac-42dd-a078-f616633118bb/overview.

130 Working Party on Non-Proliferation and Arms Exports, conventional arms exports subgroup (COARM) Public v2.0 database, https://webgate.ec.europa.eu/eeasqap/sense/app/75fd8e6e-68ac-42dd-a078-f616633118bb/overview.

131 France, Assemblée Nationale, 'Compte rendu n° 081 de la Commission des Affaires étrangères, Audition, à huis clos, de Mme Claire Landais, Secrétaire Générale de la Défense et de la Sécurité Nationale (SGDSN), sur le dispositif français d'autorisation d'exportation du matériel de guerre' [Minutes no. 081 of the Foreign Affairs Committee, Hearing, in camera, of Ms Claire Landais, Secretary General for Defense and National Security (SGDSN), on the French system for authorizing the export of military equipment war], 18 July 2018, https://www.assemblee-nationale.fr/dyn/15/comptes-rendus/cion_afetr/l15cion_afetr1718081_compte-rendu.

132 Hüllinghorst and Roll, 'German Arms Exports and the Militarisation of Arab States'.

133 Council of the European Union, General Secretariat of the Council, 'User's Guide to Council Common Position 2008/944/CFSP defining common rules governing the control of exports of military technology and equipment', 16 September 2019, pp. 80–90, https://www.consilium.europa.eu/media/40659/st12189-en19.pdf.

134 Official Journal of the European Union, 'Council common position 2008/944/CFSP of 8 December 2008 defining common rules governing control of exports of military technology and equipment', 13 December 2008, https://eur-lex.europa.eu/legal-content/EN/TXT/HTML/?uri=CELEX:32008E0944&from=EN.

135 Council of the European Union, General Secretariat of the Council, 'User's Guide to Council Common Position 2008/944/CFSP defining common rules governing the control of exports of military technology and equipment', 16 September 2019, p. 81, https://www.consilium.europa.eu/media/40659/st12189-en19.pdf.

136 Council of the European Union, General Secretariat of the Council, 'User's Guide to Council Common Position 2008/944/CFSP defining common rules governing the control of exports of military technology and equipment', 16 September 2019, p. 84, https://www.consilium.europa.eu/media/40659/st12189-en19.pdf.

137 'Qatar race is on!', Rafale News blog, 26 July 2010, http://rafalenews.blogspot.com/2010/07/qatar.html.

138 UCDP, 'Uppsala Conflict Data Program', https://ucdp.uu.se/.

139 Krista E. Wiegand, 'Bahrain, Qatar, and the Hawar Islands: Resolution of a Gulf Territorial Dispute', *Middle East Journal*, vol. 66, no. 1, Winter 2012, pp. 79–96, https://www.jstor.org/stable/41342770.

140 Dassault Aviation, 'Dassault Aviation First Rafale delivery to the State of Qatar', 6 February 2019, https://www.dassault-aviation.com/en/group/press/press-kits/dassault-aviation-first-rafale-delivery-state-qatar/.

141 Craig Hoyle, 'Qatar adds a dozen more Rafales to order', Flight Global, 7 December 2017, https://www.flightglobal.com/qatar-adds-a-dozen-more-rafales-to-order/126404.article.

142 'UAE files UN complaint over Qatar violation of airspace', 19 January 2018, Middle East Monitor, https://www.middleeastmonitor.com/20180119-uae-files-un-complaint-over-qatar-violation-of-airspace/; 'Gulf airlines deny their planes were intercepted by Qatar fighter jets', Middle East Monitor, 17 January 2018, https://www.middleeastmonitor.com/20180117-gulf-airlines-deny-their-planes-were-intercepted-by-qatar-fighter-jets/.

143 'Ex-German minister: Saudi, UAE would have invaded Qatar in 2017', Middle East Monitor, 18 December 2018, https://www.middleeastmonitor.com/20181218-ex-german-minister-saudi-uae-would-have-invaded-qatar-in-2017/.

144 'Bahrain re-opens border dispute with Qatar', Al Jazeera, 5 November 2017, https://www.aljazeera.com/news/2017/11/5/bahrain-re-opens-border-dispute-with-qatar.

145 Dassault aviation, 'Historical contract for the acquisition of 80 Rafale F4 by the United Arab Emirates', 3 December 2021, https://www.dassault-aviation.com/en/group/press/press-kits/historical-contract-for-the-acquisition-of-80-rafale-f4-by-the-united-arab-emirates/.

146 John Irish, 'Cementing ties with France, UAE places $19 bln order for warplanes, helicopters', Reuters, 3 December 2021, https://www.reuters.com/business/aerospace-defense/frances-macron-nears-uae-rafale-fighter-jet-deal-2021-12-03/.

147 'France hopeful of sale of 60 Rafale jets to UAE', Reuters, 19 June 2009, https://www.reuters.com/article/us-dassault-rafale-idUSTRE55I1OA20090619.

148 U.S. Department of State, 'UAE-Iran Island Dispute', Press release, 17 April 2012, https://2009-2017.state.gov/r/pa/prs/ps/2012/04/188049.htm; https://news.un.org/en/story/2011/09/389112-united-arab-emirates-calls-iran-take-dispute-over-islands-un-court.

149 Rajiv Chandrasekaran, 'In the UAE the United States has a quiet, potent ally nicknamed 'Little Sparta'.' *Washington Post*, 9 November 2014, https://

www.washingtonpost.com/world/national-security/in-the-uae-the-united-states-has-a-quiet-potent-ally-nicknamed-little-sparta/2014/11/08/3fc6a50c-643a-11e4-836c-83bc4f26eb67_story.html.

150 'Gulf states send forces to Bahrain following protests', BBC, 14 March 2011, https://www.bbc.com/news/world-middle-east-12729786.

151 Andrew McGregor, 'Egypt, the UAE and Arab Military Intervention in Libya', *The Jamestown Foundation Terrorism Monitor*, vol. 12, no. 17, 5 September 2014, https://jamestown.org/program/egypt-the-uae-and-arab-military-intervention-in-libya/.

152 Kenneth M. Pollack, 'Sizing up Little Sparta: Understanding UAE military effectiveness', *American Enterprise Institute*, 27 October 2020, p. 5, https://www.aei.org/research-products/report/sizing-up-little-sparta-understanding-uae-military-effectiveness/.

153 Dassault Aviation, 'Rafale export: a major contract signed with the United Arab Emirates for 80 combat aircraft', 3 December 2021, https://www.thalesgroup.com/en/worldwide/aerospace/news/rafale-export-major-contract-signed-united-arab-emirates-80-combat.

154 Caleb Larson, 'Why Does Iran Have U.S. F-4 Phantom Fighters?', *National Interest*, 24 June 2021, https://nationalinterest.org/blog/reboot/why-does-iran-have-us-f-4-phantom-fighters-188460.

155 Andrew England and Simeon Kerr, 'UAE suspends talks with US over purchase of F-35 fighter jets', *Financial Times*, 14 December 2021, https://www.ft.com/content/7ab35684-d536-4908-89d6-a730d844c8d6; Ghaida Ghantous and Humeyra Pamuk, 'U.S. says it is ready to move forward with fighter jet sale to UAE', Reuters, 15 December 2021, https://www.reuters.com/business/aerospace-defense/us-set-move-forward-with-f-35-sale-after-uae-threatens-withdrawal-2021-12-15/.

156 Rahul Bedi, J.A.C. Lewis, 'India looks to Mirage to boost strike capabilities', *Jane's Defence Weekly*, 27 March 2002.

157 'An alternate theory of the MMRCA process, p. 2', StratPost, 9 April 2012, https://stratpost.com/an-alternate-theory-of-the-mmrca-process-i/2/.

158 Vivek Raghuvanshi, 'Dassault Pulls Out Mirage from Indian Aircraft Bid', *Defense News*, 27 February 2006.

159 'France's Dassault wins $12bn Indian fighter-jet deal', France 24, 31 January 2012, https://www.france24.com/en/20120131-france-dassault-wins-multi-billion-dollar-india-fighter-jet-deal-rafale-defence.

160 Rahul Bedi and Frederic Lert, 'Modi announces Rafale buy', *Jane's Defence Industry*, 13 April 2015.

161 Dassault Aviation, 'Dassault Aviation welcomes the acquisition by India of 36 Rafale', 23 September 2016, https://www.dassault-aviation.com/en/group/press/press-kits/dassault-aviation-welcomes-acquisition-india-36-rafale/

162 UCDP, State Based Violence, 'Government of China – Government of India', https://ucdp.uu.se/statebased/569.

163 'China reveals four soldiers killed in June 2020 border clash with India', Reuters, 19 February 2021, https://www.reuters.com/article/us-china-india-border-idUSKBN2AJ04B.

164 'India uses arrival of new fighter jets to warn China', *Straits Times*, 29 July 2020, https://www.straitstimes.com/asia/south-asia/india-uses-arrival-of-new-fighter-jets-to-warn-china.

165 M Ilyas Khan, 'Kargil: The forgotten victims of the world's highest war', BBC News, 26 July 2019, https://www.bbc.com/news/world-asia-49101016.

166 UCDP, State Based Violence, 'India – Pakistan', https://ucdp.uu.se/conflict/218.

167 Sheree Sardar, 'Pakistan says Indian warplanes violated airspace', Reuters, 14 December 2008, https://www.reuters.com/article/idINIndia-37019620081214; and 'India denies violating Pakistani airspace', ABC, https://www.abc.net.au/news/2008-12-14/india-denies-violating-pakistani-airspace/239338.

168 Sanjeev Miglani and Asad Hashim, 'India says hits Pakistan-based militants, escalating tensions', Reuters, 29 September 2016, https://www.reuters.com/article/us-pakistan-india-kashmir-idUSKCN11ZolJ; and Salman Masood, 'In Kashmir, Pakistan Questions India's "Surgical Strikes" on Militants', *New York Times*, 1 October 2016, https://www.nytimes.com/2016/10/02/world/asia/kashmir-pakistan-india.html?_r=0; 'Kashmir attack: India "launches strikes against militants"', BBC, 30 September 2016, https://www.bbc.com/news/world-asia-37504308.

169 US Department of Defense, Office of the Secretary of Defense, Annual report to Congress, 'Military and security developments involving the People's Republic of China 2021', 3 November 2021, https://media.defense.gov/2021/Nov/03/2002885874/-1/-1/0/2021-CMPR-FINAL.PDF.

170 Professor Keith Hartley, 'The industrial and economic benefits of Eurofighter typhoon', *Defense Aerospace*, 16 June 2006, http://www.defense-aerospace.com/dae/articles/reports/Typhoon_studyJune2006.pdf; Ron Matthews and Rashid Al-Saadi, 'Organisational Complexity of the Eurofighter Typhoon Collaborative Supply Chain', Centre for Defence Management and Leadership, Cranfield University at the Uk Defence Academy, 14 November 2021, https://www.tandfonline.com/doi/full/10.1080/10242694.2021.1987022.

171 'Hensoldt to supply Eurofighter / Typhoon self-protection system components', Airforce Technology, 4 May 2021, https://www.airforce-technology.com/news/hensoldt-eurofighter-typhoon-self-protection-system/.

172 John N. T. Helferich, 'Arms Export Controls Under Siege of Globalisation: Defeated Nation States Or Voluntary Surrender?', 2020, pp. 45–46; and BMWI, 'Politische Grundsätze der Bundesregierung für den Export von Kriegswaffen und sonstigen Rüstungsgütern', p. 6, https://www.bmwi.de/Redaktion/DE/Downloads/P-R/politische-grundsaetze-fuer-den-export-von-kriegswaffen-und-sonstigen-ruestungsguetern.pdf?__blob=publicationFile&v=4.

173 Report: Germany OKs arms sales to Saudi Arabia', DW, 29 September, 2022, https://www.dw.com/en/german-government-approves-arms-exports-to-saudi-arabia-reports/a-63288334

174 SIPRI Arms Transfers Database, 'Importer/Exporter TIV Tables', https://armstrade.sipri.org/armstrade/page/values.php.

175 Jeong-Ho Lee, 'China's New Flash Point With U.S. Allies Is a Hotspot for Spying', Bloomberg, 4 May 2021, https://www.bloomberg.com/news/articles/2021-05-04/china-s-new-flash-point-with-u-s-allies-like-south-korea-a-hotspot-for-spying; and Steven Borowiec, 'China's Next Flashpoint?', *Diplomat*, 22 March 2012, https://thediplomat.com/2012/03/chinas-next-flashpoint/.

176 MBDA, 'Prime contractor for the TAURUS KEPD 350 weapon system', https://www.mbda-systems.com/about-us/mbda-world-wide/taurus-systems/.

177 MBDA, TAURUS KEPD 350E, https://www.mbda-systems.com/product/taurus-kepd-350/.

178 'S. Korea to buy bunker busting missiles from Europe', Reuters, 4 April 2013, https://www.reuters.com/article/korea-defense-missiles-idUSL3N0CR1D120130404.

179 윤민식, 'Parliament advises review of Taurus, Global Hawk acquisition plan', *Korea Herald*, 5 July 2013, http://www.koreaherald.com/view.php?ud=20130705000594.

180 Soon Ho Lee, 'South Korean missile acquisition boosts strike capability', East Asia Forum, 3 August 2013, https://www.eastasiaforum.org/2013/08/03/south-korean-missile-acquisition-boosts-strike-capability/.

181 Missile Defense Project, 'South Korea Tests New Taurus Missile', Missile Threat, Center for Strategic and International Studies, 12 September 2017, last modified 15 June 2018, https://missilethreat.csis.org/south-korea-tests-new-taurus-missile/.

182 Republic of Korea, Ministry of National Defense, 2017 Defense White Paper, https://www.mnd.go.kr/user/mnd/upload/pblictn/PBLICTNEBOOK_201907110548253080.pdf; and Noh Ji-won, 'Defense Ministry changes terminology for "three-axis system" of military response', Hankyoreh, 13 January 2019, https://english.hani.co.kr/arti/english_edition/e_national/878208.html.

183 Ian Bowers and Henrik Stålhane Hiim, 'Conventional Counterforce Dilemmas: South Korea's Deterrence Strategy and Stability on the Korean Peninsula', *International Security*, vol. 45.

184 The MGCS project was launched in 2012 to replace their *Leclerc* and Leopard-2 tanks by 2035. This ground combat system of the future is co-designed and developed by Krauss-Maffei Wegmann (KMW), Rheinmetall and Nexter (*via* KNDS).

185 The FCAS programme was first mentioned by France and Germany in July 2017. It was officially launched by the signature of a letter of intent (loI) by the two countries in June 2017. Then, a few months later, Spain joined the programme. The main contractors are Dassault Aviation, Airbus, and Indra. FCAS is a system of air systems that is planned to include new manned and unmanned combat aircraft. It is meant to generate next-generation combat air capabilities. FCAS should enter service around 2040.

186 Léo Géhin et Yannick Quéau, 'L'ombre d'un doute. Les divergences franco-allemandes en matière d'exportation d'armes' [The shadow of a doubt. Franco-German differences in arms exports], Groupe de Recherche et d'Information sur la paix et la sécurité (GRIP), 31 March 2021, https://grip.org/wp-content/uploads/2021/04/NA_2021-03-31_FR_LG-YQ-Exportations-FR-GE-RW.pdf.

187 France, Ministry of Foreign Affairs, 'The Treaty of Aachen on Franco-German Cooperation and Integration', 22 January 2019, https://www.diplomatie.gouv.fr/en/country-files/germany/france-and-germany/franco-german-treaty-of-aachen/.

188 France Diplomacy, 'Franco-German Agreement on Defence export controls', Press release, 14 November 2019, https://www.diplomatie.gouv.fr/en/country-files/germany/events/article/franco-german-agreement-on-defence-export-controls-14-nov-19.

189 Chaire Economie de Défense – IHEDN, Conférence annuelle 'Quelle politique d'exportation de défense pour la France ?' [What defense export policy for France?], 15 December 2021, https://ecodef-ihedn.fr/video-conference-annuelle-quelle-politique-dexportation-de-defense-pour-la-france-15-decembre-2021-a-lecole-militaire/.

190 Interview with French defence industry personnel, Le Plessis-Robinson, 11 October 2021.

191 Like Germany did in 2018 when it imposed a ban on exporting arms to Saudi Arabia, following the Khashoggi affair.

192 Allison Meakem, 'Germany Confronts Its Nuclear Demons, *Foreign Policy*, 20 June 2022.

193 *Ibid.*

AN IISS STRATEGIC DOSSIER

JAPAN

A KAWASAKI P1 MARITIME-PATROL AIRCRAFT

A Kawasaki P1 maritime-patrol aircraft with the Japanese Maritime Self Defense Force Air Squadron 3 flies near Atsugi airbase in Kanagawa. CREDIT: Damon Coulter/SOPA Images/LightRocket via Getty Images.

CHAPTER 8

Since 1949, Japan has possessed the legislative mechanisms to notionally allow arms exports. But the country's pacificist norms combined with policy guidelines and political reluctance to support weapons sales have meant exports were banned in practice. This is now changing, albeit slowly; export guidelines began to be relaxed in 2014.

In theory, Japan's Foreign Exchange and Foreign Trade Act (Law No. 228 of 1949) has, since the end of the Second World War, provided the legal basis to consider any arms export and military-technology transfer. The Ministry of Economy, Trade and Industry (METI, previously the Ministry of International Trade and Industry, MITI) would, and continues to, act as the authorising body. Weapons exports, however, were societally unacceptable and generally unsupported politically.

Rule of three

Tokyo's Three Principles on Arms Transfer were first elaborated by then-prime minister Sato Eisaku in the Japanese Diet (parliament) in 1967. The principles required Japan to refrain from arms exports to 'communist nations; countries subject to embargoes under United Nations Security Council resolutions; and countries engaged or likely to be engaged in international conflicts'.[1] Sato's statement was the result of a need to clarify the principles for arms transfer in response to criticism from the political opposition regarding the export of rockets, developed by the University of Tokyo, to Yugoslavia.[2] The Three Principles, however, did not overtly prohibit or discourage arms export by Japanese industry. A decade later, the prohibition was made explicit. In 1976, the government led by prime minister Miki

Takeo made it clear that Japan, as a peace-loving nation (*heiwakokka*), 'shall not promote arms exports', regardless of the destination, and essentially launched a blanket ban on arms exports. The policy statement came following the opposition party's criticism of the Society of Japanese Aerospace Companies (SJAC)'s 1975 proposal to export a domestically developed transport aircraft.[3]

By the early 1980s, there were already early indications that the Three Principles would need to be revised. Japanese interest in defence-related technology transfer with the US resulted in the Japan–United States Exchange of Notes on Military Technology Transfer in 1983. This was followed, just over two decades later, by the Exchange of Notes concerning the Transfer of Arms and Military Technologies to the United States of America in 2006.[4] This was aimed at facilitating joint development and production of missile-defence systems.

Following the end of the Cold War, Japan's involvement in international security cooperation and peacekeeping operations grew. The Three Principles, however, served as obstacles. Tokyo, for example, was unable to transfer an old patrol boat to Indonesia because the transfer of bulletproof glass was prohibited under the principles. The country struggled to send equipment to its Self Defense Forces (JSDF) on deployment overseas.[5] In December 2011, chief cabinet secretary Fujimura Osamu made a statement on Guidelines for Overseas Transfer of Defense Equipment and exempted the application of the Three Principles. This was based on the premise of strict control for 'cases related to peace contribution and international cooperation as well as for cases regarding international joint development and production of defence equipment, etc., that contributes to Japan's security'.[6]

Principle challenge

The Three Principles and the presumption of no arms exports were to be further stressed by Japan's involvement in collaborative programmes, particularly the development of the Lockheed Martin F-35 *Lightning* II. Japanese industrial participation in F-35 production required companies to participate in the Autonomic Logistics Global Sustainment ALGS. An international logistics support system in which user countries globally exchange parts and other items. To allow this, the chief cabinet secretary provided in 2013 an exemption to allow industrial participation, on the condition that 'under the integrated control by the Government of the United States, transfer to non-F-35 user countries is strictly restricted and transfer is restricted to those countries that conform to the purposes and principles of the Charter of the United Nations'.[7] While such a shift appeared a long way from the stringent restrictions introduced by the Miki administration in 1976, they were specific rather than general. Tokyo was struggling to adapt its defence-industrial policies to the changing security environment.

When Abe Shinzo gained power in 2012, his administration stuck with a three principles approach, but they were to be his principles, rather than those of Miki, and he ended the era of the blanket ban. Instead, arms sales and military-technology transfer were recognised, for the first time, as a tool of foreign and security policy.

Abe came into office with ambitions of implementing security-sector reform and boosting Japan's domestic defence-industrial capabilities. Japan would adopt a more extrovert security policy under the banner of a 'proactive contribution to peace' and the Free and Open Indo-Pacific (FOIP) diplomatic vision in support of the 'rules-based order'. In 2013, Japan's first-ever National Security Strategy (NSS) was adopted by the newly established National Security Council (NSC). A decision was also taken to review the Three Principles and to lay out clearer guidelines in keeping with the contemporary security environment.[8] The Cabinet adopted the Three Principles of Defense Equipment and Technology Transfer (the new Three Principles) and the Implementation Guidelines of the Three Principles of Defense Equipment and Technology Transfer (the Guidelines) on 1 April 2014.[9] In 2016, the government established the Acquisition, Technology and Logistics Agency (ATLA) to oversee advanced-technology research and development, acquisition of defence equipment and overseas transfer of arms.[10]

The new Three Principles and the Guidelines were a step change for Japan's arms-sales policy in several ways. Firstly, they clarified specific cases when defence equipment and technologies could be transferred overseas by stating cases that were previously exempted from the Three Principles through Chief Cabinet Secretary statements. Secondly, the Guidelines recognised the role of arms transfer for the 'active promotion of the maintenance of international peace and security through the timely and effective implementation of contribution to peace and international cooperation'.[11] Finally, they acknowledged that the transfer contributed to 'strengthening security and defense cooperation with Japan's ally, the United States as well as other countries' and to 'maintaining and enhancing Japan's defense production and technological bases'.[12]

Japan's 2018 National Defense Program Guidelines (NDPG), intended to shape Tokyo's defence strategy for the next decade, placed arms export and military-technology transfer within the FOIP vision laid out by Abe in 2016.[13] The NDPG further emphasised defence equipment and technology cooperation with Australia, France, India, the United Kingdom and Southeast Asia. The signing of defence-equipment and technology-transfer agreements with these countries was given precedence. Other mechanisms were also introduced to begin easing the transfer of arms to some Southeast Asian countries.

In 2015, the Cabinet revised Japan's Official Development Assistance (ODA) Charter to enable the transfer of defence material to foreign armed forces for non-military purposes. This included supporting capacity-building for law-enforcement authorities for maritime security, to combat terrorism and to counter transnational organised crime, as well as for space and cyberspace security.[14] The Japan International Cooperation Agency, administered by the Ministry of Foreign Affairs (MOFA) has transferred defence equipment to law-enforcement agencies and coastguards in several countries, including Indonesia, Malaysia, the Philippines and Vietnam.[15]

The decision-making process

Under the Foreign Exchange and Foreign Trade Act (Law No.228 of 1949), the Minister of Economy, Trade and Industry decides on the individual application for defence equipment and technology transfer under the new Three Principles and the Guidelines. The government conducts a 'strict examination' in considering arms exports based on several points. These include whether the proposed transfer will have a 'positive' effect in supporting peace and security, or in enabling international cooperation, or benefitting Japan's security. The Guidelines state that the transfer must be with a foreign government or the United Nations. Areas where a transfer or cooperation are allowed cover those 'related to international joint development and production with countries cooperating with Japan in security area including the U.S.'[16] Moreover, the Guidelines mention instances where approval would contribute to 'enhancing security and defense cooperation with countries cooperating with Japan in security areas including the U.S.'[17] The examples raised in the Guidelines include:

a) defense equipment and technology included in the provision of supplies and services in accordance with an agreement concerning reciprocal provision of logistic support, supplies and services (ACSA),
b) provision of military technology as a part of mutual exchange of technology with the U.S.,
c) provision of parts or services related to a licensed product of the U.S. or provision of repair services etc. to the U.S. armed forces,
d) defense equipment and technology related to cooperation concerning rescue, transportation, vigilance, surveillance, or minesweeping with countries cooperating with Japan in security area.[18]

Transfers and cooperation are also permitted where approval is 'necessary for supporting activities of the governmental agencies including the Self-Defense Forces … which include the activities of foreign governments or private entities etc. related to the activities of the SDF etc., or for ensuring the safety of Japanese nationals'.[19] Activities mentioned in the Guidelines include:

a) temporary export of equipment, return of purchased equipment or provision of technical information related to the activities of the SDF etc. including replacements of items which need repairing with non-defective items,
b) export of equipment for the protection or self-protection of public officials,
c) export of equipment for the self-protection of Japanese nationals operating in danger areas.[20]

Further criteria for consideration include 'the appropriateness of the destination and end user', and the 'extent the overseas transfer of such equipment and technology will raise concern for Japan's security'.[21] With regard to the destination, the government will consider the impact that 'the country or region of destination is posing to … international peace and security as well as Japan's security'.[22]

As to the appropriateness of the end user, the government will consider how the defence equipment will be used by the end user and 'the certainty of appropriate control'.[23] For the latter, the government will consider

> such factors as nature, technical sensitivity, use (purpose), quantity and form (whether finished products or parts, goods or technology, etc.) of the defense equipment and technology to be transferred, as well as the possibilities of extra-purpose use or transfer to third parties.[24]

Japan normally requires prior consent for any repurposing of the exported item or for a proposed transfer to a third country as part of its requirements.[25] Usually, the Defense Equipment and Technology Transfer Agreement stipulates this and enables the process. There are, however, other ways of ensuring appropriate control under certain conditions.[26]

While the minister of economy, trade and industry approves individual cases, the role of the NSC is growing. The Implementation Guidelines specify that the NSC will review a case 'when especially careful consideration is required as for the application of the conditions for approving the transfers' and 'when especially careful consideration is required as for the appropriateness of the destination and the extent of security concerns, etc. with particular care'.[27] Similarly, the NSC board will also deliberate cases 'when the Government has never made a decision to permit overseas transfers of similar types'.[28]

The new Three Principles also give the NSC the authority to revise the Implementation Guidelines that inform the decision-making within METI. According to the Implementation Guidelines, the ministry must prepare the draft revisions but it needs to consult with the National Security Secretariat (the administrative body of the NSC), MOFA and the Ministry of Defense (MOD) before the NSC adopts them.[29] The language of the Guidelines suggests that a decision by the minister of economy, trade and industry could be influenced by an administration's foreign-policy and security-policy goals.

Responding to war

Prime Minister Kishida Fumio's government's swift decision to revise the Guidelines at the NSC on 8 March 2022 to allow the transfer of bulletproof vests, among other non-military goods, to Ukraine after Russia's invasion in February reinforced such observations.[30] After the invasion, the Kishida government, which had been championing the promotion of the rules-based international order, aligned with the US and its European allies to condemn Russia for violating the UN Charter and implemented a series of economic sanctions.[31] It sought to meet the Ukrainian government's request for defence equipment, like US and European liked-minded partners had been doing. But the Guidelines restricted Tokyo's actions.

More specifically, Ukraine was not, according to the First Principle, 'a country party to a conflict' (i.e., Ukraine was not the aggressor),[32] meaning Japan was not prohibited from transferring arms to it. But the lack of bilateral agreements on defence equipment and technology transfer and any acquisition and cross-servicing agreement technically limited the scope of overseas transfers to 'cooperation concerning rescue, transportation, vigilance, surveillance or minesweeping with countries cooperating with Japan in security area'.[33] This did not apply in the case of transfers to Ukraine.[34] Tokyo decided to amend the Second Principle to specify that overseas transfer of equipment be allowed to 'Ukraine, which is being invaded in violation of international law'.[35] As of November 2022, Japan's transfer of bulletproof vests is among the nine cases that the NSC has considered since the adoption of the new Three Principles, but this remains small compared to the total number of approvals from METI.

While the administration and the ruling party's policies may have an effect on the decision-making through NSC deliberations, there is little room for public engagement. Neither the application nor the Implementation Guidelines are required to be debated in the Diet. Some research suggests that the Guidelines also make it difficult for the defence industry to influence decision-making. This is because it would be difficult for a private firm to explain why the transfer will have a 'positive meaning' for the contribution to peace and international cooperation or to Japan's security if it did not have support from MOFA or the MOD.[36]

Weapons sales in the real world

Since the adoption of the new Three Principles, METI's annual report on the overseas transfer of defence equipment provides an overview of the number and types of cases approved by the minister. Around 1,000 transfers have been sanctioned annually by the minister. But almost all of these (90%) are to support JSDF overseas activity.[37] Though the number remains low, Tokyo has, under the new Three Principles, increased its participation in collaborative programmes and its pursuit of the export of arms.[38]

The defence-aerospace sector is represented strongly in terms of Japan's collaborative programmes, with the US as its main partner. Over the past three decades, Tokyo has carried out 25 joint research projects and one joint development project with Washington.[39] Since 2014, Japan has been working with the United Kingdom on the Joint New Air-to-Air Missile, which was approved for co-development in 2022.[40] Tokyo has also become increasingly involved with a UK-led future combat-aircraft programme, generally referred to as *Tempest*. Areas of cooperation include sensor and propulsion technology development applicable to Japan's future combat-aircraft programme and to *Tempest*. Tokyo has, since 2018, also been cooperating with France on mine countermeasures, and from the same year with India on navigation technology applicable to uninhabited vehicles. In 2021 Japan and Australia announced a joint research programme on maritime hydrodynamics and hydroacoustic and uninhabited ground-vehicle technology.

While a number of attempts were made to sell finished products overseas, the sales of Mitsubishi Electric's air surveillance system to the Philippines, concluded in August 2020, was the first and only case of successful arms sales of a finished product since the principles were changed.[41] The unsuccessful bid in 2016 of Japan's *Soryu*-class attack submarine for an Australian requirement showed the lack of government and industrial experience in pursuing export business. This will continue to challenge Tokyo's ability to become a competitive arms exporter irrespective of the quality of defence equipment and technology on offer.

Despite the 2014 policy shift by Tokyo towards taking a more proactive approach to arms sales and military-technology transfer, decades-long inexperience in international sales and the isolated nature of Japan's defence industry from major Western defence-industrial ecosystems will hamper Japan's purpose as an arms exporter. The nature of Japan's defence-industrial ecosystem – in which traditional defence businesses are part of a larger commercial conglomerate, making less than 10% of the total revenue to meet the requirements of a single client, Japan's MOD – presents another structural challenge that Tokyo needs to tackle to strengthen Japanese firms' business capabilities.[42]

Conclusion

Given the Japanese defence industry's lack of international experience and the lack of business incentive to further invest in its defence business, the government's role will be key in forging export and collaborative opportunities. The government's review of Japan's three core defence documents – the NSS, the NDPG and the Medium Term Defense Program (MTDP) in 2022 – creates an opportunity for Tokyo to adopt a more active posture on arms sales. Senior officials have stated the need to promote Japan's defence-equipment transfer in relations, alongside its effort to maintain and enhance Japan's defence-equipment production and technology capabilities, and implied that the topic will be debated further in the defence and security review.[43] The FY2022 defence budget also included several policy items designed to enhance the defence-production and technology base by identifying and supporting Japan's industries and to mitigate the various risks to their businesses from getting involved in defence, most notably cyber-security challenges.[44] In the near to medium term, however, joint research and development with key allies will be the predominant pattern, rather than the export of major weapons.

NOTES

1 Alexandra Sakaki and Sebastian Maslow, 'Japan's new arms export policies: strategic aspirations and domestic constraints', *Australian Journal of International Affairs*, vol.74, no.6, 2020. p. 652, https://www.tandfonline.com/doi/pdf/10.1080/10357718.2020.1781789?needAccess=true.

2 Morimoto Satoshi, *Why the Three Principles for Arms Transfer was Reviewed* [Bukiyushutsu Sangensoku wa Doshite Minaosareta no ka] (Tokyo: Kairyūsha, 2014), p. 2.

3 *Ibid.*

4 Japan issued a statement by the Chief Cabinet Secretary on 10 December 2004, saying that 'If Japan decides that it will engage in joint development and production of ballistic missile defense systems with the United States, however, the Three Principles will not be applied, under the condition that strict control is maintained, because such systems and related activities will contribute to the effective operation of the Japan-U.S. security arrangements and are conducive to the security of Japan'. See, for example, Ministry of Foreign Affairs of Japan (MOFA), 'Exchange of Notes concerning the Transfer of Arms and Military Technologies to the United States of America', 23 June 2006, https://www.mofa.go.jp/announce/announce/2006/6/0623-2.html.

5 Honda Tomoaki,'Reassessment of International Peace Cooperation under the Democratic Party of Japan [*Minshutō seiken ni youru kokusaiheiwa kyōryoku no saihyōka*]', *Nenpo Seijigaku*, vol.1, p. 186, https://www.jstage.jst.go.jp/article/nenpouseijigaku/71/1/71_1_178/_pdf/-char/ja/.

6 Prime Minister's Office, 'Statement by the Chief Cabinet Secretary on Guidelines for Overseas Transfer of Defense Equipment etc', 27 December 2011, pp. 2–3, https://japan.kantei.go.jp/noda/topics/201112/20111227DANWA_e.pdf.

7 'Statement by the Chief Cabinet Secretary on the participation of industries of Japan to the production etc. of F-35', Prime Minister of Japan and His Cabinet, 1 March 2013, https://japan.kantei.go.jp/96_abe/decisions/2013/0301danwa_e.html.

8 'National Security Strategy (Provisional Translation)', Prime Minister's Office and His Cabinet, 17 December 2013, p. 19, https://www.cas.go.jp/jp/.siryou/131217anzenhoshou/nss-e.pdf.

9 'About the Three Principles on Defense Technology and Transfer [Bōei sōbihin iten san gensoku nitsuite]', Cabinet Secretariat, https:// www.cas.go.jp/jp/gaiyou/jimu/bouei.html.

10 'Missions of ATLA', Ministry of Defense, https://www.mod.go.jp/atla/en/soubichou_gaiyou.html.

11 MOFA, 'The Three Principles on Transfer of Defense Equipment and Technology', 1 April 2014, p. 1, https://www.mofa.go.jp/files/000034953.pdf.

12 *Ibid.*

13 Ministry of Defense of Japan, 'National Defense Program Guidelines for FY 2019 and beyond', 18 December 2018, p. 15, https://www.cas.go.jp/jp/siryou/pdf/2019boueikeikaku_e.pdf.

14 MOFA, 'Cabinet decision on the Development Cooperation Charter (Provisional Translation)', 10 February 2015, p. 6 and pp. 10–11, https://www.mofa.go.jp/files/000067701.pdf.

15 Jun Ishimaru, 'Japan's cooperation for ASEAN Region in the Areas of Maritime Security', MOFA, p. 2, https://aseanregionalforum.asean.org/wp-content/uploads/2019/02/Annex-7-Japans-ODA-Cooperation-for-the-ASEAN-Region-in-the-Areas-of-Maritime-Security-9th-ISM-MS.pdf.

16 National Security Council of Japan, 'Implementation Guidelines for the Three Principles on Transfer of Defense Equipment and Technology (Provisional Translation)', MOFA, 1 April 2014, p. 1, https://www.mofa.go.jp/files/000121050.pdf.

17 *Ibid.*

18 *Ibid.*, pp. 1–2.

19 *Ibid.*, p. 1.

20 *Ibid.*, p. 3.

21 *Ibid.*, p. 2.

22 *Ibid.*

23 *Ibid.*

24 *Ibid.*

25 Morimoto, *Why Was the Three Principles for Arms Transfer was Reviewed*, pp. 5–6.

26 The Guidelines state that '1) the transfer is judged to be appropriate for active promotion of peace contribution and international cooperation, and when: A. the transfer is in urgent need or highly important from humanitarian perspective, B. the recipient is the UN System or organizations conducting the activities based on a UN resolution. C. the transfer is for the provision of technical information or specimens which are necessary for participating in an international tendering. D. the defense equipment to be transferred is small in price and quantity and thus deems to have small security concern. 2) the transfer involves participation in an international system for sharing parts etc. , 3) the transfer involves delivery of parts etc. to a licenser, 4) the contribution of parts or technology to be transferred to the recipient country is judged to be considerably small, 5) the overseas transfer is necessary for the activities of the SDF etc. or for ensuring the safety of Japanese nationals, or 6) the transfer is judged to have very small impact from the viewpoint of Japan's security such as return of misdelivered items, export of samples to be returned later and temporary landing of goods.' See 'Implementation Guidelines', p. 3.

27 'Implementation Guidelines', p. 4.

28 *Ibid.*, p. 4.

29 *Ibid.*, p. 5.

30 METI, 'Annual Report on Permission Status of Overseas Transfer of Defense Equipment [*bōeisōbi no kaigaiiten no kyoka no jyōkyō ni kansuru nenjihōkoku*]', 4 April 2022, p. 21, https://www.meti.go.jp/policy/anpo/set_annualreport_220408.pdf.

31 For Japan's responses to the situation in Ukraine, see, for example, MOFA, 'Responses to the situation in Ukraine', 2 May 2022, https://www.mofa.go.jp/erp/c_see/ua/page3e_001171.html.

32 MOFA, 'Three Principles', p. 1.

33 National Security Council of Japan, 'Implementation Guidelines', p. 1.

34 According to the Three Principle, 'a country party to a conflict is defined as "a country against which the United Nation's Security Council is taking measures to maintain or restore international peace and security in the event of an armed attack"'. See 'Three Principles', pp. 1–2.

35 The author's translation of the 3 March 2022 revision to 'The Three Principles on Transfer of Defense Equipment and Technology [*Bōeisōbihin Iten Sangensoku no Unyō Shishin*]', 1 April 2014, https://www.cas.go.jp/jp/gaiyou/jimu/pdf/bouei3.pdf.

36 Morimoto, *Why Was the Three Principles for Arms Transfer was Reviewed*, p. 4.

37 METI, 'Annual Report on Permission Status of Overseas Transfer of Defense Equipment', 4 April 2022, p. 5.

38 See, for example, MOD, 'Defense Equipment and Technology Cooperation with Other Countries', https://www.mod.go.jp/en/equipment/tec_cooperation/index.html.

39 Japan, Ministry of Defense, 'Defense of Japan 2021', p. 457, https://www.mod.go.jp/en/publ/w_paper/wp2021/DOJ2021_EN_Full.pdf.

40 Kyosuke Takahashi, 'Japan approves JNAAM co-development', Janes, 22 February 2022, https://www.janes.com/defence-news/news-detail/japan-approves-jnaam-co-development.

41 Mike Yeo, 'Japan secures first-ever major defense export with Philippine radar order', *Defense News*, 28 August 2020, https://www.defensenews.com/global/asia-pacific/2020/08/28/japan-secures-first-ever-defense-export-with-philippine-radar-order/; For past research on Japan's attempt to sell, donate, and aid defence equipment to Southeast Asia, see Victor Teo, 'Japan's Weapons Transfers to Southeast Asia: Opportunities and Challenges', ISEAS, *Perspective*, vol. 2021, no.70, https://www.iseas.edu.sg/wp-content/uploads/2021/04/ISEAS_Perspective_2021_70.pdf.

42 Alexandra Sakaki and Sebastian Maslow, 'Japan's new arms export policies: strategic aspirations and domestic constraints', p. 660.

43 'Hamada boeisho "Takaha no toki mo, hato no toki mo"' [Defense Minister Hamada "Even when it's a hawk or a pigeon" Emphasizes the importance of balance and calmness], Asahi Shimbun, 30 August, 2022, https://www.asahi.com/articles/ASQ8Y6TZXQ8YUTFK003.html

44 Ministry of Defense of Japan, 'Defense Programs and Budget of Japan,' 31 August, 23, https://www.mod.go.jp/j/yosan/yosan_gaiyo/2023/yosan_20220831.pdf.

CONCLUSION

SAUDI DEFENCE EXHIBITION

An armed uninhabited aerial vehicle (UAV) is displayed at Saudi Arabia's first World Defense Show, north of the capital Riyadh, 8 March 2022. CREDIT: FAYEZ NURELDINE/AFP via Getty Images.

CONCLUSION

That the export of major weaponry continues to be contested territory is beyond dispute. Arms sales are often politically divisive and on occasion prompt wider societal concern, discomfort and opposition. This, furthermore, is compounded by continuing debate over the extent to which such sales can or do act as a destabilising or stabilising factor in regional security. All the countries assessed in this volume clearly factor in regional stability before deciding to export major weapons. But the weighting it is given in the national decision-making process varies from state to state, within national processes, and department to department, depending on a range of factors. Perhaps most importantly, it is seldom the determining consideration. It is difficult to accurately assess the impact of major-weapons sales without first taking into account the context of the system being supplied, the buyer country and its regional security environment.

Motivating factors

Influence and economics are the two fundamental reasons why countries that export major weapons behave as they do. The United States, given the size of its internal market combined with its geopolitical outlook, can predicate its decisions more on the former than the latter. Washington does not need to export major weapons to support a defence-industrial base capable of meeting national requirements, given its levels of defence expenditure. Exports, however, may allow it to sustain a larger defence industry, with a greater number of manufacturers, than would be the case if it did not sustain sales on broadly the present scale.

Influence trumping economics was also evident with the Soviet Union, though through the different model of a command economy. Arms export in the Soviet era was primarily ideological, though this is no longer the case with Moscow. In the post-Soviet era, economics became the primary driver behind major-weapons sales. For some companies, it was a matter of survival as sales brought in desperately needed business for a sector where domestic demand had collapsed. While US defence expenditure fell during the 1990s, the economic turmoil of the same period saw swathes of Russia's defence industry with empty order books.

For instance, in the defence-aerospace sector, China and India were to provide vital work in the 1990s and early 2000s for combat-aircraft assembly lines in Komsomolsk-on-Amur and Irkutsk. During this period Moscow took a liberal approach to what the industry could offer for sale. At times, this involved promoting for sale designs of conventionally armed land-attack missiles that strayed over the payload and range limitations of the Missile Technology Control Regime (MTCR). But in the 1990s and early 2000s Russia exercised much restraint regarding some conventional systems. For example, reported Chinese interest in the Tupolev Tu-22M3 *Backfire* C has so far not met with Moscow's approval, even at a time in the early 2000s when the production site associated with the aircraft, the Gorbunov plant in Kazan, had little work, and a modification or refurbishment project would have helped.

European countries, such as the United Kingdom and France, no longer have national requirements of the scale needed to independently support an industrial base with the capacity to meet all major platform requirements. London and Paris have used the export of major weapons as a means of sustaining defence-industrial research and development and manufacturing capacity at a level beyond that which could be supported by national needs alone. While regional-stability concerns do figure in export considerations, they are not given as much prominence as in Washington. London and Paris, certainly in the combat-air sector, have vied for decades to secure lucrative export deals in the Middle East to bolster the domestic military-aerospace industry. France and the UK, for instance, competed for business in Saudi Arabia in the 1980s, with the political leadership of the first two attempting to secure orders for their respective industries. Today, a similar rivalry is playing out in the Kingdom.

Unintended outcomes

In Saudi Arabia in the mid-1980s, the UK won out not just against France but also the US, though Washington had in effect removed itself from any contest. Riyadh was interested in the then-McDonnell Douglas F-15E *Strike Eagle* as a complement to the F-15C. But Washington in the mid-1980s was unwilling to sanction the sale of the former, given its long-range and surface-attack capability. London was able to offer the Panavia *Tornado* IDS as an alternative, at a time when there was increasing political and industrial concern over the looming lack of production work for the UK sites involved in the trinational aircraft.

The eventual result was the al-Yamamah programme, signed in 1985. Unilateral restraint on the part of Washington had not stymied Riyadh's ambition but rather forced the Saudis to buy elsewhere. The outcome was echoed in the United States' approach to the sale of land-attack cruise missiles and medium-altitude long-endurance uninhabited aerial vehicles (UAVs). In neither case did restraint on the part of Washington halt the spread of such systems. In the case of the former, Europe provided an alternative, and with the latter it proved to be China that was more than willing to market its armed UAVs. Beijing's lead has since been followed by Ankara, with Turkey emerging as the alternative supplier of choice. Furthermore, the demand for UAVs provided Beijing with a surer foothold in Middle Eastern markets, a growing presence that is of concern to Washington. Unilateral restraint, while salving national concerns or qualms, is often ineffective in managing or slowing the spread of major weapons, nor does it ensure regional stability. Although far more difficult to agree upon, a multilateral approach promises to be more effective. Even here the extent of any impact risks being diluted by differing national interpretations of any multinational accord. The MTCR has proved more successful in slowing the spread of ballistic missiles than it has in curtailing the adoption of cruise missiles or latterly armed UAVs. The threshold of any acceptability for the export of the first was far lower, and far less opaque, than for the other two.

A question of stability

Behind the boilerplate of the US Defense Security Cooperation Agency that a 'proposed sale ... will not alter the basic military balance in the region' sit an array of assessments and assumptions. Furthermore, 'stability', in the company of a variety of adjectives, is scattered confetti-like among the agency notifications, foregrounding the US aim of sustaining, or supporting, the development of stability within a region. As suggested in this volume, regional stability is not a static notion or a status quo concept when it comes to considering major-weapons sales.

That there is no agreed definition of what constitutes stability is an additional complicating factor, as is the general lack of transparency concerning the seller country's assessment. Additionally, given a major weapons system's service life, a region may experience dynamic and/or unforeseen changes over time. Projecting accurately the security trajectory of a region over the better part of the next 25 years or so is a demand that forecasting has so far understandably failed to meet.

There is also a lack of clarity as to what constitutes a defensive versus an offensive weapon. For instance, an apparently defensive capability, such as an advanced air- and missile-defence system, could have a wider impact if the recipient state felt that such an acquisition gave it the ability to mount offensive activity and be better able to repel any response.

National and multinational outlooks

The risk of great-power conflict abated in the wake of the Cold War. While in the 1990s and early 2000s the US led several regional interventions and became entangled in prolonged counter-insurgency conflicts in Afghanistan and Iraq, the early years of the twenty-first century continued to reflect a much-reduced risk of armed confrontation between Russia and the US. The security environment, however, has deteriorated markedly. Relations between Beijing and Washington have become fractious, with the former's rhetoric and behaviour regarding Taiwan increasingly aggressive. Russia's war of aggression against Ukraine, meanwhile, has served to underscore further, were it needed, the gulf in security perceptions between Moscow, the US and almost all European nations. Such a dark backdrop appears unlikely to foster restraint on the part of purchasing states, while the supplier countries may be encouraged increasingly to support client states in moves perceived to bolster their security. Competition among the major powers and their interests in building influence, particularly among 'swing states', may also encourage a yet more liberal approach in arms-export policy.

As of November 2022, US President Joe Biden's administration had yet to issue a revised conventional-arms transfer policy. Reports suggested the review will place a greater emphasis on human rights when evaluating a potential arms sale than Trump's more transactional approach. As of the third quarter of 2022, there also remained the question of whether the US will ratify the Arms Trade Treaty (ATT). Whether the emergence and adoption of a revised policy and any ATT ratification would be adhered to in a way that had a material effect on US sales also remains a matter for conjecture.

China and Russia are both likely to continue pursuing the sale of major weapons, even if the impetus for each differs, and each faces different challenges. China, Russia and the US will continue to seek geostrategic influence and to secure business in the Middle East. Moscow, however, may be forced to carry out further import substitution on some of its export offerings, for example in microprocessors, because of a US and European Union embargo. Beijing, meanwhile, became a modern major-weapons provider and is near certain to look to build on its position. It is unlikely all three share the same vision of regional stability, either generally or regarding specific locales.

The EU's Common Position, meanwhile, remains flexible, or lax, enough to accommodate stances as apparently diverse at the national level as those of France and Germany. Considerably different national approaches do not necessarily seem to result in notably different outcomes. Berlin's restrictive policies are not reflected fully in the country's comparatively large volume of arms exports.

The main sellers of major-weapons systems face an increasingly competitive market. Some key customers are transitioning from being consumers to becoming producers and are seeking to establish themselves as providers. This may have several effects: traditional producers could offer access to more-capable technology or provide technology transfer and manufacturing capacity to secure sales; it could also lessen the extent to which stability is given consideration in these providers' export decisions. At the same time, new entrants to the arms-sales market may bring further differing interpretations of regional stability as they attempt to forge relationships, while potentially adopting more liberal export policies.

There are only two absolute positions when it comes to the sale of major weapons: one is based on moral repugnance and ethical concern over such trade, the other that it is a mercantile activity like any other. Neither properly engages with the question of regional stability. For the rest, the difficulties are manifold, with ambiguity and opacity at the fore. In an increasingly fraught security environment, it should be down to all governments to provide greater transparency in their decision-making criteria and to better explain the impact, for better or worse, on stability when approving an arms sale into a region, be it the Middle East, the Indo-Pacific or elsewhere. In a deteriorating security environment that will only increase demand for major weapons, the interplay between arms-export policy and regional stability is ever-more important.

Index

INDEX